"The eclipse of the family in hui
trous developments of our age. Sac
marriage and family has also happ
churches. Andreas and Margaret Köstenberger come to the rescue with
biblical and theological insight and practical wisdom."

> **R. Albert Mohler Jr.**, President and Joseph Emerson Brown Professor
> of Christian Theology, The Southern Baptist Theological Seminary

"Models the best of Christian discernment about matters of gender, theology, justice, roles, and gifts. It is faithful in its representation both of
God's character and our own propensity to sin, pastoral in its application
of faithful biblical hermeneutics, insightful in its explanation of original
word usages and their application, concise in its framing of hot-button
issues and the hermeneutical fallacies that often fuel them, and charitable
in its handling of the motives of those who disagree."

> **Rosaria Butterfield**, former tenured Professor of English at Syracuse
> University; author, *The Secret Thoughts of an Unlikely Convert*; mother;
> pastor's wife; and speaker

"A refreshingly clear, well-informed, balanced, thorough, biblically faithful
overview of the teachings of the entire Bible about manhood and womanhood as designed by God and intended for the joy and well-being of both
women and men. A significant achievement!"

> **Wayne Grudem**, Research Professor of Theology and Biblical Studies,
> Phoenix Seminary

"Scriptural, thorough, scholarly, irenic, and practical, this vital resource
will help any serious student of the Bible understand God's good, wise,
and wonderful design."

> **Mary A. Kassian**, Professor of Women's Studies, The Southern Baptist
> Theological Seminary; author, *Girls Gone Wise in a World Gone Wild*

"The brilliant and respected Andreas and Margaret Köstenberger are wise
experts, guiding us through the Bible for a substantive, gospel-rich, and
pastorally applied theology of masculinity, femininity, and the goodness
of our differences by God's design."

> **Russell D. Moore**, President, The Ethics and Religious Liberty
> Commission; author, *Tempted and Tried*

"Whenever we consider our God-given design, we must do so with humble
hearts. What a gift to be able to appreciate how the triune, eternal God
made us! This study on God's design will be useful in every field of Christian work all over the world."

> **Gloria Furman**, pastor's wife, Redeemer Church of Dubai; mother of
> four; author, *Glimpses of Grace* and *Treasuring Christ When Your Hands
> Are Full*

"Some books are unhelpful, others are helpful, and a select few are spectacularly helpful. *God's Design for Man and Woman* belongs with that select few. With thoroughness, nuance, and textual insight, it simultaneously unfolds biblical complementarianism as a coherent, life-giving worldview and answers common questions related to it."

> **Owen Strachan,** Assistant Professor of Christian Theology and
> Church History, Boyce College; Executive Director, The Council on
> Biblical Manhood and Womanhood

"As the consequences of gender distortions permeate more relationships, families, and churches, the need is urgent for biblical clarity about God's design and the work of the Spirit in restoring us to our original purpose. Here is a faithful guide to living as God created us, for our good and his glory."

> **Candice Watters,** Cofounder, Boundless.org; coauthor, *Start Your
> Family*; Associate Editor, CBMW Family

"Andreas and Margaret Köstenberger have teamed up to write one of the most helpful, comprehensive, and practical books to date on what Scripture teaches about God's design for men and women and its implications for marriage, families, relationships in the church, and society."

> **Stephen J. Wellum,** Professor of Christian Theology, The Southern
> Baptist Theological Seminary; Editor, *The Southern Baptist Journal of
> Theology*

"*God's Design for Man and Woman* is rigorously biblical, and the exegetical work is what we have come to expect of the Köstenbergers. Those who believe in the inspiration of the Bible will find this presentation compelling and hard to dismiss. Even those who do not accept biblical authority will, if honest, respect the arguments that are made. This book will serve the church of the Lord Jesus well."

> **Daniel L. Akin,** President, Southeastern Baptist Theological Seminary

"Returning to a topic on which the Köstenbergers have already shown mastery, they here round off their achievements with a full, lucid, and compelling demonstration that all Scripture treats male leadership as the creational pattern. Complementarians in particular will find here an invaluable resource, as indeed will any other open-minded Bible students."

> **J. I. Packer,** Board of Governors' Professor of Theology, Regent College

"From Genesis to Revelation, Andreas and Margaret Köstenberger masterfully present God's plan for manhood and womanhood in the home, church, and society. This thought-provoking, insightful, and theologically grounded resource could not be timelier. This is a must-read that I highly recommend!"

> **Monica Rose Brennan,** Associate Professor and Director of Women's
> Ministries, Liberty University

"The authors break no new ground; they do not intend to. What they have done is put together biblical material in convenient and broadly comprehensive textbook format—material that brings together historical surveys, along with some exegesis, biblical theology, and pastoral application. One need not agree with every detail of the argument to see that this book meets a need to inform students and others who are new to the debate of some of its most inescapable parameters."

D. A. Carson, Research Professor of New Testament, Trinity Evangelical Divinity School

"This unique and accessible book presents a positive, constructive, and winsome case for the whole gamut of biblical teaching about the divine design for men and women, as well as much practical application for how to live it out in both the home and the church."

Gregg R. Allison, Professor of Christian Theology, The Southern Baptist Theological Seminary

"While academic in nature, the text clearly interprets Scripture and makes practical life application. I wholeheartedly recommend this book for *all* Christians and encourage teachers in Christian colleges and universities to use it as a textbook."

Rhonda Harrington Kelley, Professor of Women's Ministry; president's wife, New Orleans Baptist Theological Seminary

"This meaty (but not technical) volume will equip readers to grasp the beauty, utility, and missional importance of being created in God's image, male and female. It deserves a wide readership in church and college or seminary classroom."

Robert W. Yarbrough, Professor of New Testament, Covenant Theological Seminary

"Using the primary picture of the household and pointing to a call for men to carry out their calling, this book is a careful and sober study of biblical texts. It calls on us to reflect on what Scripture teaches, making many important points along the way."

Darrell L. Bock, Executive Director of Cultural Engagement, Howard G. Hendricks Center for Christian Leadership and Cultural Engagement; Senior Research Professor of New Testament Studies, Dallas Theological Seminary

"We live in a day when God's order has been turned on its head, resulting in confusion and heartache—even in the church. Margaret and Andreas Köstenberger team up to present a comprehensive and thoroughly biblical exposition of manhood and womanhood."

Teresa Wigington Bowen, pastor's wife; mother; Founder, *Candle in the Window Hospitality Network*

Other Crossway books by Andreas Köstenberger and Margaret Köstenberger:

The Final Days of Jesus: The Most Important Week of the Most Important Man Who Ever Lived, Andreas J. Köstenberger and Justin Taylor with Alexander Stewart (2014)

Marriage and the Family: Biblical Essentials, Andreas J. Köstenberger with David W. Jones (2012)

Excellence: The Character of God and the Pursuit of Scholarly Virtue, Andreas Köstenberger (2011)

Understanding the Times: New Testament Studies in the Twenty-First Century: Essays in Honor of D. A. Carson on the Occasion of His Sixty-Fifth Birthday, Andreas J. Köstenberger and Robert W. Yarbrough, editors (2011)

God, Marriage, and Family: Rebuilding the Biblical Foundation, 2nd edition, Andreas Köstenberger with David W. Jones (2010)

The Heresy of Orthodoxy: How Contemporary Culture's Fascination with Diversity Has Reshaped Our Understanding of Early Christianity, Andreas Köstenberger and Michael J. Kruger (2010)

Quo Vadis, Evangelicalism? Perspectives on the Past, Direction for the Future: Nine Presidential Addresses from the First Fifty Years of the Journal of the Evangelical Theological Society, Andreas J. Köstenberger, editor (2008)

Jesus and the Feminists: Who Do They Say That He Is?, Margaret Köstenberger (2008)

GOD'S DESIGN

for

MAN

and

WOMAN

A BIBLICAL-THEOLOGICAL SURVEY

ANDREAS J. KÖSTENBERGER AND
MARGARET E. KÖSTENBERGER

CROSSWAY

WHEATON, ILLINOIS

Library of Congress Cataloging-in-Publication Data

Köstenberger, Andreas J., 1957-
  God's design for man and woman : a biblical-theological
survey / Andreas J. Köstenberger and Margaret E.
Köstenberger.
     pages cm.
  Includes bibliographical references and index.
  ISBN 978-1-4335-3699-1 (tp)
  1. Theological anthropology—Biblical teaching.
2. Theological anthropology—Christianity. 3. Men—Biblical
teaching. 4. Man (Christian theology) 5. Women—Biblical
teaching. 6. Women—Religious aspects—Christianity.
7. Bible—Criticism, interpretation, etc. I. Title.
BS670.5.K67   2014
233—dc23   2013044702

Crossway is a publishing ministry of Good News Publishers.

VP		24	23	22	21	20	19	18	17	16	15	14
15	14	13	12	11	10	9	8	7	6	5	4	3	2	1

To our children:
Lauren, Tahlia, David, and Timothy
We love you!

Contents

List of Tables

Introduction

Following Andreas's graduation from high school, he went on an extensive tour of southern Europe. On returning home to his native Austria, he opened the door to his family apartment and immediately noticed his parents' dresser drawers pulled out and in seeming disarray. He stopped. What had happened? Eventually, it dawned on him: the apartment hadn't been burglarized; his dad had moved out! In a mild state of panic, he called his dad and asked what was going on. Matter-of-factly, his father replied, "I don't live at home anymore." Andreas didn't know what to say. He tried to engage his father in conversation but to no avail. His father had made his decision.

As we all know, a marriage doesn't break up overnight. Even though Andreas's parents had been married for over twenty years, as he looked back over the years prior to his father's leaving the family, he saw that his father had already been absent from the home for many years, not only physically but, more importantly, spiritually. Andreas's mother had been left to raise him and his younger sister by herself, teaching them responsibility and whatever values she could. And though she strove valiantly to do so, she couldn't replace his father.

Andreas found himself adrift morally and spiritually during the bulk of his high school and college years. Searching for an anchor for his soul, he eventually found the Lord Jesus Christ. He forgave his dad and entreated his father to have the opportunity to explain to him about salvation and the new life that he could have in Christ. Though his father was not receptive spiritually, in God's mercy, over time, Andreas grew in his practical understanding of what it means to be a Christian husband and father.

Perhaps it is in these traumatic times that God, in his providence, sows the seeds of a passion for righteous living and the healing found only in Christ. We share this part of Andreas's story not because we base our beliefs and actions on reactions to our experiences;[1] nor do we mean to emotionalize the issues we're about to discuss. We do so because it illustrates the terrible price we often pay when we fail to live out God's design for us obediently, by grace, despite the challenges and effects that sin has on us.

Purpose of This Book

We've written this book because we're convinced that it's vital to wrestle with our identity as men and women for the sake of healthy marriages, families, and churches but, more importantly, for the true expression of the gospel of Jesus Christ in our world. We're committed to go about exploring the topic with an open mind and to reach out in love and ministry while doing so. What we believe about our identity as man or woman is central to who we are as individuals, couples, and families and how each of us pursues our life calling. It will determine the way in which we act as wife or husband, as parents, as church members, and in the culture as we identify with the God who created us by design as man or woman. Biblical manhood and womanhood is too important a subject not to think through carefully as a Christian.[2]

While it is undeniable that there's no current consensus on this issue in the church, the probable reason isn't that Scripture is inconclusive or conflicted. We don't believe that God would have left his people without clear guidance on an issue as foundational and important as male-female identity and roles. More likely, there are other reasons. Is it contemporary culture, influenced by various philosophical and theological sets of beliefs, that makes it more difficult for people to grasp the biblical message? Maybe the fact that we're sinful

---

[1] If you're interested in reading the rest of the story of Andreas's conversion, you can find it in Andreas J. Köstenberger, *Excellence: The Character of God and the Pursuit of Scholarly Virtue* (Wheaton, IL: Crossway, 2011), chap. 1.

[2] R. Albert Mohler Jr., "A Call for Theological Triage and Christian Maturity," *The Tie* 74 (Summer 2006): 2–3, outlines a three-part framework for understanding theological priorities: (1) first-order issues—doctrinal points that distinguish Christians from non-Christians (e.g., the Trinity, orthodox christology); (2) second-order issues—doctrinal points that distinguish Christians from other Christians that render it difficult if not impossible for them to fellowship together in a local church context (e.g., baptism); and (3) third-order issues—doctrinal points over which Christians disagree without rift in local church fellowship (e.g., the timing of the rapture). Mohler (rightly, in our opinion) identifies the "women in ministry" question as a second-order (but not third-order) issue.

and unspiritual in our bent has something to do with it. Few naturally like to submit to others; many of us would rather be independent and autonomous. So any teaching like this that calls on certain people to submit to others is a tough sell.

Certainly, the first order of business for any person—male or female—is to trust in the crucified and risen Savior and then to be taught how to grow spiritually as Christ's follower in the context of a local church. There are many things to learn in the Christian life that are true universally, regardless of whether a person is a man or a woman. But certainly no later than when a couple receives premarital counseling; when a baby is born (male or female); or when we sit down to write a church constitution and bylaws after planting a new church, the question of male-female identity and roles needs to be addressed. To clearly address from Scripture our mission from God as man and woman in partnership, and as individuals, is vital for serious spiritual impact on the world.

God's Design for Men and Women and Contemporary Culture

Both Andreas and Margaret became Christians in part because they were drawn to Christianity by what they saw in the relationships of the believers they met. Shortly after his conversion to Christ, Andreas remembers Gary and his wife, Ann, and their family, missionaries in his native Austria. Gary's robust masculinity in "hanging out with the guys," coupled with his tender gentleness toward Ann and his caring fatherly concern for his boys, left a deep impression on him. Andreas can still recall one evening when Ann threw a birthday party for her husband, asking everyone to go around the room and tell Gary what they appreciated about him. Ann was great at encouraging and affirming her husband, and Gary was a true servant in the way in which he nurtured and ministered to his wife and the entire family. It wasn't until later when Andreas started reading in the Bible about God's plan for men and women that he gradually realized that Gary and Ann had consciously been living out the divine design for what it means to be a man and a woman.

The summer before Margaret went to college, a group of young adults invited her to join their college and career group for a weekend trip away to the ocean. She was told to bring a Bible and otherwise just pack for a trip at the beach. Though never having really understood the Bible, she did have one on the shelf in her room. She grabbed the Bible and her bag and headed out for the weekend away. It was a lot of fun and truly enlightening for her. Years later, she recalls how Mark and Kevin, both engaged to be married, were contagious in their love for the Lord and in their desire to be submissive and obedient to God's plan for them. They led the group in a passionate pursuit of the truths of God, and their confidence and hope in these truths drew Margaret herself to seek after God. After becoming a Christian, she had an immediate desire to make sense of her place in the world as a woman. She visited different churches in the vicinity of Toronto, Canada, where she was living, listened to numerous sermons, read several books on how to grow in her relationship with Christ, and sought out role models. She heard a variety of viewpoints on the topic of biblical manhood and womanhood, but after studying the Bible for herself, she realized that Scripture spoke with a unified voice and she committed herself to living out God's design for her as a woman.

People in our culture have a great need to see role models of biblical manhood and womanhood that flesh out God's design for men and women. We don't need to tell you that our world is in greater ferment on the issue of masculinity and femininity today than when we went to college years ago. Terms such as "transgender," "gender-fluid," or "gender-variant" have made their way into the English language, and the past decades have witnessed an increasing trend toward an erosion of marital roles and male-female identity.

Today, many see marriage as little more than a convention, a social contract to be entered largely out of convenience. No longer is marriage viewed as a necessary and healthy relational context for conceiving children, and many women and men are indifferent toward what used to be standard societal expectations. Divorce is rampant, and the sins of fathers and mothers are visited upon their children. Comparatively few are concerned about the biblical teaching on the matter, even in the church.

We've entered a post-Christian, pluralistic, postmodern phase in Western culture's approach to gender roles. But the "new tolerance" of diversity on gender issues raises several important questions.[3] Is marriage really best left to subjective social arrangement with no basis in divine truth? Are male-female relationships simply a matter of consensual patterns of relating that are subject to ever-changing societal preferences and values? Is gender merely a social phenomenon as many feminists and others insist?

Or does Scripture provide us with abiding truth based on God's plan for men and women? Is maleness or femaleness a characteristic with which we are born, an indelible mark of who we are that we can embrace, even celebrate, and live out to the glory of the God who gave it to us in the first place? What if our creation as male or female grounds us in a true and meaningful supernatural reality that we ignore to our loss and peril in both this life and the life to come?

And if so, what is this divine design?

In this book, we'll take a closer look at what the Bible teaches on the way God designed male-female identity and relationships in order to help us to get closer to this reality.

The Contribution and Method of This Book

We've chosen to address the topic by presenting a positive and constructive (and, we hope, winsome) case for what the Bible, carefully interpreted, teaches regarding God's design for men and women. As you join our guided tour through the biblical landscape, we hope you'll witness with us the gradual unfolding of God's plan through Scripture.

This book attempts to fill a gap.[4] While there are more popular works touching on God's design for men and women, few are written from a perspective that traces the thread of manhood and womanhood as it unfolds from Genesis to Revelation.[5] Also, many treatments

---

[3] The allusion is to the important book by D. A. Carson, *The Intolerance of Tolerance* (Grand Rapids, MI: Eerdmans, 2012). See also the update by the same author, "More Examples of Intolerant Tolerance," *Themelios* 37 (November 2012), http://thegospelcoalition.org/themelios/article/more_examples_of _intolerant_ tolerance (accessed June 28, 2013).

[4] In some ways, this volume is a companion volume to Andreas J. Köstenberger with David W. Jones, *God, Marriage, and Family: Rebuilding the Biblical Foundation*, 2nd ed. (Wheaton, IL: Crossway, 2010). While *God, Marriage, and Family* focuses primarily on recovering the biblical teaching on marriage in today's culture, the present volume probes the question of our fundamental identity as men and women and our proper, God-ordained roles not just in marriage but also in the church and in society.

[5] One book that has exerted considerable influence is the collection of essays in *Recovering Biblical Manhood and Womanhood: A Response to Evangelical Feminism*, ed. John Piper and Wayne Grudem (Wheaton, IL: Crossway, 1991). See also Mary Kassian, *Women, Creation, and the Fall* (Wheaton, IL: Crossway, 1990). A more recent summary of the biblical teaching is Kevin DeYoung, *Freedom and Boundaries: A Pastoral*

on the topic deal primarily, if not exclusively, with women's roles.[6]
Fewer volumes deal with biblical manhood. Even fewer explore men's
and women's roles jointly. What is missing is an effort to show God's
design in a holistic, comprehensive manner. In utilizing this approach,
we're convinced that God's plan can only be adequately highlighted as
men's and women's roles are considered progressively through Scripture and in relation to one another.

Our approach will therefore involve reflection on Scripture as a
whole, with the use of what we consider to be the best interpretive
work available on various aspects of this subject, in order to help draw
connections between different passages and themes in Scripture.[7] In
performing a biblical-theological survey, we'll draw our primary cues
not from contemporary sensibilities or debates but from the historical
setting of the biblical documents, whether the book of Genesis or the
book of Ephesians. Also, while we're of course interested ultimately
in applying what we've learned from studying Scripture, we'll at first
be primarily concerned with biblical terminology rather than with
modern concepts or topics.[8]

Our goal will be to provide an accessible and helpful tool for serious Bible students and people in the churches. In the process, we'll
be reflecting on the major didactic passages in the Bible on the topic,

Primer on the Role of Women in the Church (Enumclaw, WA: Pleasant Word, 2006). Written from an egalitar-
ian perspective is Ronald W. Pierce, *Partners in Marriage and Ministry* (Minneapolis: Christians for Biblical
Equality, 2011). An attempt to cover the entire sweep of Scripture in a very short amount of space is
N. T. Wright, "Women's Service in the Church: The Biblical Basis," conference paper for the symposium
"Men, Women and the Church," St. John's College, Durham, September 4, 2004; though see below the
disagreements we register regarding some of his conclusions. See also the popularly written volume
by Michael F. Bird, *Bourgeois Babes, Bossy Wives, and Bobby Haircuts: A Case for Gender Equality in Ministry*,
Fresh Perspectives on Women in Ministry (Grand Rapids, MI: Zondervan, 2014), who says a woman
once called him a "patriarchal, androcentric, chauvinistic misogynist" but who now describes himself
as "almost-complementarian or nearly-egalitarian." Among others, he cites as reasons for his change of
mind the lack of female worship leaders (and ushers) in his church, the presence of female coworkers
in Acts and Paul's letters, and the similar rationale in 1 Cor. 11:2–16 and 1 Tim. 2:11–14 (leading him to
believe both are merely cultural).
[6] This is true even for books that have "men and women" in the title or subtitle but discuss mostly
passages dealing with women, and men only where they're inevitably mentioned alongside women
(e.g., Genesis 1–3; Eph. 5:21–33).
[7] Since this book is written primarily for nonspecialists, we won't extensively document sources of
the various views with which we interact (though we'll refer to strategic works). For bibliographic
information, see the relevant literature such as Wayne Grudem, *Evangelical Feminism and Biblical Truth:
An Analysis of More Than 100 Disputed Questions* (Wheaton, IL: Crossway, 2012).
[8] Case in point: equality. While today we're very concerned about equality, whether pertaining to race,
class, or gender, is it really accurate to interpret the statement in Gen. 1:28, for example, that God created humanity male and female, in terms of gender equality? Is this what the ancient author intended
to convey, and is this what his original readers would have understood him to communicate? This is
a question of biblical theology, in distinction from systematic theology. See further the discussion of
biblical theology at the end of appendix 2.

many of which are in Paul's letters. We'll look at the key leadership institutions in the life of Israel (patriarchs, kings, priests) and in the New Testament period (the Twelve, the Pauline circle). We'll also cull sketches of some important male and female characters from the narrative portions of Scripture in order to give more information about specific individuals and their part in God's plan (Old Testament historical narratives, the Gospels, the book of Acts).

Perhaps most importantly, we've included a fairly full chapter discussing how to apply the biblical teaching on manhood and womanhood (chapter 8). If you're primarily interested in application, go ahead and dive straight into that last chapter. Then backtrack and read the biblical-theological survey or just use it as a reference. Technically, biblical theology is supposed to be primarily descriptive, so in our survey we focus on giving an accurate presentation of what Scripture actually says (though we try to sprinkle in relevant application points throughout).

Finally, we've also chosen to provide appendices on a cultural women's history survey and on biblical interpretation (general interpretive issues and special issues in interpreting gender-related passages in Scripture), canvassing the context for our study of the biblical teaching on men's and women's identities and roles. We've included these in the conviction that our method and the context in which we study Scripture matter a great deal. Some of you may want to read these appendices first, if you're interested in a general introduction to these issues before delving into Scripture; others may want to start with the biblical-theological survey in chapters 1–8 and read the appendices last.[9] Lastly, make use of the tables throughout and the Scripture index along with the general index at the back of the book.

On a Personal Note

Speaking personally, we didn't start out writing this book as a blank slate. Our personal life experiences have highlighted the importance of this study, and since then we have invested in much study of Scripture

[9] If you're teaching a class on biblical manhood and womanhood, you may want to consider asking your students to read the appendices prior to class. In this way, they'll be prepared for the discussion of the biblical portion of your class on male-female identities, relationships, and roles.

along with teaching classes on the topic. We've approached our subject in the understanding that the Bible, in both Testaments, teaches both male-female partnership and male leadership.[10] Working on this book has only deepened this conviction and grounded it even more firmly in Scripture.

While our basic conviction regarding the biblical teaching on our topic hasn't fundamentally changed, we've learned a lot from continuing to search the Scriptures, especially as we've connected the different parts of Scripture to one another. For example, we learned something new about the role of Deborah and about the role of Old Testament judges and prophets. We learned more about the teaching on male-female roles in the General Epistles and in the book of Revelation. We've also come to understand better where feminists are coming from in their interpretation of certain biblical passages, as we sought to interact with those arguments at various points in the book.

Above all, working on this book together has been a unifying experience in our marriage. It's deepened our shared conviction regarding God's design for male-female relationships and led us to be more committed than ever to living it out in our lives individually and jointly in the context of our family and in the church. We've also been further impressed by the urgency and priority of mentoring our own daughters and sons in biblical womanhood and manhood as well as passing on these biblical insights to other men and women.

We hope that you see in this book evidence of our personal pilgrimage and wrestling with the texts as well as honest, open, fair, and balanced engagement with significant questions that arise. We offer you our service as guides through the biblical landscape, but we want to make sure that the focus isn't on the guides but on what we're about to see—God's beautiful, wise, and good plan for men and women of all ages, backgrounds, and cultures.

A book such as this one doesn't get written without the encouragement and support of many others. We're grateful to God for each other

[10] Two decades ago, I wrote in Andreas J. Köstenberger, "Gender Passages in the NT: Hermeneutical Fallacies Critiqued," *Westminster Theological Journal* 56 (1994): 259–83, "What is needed is a systematized biblical theology of manhood and womanhood that is based on a careful exegesis of the relevant passages but transcends such exegesis by integrating interpretive insights into a systematic whole" (p. 279). The present volume is a modest step in this direction.

and for the twenty-four years of marriage (and counting!) he's allowed us to enjoy. We're grateful also for our family—our two precious girls, Lauren and Tahlia (both now in college), and two precious boys, David and Timothy (homeschooled this year), a constant source of joy, challenge, and opportunity for growth.

Thanks are also due those who read the book in manuscript form prior to publication—endorsers as well as some who offered helpful feedback, especially John Burkett (director of the Writing Center at SEBTS), Sarah Carr, Theresa Bowen, Chuck Bumgardner, Anne Ballou, and Lauren Köstenberger. We're also grateful for the students in the classes we've been privileged to teach jointly on this subject as well as for the brothers and sisters who attended marriage seminars at which we spoke and engaged us in lively discussion. Iron sharpens iron! We've used this material repeatedly in the classroom and in small-group settings and are regularly amazed how compelling an open-minded study of Scripture on biblical manhood and womanhood is proving to be.

We're grateful particularly to Andreas's one-time research assistant, Alexander Stewart, for transcribing our initial set of classroom lectures that formed the point of departure for this manuscript.

If the quest resonates with you to know more fully what the Bible teaches regarding God's plan for men and women, then we invite you to join us on this journey—to be all God wants you to be and to discover God's good, wise, and wonderful design. Certainly God's plan for women and men—whatever it is—matters, and matters a great deal! Join us as we walk step-by-step through the sacred pages of God's Word, and may he richly bless you as you seek his will in this crucial area of your life.

1

God's Original Design and Its Corruption

Genesis 1–3

Have you not read that he who created them from the beginning made them male and female?

—Jesus (Matt. 19:4)

"Begin at the beginning," the King said, very gravely, "and go on till you come to the end: then stop."

—Lewis Carroll, *Alice in Wonderland*

Key Points

1. Genesis 1–3, cited by both Jesus and Paul, provides the foundational biblical teaching on men's and women's identities and roles.
2. Genesis 1 makes clear that humanity, male and female, was created in God's image to rule the earth jointly as God's representatives.
3. Genesis 2 indicates that men and women have different roles or functions in the fulfillment of God's creation mandate to humanity to multiply and subdue the earth. The man is ultimately responsible for leading in the marriage and the fulfillment of God's mandate, while the woman is his partner, his suitable helper. Different functions or roles don't convey superiority or inferiority.
4. The Old Testament bears witness to several ways in which humanity compromised God's design for marriage, such as polygamy, divorce, adultery, and homosexuality.

5. Even after the fall, God's ideal for men and women continues unabated and constitutes the abiding standard for male-female relationships.

At a recent lunch stop at a Cracker Barrel on the way back from a
family road trip north to Canada and New York City, we got into one
of our lively family discussions. We were reflecting on the *Cinderella*
Broadway performance the girls had just seen. One of our daughters
mentioned that this Rogers and Hammerstein musical was a feminist
version of the fairy tale. Though we didn't all agree with this opinion,
the topic of male-female roles and identities came up. In the middle of
the discussion, our teenage daughter expressed her opinion that men
and women are "equal." She assumed we would all understand what
she meant without further elaboration. Trying to tease out her thinking, we asked her in what way she thought women and men are equal
since, after all, there are also some obvious differences! "Are there
not also unique identities and roles associated with men and women
being created unique?," we asked. Our daughter retorted, "Well, of
course, everybody knows *that*!" Andreas then talked about the man's
responsibility to provide for his family. Our teenage son quickly added
that men who let their wives bear the main load of providing for the
family are "wimps." Trying to wrap up our discussion (our food was
just about to be served), Andreas pointed out that many people in our
culture believe that our male and female roles are simply determined
by preferences and personal arrangements and that fewer and fewer
people seem to base our male-female identities on the way in which
we've been created by God.

Creation (Genesis 1–2)

You only have to look at the starry sky or a butterfly's wings to see that
God is a master designer. The psalmist exclaims,

O LORD, our LORD,
    how majestic is your name in all the earth!
You have set your glory above the heavens. . . .
When I look at your heavens, the work of your fingers,
    the moon and the stars, which you have set in place,

> what is man that you are mindful of him,
> > and the son of man that you care for him?
> Yet you have made him a little lower than the heavenly beings
> > and crowned him with glory and honor.
> You have given him dominion over the works of your hands;
> > you have put all things under his feet. (Ps. 8:1–6)

The apostle Paul concurs: "For his invisible attributes, namely, his eternal power and divine nature, have been clearly perceived, ever since the creation of the world, in the things that have been made" (Rom. 1:20). God, our creator, has put an indelible imprint on all of his creation, whether the starry skies or his crowning work, the making of man and woman, which the Creator himself pronounced "very good" (Gen. 1:31).

What ought to give cause to much wonder and amazement, however, is also the cause of much consternation. A large part of humanity, in the first (and, sadly, also in the twenty-first) century, has set aside God's design for men and women. As Paul continues in his epistle to the Romans,

> So they are without excuse. For although they knew God, they did not honor him as God or give thanks to him, but they became futile in their thinking, and their foolish hearts were darkened. Claiming to be wise, they became fools, and exchanged the glory of the immortal God for images resembling mortal men. . . . Therefore God gave them up in the lusts of their hearts to impurity, to the dishonoring of their bodies. (Rom. 1:20–26)

We see that God's design, in all of its beauty, wisdom, and goodness, is ignored at great peril. While God loves the man and the woman he has made, judgment awaits those who treat lightly the purpose for his creation. So whether our motive is the love of God or the fear of God, we should strive to rediscover and seek to live in accordance with his divine design.

What, then, is God's design for men and women? As we will see, an engaging study of what Scripture teaches about God's plan for males and females from beginning to end provides clear and abundant guidance on the purpose for our gender. We'll start at the very beginning:

the biblical account of creation (Genesis 1–3). This part of the Bible lays the foundation for God's purpose in creating man and woman unique and different and shows the serious consequences of the fall on the male-female relationship.[1]

After this, we will begin to engage the important matters of how these truths relate to our lives. We will also cull Israel's history and demonstrate how the divine ideal continues unabated.[2] Later in the book, we will move on to the rest of the story and discover that God's original plan is abiding, consistent, and missional.

Overview of the Creation Narrative

Before we delve into the teaching of Genesis 1–3 on biblical manhood and womanhood in greater depth, it will be helpful to catch a birds' eye view of the scriptural narrative of humanity's creation and fall into sin. The biblical creation story provides us with a wonderful, coherent presentation of God's creation of the man and the woman according to his divine design.[3] In the Genesis story, read as a continual narrative, we move from a general account of God's creation to a more specific presentation focusing on the male-female relationship and then to the fall. Chapter 2 acts as a necessary link between chapters 1 and 3 and has often been compared to a zoom lens that focuses on the general presentation of creation in chapter 1 in greater detail.

Read as part of a consecutive narrative, Genesis 1 tells the story of God's creation of the universe, culminating in the creation of humanity as male and female in God's image (Gen. 1:26–27). Genesis 2, then,

---

[1] Some of the material in this chapter overlaps with Andreas J. Köstenberger with David W. Jones, *God, Marriage, and Family: Rebuilding the Biblical Foundation*, 2nd ed. (Wheaton, IL: Crossway, 2010), chap. 2. Used by permission.

[2] For a concise discussion see Daniel I. Block, "Leader, Leadership, OT," in *New Interpreter's Dictionary of the Bible*, vol. 3: I–Ma, ed. Katharine Doob Sakenfeld (Nashville: Abingdon, 2008), 620–26.

[3] Not everyone agrees on the proper interpretation of the opening chapters of Genesis. Over a century ago Elizabeth Cady Stanton, based on her view that the Bible was unnecessarily patriarchal and an obstacle to women's rights, argued in her *Woman's Bible* that the "wily writer" of Genesis 2 was trying to put women in their place in order to subvert the presentation of men and women as equals in Genesis 1. Julius Wellhausen, a nineteenth-century German theologian, set forth the proposal that Genesis 1 and 2 reflect two competing creation accounts penned by different writers based on two different names used for God (i.e., *Elohim* in chap. 1 and *Yahweh* in chap. 2). However, neither Stanton's nor Wellhausen's view is adequately borne out by the text. Both are heavily influenced by their respective sets of presuppositions. The conventional way to read the first two chapters of Genesis is to understand Genesis 1 as referring to the creation of humanity at large and Genesis 2 as focusing specifically on the creation of man and woman. In this context, *Elohim* is the proper way to speak of God in his relation to the entire earth, while *Yahweh* is more appropriate in speaking of his special relationship to his covenant people Israel. In the NT, both Jesus (Matt. 19:4–5; Mark 10:6–8) and Paul (Eph. 5:31; 1 Tim. 2:12–13) refer to Genesis 1 *and* 2 as authoritative Scripture.

goes on to elaborate more specifically on God's purpose and manner of creating the man and the woman and the divine design expressed in distinct male-female roles: the man is to serve as the leader while the woman has been created to come alongside him as his partner, his suitable helper (vv. 18, 20). We also learn that the fact that God made the man first constitutes a deliberate act and important indication of the man's primary responsibility to God for the marriage relationship.[4]

Table 1.1: Basic Contents of Genesis 1–3

Chapter	Description
Genesis 1	God's creation of the universe generally (including man and woman)
Genesis 2	God's creation specifically of man and woman in relation to each other (zoom lens)
Genesis 3	Woman's and man's transgression of the Creator's command (the fall)

Looking at Genesis 2 in greater detail, we see that following the creation of the first man, God then makes the woman. God's purpose for creating the woman is to bring her to the man to alleviate his aloneness, to provide him with companionship, and to enable humankind to fill the earth and to help govern it for God. We see that the woman is the result of a unique creative act of God who fashioned her from a rib of the man, an act that sets her apart from the manner of creation of the animals. The way Scripture tells the story, the woman was created for a special purpose. She was created both from the man and for the man.

Following the dual creation narrative, then, Genesis 3 tells the story of an ominous role reversal at the fall of humanity where the Serpent (Satan) approaches the woman, who leads the man to join her in transgressing their Creator's command. This turns biblical lines of authority on their head, according to which God rules over the man who is responsible to lead and care for his wife and together with her

---

[4] See Paul's comments on 1 Tim. 2:12–13 (on which see the discussion in chap. 6).

is given charge of the animal world.[5] Consequently, God holds each party accountable and pronounces a series of judgments on the Serpent, the woman, and the man.

Created in God's Image to Rule the Earth for God (Gen. 1:26–28)

We'll pick up the creation narrative in chapter 1 at its climax:

> Then God said, "Let us make man in our image, after our likeness. And let them have dominion . . . over all the earth. . . ."
>
> So God created man in his own image,
>> in the image of God he created him;
>> male and female he created them.
>
> And God blessed them. And God said to them, "Be fruitful and multiply and fill the earth and subdue it, and have dominion." (Gen. 1:26–28)

Strikingly, at the outset of the passage, God emphatically announces his intention to make humanity in his own image.[6] In verse 26, he declares his intention and purpose for creating humanity: to have dominion over all the earth as his representatives.[7] In verse 27, the narrative switches from prose to poetry, each of the three lines registering an important point: (1) humanity has God as its source; (2) humanity bears resemblance to God; and (3) humanity exists in the plurality of male and female. Verse 28 records God's blessing of humanity and his mandate for the man and the woman: to be fruitful and multiply and to fill the earth and subdue it.[8] Let's now briefly discuss some of the most salient points in interpreting this important passage.

First, what are we to make of the plural in the divine declaration,

---

[5] See table 1.5, "Role Reversal at the Fall," in the discussion of Genesis 3.

[6] The insights in this paragraph are indebted to Raymond C. Ortlund Jr., "Male-Female Equality and Male Headship: Genesis 1–3," in *Recovering Biblical Manhood and Womanhood: A Response to Biblical Feminism*, ed. John Piper and Wayne Grudem (Wheaton, IL: Crossway, 1991), 96–97. For a systematic theological treatment of "image of God," including further bibliographic references, see Wayne Grudem, *Systematic Theology: An Introduction to Biblical Doctrine* (Grand Rapids, MI: Zondervan, 1994), chap. 21.

[7] As John H. Sailhamer, "Genesis," in *Genesis–Leviticus*, vol. 1 of Expositor's Bible Commentary, ed. Tremper Longman III and David E. Garland, rev. ed. (Grand Rapids, MI: Zondervan, 2008), 69, points out, the customary impersonal "Let there be" is replaced by the personal "Let us make." Also, while the other creatures were each made "according to their own kind," humanity is made "in God's image": "They are not merely like themselves, they are also like God" (ibid.).

[8] Sailhamer (ibid., 70–71) notes the importance of the blessing and its connection to the notions of "seed" and "life," which are exceedingly significant in the ensuing biblical narrative.

"Let *us* make man," in verse 26? Is it: (1) a reference to the Trinity? (2) a reference to God and the court of heavenly angels? Or (3) a reference to God's deliberation within himself? A reference to angels is rendered unlikely by the fact that humanity is made in God's image, not that of angels. A reference to God's deliberation within himself is also rather unlikely because in passages such as Genesis 18:17, the first-person singular is used in such instances ("Shall I hide from Abraham what I am about to do?"). Most likely, therefore, the reference is to a plurality within the Godhead ("Let *us* make man") issuing in a plurality in humanity, male and female ("male and female he created *them*").[9]

Second, what are we to make of the equally momentous affirmation that God made humanity in his image (Gen. 1:27)? The declaration that humanity bears God's likeness is startling, awesome, and almost incredible, but what exactly does it mean?[10] Scholars debate the specifics.[11] Two primary, and not necessarily contradictory, views are: (1) the substantive view, according to which humans share some aspects of the nature of God (intelligence, emotions, etc.); and (2) the functional view, according to which humans act like God in their divinely given role to rule the earth. The immediate context, with the language of dominion and subjugation, suggests that the functional interpretation is primary. Let's stay close to the text, then, and interpret this passage in the context of the Bible's overall story line.

On the heels of the statement that God created the man and the woman in his image is God's foundational mandate for humanity, which is expressed in a series of five imperatives: "And God blessed

---

[9] See Sailhamer (ibid., 70): "The divine plurality of persons . . . can be seen as an anticipation of the human plurality of persons reflected in man and woman, thus casting human personal relationships in the role of reflecting God's own personhood."

[10] Curiously, N. T. Wright denies that "the creation of man and woman in their two genders is a vital part of what it means that humans are created in God's image," primarily because plants and animals, not merely humans, procreate, warning against "collaps[ing] into a kind of gnosticism" ("Women's Service in the Church: The Biblical Basis," conference paper for the symposium "Men, Women and the Church," St. John's College, Durham, September 4, 2004, 2). However, it's hard to escape the explicit link established between creation in God's image and humanity as male and female in Genesis 1:27: "So God created man *in his own image, in the image of God* he created him; *male and female* he created them. And God blessed them. And God said to them, 'Be fruitful and multiply.'" See Köstenberger with Jones, *God, Marriage, and Family*, 21–28.

[11] See, e.g., Kristina LaCelle-Peterson, *Liberating Tradition: Women's Identity and Vocation in Christian Perspective* (Grand Rapids, MI: Baker Academic, 2008), who argues that we need to be liberated from the notion of "gender essentialism" (i.e., the notion that God created humanity male and female). See the review by Rebecca Jones in *Journal of Biblical Manhood and Womanhood* 16 (Fall 2011): 40–47.

them. And God said to them, '*Be fruitful* and *multiply* and *fill* the earth and *subdue* it, and *have dominion* over the fish of the sea and over the birds of the heavens and over every living thing that moves on the earth'" (v. 28). The fact that humanity is said to have been made in God's image as a plurality ("male and female he created *them*," v. 27), along with the plural pronouns "them" at the beginning of verse 28 ("And God blessed *them*. And God said to *them*"), indicates that ruling the earth is a joint function of the man and the woman. Humanity is conceived as a plurality.

Understood in this way, verse 28 teaches that the primary means of carrying out humanity's representative rule is that of procreation. Neither the man nor the woman can fill the earth and subdue it without the other. Fulfilling the mandate to "be fruitful and multiply and fill the earth and subdue it" takes both a man and a woman.[12] Being made in God's image thus involves joint dominion of the earth involving procreation. This truth has abiding relevance. In a day when birthrates drop in the civilized world and when many choose to have fewer or no children at all for lifestyle reasons, and when some countries, in order to curb population growth, limit the number of children a couple may legally produce, Scripture reminds us that procreation is at the very heart of God's creation purpose and mandate for humanity as male and female.

So what's the ancient cultural background? Today, when you hear the word *image*, you may think of a picture or drawing, but in the day when Genesis was written, the term carried a slightly different connotation.[13] In the ancient Near East, the image of a ruler commonly represented the potentate's presence in his kingdom. A ruler's image thus signified his rule, such as when his or her likeness was minted on a coin. In the case of humans, as the male-female image of God, they symbolize his rule, having been created to reflect his glory to all creation (see Ps. 8:6–8). Neither the angels nor the animals are in charge of creation—humans are, created in God's image. At the same

---

[12] The implications for same-sex marriage are obvious.
[13] Hans Walter Wolff, *Anthropology of the Old Testament* (Philadelphia: Fortress, 1973), 160: "In the ancient East, the setting up of the king's statue was the equivalent to the proclamation of his domination over the sphere in which the statue was erected (see, e.g., Daniel 3:1, 5–6). . . . Accordingly, man is set in the midst of creation as God's statue."

time, they are to exercise dominion not in an abusive or oppressive manner but as responsible guardians of the earth for God.[14]

Essentially, therefore, God at creation commissioned humanity to serve as representative rulers of the earth on his behalf. As the sovereign ruler and creator of the universe, God delegated to humanity as male and female the power to rule and to procreate. He put humans on the earth to take care of it for him, requiring them to reproduce as male and female. While there is not yet in the creation narrative any clear indication as to the exact role differentiation between the man and the woman, male headship is suggested by the fact that the name for the man (*ādām*) in Genesis 1:26–27 (and later in 5:1–2) is the Hebrew name for the race at large.[15] Table 1.2 shows how God made hu-man-ity (*ādām*) male and female, while at the same time the man (*ādām*) is given primary responsibility for humanity at large.[16]

Table 1.2: The Term *ādām* as a Name for the Human Race in Genesis 1–5

Genesis	English Translation with Hebrew Term for "Man"/"Woman" (*hā* = Hebrew article)
1.	*Creation of Humanity (1:26–28)*
1:26 1:27	**"Let us make *ādām* in our image."** **So God created *hā-ādām* in his own image,** **in the image of God he created *him*,** **male and female he created *them*.**
1:28	And God blessed *them*. And God said to *them*, "Be fruitful and multiply."

[14] Noah J. Toly and Daniel I. Block, eds., *Keeping God's Earth: The Global Environment in Biblical Perspective* (Downers Grove, IL: InterVarsity, 2010), provides reflections on how Christians ought to be involved in carrying out this mandate.
[15] See, e.g., Ortlund, "Male-Female Equality and Male Headship," 98: "*God's naming of the race 'man' whispers male headship*, which Moses will bring forward boldly in chapter two" (emphasis added). See also the important clarification that the man and the woman reflect the divine image individually, not just collectively (pp. 98–99, citing Gen. 5:1, 3). See further the important discussion in Sailhamer, "Genesis," 106–7.
[16] See, e.g., God's judgments addressed to "the woman" and "to Adam," the head of the human race—not merely "to the man"—in Gen. 3:16–17. Some point to the plural pronoun "them" in Gen. 1:28 as evidence that God assigned stewardship of the earth to the man and the woman jointly, apart from any male leadership. However, this insufficiently takes into account that the specific roles of the man and the woman in relation to each other are elaborated upon further in Genesis 2 (see below).

Genesis	English Translation with Hebrew Term for "Man"/"Woman" (hā = Hebrew article)
2.	*The Creation of the Man (2:7–8)*
2:7	Then the LORD God formed *hā-ādām* of dust from the *adāmāh* [ground] and breathed into his nostrils the breath of life, and *hā-ādām* became a living creature.
2:8	And the LORD God planted a garden in Eden, in the east, and there he put *hā-ādām* whom he had formed.
3.	*The Creation of the Woman for the Man (2:23–25)*
2:23	Then *hā-ādām* said, "This at last is bone of my bones and flesh of my flesh; she shall be called *ishah* because she was taken out of *ish*."
2:24	Therefore an *ish* shall leave his father and his mother and hold fast to his *ishah*, and they shall become one flesh.
2:25	And *hā-ādām* and his *ishah* were both naked and were not ashamed.
4.	*God's Judgment on the Woman and the Man (3:16–17)*
3:16	And to *hā-ishah* he said . . .
3:17	And to *ādām* he said . . .
5.	*Creation of First Offspring (4:1)*
4:1	Now *hā-ādām* knew Eve his wife, and she conceived and bore Cain, saying, "I have gotten a man (*ish*) with the help of the LORD."
6.	*Recap of Creation of Humanity (5:1–3)*
5:1	This is the book of the generations of *ādām*. When God created *ādām*, he made *him* in the likeness of God.
5:2	**Male and female he created *them*, and he blessed *them* and named *them* *ādām* when they were created.**
5:3	When *ādām* had lived 130 years . . .

The Man's Leadership in the Marriage and the Wife's Role as His Suitable Helper (Genesis 2)

We've seen that Genesis 1 focuses primarily on the creation of humanity as male and female in God's image. How does Genesis 2, then, build on and supplement Genesis 1?[17] In Genesis 2:4, the narrative returns to the creation of humankind that was mentioned in Genesis 1:26–28, yet provides additional details. Genesis 2:7–8 describes how God forms the man from the dust of the ground, breathes life into him, and places him in the garden of Eden. Genesis 2:15–17 records God's command to the man to work the garden and his gracious permission for him to eat from every tree except for the Tree of the Knowledge of Good and Evil. The woman is not present to hear the command (she hasn't been created yet!), so it's the man's responsibility to pass it on to her at a later time.[18]

In Genesis 2:18 we are given important information regarding God's purpose for creating the woman and her design in relation to the man: "It is not good that the man should be alone; I will make him a helper fit [i.e., suitable] for him."[19] The Creator is about to make a special companion and soul mate for the man. Yet rather than record this creative act immediately, the following verse describes how God brings all the animals to Adam so he can name them. What's going on here? Most likely, God is leading the man through a process of

---

[17] Note the recent proposal of a "new wave complementarianism" that understands male-female roles "not so much from the perspective of Genesis 2:18 . . . but more from Genesis 1:27" (Wendy Alsup, "A New Wave of Complementarianism," http://www.theologyforwomen.org/2013/04/a-new-wave-of-complementarianism.html). For a trenchant critique, see Kevin DeYoung, "New Wave Complementarianism: A Question and a Concern," http://thegospelcoalition.org/blogs/kevindeyoung/2013/05/03/new-wave-complementarianism-a-question-and-a-concern.

[18] When Paul mentions that the man was created first and that the woman was made for the man (1 Cor. 11:9; cf. Gen. 2:18, 22) and from the man (1 Cor. 11:8, 12; cf. Gen. 2:21), and elsewhere observes that Adam was created first, and then Eve (1 Tim. 2:13), he's simply registering observations from the text. Paul took the text literally, historically, and factually. The assumption is that because the man was created first, he was placed in a position of ultimate responsibility for the marriage. William Webb, however, argues that this is just a matter of the ancient custom of primogeniture, essentially the custom of the firstborn (*Slaves, Women, and Homosexuals: Exploring the Hermeneutics of Cultural Analysis* [Downers Grove, IL: InterVarsity, 2001], 136–42). He asserts that usually the firstborn had rights and privileges and that this was a mere cultural convention with no abiding normative ramifications. Genesis 2, however, is not merely a culture-bound expression of firstborn rights but refers to the creation of all of humanity in two genders and thus is vital in understanding our essential nature as creatures made for a specific, God-designed, and intended purpose. See the interaction with Webb on this point in Thomas Schreiner, "An Interpretation of 1 Timothy 2:9–15: A Dialogue with Scholarship," in *Women in the Church*, 2nd ed., ed. Andreas J. Köstenberger and Thomas R. Schreiner (Grand Rapids, MI: Baker, 2005), 106–8.

[19] The Hebrew phrase is *ezer kᵉnegdo*, which literally means "helper corresponding to him" (*k* = "like," *negd* = "corresponding," *o* = "to him"). The first term, *ezer*, conveys more the sense of subordination, while *kᵉnegdo* stresses the woman's congeniality to the man.

understanding, helping him to realize that he needs a counterpart, human but different, with whom he shares the image of God and can exercise representative rule through the procreation of offspring. In verse 20, then, the same phrase recurs once again: "no suitable helper was found for him."

After the temporary letdown resulting from the declaration that no suitable helper was found for the man from among the animals, verse 21 narrates how God at last takes action: "So the LORD God caused a deep sleep to fall upon the man, and while he slept took one of his ribs and closed up its place with flesh." It's not that God couldn't get it right the first time. Rather, he led the man to see that none of the animals could meet his need for companionship. What is more, we see that the woman's creation isn't man's idea; it's an act of divine grace. In fact, the man doesn't contribute anything at all to the entire process. To be sure, he himself was created first, but he has no part in the creation of the woman (except for providing one of his ribs, and even that not by his own choice).

"What's going on here? Most likely, God is leading the man through a process of understanding . . . that he needs a counterpart, human but different, with whom he shares the image of God and can exercise representative rule through the procreation of offspring."

Verse 22 states, "And the rib that the LORD God had taken from the man he made into a woman and brought her to the man." We've already seen that, according to Genesis 1:26–27, God created humanity male and female. Now we see the process by which God fashions the man and the woman: he makes them separately (the man first, then the woman), but for each other. They are products of separate acts of divine creation. The man is formed from the ground, signifying that humanity is part of creation at large; then the woman is created from the man, signifying their close bond.[20] The man exclaims, "This at last is bone of my bones and flesh of my flesh" (Gen. 2:23), joyfully affirming what God has done in the creation of the woman. And he is given the privilege of assigning the woman a name derived from his own (ish, ishah; Gen. 2:23; cf. 3:20).

We see that the biblical text doesn't pit the man and the woman

---

[20] Regarding the creation of the woman from one of the man's ribs, see Sailhamer, "Genesis," 81–82.

against each other but rather presents their union as exceedingly intimate and harmonious. The idea that the genders are locked in an adversarial, antagonistic relationship is utterly foreign to the biblical creation account. To the contrary: Adam and Eve are super-excited! The claim that the man's headship and the woman's role as his suitable helper reflect the man's superiority and the woman's inferiority is likewise not borne out by the Genesis account. Rather, God's plan for humanity is one of partnership in which the man, as God-appointed leader, and his wife alongside him jointly represent the Creator by exercising dominion over the earth. In this vein, God places the man in a position of accountability and responsibility to his Creator.

What? I'm Supposed to Be Your "Helper"? (Gen. 2:18, 20)

Before we move on to Genesis 3, let's take a closer look at the term *suitable helper*.[21] "What?" you may say if you're a woman reading this. "Am I supposed to be *his* helper?" What does this phrase mean? To begin with, it may seem obvious, but it is nonetheless important to note that the woman is called the man's helper; not the other way around. From a fair reading of Genesis 2, it doesn't seem that male-female roles are reversible. At the same time, the expression clearly conveys that the woman is congenial to the man in a way that none of the animals is (vv. 19–20; cf. v. 23: "bone of his bones and flesh of his flesh") and that she is God's perfect provision for him in his need of companionship (v. 18). If you had asked Eve, she probably would have said the same about Adam. He was exactly what she needed!

> "The claim that the man's headship and the woman's role as his suitable helper reflect the man's superiority and the woman's inferiority is likewise not borne out by the Genesis account. Rather, God's plan for humanity is one of partnership in which the man, as God-appointed leader, and his wife alongside him jointly represent the Creator by exercising dominion over the earth."

With regard to God's mandate for humanity to be fruitful and multiply and to fill the earth and subdue it (Gen. 1:28), the woman is

---

[21] A really good book on what it means practically to be a "helper" is Susan Hunt, *By Design: God's Distinctive Calling for Women* (Wheaton, IL: Crossway, 1994).

shown to be the man's suitable partner in both procreation (becoming "one flesh" with him, which means more, but not less, than fruitful sexual union; Gen. 2:24) and in the earth's domestication (Gen. 1:28).[22] The woman's role is distinct from the man's (in fact, their roles are complementary), yet the contribution of both sexes is absolutely vital. While assigned to the man as his helper and thus placed under his overall care and responsibility, the woman is the man's partner in ruling the earth for God. This much seems clear from reading the references to the woman as suitable helper in the immediate context, but let's now look at the phrase itself.

In Genesis 2:18 and 20, the word "helper" (*ezer*) is used to describe the woman's role in relation to the man. Many of us women today have trouble seeing ourselves as helpers of the man. Why should we help him? Isn't this an inferior role? Why shouldn't he help us? In working this through, it's helpful to note that the term *helper* is applied several times throughout the Old Testament to none other than God himself.[23] Although God takes on the role of helper only temporarily to come to the aid of a given individual (in contrast to the woman who is said to be the man's helper permanently), the fact that God can be said to be a helper lends great dignity and value to this role. Since God is clearly not inferior to anyone, whatever the term *helper* entails, it's certainly not inferiority.

On the other hand, it wouldn't be accurate to adduce the scriptural references to God submitting himself to a person as his or her helper as proof that male-female roles are interchangeable.[24] In God's case, being a helper means that he may choose to subordinate himself to humanity to render some kind of assistance. This doesn't affect his

---

[22] See esp. Sailhamer, "Genesis," 81, who notes that the church father Augustine interpreted the woman's role as the man's "helper" in terms of her task of bearing children while others support a wider sense. Sailhamer himself sides with Augustine, noting that "it appears most likely that the 'help' envisioned is tied to the bearing of children." He notes both the possible wordplay between "helper" (*ezer*) and "offspring" (*zera*, lit. "seed") and the fact that the woman's judgment is tied to her childbearing role (Gen. 3:16; cf. v. 15).

[23] See Ex. 18:4; Pss. 20:2; 33:20; 70:5; 115:9–11; 121:1–2; 146:5. See the helpful discussion of the phrase "suitable helper" in Ortlund, "Male-Female Equality and Male Headship," 103–5, who writes, "Therefore, the fact that the Old Testament portrays God as our Helper proves only that the helper's role is a glorious one, worthy even of the Almighty" (p. 104).

[24] See, e.g., Jim and Sarah Sumner, *Just How Married Do You Want to Be? Practicing Oneness in Marriage* (Grand Rapids, MI: Baker, 2009), 54, who claim that in the Hebrew phrase *ezer kᵉnegdo* the term *kᵉnegdo* denotes a "correspondent" or "counterpart," and *ezer* refers to a "powerful type of helper" because it pertains to God in sixteen of its nineteen OT occurrences.

divinity in any way. For the woman to be subordinate to the man (albeit not by her own choice but by God's creative will) doesn't alter the fact that she is part of humanity created in God's image as male and female. Some try to reinterpret the meaning of the word *helper* in order to remove any notion of subordination because they (erroneously) believe this to be an inferior role, maintaining that God could never be subordinate in role to anyone at any time, but, as mentioned, this is unnecessary.

The argument from God and the woman sharing the term *helper* also insufficiently recognizes the fact that the woman isn't directly comparable to God in his essence or variety of roles. Just because the term is applied to both God and the woman doesn't establish an analogy as to their nature or all of their other roles. Otherwise, to be consistent, the woman would be superior to the man by virtue of being called his helper, since God is most certainly superior to humans! Also, God is our creator and Lord; the woman is not. The fallacy in the above-stated argument, therefore, is the assumption that subordination necessarily implies personal inferiority. It does not. For children to be entrusted to their parents' care, for example, doesn't mean they're inferior persons. Neither are employees inferior to their bosses because they report to them.

> "The fallacy in the above-stated argument, therefore, is the assumption that subordination necessarily implies personal inferiority. It does not. For children to be entrusted to their parents' care, for example, doesn't mean they're inferior persons. Neither are employees inferior to their bosses because they report to them."

An analogy from the Trinity may also help.[25] Some reject any form of subordination in the Trinity. But Scripture does seem to affirm such a notion. In John's Gospel, for example, Jesus states, "I and the Father are one" (John 10:30), and later on says, "The Father is greater

---

[25] See Bruce Ware, "Tampering with the Trinity: Does the Son Submit to His Father?," *Journal of Biblical Manhood and Womanhood* 6 (Spring 2001): 4–12; "Equal in Essence, Distinct in Roles: Eternal Functional Authority and Submission among the Essentially Equal Divine Persons of the Godhead," *Journal for Biblical Manhood and Womanhood* 13 (2008): 43–58. More recently, see Ware's review of Thomas H. McCall, *Which Trinity? Whose Monotheism? Philosophical and Systematic Theologians on the Metaphysics of Trinitarian Theology* (Grand Rapids, MI: Eerdmans, 2010), in *Journal of Biblical Manhood and Womanhood* 16 (Fall 2011): 41–46. See also Christopher W. Cowan, "The Father and Son in the Fourth Gospel: Johannine Subordination Revisited," *Journal of the Evangelical Theological Society* 49 (2006): 115–35; Robert Letham, "The Man-Woman Debate: Theological Comment," *Westminster Theological Journal* 52 (1990): 65–78; and Stephen D. Kovach and Peter R. Schemm Jr., "A Defense of the Doctrine of the Eternal Subordination of the Son," *Journal of the Evangelical Theological Society* 42 (1999): 461–76.

than I" (John 14:28). John thus presents unity of purpose and subordination side by side.[26] Jesus's prayer in the garden of Gethsemane, "Not my will, but yours be done" (Luke 22:42), likewise illustrates the Son's submission to the Father without diminishing his inclusion in the plurality of the Godhead in terms of being. The Son's subordination doesn't imply personal inferiority. The Trinity illustrates the possibility of two beings forming an intimate oneness, accomplishing their mission by fulfilling distinct, complementary roles (see 1 Cor. 11:3). The Father didn't die on the cross for our sins; the Son did. Role distinctions within the Godhead don't imply difference in essential being.

Some contemporary biblical scholars present headship and submission as if they're merely a result of the fall. However, this fails to account for the fact that the man was exercising dominion prior to the creation of the woman (receiving the divine command, naming the animals, etc.; see table 1.3). What is more, those who interpret the phrase *suitable helper* as conveying undifferentiated equality fail to observe other indications of male headship in the foundational Genesis account. If the original creation was egalitarian, how do we account for the fact that there are clear indications of the man's ultimate responsibility for humanity at large? And why is Adam, rather than Eve, contrasted with Christ as the first human being through whom sin entered the world (Rom. 5:12–21), when, according to the Genesis account, it was Eve who sinned first?[27] The most likely explanation is that even though Eve sinned first, it was Adam who was held ultimately accountable by God as representing the human race.

Table 1.3: Does the Term "Helper" in Genesis 2:18, 20 Denote Equality?

Claim:
The term *helper* is applied in Scripture to God; since God is not an inferior being, the term *helper* doesn't convey the woman's inferiority to the man. *Helper* means "equal."

[26] For more details, see Andreas J. Köstenberger and Scott R. Swain, *Father, Son, and Spirit: The Trinity and John's Gospel*, New Studies in Biblical Theology 24 (Downers Grove, IL: InterVarsity, 2008).
[27] See Ortlund, "Male-Female Equality and Male Headship," 107.

> **Response:**
>
> It's true that *helper* is applied to God in Scripture. However, this doesn't diminish the fact that *helper* is a subordinate role. It only shows that we must distinguish between a person's *being* and his or her *role*.
>
> God, the creator and Lord of the universe, may choose to take on a subordinate role (temporarily) to help his people. The woman was created by God to come alongside the man (permanently and constitutionally) as his helper.
>
> While *suitable* connotes the sense "corresponding to" (sometimes translated "fit for"), "helper" doesn't mean "equal," but in context suggests a subordinate role.

To conclude, the fact that the woman is called a helper in Genesis 2—just like God is called a helper repeatedly in the Psalms—shows how significant and special the woman's role toward the man really is. At the same time, claiming that the use of the term *helper* with regard to the woman requires undifferentiated male-female equality (if not female superiority) fails both logically and theologically.[28] The woman was created to meet the man's need for companionship and to assist him and partner with him in subduing the earth, particularly through procreation. In this regard, the man needs the woman, and the woman needs the man; neither is able to multiply and subdue the earth without the other. The woman comes alongside the man as his companion with whom he procreates children, additional image bearers who join in the task of multiplying, filling the earth, and exercising dominion over it.

Table 1.4: Indications of the Man's Leadership in Genesis 1–3

Passage in Genesis	Significance
1:27; 5:2	The name for humanity is the same as for the male (*ādām*; see table 1.2).
2:7	God created the man first.

---

[28] Philip B. Payne, *Man and Woman, One in Christ: An Exegetical and Theological Study of Paul's Letters* (Grand Rapids, MI: Zondervan, 2009), attempts to read Genesis 1–3 consistently from an egalitarian vantage point, though his reasoning is largely unpersuasive. For a summary of Payne's arguments and a concise critique, see Thomas Schreiner, review of Philip Payne, *Man and Woman, One in Christ*, in *Journal of Biblical Manhood and Womanhood* 15 (Spring 2010): 33–34.

Passage in Genesis	Significance
2:15–17	The man is the recipient of the divine command prior to the creation of the woman.
2:15, 19–20	The man is put in the garden to work and name the animals.
2:18, 21–22	God created the woman for the man and from the man.
2:18, 20	The woman is called the man's suitable helper.
2:23	The man names the woman.
3:16	As a result of the fall, the woman's desire is to elevate herself above her husband in a struggle for control.

Husband and Wife Become "One Flesh" (Gen. 2:24)

In verse 24, then, Moses explains how, in marriage, a man leaves his paternal home, is joined to his wife in matrimony, and becomes one flesh with her, establishing a distinct family unit and creating offspring through procreation. What does it mean for the man and the woman to become "one flesh"? As Raymond Ortlund Jr. points out, becoming "one flesh" means a lot more than sex: "It is the profound fusion of two lives into one, shared life together, by the mutual consent and covenant of marriage. It is the complete and permanent giving over of oneself into a new circle of shared existence with one's partner."[29]

The narrative of the creation of the man and the woman concludes with the statement, "And the man and his wife were both naked and were not ashamed" (v. 25). At this juncture, all is well in Paradise. In this idyllic state, the man and the woman are completely innocent, obediently resting in God's word, trusting in him and depending on his care and provision, and their union is close, trusting, and intimate.[30]

---

[29] Ortlund, "Male-Female Equality and Male Headship," 101.

[30] Victor P. Hamilton, *The Book of Genesis, Chapters 1–17*, New International Commentary on the Old Testament (Grand Rapids, MI: Eerdmans, 1990), 181, remarks that the couple's unashamed nakedness indicates that "no barrier of any kind drove a wedge between Adam and Eve." Gordon J. Wenham,

Together, they exercise dominion over the earth in keeping with God's purpose and design. And as the man is entrusted with the care of his wife, he is to exercise this responsibility in an atmosphere of self-giving love, unbroken trust, and perfect unity.[31]

The Fall (Genesis 3)

The fall of humanity, as mentioned, was engineered by a complete reversal of the divine design. Instead of God's authority being mediated from Adam to Eve to the rest of creation, the biblical fall narrative recounts how the Serpent (Satan) approached Eve, who took the initiative, with Adam following her lead, in breaking God's commandment. Nevertheless, despite Eve's role in the rebellion, God held the man, not the woman, primarily responsible for the rebellious act (Gen. 3:9; cf. 3:17; Rom. 5:12–14).[32] Adam bears ultimate responsibility for humanity's sin because he was the one God had put in charge in the first place. This is a standard feature of any authority structure, whether in government, the military, or a properly run business—the one in charge is primarily responsible for everything that takes place in his or her realm of responsibility. As Harry Truman memorably put it, "The buck stops here."

Table 1.5: Role Reversal at the Fall

Lines of Authority at Creation	Lines of Authority at the Fall	Realigned Lines of Authority
God Man Woman Serpent (Satan)	Serpent (Satan) Woman Man God	God Man Woman Serpent (Satan)

<hr/>

Genesis 1–15, Word Biblical Commentary 1 (Waco, TX: Word, 1987), 72, observes that the verse "reiterates the contentment of the couple with God's provision."

[31] Daniel I. Block, "Marriage and Family in Ancient Israel," in *Marriage and Family in the Biblical World*, ed. Ken M. Campbell (Downers Grove, IL: InterVarsity, 2003), 33–102, presents the largely positive function of male headship throughout the OT. In contrast to this harmonious picture of the man and the woman jointly trusting in God's care and provision, some feminists cast the sexes as autonomous, independent agents. Some also tend to exaggerate the degree to which nonfeminists are preoccupied with male authority. However, some feminists reject the notion of authority altogether, positing a kind of "servant leadership" devoid of authority altogether. The late Stanley Grenz, for example, in *Women in the Church*, argues for this notion of servant leadership. Stanley J. Grenz and Denise Muir Kjesbo, *Women in the Church: A Biblical Theology of Women in Ministry* (Downers Grove, IL: InterVarsity, 1995), 222–30.

[32] For the NT's "Adam christology," which has a crucial bearing on the biblical theology of manhood and womanhood, see Rom. 5:12–21; 1 Cor. 15:21–23, 44–49.

Scenario at the Fall (Gen. 3:1–7)

The Serpent. How exactly did the fall occur? The narrator of the Genesis account draws attention to the Devil's devious character, describing him as "crafty," that is, shrewd or subtle with intent to deceive. The Serpent's cunning nature becomes apparent when we compare and contrast God's actual words with the Devil's distorted version used to cast doubt in the mind of his unsuspecting victim.

Table 1.6: Satan's Deception of the Woman

God's Original Command (Gen. 2:16–17)	Satan's Deception (Gen. 3:1, 4)
And the Lord God commanded the man, saying, "You may surely eat **of every tree of the garden**, but of the tree of the knowledge of good and evil <u>you shall not eat</u>, for in the day that you eat of it *you shall surely die."*	"'<u>You shall not eat</u> **of any tree in the garden**'?" *"You will* **not** *surely die."*

In the Hebrew original, the Devil's craftiness is even more apparent. His first word is "actually," by which he immediately calls into question God's goodness and generosity. While God in fact was generous, the Devil casts him as stingy.[33] It's as if the Serpent said, "Really? What else does the Creator intend to withhold from the woman?" In the original word order, God's original prohibition is framed by his gracious permission: "Of every tree of the garden, you may eat." The Devil, however, in feigned surprise, subtly conflates God's good gift with the prohibition: "Not [in the original word order] shall you eat of any tree of the garden?"

Then, even more shockingly, the Devil casts off all subtlety and proceeds to frontally contradict God's pronouncement, casting doubt on his integrity and truthfulness. Where the Creator had said, "In the day that you eat of it you shall surely die" (Gen. 2:17), the Devil flatly asserts, "You will *not* surely die" (Gen. 3:4). Not only is God withholding good things from the man and the woman, the Serpent alleges, but

---

[33] Wenham (*Genesis 1–15*, 73) calls this "a total travesty of God's original generous permission."

also he lied to them about the consequences of transgressing the divine commandment![34] Finally, the Serpent casts doubts on God's motives: "For God knows that when you eat of it your eyes will be opened, and you will be like God, knowing good and evil" (v. 5). Somehow, the Serpent insinuates, God has sinister motives in issuing his directives to the first human couple. As the narrative progressively makes clear, the Devil is a devious, deceptive seducer who opposes God and his word and successfully tricks the woman into disobeying her Creator.[35]

Table 1.7: The Serpent's Strategy (Gen. 3:1–5)

Passage	Words	Strategy
Verse 1	"Did God actually say?"	Cast doubt on God's generosity
Verse 4	"You will *not* surely die."	Cast doubt on God's integrity
Verse 5	"For God knows . . . you will be like God."	Cast doubt on God's motives

The woman. What about the woman? Essentially, she seems to be innocently (even naïvely) assuming that the Devil's question is genuine and answers it straightforwardly (albeit inaccurately). Again, compare the woman's words with God's original command in table 1.8.

Table 1.8: The Woman's Misrepresentation

God's Original Command (Gen. 2:16–17)	The Woman's Misrepresentation (Gen. 3:2–3)
"You may surely **eat of every tree of the garden**, but of the tree of the knowledge of good and evil you shall not eat, for in the day that you eat of it you shall surely die."	"We may **eat of the fruit of the trees in the garden**, but *God* said, 'You shall not eat of the fruit of the tree that is in the midst of the garden, <u>neither shall you touch it</u>, lest you die."

---

[34] Other subtle misrepresentations include the fact that the Serpent asks, "Did God *say*?" when the narrative states that God *commanded*. Cf. Kenneth A. Mathews, *Genesis 1–11:26*, New American Commentary 1A (Nashville: Broadman, 1996), 235.

[35] See the similar chart in Carrie Sandom, *Different by Design: God's Blueprint for Men and Women* (Fearn, Ross-shire, UK: Christian Focus, 2012), 71.

Again, there are several differences between God's actual command and the woman's representation of it. First, "Eat of *every* tree of the garden" has become "Eat of the *fruit* of the trees in the garden." Second, on a subtle note, she follows the Devil's designation of God as *Elohim* ("God") rather than *Yahweh Elohim* ("Lord God"). Most importantly, third, she adds the prohibition, "Neither shall you touch it." Regardless of what one should make of these more or less subtle differences, what's clear is that the woman is for the first time pressed to explain and defend the word of God. The Serpent has successfully engaged Eve in an exercise in which she must discern truth from error, and he has awakened the woman's mind to the possibility that there might be another way to interpret God's word.[36]

Essentially, the Serpent's message to Eve is: "You can transgress your Maker's command with impunity. There will be no negative consequences. In fact, you will be wiser and more fulfilled if you do." And the woman, deceived by the Serpent's guile, takes the bait: "So when the woman saw that the tree was good for food, and that it was a delight to the eyes, and that the tree was to be desired to make one wise, she took of its fruit and ate" (Gen. 3:6). Somehow, she reasons, following the Devil's twisted logic, by transgressing God's command, she will become more like God.

What constitutes the primary appeal for the woman? The tree is "good for food": there is an appeal to her taste. The fruit is a "delight to the eyes": there is an appeal to aesthetic pleasure. Finally, and climactically, there is an appeal to deeper wisdom.[37] Later, when held accountable by God, the woman laments, "The serpent deceived me, and I ate" (v. 13). Her eyes had been opened, and she now understands that the Serpent misrepresented reality, including God's original command and the threatened consequences for disobedience. The Devil, not God, turns out to be the actual liar, and God's word is vindicated.

The man. Now, what about the man? During the entire conversation between the Serpent and Eve, Adam is conspicuously silent (vv. 1–5), though the narrative doesn't say whether he is present during part

---

[36] See Greg Stiekes, "The Fall of Eve in the Letters of Paul," seminar paper, Southeastern Baptist Theological Seminary (Wake Forest, NC, 2013), 7. Greg is currently working on a dissertation on the subject.
[37] For a practical book on women's contentment, see Melissa B. Kruger, *The Envy of Eve: Finding Contentment in a Covetous World* (Fearn, Ross-shire, UK: Christian Focus, 2012).

or all of the conversation. The narrative only refers to Adam as Eve's husband, "who was with her" when she gives him the forbidden fruit (v. 6). Nevertheless, some dialogue between the man and the woman preceding the man's partaking of the fruit seems implied in the wording of the divine pronouncement: "Because you have listened to the voice of your wife" (v. 17). As Victor Hamilton notes, "The woman does not try to tempt the man. She simply gives and he takes. He neither challenges nor raises questions. . . . Hers is a sin of initiative. His is a sin of acquiescence."[38] The man follows his wife's lead, when God had made him the leader.

The Aftermath

God calls the man and the woman to account for their sin (Gen. 3:8–13). Following the fall, God is shown to take the initiative in calling the man and the woman to account for their sin (Gen. 3:8–13). When they hear "the sound of the LORD God walking in the garden in the cool of the day," the man and his wife hide from God's presence among the trees of the garden (v. 8). While they were created to live in God's presence and in communion with him (the narrative seems to suggest that God's "walking in the garden" was a customary occurrence), the man and the woman now seek to elude their Creator's presence. How things have changed! But there's no place to hide from God.

The Lord first calls the man, not the woman, even though the woman sinned first, an indication of the man's ultimate responsibility for the couple (v. 9). The man acknowledges that he hid from God because he was afraid and because he was naked (v. 10). God probingly responds, "Who told you that you were naked? Have you eaten of the tree of which I commanded *you* not to eat?" In fact, it was the man to whom God directed the original command (Gen. 2:17). In response, the man has the chutzpah to blame not only the woman but even the Creator himself for his sin: "*The woman* whom *you gave to be with me, she* gave me fruit of the tree, and I ate" (Gen. 3:12). It's as if the man was saying, "Remember the suitable helper you gave me? It's all your fault! Obviously, she wasn't so suitable after all! What was I supposed to do?

---

[38] Hamilton, *Genesis*, 191.

Next time don't make somebody who leads me into sin!" No response from God. No response necessary.

God then proceeds to call the woman to account: "What is this that you have done?" (v. 13). The Creator here focuses on the woman's action and calls on her to accept responsibility for her choice to transgress his command. Lamentably, though by now somewhat predictably (and consistent with her fallen nature), the woman replies, "*The serpent deceived me*, and I ate." In other words, "Don't blame me; blame the Serpent!" It's almost as if the woman was saying, "What did you expect? Of course I ate from the forbidden tree! I practically had no choice!"

Again, God doesn't dignify the woman's excuse with a response but instead proceeds to pronounce a series of judgments on the Serpent, the woman, and the man (note that God doesn't call the Serpent to account, perhaps because, in God's mysterious providence, fallen angels are not subject to redemption, though he does pronounce judgment on the Devil). Thus we see that God calls the man and the woman to account separately, treating both as responsible agents, though because of their fallen sin nature both fail to accept responsibility for their action and instead try to shift the blame to others (the Serpent, the woman, and even God). So we see that their sin didn't separate the man and the woman only from their Creator; it also separated them from each other.

God's judgment on the Serpent, the woman, and the man (Gen. 3:14–19). God's judgment swiftly ensues, climactically proceeding from the Serpent to the woman and finally to Adam, the man (possibly indicating his ultimate responsibility for humanity's fall into sin). Tellingly, the consequences of the sin and the ensuing judgments on the man and on the woman observably relate to their primary realms of responsibility and role, striking each at the heart of their existence and identity as persons created according to God's design.[39]

The judgment on the Serpent "because you have done this" (i.e., caused the fall by deceiving the woman) entails a curse: "Cursed are you above all livestock and above all beasts of the field; on your

---

[39] For the connection between the divine judgments and God's original mandate to the man and the woman, see Mitchell Chase, "God's Judgment on His Blessing: How Genesis 1:28 Informs the Punishments on Adam and Eve," *Journal of Biblical Manhood and Womanhood* 18 (Spring 2013): 16–21.

belly you shall go, and dust you shall eat all the days of your life" (Gen. 3:14).[40] It also entails continual spiritual warfare between Satan and humanity in the context of God's promise of a Messiah: "I will put enmity between you and the woman, and between your offspring and her offspring: he shall bruise your head, and you shall bruise his heel" (v. 15). Following the fall, spiritual warfare will be a continuing reality, and history will gradually move toward humanity's redemption in Christ.

The consequences for the woman pertain to her roles as wife and mother: "I will surely multiply your pain in *childbearing*; in pain you shall bring forth *children*. Your desire shall be for your *husband*, and he shall rule over you" (v. 16). Unlike in the case of the divine judgment on the Serpent and the man, no reason for the punishment of the woman is given, perhaps because the reason is obvious: the woman transgressed the divine command. The woman should have worked in tandem with her husband as his "helper"; instead, she followed the Serpent's lead. As a result, she is destined to experience increased pain in childbearing and a negative change in her relationship with her husband.[41] This increased pain in childbearing might cause some women not to want to have children, even today, though this would place them in a state of disobedience with regard to God's original command for humanity to multiply.[42] The loving harmony that prevailed before the fall will be replaced by a pattern of struggle in which the woman will seek to exert control over her husband (interpreting "desire" as "desire for control," cf. Gen. 4:7), who will respond by asserting his authority.[43] In failing to exercise his God-given leadership

---

[40] Note that while the Serpent (v. 14: "cursed are you") and the ground (v. 17: "cursed is the ground") are cursed, the woman and the man are not, though God does pronounce judgments on them and delineates the negative consequences of the fall on the woman and the man in their respective roles. See John H. Walton, *Genesis*, NIV Application Commentary (Grand Rapids, MI: Zondervan, 2001), 236–39.

[41] There is a play on words in the original Hebrew: while in Genesis 1:28, the man and the woman were told to multiply, now the woman is told that the pain she will experience in childbirth will multiply. See C. John Collins, "What Happened to Adam and Eve? A Literary-theological Approach to Genesis 3," *Presbyterion* 27 (2001): 26.

[42] Sailhamer, "Genesis," 93, points out that "after the fall, childbirth becomes the means by which the snake is defeated and the blessing restored. The pain of every birth is a reminder of the hope that lies in God's promise" (citing Rom. 8:22–24; cf. Matt. 24:8).

[43] See Sailhamer (ibid.): "The sense of 'desiring' in 3:16 should be understood as the wife's desire to overcome or gain the upper hand over her husband." The parallels in wording between Genesis 4:7 ("Sin is crouching at the door. Its desire is for you, but you must rule over it") and 3:16 are very strong. See also Susan T. Foh, "What Is the Woman's Desire?," *Westminster Theological Journal* 37 (1975): 376–83; against those (e.g., Walton, *Genesis*) who interpret "desire" here as sexual desire in keeping with the word's meaning in Song 7:10.

role, he might exhibit passivity, as he did when Satan tempted the woman in the garden and he failed to protect her. Or the man might harshly dominate his wife.[44] In either event, following the fall the male-female relationship is mired in a perennial struggle for control.

Table 1.9: Parallels between Genesis 3:16 and 4:7

Genesis 3:16	Genesis 4:7
"Your *desire* shall be for your husband, and he shall *rule over* you."	"Its *desire* is for you, but you must *rule over* it."

The consequences for the man's sin ("because you listened to the voice of your wife") include increased hardship in fulfilling God's command to subdue the earth (cf. Gen. 1:28). Like the woman, he will experience pain (Gen. 3:17); while pain for the woman will come in giving birth to children, for the man it will come in his work. He must now extract the fruit of the land from thorns and thistles and eat his bread by the sweat of his brow (vv. 17–19).[45] God's pronouncement of judgment on the man for listening to his wife constitutes an indirect acknowledgment of the man's responsibility as God-appointed leader in the relationship. Remember, God's original command had been addressed to the man: "And the LORD God commanded the *man*, saying, 'You may surely eat of every tree of the garden, but of the tree of the knowledge of good and evil you shall not eat, for in the day that you eat of it you shall surely die'" (Gen. 2:17). God had made clear his intention that the man was to assume responsibility for ensuring the couple's obedience and compliance, but at the fall the man remained passive and allowed the woman to take the lead instead.

The naming of the woman and the expulsion from the garden (Gen. 3:20–24). Now that the divine judgments have been pronounced, the narrative proceeds to recount the naming of Eve by the man (Gen. 3:20),

[44] The word "shall" in verse 16, "and he *shall* rule over you," could be either descriptive (That's what'll happen—though it's wrong; negative connotation of "rule") or prescriptive (That's what I want him to do—because that's how I set up the relationship in the first place; positive or neutral connotation of "rule").

[45] Sailhamer ("Genesis," 92) draws attention to the importance of "eating" in the opening chapters of Genesis. While prior to the fall they were "free to eat" from any tree in the garden (Gen. 2:16), the woman and the man both succumbed to temptation, which is simply narrated in terms of eating: "She *ate* it . . . and he *ate* it" (Gen. 3:6). Now, in God's judgment on the man, he is told that he will "eat" of the ground only through painful toil.

God's provision of clothing for Adam and his wife (v. 21), and the expulsion of the man and the woman from the garden of Eden (vv. 22–24). The naming of Eve is narrated as follows: "The man called his wife's name Eve, because she was the mother of all living" (v. 20). In the Hebrew original, the name Eve constitutes a wordplay on the word for "life." There is irony in the fact that in the same textual unit, the man and his wife are barred from accessing the "tree of life" lest they

> "God's pronouncement of judgment on the man for listening to his wife constitutes an indirect acknowledgment of the man's responsibility as God-appointed leader in the relationship."

"live forever" (v. 22). Similarly, the man's name, Adam, represents a wordplay with the Hebrew word for "ground," *adāmāh* (vv. 19–20; see also Gen. 2:7). This is now the second time Adam names the woman; her first name, *ishah* (see Gen. 2:23), designated her origin or source (taken from *ish*, the man); her second name indicates her destiny ("mother of all the living").[46] It is likely that the man's naming of the woman implies authority, just as the man's naming of the animals prior to the creation of the woman was part of the fulfillment of God's mandate to govern the earth. Similarly, in both ancient cultures and today, the privilege of naming a child is part of the parents' authority over a child.

In the end, both the man and the woman will die (Gen. 3:19, 22), but in the meantime, they're expelled from the garden (v. 24). Nevertheless, as an indication of his great mercy and love for his creatures and image bearers, God clothes the man and the woman (v. 21). What is more, in his judgment on the Serpent, as mentioned, God holds out the promise of a future Messiah who will defeat the Serpent and undo the effects of the fall (v. 15). In his wisdom, goodness, and love, God had appointed the man as the leader and brought the woman alongside him as his helper for their own protection and good. But, sadly, the couple sinned against their Creator by transgressing his instructions. In subsequent history, the woman is often blamed for the fall,[47] but the

---

[46] Ibid., 93.

[47] See, e.g., the intertestamental work Sirach 25:24: "From a woman sin had its beginning, and because of her we all die." In Josephus's account of the fall, Adam says, "It was her [the woman's] deception that had caused him to sin" (*Jewish Antiquities* 1.48). See also the work *Life of Adam and Eve*, which may have been written toward the end of the first century AD. But see Paul in Romans 5:12: "Sin came into the world through one man"; 5:15: "Many died through one man's trespass."

truth is that the man and the woman sinned jointly and together are in need of divine redemption.[48]

Life after the fall. There are numerous lessons to be learned and implications that arise from the biblical fall narrative. Perhaps most important, men, in keeping with God's original design, should live out their roles as the spiritual leaders in their marriages and families, and women should follow their lead rather than try to usurp their husband's role. Rather than let Satan divide them or take advantage of the woman's vulnerable position when she is without her husband, couples should work together in tandem, develop a habit of praying together, and continually seek each other's advice, counsel, and support. In this way, they are to strive, with the Lord's help, to withstand Satan's attempts to intrude into their relationship, to divide them, and to wreak havoc in their marriage and family. They should be faithful to each other, enjoy their sexual relationship, and continue to live out God's mandate to be fruitful and multiply and fill the earth and subdue it.

Developments in the History of Israel Subsequent to the Fall

The fall and sin significantly subverted God's original design for the male-female relationship, though the original design continues to be upheld.[49] The Old Testament describes several ways in which humanity at large and Israel in particular fall short of God's ideal for marriage: polygamy, divorce, adultery, and homosexuality. The state of marriage and family in the Old Testament, along with all of life, subsequent to the fall thus presents itself as in great need of redemption and restoration in the Messiah. The big picture is clear: God's perfect original design was subverted, though far from eradicated and certainly not set aside as the ideal.

Polygamy

It is evident very early on that humanity compromised God's original monogamous design in which one man and one woman would

---

[48] New Testament references to the fall in general and to Eve's role in particular include 2 Cor. 11:3; 1 Tim. 2:14; and possibly also Rom. 7:11 and 16:17–20 (see Stiekes, "Fall of Eve").

[49] This is something that's still with us because we've inherited the sin nature and are still sinners. There are times when wives struggle with temptation to manipulate their husbands and to subtly try to subvert his God-given role as the leader. Conversely, husbands may respond in a number of inappropriate ways, whether by abdicating their God-given responsibility or by treating their wives harshly.

become one flesh (Gen. 2:24) and in which a man would leave his father and mother and be united with his wife, not his wives. Within six generations, shortly after Adam had died, we read that "Lamech took two wives" (Gen. 4:19). It doesn't take too long before we see a violation of God's plan for there to be one man and one woman in a marriage relationship.

While God's plan for marriage hadn't changed, polygamy was nonetheless quite prevalent in Old Testament times, and, sadly, the list of individuals who had multiple wives reads like a "Who's Who" in the Old Testament. Abraham (Gen. 16:3), Esau (Gen. 26:34; 28:9), Jacob (Gen. 29:30), Gideon (Judg. 8:30), Elkanah (1 Sam. 1:1–2), David (2 Sam. 3:2–5; 5:13), Solomon (1 Kings 11:3), and many others had multiple wives, even though there were Old Testament laws against polygamy (Lev. 18:18: "And you shall not take a woman as a rival wife to her sister"; Deut. 17:17: "And he shall not acquire many wives for himself"). However, the narratives featuring patriarchs who had multiple wives indicate that there were invariably negative consequences, whether disruptive favoritism in the marriages of Jacob (Gen. 29:30), Elkanah (1 Sam. 1:4–5), and Rehoboam (2 Chron. 11:21) or jealousy in the marriages of Abraham (Gen. 21:9–10), Jacob (Gen. 30:14–16), and Elkanah (1 Sam. 1:6). Solomon's foreign wives turned away his heart after other gods (1 Kings 11:4).

Monogamy continued to be upheld and presented as God's ideal (e.g., Prov. 12:4: "An excellent wife is the crown of her husband"; 18:22: "He who finds a wife finds a good thing and obtains favor from the Lord"; 19:14: "a prudent wife is from the Lord"; see also Ps. 128:3; Prov. 31:10–31; Ezek. 16:8). While explicit prohibitions of polygamy in the Old Testament are rare, no one could read the Old Testament and walk away thinking polygamy represented God's ideal. In the New Testament, Jesus himself reiterated God's original design of marriage as between one man and one woman (Matt. 19:4–6; Mark 10:6–9 citing Gen. 2:24), and one looks in vain for references to polygamy anywhere in the New Testament, indicating that this was not likely a practice of New Testament believers or acceptable in the early church.

Adultery
Adultery also constitutes a violation of the sacred bond between a man and a woman pledged to marital fidelity. The instructions in Genesis

2:24 for the man to hold fast to his wife and for the two to become one flesh imply that there should be no other wives or women alongside the man's wife (nor, by implication, should there be any other husbands or men in the wife's life). The most notorious instance of adultery in the Old Testament is David's sin with Bathsheba (2 Samuel 11); other lesser-known descriptions of the sin of adultery include Reuben with Bilhah (Gen. 35:22; cf. 49:3–4), Hosea's wife Gomer (Hos. 3:1), and the adultery of a host of other unnamed Israelites (Jer. 3:2; 5:7–8; 7:9–10; etc.).

The Old Testament clearly upholds God's ideal of marital fidelity in the seventh commandment: "You shall not commit adultery" (Ex. 20:14; Deut. 5:18). The Levitical holiness code prohibits adultery in Leviticus 18:20, stipulating death as the penalty—an indication of the seriousness of this offense. Proverbs repeatedly describes adultery as foolish and dangerous (2:16–19; 5:3–22; 6:32–33; 7:5–23; 9:13–18; 22:14; 23:27–28; 30:20). In addition, adultery is frequently used throughout the Old Testament as an analogy to depict the spiritual unfaithfulness of Israel when she engaged in idolatry and the worship of other gods (Jer. 3:8–9; Ezek. 16:32, 38; Hos. 1:1–3:5). This analogy indirectly supports the ideal of marital fidelity.

No one could legitimately argue from the Old Testament that adultery is a good thing, and Jesus set the bar even higher, prohibiting men from even looking lustfully at a woman (Matt. 5:28). This removes all potential technicalities concerning what might be meant by adultery. God is interested in the heart and faithfulness, not just conforming to an external command. What's more, even though Scripture focuses primarily on men's responsibility to be faithful to their one wife (see also the stipulation that church leaders be "faithful husbands," 1 Tim. 3:2, 12; Titus 1:6), women, too, ought to be faithful to their husband and submit to "their own husband" (Eph. 5:22; Col. 3:18; Titus 2:5).

Divorce

Divorce is another destructive pattern that issued from the sinful departure from God's original design for marriage. Divorce compromises the permanence and durability of marriage. According to Genesis 2, the man was to leave his father and mother and enter into a one-flesh union with his wife in lifelong, monogamous marriage. In Deuteronomy 24:1–4, the Mosaic law regulates cases of divorce in ancient Israel. The Old Testament records several examples of divorce (Ezra 9–10; Neh. 13:23–31; Mal. 2:14–16).[50] At times, divorce is also used as a metaphor for spiritual apostasy (e.g., Isa. 50:1; Jer. 3:8), also a negative and unspiritual state of being. What is clear is that divorce is a violation of God's original design, which is that marriage be lifelong.[51]

In the New Testament, Jesus shows his disapproval of divorce when commenting on Deuteronomy 24:1–4, indicating that the Mosaic Law regulated divorce merely because of the Israelites' "hardness of heart" (Matt. 19:8). In Matthew 19:9, Jesus affirms that adultery constitutes an exception to the universal prohibition of divorce ("except for sexual immorality") in continuity with the Old Testament condemnation of adultery (Lev. 20:10; see also Num. 5:11–31; Deut. 22:22). Yet even in cases of adultery, remember that divorce is only permitted and not mandated. To the contrary, reconciliation and forgiveness are the Christian obligation and the first direction in which couples should strive when dealing with adultery.[52]

Homosexuality

Homosexuality is an obvious breach of God's creation design of man as deliberately masculine and of the woman as deliberately feminine and of the creation ordinance of marriage as between a man and a woman. It represents aberrant, unnatural behavior (see esp. Rom. 1:24–27; see also Jude 7, on which see further the discussion below) epitomizing rebellion against the Creator's design of marriage as heterosexual. It almost goes without saying that God created Adam and Eve, a man and a woman, not a man and a man or a woman and a woman, and that he

[50] Malachi speaks of hatred and divorce in a statement that can be understood in various ways (Mal. 2:16). Traditionally, the passage has been rendered as indicating that God hates divorce. More recently, however, the interpretation has gained ground that the passage may be pointing to a *man's* hatred of his *wife* rather than to *God's* hatred of *divorce*. The HCSB translates the passage as follows: "'If he [the man] hates and divorces [his wife],' says the LORD God of Israel, 'he covers his garment with injustice'" (similarly, ESV). In any case, the biblical case against divorce does not depend upon any one passage.
[51] See Köstenberger with Jones, *God, Marriage, and Family*, 275–85. More broadly, see ibid., chap. 11.
[52] In addition, Paul acknowledged that non-Christian spouses may leave a marriage because the other spouse becomes a Christian, in which case the believing spouse is not bound and should let the unbelieving spouse go (1 Cor. 7:12–16). Evangelicals differ on how to respond biblically to complex situations that Scripture does not address directly, such as spousal abuse. Divorce raises many complex issues that cannot be addressed here; it will suffice at this point to note that humanity in this case, too, rapidly fell short of God's design for marriage.

united this man and woman in lifelong marriage. In Genesis 2:24, the inspired author says that it is the man who is to hold fast to his wife.

Early on in the book of Genesis, we see the men of Sodom and Gomorrah committing the sin of homosexuality and being severely judged for it (Gen. 19:1–29), similar to the Gibeonites in the days of the judges (Judg. 19:1–21:25).[53] Some pro-homosexual interpreters contend that the sin of Sodom and Gomorrah is that of inhospitality, not homosexuality, but this is plainly contradicted in passages such as Jude 7 (in the context of Jude 4), which states, "For certain people have crept in unnoticed who long ago were designated for this condemnation, ungodly people, who pervert the grace of our God into sensuality and deny our only Master and Lord Jesus Christ, . . . just as Sodom and Gomorrah and the surrounding cities, which likewise *indulged in sexual immorality* and *pursued unnatural desire*, serve as an example by undergoing a punishment of eternal fire." This makes clear that the sin of Sodom and Gomorrah that incurred the most severe divine judgment was of a sexual nature and was in fact homosexuality, not merely inhospitality.

As it does with adultery, the Levitical holiness code stipulates death as the punishment for homosexuality, not merely for a more narrowly construed offense but in cases where "a man lies with a male as with a woman," in which case "both of them have committed an abomination" (Lev. 20:13; cf. 18:22; Deut. 23:17).[54] The reason for this is that, according to Paul in Romans 1:26–27, homosexuality (broadly conceived) is unnatural, contrary to the nature God has assigned to men and women (cf. Jude 7), not merely a more narrowly conceived offense in Greco-Roman culture. Because procreation is not intended to be between two males or two females, it goes against God's design and his very purpose for creating marriage in his created order in the first place (cf. procreation "according to their kinds," Gen. 1:21, 24, 25).[55] Notice the strong language Paul uses in Romans 1:25, 28, where he writes that such people "exchanged the truth about God for a lie and worshiped and served the creature rather than the Creator" and "did not see fit to acknowledge God." The Bible is quite clear on this issue.

---

[53] Köstenberger with Jones, *God, Marriage, and Family*, 201–5.
[54] Ibid., 205–7.
[55] Ibid., 208–9.

Table 1.10: Departures from God's Creation Design
in Israel's History Subsequent to the Fall

Departure	Description
Struggle for control	Man's authority challenged or usurped by the woman
Polygamy	Multiple wives rather than one man, one woman
Divorce	Breaking of lifelong marriage covenant between man and woman
Adultery	Breaking of one-flesh bond of marriage
Homosexuality	Violation of God's design for marriage between one man and one woman

God's Plan Continues Unabated

Amidst all these scenarios of God's people falling short of his original creation purpose, the Old Testament features many positive instances of those who celebrate monogamous marriage and the beauty of the marriage relationship within the family.[56] The picture of the virtuous wife in Proverbs 31 and the celebration of the beauty of sex in the Song of Solomon provide positive examples.[57]

Despite the violations noted above, the creation order and mandate did not cease serving as the standard for marriage and family in the Old Testament. Thus we see that the image of God in the man and the woman was distorted but not eradicated. In fact, even in its distorted form, God's beauty in male-female relationships and particularly in marriage still shines through. Nevertheless, sin had strong negative effects on the male-female relationship on an interpersonal

---

[56] See the extensive treatment in Block, "Marriage and Family in Ancient Israel," 33–102.

[57] On the Proverbs 31 woman, see Köstenberger with Jones, *God, Marriage, and Family*, 39–43 (with further bibliographic references); see also Bruce K. Waltke, *The Book of Proverbs: Chapters 15–31* (Grand Rapids, MI: Eerdmans, 2005), 510–36; and Al Wolters, *The Song of the Valiant Woman: Studies in the Interpretation of Proverbs 31:10–31* (Carlisle, UK: Paternoster, 2001). See also Douglas Sean O'Donnell, *The Beginning and End of Wisdom: Preaching Christ from the First and Last Chapters of Proverbs, Ecclesiastes, and Job* (Wheaton, IL: Crossway, 2011), who argues that Proverbs 31 is intended as instruction to young men on what kind of woman they should look for in a prospective wife (a woman who serves and puts others ahead of herself). On sex, see Köstenberger with Jones, *God, Marriage, and Family*, 79–84. See also the bibliography in ibid., 297–98; John Piper and Justin Taylor, eds., *Sex and the Supremacy of Christ* (Wheaton, IL: Crossway, 2005); and Christopher Ash, *Marriage: Sex in the Service of God* (Leicester, UK: Inter-Varsity, 2003).

"Amidst all these scenarios of God's people falling short of his original creation purpose, the Old Testament features many positive instances of those who celebrate monogamous marriage and the beauty of the marriage relationship within the family."

level and disrupted the trust, intimacy, and fidelity among marriage partners.

In the following chapter, we'll move past the discussion of God's original design for man and woman in marriage (though assuming it as the continuing norm for male-female relationships). We'll discuss Old Testament institutions such as patriarchy, the monarchy, the priesthood, and the ministry and role of prophets in ancient Israel in order to see how God's rule was manifested among his people in the days following the fall but prior to the coming of the Messiah. This will help us see how God's original design played itself out in subsequent history.

Key Resources

Ash, Christopher. *Marriage: Sex in the Service of God*. Leicester, UK: Inter-Varsity, 2003.

Block, Daniel I. "Marriage and Family in Ancient Israel." In *Marriage and Family in the Biblical World*, edited by Ken M. Campbell, 33–102. Downers Grove, IL: InterVarsity, 2003.

Köstenberger, Andreas J., with David W. Jones. *God, Marriage, and Family: Rebuilding the Biblical Foundation*. 2nd ed. Wheaton, IL: Crossway, 2010. Chap. 2.

Ortlund, Raymond C., Jr. "Male-Female Equality and Male Headship: Genesis 1–3." In *Recovering Biblical Manhood and Womanhood: A Response to Evangelical Feminism*, edited by John Piper and Wayne Grudem, 95–112. Wheaton, IL: Crossway, 1991.

Ware, Bruce A. "Male and Female Complementarity and the Image of God." In *Biblical Foundations for Manhood and Womanhood*, edited by Wayne A. Grudem, 71–92. Wheaton, IL: Crossway, 2002.

2

Patriarchs, Kings, Priests, and Prophets

Old Testament

> The head of the family functioned as its center. Like the spokes of a wheel, family life radiated outward from [the father].
>
> —Daniel I. Block[1]

Key Points

1. The Old Testament continues to exhibit a pattern of male leadership, including patriarchs, kings, and priests.
2. As a rule, women didn't occupy governing offices in ancient Israel (Deborah, Esther, and Athaliah are no real exceptions).
3. Both men and women served as prophets (female prophets included Miriam, Deborah, and Huldah), though the writing prophets were all men. Prophets had no institutional authority to command people's compliance with their prophetic utterances.

The world of ancient patriarchs, kings, priests, and prophets is far removed from our everyday experience. In some ways, it's hard to see how the way they lived so long ago and so far away has any relevance for our busy, advanced technological age today. If it weren't for our belief that Scripture is inspired and profitable across the centuries, it would be easy to dismiss the bygone era as irrelevant for our discussion of male and female identities and roles in our day. In fact, there

---

[1] Daniel I. Block, "Marriage and Family in Ancient Israel," in *Marriage and Family in the Biblical World*, ed. Ken M. Campbell (Downers Grove, IL: InterVarsity, 2003), 41.

is one group of translators that has forthrightly stated that it set itself the task of "muting the patriarchalism" of the Old Testament writings in order to level the playing field between our contemporary sensibilities and way of life and the archaic mores of the biblical documents.[2] Are blunt admissions such as these helpful, or are they unnecessary, perhaps even misguided? It's time to see if we can close the gap and discern what the times of the patriarchs, judges, and kings in Israel contribute to our understanding of the biblical teaching on male and female identities and roles.

In our study of Genesis 1–3 in the previous chapter, we saw God's original design for the woman and the man: God created humanity male and female in his image as a plurality and complementary in role. In this chapter, we'll continue our journey through Scripture by walking through the remainder of the Old Testament. At the end of the previous chapter, we observed that while the fall had serious negative consequences for the male-female relationship, the divine ideal continued unabated.[3] As we continue our study, we'll take a closer look at the major ancient patterns of leadership in ancient Israel: patriarchs, kings, and priests. We'll also attempt to develop a better understanding of the role of prophet during the same period.[4] It'll certainly be interesting and highly instructive to see how God's creation design plays itself out in Israel's history in and through the lives of key players such as Abraham, Moses, David, and many others. Notable women of this period will be addressed as well. Probing the implications of these observations for our own lives as women and men today will also be helpful.

---

[2] "Preface to Inclusive Language NIV," in *The Holy Bible: New International Version Inclusive Language Edition* (London: Hodder & Stoughton, 1996), vii. The full statement reads: "At the same time, it was recognised that it was often appropriate to mute the patriarchalism of the culture of the biblical writers through gender-inclusive language when this could be done without compromising the message of the Spirit."

[3] See Rebekah Josberger, *Between Rule and Responsibility: The Role of the 'ab as Agent of Righteousness in Deuteronomy's Domestic Ideology*, PhD dissertation, The Southern Baptist Theological Seminary (2007), who examines all the texts involving the male head of the household and the women of his household, whether wife or children.

[4] See Daniel I. Block, "Leader, Leadership, OT," in *New Interpreter's Dictionary of the Bible*, vol. 3: I–Ma, ed. Katharine Doob Sakenfeld (Nashville: Abingdon, 2008), esp. "Women and Leadership," 625–26. Thanks are due Mark Catlin, who under Andreas's direction wrote an initial rough draft of parts of this chapter.

Table 2.1: Significant Leaders in the Old Testament

Time Period	Biblical Character	Description
Creation	Adam	Head of the human race
Patriarchs	Abraham	Father of the Jewish people and of all believers
	Isaac	Promised son of Abraham
	Jacob	Renamed Israel, patriarch of twelve tribes
Exodus and Conquest	Moses	The lawgiver, leader of Israel at the exodus
	Aaron	Moses's brother and spokesman, priestly role
	Joshua	Moses's successor, conquest of Promised Land
Kings	Samuel	Anointed first Saul, then David, as king
	Saul	Israel's first king
	David	Man after God's own heart, Messiah son of David
	Solomon	Literal son of David, rules over vast empire

Patriarchs (the Pentateuch)[5]

Let's start with the patriarchs. The patriarchs exhibit a male pattern of leadership in ancient Israel. Abraham, Isaac, and Jacob are commonly identified as Old Testament patriarchs. As in most ancient Near Eastern cultures, Israelite families were patrilineal (official descent was traced through the father's line), patrilocal (married women became part of their husband's household), and patriarchal (the father was in charge of

---

[5] "Pentateuch" refers to the five books of Moses, that is, Genesis, Exodus, Leviticus, Numbers, and Deuteronomy.

the household).[6] In this way, "leadership within the family was focused on the male head, hence the designation of a household as a *beth 'av*, 'house of the father.'"[7] In describing the role of the father in ancient Israel, *patricentrism* ("father-centeredness") may be a more appropriate term than *patriarchy* ("father-rule"), for the following reasons.

First, in our day feminism has widely discredited the term *patriarchy* even in its nonabusive forms by giving it a strongly pejorative connotation.[8] Second, *patricentrism* better reflects the "normative biblical disposition toward the role of the head of a household in Israel."[9] Similar to the hub on a wheel, the father resided at the center of the ancient Jewish family, and, like spokes, life radiated outward from the father to the members of the extended household.[10] Third, while the father was indisputably in charge of those under his care, the Old Testament rarely focuses on his power. Rather than functioning as a despot, the head of household usually commanded the trust and provided for the security of its members. For this reason it was not primarily the father's authority that was emphasized but rather his responsibility for the welfare of the members of his household.[11]

While the Old Testament patriarchs were far from perfect, therefore, patriarchy as an institution was benevolent and beneficial rather than intrinsically abusive or oppressive. It is therefore important to distinguish between patriarchy as a historical, cultural expression of God's plan and the larger biblical pattern of male leadership of which patriarchy is one early expression. Cultural aspects of patriarchy, such as people (including slaves) living together in ancient Israel in ex-

---

[6] Block, "Marriage and Family in Ancient Israel," 40–43.

[7] Block, "Leader, Leadership, OT," 622. He elaborates, "When the extended family unit included several generations, the oldest male relative provided overall leadership, while the heads of individual marital units led in issues limited to the immediate family . . . communities consisting of more than one clan tended to be governed by elders, men recognized for their maturity by virtue of age and experience" (ibid.).

[8] For background, see the women's history survey in Appendix 1. See also the SBL presidential address by Carol L. Meyers, "Was Ancient Israel a Patriarchal Society?," *Journal of Biblical Literature* 133, no. 1 (2014): 8–27, who notes that the validity and appropriateness of this concept in relation to OT Israel has recently been questioned in several disciplines, including classical scholarship, OT scholarship, and third-wave feminism. Meyers believes "these challenges provide compelling reasons for abandoning the patriarchy model as an adequate or accurate descriptor of ancient Israel" (p. 8). Meyers calls on researchers to move "beyond patriarchy" in order to be able to understand "the complex gendered patterns of life in ancient Israel" (p. 26).

[9] Block, "Marriage and Family in Ancient Israel," 41.

[10] See figure 3 in ibid., 42.

[11] Andreas has delineated the father's responsibilities in greater detail in Andreas J. Köstenberger with David W. Jones, *God, Marriage, and Family: Rebuilding the Biblical Foundation*, 2nd ed. (Wheaton, IL: Crossway, 2010), 86–88.

tended households on large compounds, are not necessarily normative or historically transferable, but the broader principle of male leadership is. In this regard, we must resist the characterization of patriarchy, and by extension of all forms of male leadership, as necessarily bad, evil, or sinful.

While there is certainly a cultural dimension to the Old Testament pattern of patriarchy, the practice of patriarchy in ancient Israel therefore provides a positive vision for the father's role as a blessing to those around him who depend on him for provision, protection, and leadership. On a biblical-theological level, this means that there is no radical discontinuity between the New Testament pattern of male headship in the church and the Old Testament pattern of male leadership. To the contrary, both Testaments consistently affirm this pattern of male leadership. As we've seen, God's original design calls for male leadership, and the fall demonstrates the negative consequences when the original design is subverted (see esp. Gen. 3:17). As we'll observe in the remainder of this chapter, subsequent history witnesses to the continuation of the original pattern of male leadership.

Kings (1–2 Samuel; 1–2 Kings; 1–2 Chronicles)

The monarchy is an institution in ancient Israel that clearly exhibits the continuity of God's design of a male pattern of leadership. While in the first instance God ruled his people directly, he later prepared the way for kings to rule the people of Israel. In Deuteronomy 17:14–15 (HCSB), Moses anticipates people's desire for a king: "When you enter the land the LORD your God is giving you, take possession of it, live in it, and say,

> "While there is certainly a cultural dimension to the Old Testament pattern of patriarchy, the practice of patriarchy in ancient Israel therefore provides a positive vision for the father's role as a blessing to those around him who depend on him for provision, protection, and leadership."

'We want to appoint a king over us like all the nations around us,' *you are to appoint over you the king the Lord your God chooses.* Appoint a king from your brothers. You are not to set a foreigner over you, or one who is not of your people." There were virtually no women serving as monarchs. From the outset, God set up a political system in which men were designated to rule.

The above-cited passage goes on to describe what sort of king this man must be: "However, he must not acquire many horses *for himself* or send the people back to Egypt to acquire many horses, for the LORD has told you, 'You are never to go back that way again.' He must not acquire many wives *for himself* so that his heart won't go astray. He must not acquire very large amounts of silver and gold *for himself*" (vv. 16–17 HCSB). He must not use political power for selfish gain but must serve the people by performing one essential duty: "When he is seated on his royal throne, he is to write a copy of this instruction for himself on a scroll in the presence of the Levitical priests. It is to remain with him, and he is to read from it all the days of his life, so that he may learn to fear the LORD his God, to observe all the words of this instruction, and to do these statutes" (vv. 18–19 HCSB).

A good king must keep God's Word close to his heart at all times in order to rule the people according to the Law's commands and ordinances. If the king doesn't amass wealth for himself but keeps the law close at hand and fears God, he'll be a humble monarch who considers his people more important than himself. As the above-cited passage concludes, *"Then his heart will not be exalted above his countrymen, he will not turn from this command to the right or the left, and he and his sons will continue ruling many years over Israel"* (v. 20 HCSB). The entire passage, Deuteronomy 17:14–20, highlights the fact that a person's possession of authority doesn't equal his or her value in God's economy. The fact that only men were to rule Israel therefore doesn't diminish the value of women in the community of faith, as we'll see (though it does continue to exhibit the divinely instituted pattern of male leadership).

The above ideal notwithstanding, the history of Israel, as recorded especially in 1–2 Kings, reveals that a vast majority of kings didn't follow these admonitions. Solomon's kingship reads almost as a direct contradiction to these stipulations as he amasses wealth and a vast number of wives. As a result, he falls into idolatry, the kingdom is split in two, and Israel's history from that point on is a sad story of successive leadership failure resulting in eventual exile. The failure of these kings, however, isn't a result of the fact that the office of those who ruled over Israel was restricted to males. Rather, these kings failed to cultivate godliness in leading their people according to God's law. Because of their failure to humble themselves before God and the people, Israel experienced the negative consequences stipulated in the law. Nevertheless, the future redemption doesn't look forward to a time when there will be no authority at all, or authority will be opened up to both men and women. Rather, it anticipates godly (male) leadership ultimately epitomized by none other than the Messiah himself.

One exception to male rule seems to be found in 2 Kings 11:1–16, where Queen Athaliah rules over Israel for six to seven years. This intermezzo, however, doesn't provide much information concerning the roles men and women are to play within the community of faith. In fact, from beginning to end,

> "Nevertheless, the future redemption doesn't look forward to a time when there will be no authority at all, or authority will be opened up to both men and women. Rather, it anticipates godly (male) leadership ultimately epitomized by none other than the Messiah himself."

the story is quite tragic. The narrative opens on a gruesome note: "When Athaliah, Ahaziah's mother, saw that her son was dead, she proceeded to annihilate all the royal heirs" (HCSB). Athaliah isn't chosen or anointed by God according to the law. Rather, she takes the throne by killing all the heirs to the throne in Judah. However, one rightful heir, Joash, is rescued and kept a secret for the duration of Athaliah's reign. In Athaliah's seventh year, Joash is anointed king "according to the custom" (vv. 12–14). Athaliah is then put to death, and Joash ascends to the throne of Judah at the age of seven. This story serves more to display the depraved spiritual state of Israel than to demonstrate the right of women to the throne.

Women, however, are very important to the kings who rule. An obvious and important Old Testament example is Queen Esther whom God sovereignly elevates to her position "for such a time as this" so she can be his instrument to save his people from extinction.[12] Also, as Thomas Finley notes, "the position of queen mother seems to have been especially important and influential. She could have some say in the naming of her son as successor to the king. She could also have a strong spiritual influence on her son that would have an effect on

---

[12] But note the fact that "no Israelite woman is ever designated 'queen' in the courts of Jerusalem or Samaria" (Block, "Leader, Leadership, OT," 625).

the quality of his reign (1 Kings 15:13; 22:52), and Scripture often preserved her name along with that of her son (1 Kings 11:26; 14:21; 15:2, 10; 22:42; 2 Kings 12:1; 14:2; 15:2, 33; 18:2; 21:1, 19; 22:1; 23:31, 36; 24:8, 18)."[13] The role of queen mother in ancient Israel accentuates the important influence of a mother on future (and present) leaders. While these women don't have the same authority as the king, they serve an important, necessary, and valuable role in the political life of Israel.[14]

Table 2.2: Queens in the Old Testament

Name	Description
Athaliah	Mother of Ahaziah and queen of Israel
Esther	Jewish queen in Persia who helped save Jewish people from extinction

Priests (Leviticus and Subsequent History of Israel)

One of the most unequivocal instances of the pattern of male leadership in ancient Israel and in all of Scripture is that of the Old Testament priesthood. Priests exercised authority in Israel by mediating Yahweh's relationship with Israel through the sacrificial system, temple worship, and teaching of God's Word. In this way, priests represented God to the people, and the people before God. Women were excluded from the priesthood in Israel because the priesthood continued through hereditary succession of priests' sons. However, women did serve at the tent of meeting (Ex. 38:8; 1 Sam. 2:22). Nevertheless, these women were not part of the official priesthood.

Women also brought sacrifices to the priests and prayed to God. Leviticus 12:1–8 deals with a woman's purity after childbirth. The law concerning her purification concludes, "When her days of purification are complete, whether for a son or daughter, *she is to bring to the priest at the entrance to the tent of meeting a year-old lamb for a burnt offering, and a*

13 Thomas Finley, "The Ministry of Women in the Old Testament," in *Women and Men in Ministry: A Complementary Perspective*, ed. Robert L. Saucy and Judith K. TenElshof (Chicago: Moody, 2001), 76.
14 On the exclusion of queenship as an authoritative office, see Carol Smith, "Queenship in Israel: The Cases of Bathsheba, Jezebel and Athaliah," in *King and Messiah in Israel and the Ancient Near East*, ed. John Day (Sheffield, UK: Sheffield Academic Press, 1998), 142–62.

young pigeon or a turtledove for a sin offering. He will present them before the Lord and make atonement on her behalf" (vv. 6–7a HCSB). The woman, apart from her husband, could bring a sacrifice to the sanctuary for her ritual restoration.

In 1 Samuel 1–2, Hannah demonstrates great faith through fervent prayer to the Lord. Because of her barrenness, Hannah prays to God to open her womb and give her a son. The Lord answers her prayer and gives her a son, and Hannah takes him to Eli the priest and says, "Oh, my lord! As you live, my lord, I am the woman who was standing here in your presence, praying to the Lord. For this child I prayed, and the Lord has granted me my petition that I made to him. Therefore I have lent him to the Lord. As long as he lives, he is lent to the Lord" (1 Sam. 1:26–28). This boy, Samuel, would serve faithfully and anoint the first king of Israel. In displaying a godly disposition when told that she would give birth to a special son, Hannah serves as a precursor to Mary, the mother of Jesus. While Hannah holds no official position in the political or religious life of Israel (though she issues a prophetic utterance, 2:1–10, anticipating Mary), God values her faith as a member of his covenant people. Like Mary after her, Hannah serves as a major biblical example of godly motherhood.

Prophets and Prophetesses (Old Testament Prophetic Books)

The Old Testament provides more evidence for women functioning as prophetesses than for women serving in governing or priestly offices. In fact, the affirmation of women serving in prophetic ministry spans both Testaments.[15] Thomas Finley identifies a possible reason for this difference: "The two basic institutions of leadership in ancient Israel were the priesthood and the monarchy. Prophets also stepped in to bring a word from the Lord to his people, but the phenomenon of prophecy was more situational than constant in nature."[16] In other words, prophecy was a recognized way through which God moved and revealed his will but not an institution like the offices of king and priest that were perpetual in nature.

---

[15] In addition to the women mentioned below, note Hannah in the OT (1 Sam. 2:1–10) and Elizabeth and Mary in the New (Luke 1:42–55), as well as Philip's daughters (Acts 21:9; cf. 2:17; see also the reference to women prophesying in 1 Cor. 11:2–16).
[16] Finley, "Ministry of Women," 74.

In fact, the "prophetic institution seems to represent a special case. . . . Unlike the hereditary priestly and royal institutions, in Israel the prophetic institution especially bore an *ad hoc* flavor."[17] God appointed a prophet when he needed someone to convey a message to his people. There was no succession of prophets, whether hereditary or otherwise, as in the case of kings and priests: "With few exceptions (Moses, Samuel), prophets had no enduring governmental authority over the people; they had no subjects obliged to follow their directives, and no territory over which they ruled. Although ultimately God would hold the people responsible for their responses to prophetic utterances, there was no human sanction for ignoring what the prophets said."[18]

For this reason the nature of a prophet's authority differed from that of kings (politically) and priests (ritually): "God revealed His will and gave direction to His people through the prophets. They could function as a check on the monarchy and the priesthood, in that God often sent a prophet when the king or priests became corrupt. Of course it would be up to the king or priest to recognize the divine authority of the prophet or to reject him or her."[19] In a sense, therefore, the prophet was subject to the authority of the king or priest (though in another sense he occupied an independent function and "reported" directly to God). Thus people weren't called to submit to the prophet as they were subject to the authority of the king or priest. These insights will prove important as we consider the significance of the presence of at least three prophetesses in the Old Testament: Miriam, Deborah, and Huldah.[20]

Table 2.3: Prophetesses in the Old Testament

Name	Description
Miriam	Moses's sister
Deborah	Prophetess during the period of the judges
Huldah	A Jerusalem prophetess

[17] Block, "Leader, Leadership, OT," 622.
[18] Ibid.
[19] Finley, "Ministry of Women," 74.
[20] We won't deal with Isaiah's wife, who is briefly referred to as "the prophetess" in Isa. 8:3.

Miriam

Miriam, Moses's older sister, took care of Moses when she was young (Ex. 2:4–8) and later on apparently exercised the prophetic gift along with her brother Aaron. In one instance, when she took the lead alongside Aaron in inappropriately challenging Moses's authority, the Lord struck her with a disease (Num. 12:1–15). Exodus 15:20 identifies Miriam as a prophetess, stating, "Then Miriam the prophetess, Aaron's sister, took a tambourine in her hand, and all the women followed her with their tambourines and danced" (HCSB). Miriam then leads the women in song, celebrating the victory the Lord granted the people of Israel in perhaps the most defining event in Old Testament Israel's history—the exodus. Later, when Scripture records her death, it highlights Miriam's importance in the history of Israel (Num. 20:1).

Deborah

Deborah, the wife of Lappidoth, served as a prophetess (e.g., Judg. 4:14), and possibly as a judge, during the time of the judges prior to the monarchial period (Judges 4–5).[21] During a time of national crisis, at the people's bidding, she summoned the military leader Barak to lead the people in war and accompanied him upon his request (Judg. 4:6–10). The Lord accomplished military victory through Barak, Deborah, and another woman, Jael (vv. 11–24). Deborah also composed a song together with Barak that takes up nearly all of chapter 5 of Judges. The book of Judges portrays Deborah in a positive light, as a woman of faith serving the Lord at a time when the priesthood was corrupt.[22]

The text also provides hints that this may not have been the ideal situation, however. When Deborah summons Barak to fight in battle, and he refuses to do so unless Deborah goes with him, Deborah responds, "I will surely go with you. Nevertheless, the road on which you are going will not lead to your glory, for the LORD will sell Sisera into the hand of a woman" (Judg. 4:9). Later in the story, a woman named Jael kills Sisera, driving a tent peg through his temple (vv. 17–

---

[21] In Judg. 4:5 we read that Deborah "used to sit under the palm of Deborah between Ramah and Bethel in the hill country of Ephraim, and the people of Israel came up to her for judgment." At the very least, this would indicate that Deborah had the gift of wisdom and discernment.

[22] See the helpful study by Barbara K. Mouser, "The Womanliness of Deborah: Complementarian Principles from Judges 4–5," *Journal of Biblical Manhood and Womanhood* 11 (Fall 2006): 19–36.

21). Jael then brings Barak into the tent to show him what she's already done (v. 22). The Lord thus accomplishes this victory by a woman. In context, it becomes clear that this happened to Barak's *shame* rather than serving as a positive model (cf. Judg. 9:53–54 where a "certain woman" throws a millstone on Abimelech's head and crushes his skull and the latter tells his armor bearer, "Draw your sword and kill me, lest they say of me, 'A woman killed him'").

On the whole, Deborah's role was primarily that of prophetess (Judg. 4:4: "Deborah, a prophetess") rather than military or political ruler. In fact, the term *judge* may be misleading, because at that time judges were essentially national deliverers, not judges in the modern sense. What's more, Deborah didn't serve as deliverer herself but recruited Barak to this task. For this reason, "within the broader context, the 'judgment' [Deborah exercised; vv. 4–5] probably refers not to settling legal disputes among the people but to the divine response to the crisis for the nation created by Jabin and the Canaanites. The answer is the charge to Deborah to go and call Barak to lead the troops against the enemy."[23] The author of Hebrews lists Barak but not Deborah among those who "through faith conquered kingdoms" and "enforced justice" (Heb. 11:32; cf. 1 Sam. 12:11: "And the LORD sent Jerubbaal and *Barak* and Jephthah and Samuel and delivered you out of the hand of your enemies on every side, and you lived in safety").

Huldah

Second Chronicles 34:22 identifies Huldah as a prophetess: "So Hilkiah and those the king had designated went to *the prophetess Huldah*, the wife of Shallum son of Tokhath, son of Hasrah, keeper of the wardrobe. She lived in Jerusalem in the Second District. They spoke with her about this" (HCSB). Here Josiah, a godly king of Israel, sends a convoy to consult a prophetess concerning the fate of the nation. The text implies that Huldah is well known as a prophetess who truly speaks the word of the Lord. Otherwise, Josiah would have no reason to send his people to her.

In keeping with this implication, the prophetic word Huldah gives

---

[23] Block, "Leader, Leadership, OT," 626. See also Block, *Judges, Ruth*, New American Commentary (Nashville: Broadman, 1999), 191–211, esp. 193–97.

to Josiah's messengers comes directly from the Lord. We see here the Lord speaking directly through a woman in order to inform the ruler of Israel. It should be noted, however, that there is no presumption of authority exercised over Josiah, especially since he sends out to hear from Huldah. Scripture records other instances of women providing wise or prophetic words as well (1 Sam. 25:23–33; 28:6–19; 2 Sam. 20:14–22).

Summary

The examples of Miriam, Deborah, and Huldah show that several women provided a valuable service to the people of God at crucial times in redemptive history.[24] Miriam, Moses's sister, composed a song and led the women of Israel in worship during the time of Israel's exodus from Egypt. Deborah, a godly woman of faith, summoned a male military leader, Barak, to lead Israel's army to defeat the Canaanites in a time of national crisis during the period of the judges. Huldah conveyed a message from God to the people during the reign of godly king Josiah.

On the whole, the Old Testament exhibits a male pattern of leadership during the period of the patriarchs and in the two major political and religious institutions of Jewish life, that is, the monarchy and the priesthood. Deborah recruited a male military leader in the period of the judges but probably does not constitute a paradigm of female political leadership.[25] Neither do Esther (Xerxes's wife) or Athaliah (illegitimate queen). Most likely because the prophetic calling is less permanent and more situational, women as well as men served as prophets.

Notable Women in the Old Testament

Other women featured in the Old Testament are notable primarily because of their connection to a noted patriarch or other major male figure. The first woman, Eve, Adam's wife, has already been mentioned above as the woman through whom sin entered the world when she

---

[24] The presence of prophetesses in the OT is consistent with the NT reference to both men and women prophesying in Acts 2:17–18 (see also the reference to Philip's daughters in Acts 21:9) and the mention of women exercising the gift of prophecy in the local church context in 1 Corinthians 11. See further chaps. 4 and 5 below.

[25] Consider especially the following three factors: (1) A solitary woman judge doesn't constitute a paradigm. (2) The time of the judges is hardly an exemplary chapter in Israel's history; as the constant refrain in the book has it, during this period "everyone did what was right in his own eyes." (3) Barak's reluctance to assume authority leads Deborah and another woman to fill the resulting power vacuum.

succumbed to temptation by the Devil. Other notable women include Sarah, wife of Abraham, mother of Isaac, who is upheld in 1 Peter 3 as an example of wifely submission; Rebekah, wife of Isaac, mother of Esau and Jacob; and Leah and Rachel, wives of Jacob. Ruth, a Moabite woman, the great-grandmother of David and one of two women after whom an Old Testament book is named (the other being Esther), was the wife of Boaz, the great-grandmother of David, and an ancestor of the Messiah. Hannah, wife of Elkanah and mother of Samuel, in her godly disposition anticipated the godly disposition of Mary, the mother of Jesus. Other women that should be mentioned are two notable wives of David, Abigail (the former wife of Nabal) and Bathsheba (former wife of Uriah the Hittite and mother of Solomon). Jezebel, the evil wife of King Ahab, achieved dubious notoriety by opposing the prophet Elijah.[26]

Table 2.4: Other Well-Known Women in the Old Testament

Name	Description
Eve	First woman, Adam's wife, succumbed to temptation by the Devil
Sarah	Wife of Abraham, obeyed her husband, calling him "lord" (1 Peter 3)
Rebekah	Wife of Isaac, mother of twins Esau and Jacob
Leah, Rachel	Wives of Jacob
Rahab	Gentile woman who welcomed Israel's spies and had faith in God
Ruth	Wife of Boaz, her kinsman-redeemer, ancestor of the Messiah
Hannah	Godly wife of Elkanah, mother of Samuel, precursor of the mother of Jesus

[26] Within the scope of this biblical-theological survey, we will not be able to engage in detailed discussions of each of these notable women. For insightful studies of many of them, see Jerram Barrs, *Through His Eyes: God's Perspective on Women in the Bible* (Wheaton, IL: Crossway, 2009). We'd also encourage you to read the biblical accounts of these women directly and to engage in inductive study of their lives and contributions to the story of the Bible and God's people, perhaps using a good study Bible such as the *ESV Study Bible*, ed. Wayne Grudem (Wheaton, IL: Crossway, 2008).

Name	Description
Abigail	Wise and discerning wife of David
Bathsheba	Wife of David, mother of Solomon, former wife of Uriah
Jezebel	Evil wife of Ahab, opposed Elijah

The Status of Women in Old Testament Times

As we've seen, in the beginning God created humanity male and female, in his image. He created the man first, and then the woman,
with the man as the leader and the woman as his partner and suitable
helper. At the fall, the husband's loving headship and the woman's
gracious submission were subverted into a struggle for control. The
woman acted apart from her husband, and the man failed to exercise
his God-given leadership role. The remainder of the Old Testament
exhibits the negative consequences of the fall (including polygamy,
adultery, divorce, and homosexuality), yet affirms the continuing validity of God's plan. In the case of patriarchs, kings, and priests, we
see authority vested firmly in the hands of men, while men as well as
women serve in a prophetic role.

Some, however, are troubled by the treatment of women in the Old
Testament.[27] In some cases, these writers don't believe in the reality
of sin and consider the biblical accounts of creation and the fall to
be a myth, laying the blame squarely at the feet of the institution of
patriarchy (which they consider oppressive) and alleging male bias on
the part of the biblical writers (who, they contend, are insensitive to
the plight of women). Such writers typically point to places in the Old
Testament law where women are considered their husband's property.
They also criticize the male-centered outlook in books such as Proverbs and take strong objection to the apparent Old Testament approval
of polygyny (multiple wives).

How are we to assess the merits of these observations in light

[27] E.g., Christopher Rollston, "The Marginalization of Women: A Biblical Value We Don't Like to Talk
About," *Huffington Post* (October 16, 2012), http://www.huffingtonpost.com/christopher-rollston/the
-marginalization-of-women-biblical-value-we-dont-like-to-talk-about_b_1833648.html#slide=more
212657; Rachel Held Evans, *A Year of Biblical Womanhood: How a Liberated Woman Found Herself Sitting on
Her Roof, Covering Her Head, and Calling Her Husband "Master"* (Nashville: Thomas Nelson, 2012), 48–51.

of the biblical evidence?[28] First, as mentioned, Scripture makes clear that humanity's fundamental problem is sin—rebellion against the Creator—not male oppression. God's design is for men to serve as leaders in a way that treats others (including women) with love, dignity, and respect. At the root, therefore, the solution to humanity's problem is not freeing women from all forms of male leadership—though where such is exercised in an abusive manner, this should certainly be addressed and rectified—but for both men and women to repent of their sin and to confess their need for a Savior, the Lord Jesus Christ. He alone is able to help men and women to restore their relationship to God's original design.

Second, because some of those charging the Old Testament with inferior treatment of women deny the reality of sin and the historicity of the fall narrative, these writers also fail to adequately appreciate the gravity of the negative consequences of the fall for humanity in subsequent Old Testament history. As we tried to show in the previous chapter, polygamy was not God's original design, and where it's found in the Old Testament, this marks the consequences of sin, not an alternative lifestyle approved by God. The apparent allowance for polygyny in certain Old Testament passages must be understood within the larger framework of the Old Testament, which, as mentioned, shows the negative consequences of polygyny on marriage and people's relationship with God. Ever since the fall, conditions for humanity had deteriorated, and nothing short of the coming of the Messiah would be able to restore humanity spiritually to its pre-fall condition (or at least enable humanity to overcome the consequences of the fall in the power of the Holy Spirit).

Third, while Old Testament laws may not always restore women to their status as partners with men, they are regularly designed to

[28] In personal correspondence dated May 29, 2013, Daniel Block writes in this regard, "I think the biblical ideals of marriage and the relationship of men and women are timeless, and that the constitutional material of the Pentateuch, for instance, seeks to promote those ideals throughout. . . . I do not think marital and gender values change as we move to the New Testament (any more than other ethical values change), but the way in which people are to respond to breaches of ideals change. So long as the agent of God's missional agenda is a particular people in a particular land, we find a particular concern to prescribe specific (and often in our minds severe) prescriptions for response. In my view, the breaching of the ethnic boundaries (the book of Acts recounts this breaching in four stages beginning at Pentecost) does not change these ideals, but opens up other possibilities for response, as in Jesus's response to the woman caught in adultery. I do not think he is softening YHWH's abhorrence of adultery, but exposing the Pharisaical hypocrisy in the way they approach the issues."

protect women. This is true for divorce laws as well as for laws protecting an unborn child in her mother's womb. While some aren't satisfied with the commandment calling on people not to covet another's wife because the corresponding command for a wife not to covet another's husband isn't given, we shouldn't lose sight of the fact that the command for a man not to covet another's wife is given to restrain the man and to protect the woman. And just because a man's wife is listed along slaves and farm animals doesn't mean she's considered as being on the same level as a farm animal or slave. Logically, this doesn't follow. To the contrary, the "cumulative weight of this evidence raises questions about the commonly held view that in ancient Israel women had no legal status and that they were merely personal property owned first by their fathers and then by their husbands."[29]

Fourth, some object that the Bible was written by men and from a male perspective. However, given the male pattern of leadership in Scripture, this is to be expected and not necessarily problematic. If the book of Proverbs, for example, was written for young men in order to equip them for leadership, the lack of equivalent instructions for young women makes sense if they weren't normally trained for leadership roles in ancient Israel. And warning young men against adulterous women seems entirely appropriate also because any such relationships would be immoral. Also, remember that women are also used in Proverbs to personify various other virtues and vices, such as wisdom or folly.

Fifth, and perhaps most important, critics of the treatment of women in Old Testament times don't sufficiently read the Bible in the context of its unfolding salvation-historical narrative. This is why biblical theology is so important. Only if we understand God's plan for men and women within the larger framework of creation, fall, and redemption will we be able to appreciate God's original design

---

[29] Block, "Leader, Leadership, OT," 625. Block notes the woman's participation in naming a couple's children (twenty-eight out of forty-six OT instances of naming of a child refer to women); her role in the arranging of marriages; her important part in the household economy by managing the many aspects of household life, especially in rearing children, managing the servants, supervising food production and other domestic needs (e.g., Prov. 31:10–31); her instruction of her children (e.g., Prov. 1:8; 6:20); and the injunction for children to extend the same honor to their mothers as they do to their fathers (Ex. 20:12; Deut. 5:16; cf. Lev. 19:3).

for men and women, the depths of humanity's fall from grace, and the magnitude of redemption in Christ and the restoration of God's original plan for men and women. The Old Testament subsequent to Genesis 3 is not a sufficient primary reference point by itself when discussing "biblical values" regarding women, because it deals with a stage in salvation history where humanity had fallen and was awaiting redemption. If we want to see men's and women's roles restored in Christ, we need to consult the New Testament as well.

"Only if we understand God's plan for men and women within the larger framework of creation, fall, and redemption will we be able to appreciate God's original design for men and women, the depths of humanity's fall from grace, and the magnitude of redemption in Christ and the restoration of God's original plan for men and women."

In this regard, it is appropriate to point people to passages such as Galatians 3:28 that affirm that with regard to salvation, there's no distinction between men and women—all are children of God by faith in Christ. It is also appropriate to point them to Luke's Gospel—faithfully reflecting Jesus's own teaching—which regularly balances references to male and female characters.[30] There's a legitimate development from the treatment of women in Old Testament times to Jesus's and Paul's teaching regarding women, and it's illegitimate to flatten this distinction and to make it appear that the Old Testament treatment of women by itself is a necessary indication of the Bible's disregard for women.

Sixth and finally, the criticisms that the Bible is written from a male perspective and that (particularly in the Old Testament and to a lesser extent in the New) women are not treated as equals, while open to the above-stated rebuttals, rightly discern that Scripture affirms a pattern of male leadership. To the extent that people's concern with the treatment of women in the Old Testament is rooted in opposition to God's design for men to serve as leaders, none of the above responses will likely satisfy. God's creation of humanity as male and female in his image and the fact that Christian women are fellow heirs of salvation together with their Christian husbands show that Scripture assigns a very high value to women in both Testaments.

---

[30] See chap. 3 below.

The Nature of Leadership

Before we conclude this chapter, it will be helpful to reflect a bit more on the nature of leadership. Overall, "leadership involves primarily the exercise of responsibility, rather than the exercise of power."[31] In fact, "according to Old Testament ideals, leaders are servants of those whom they are called to lead, and are to operate in the interests of those whom they lead, rather than in self-interest."[32] Unfortunately, as mentioned, Israel's history is full of examples of the "corruption of leadership from a position of responsibility to the abuse of power."[33] The Old Testament expectation is that adult male heads of households (to whom the Ten Commandments were ultimately addressed) "will see to the well being [*sic*] of their wives, children, servants, neighbors, and even their livestock."[34] In this regard, God himself served as the paradigm for leadership (see esp. Deut. 10:17–19). While he is supreme over all, he "exercises leadership in the interests of the least, executing justice for the marginalized and showing love to aliens by giving them food and clothing."[35] Kings, likewise, must not abuse their office for personal advantage (1 Kings 17:14–20), and leaders must be willing to sacrifice themselves for their followers (see, e.g., Moses and the golden calf incident in Ex. 32:31–32).

As mentioned, the Old Testament teaching on male rule in terms of patriarchy has often been given a pejorative connotation and has put on the defensive those who believe in distinct male-female roles with ultimate male leadership. However, those who cast male leadership in ancient Israel in negative terms can sustain their argument only by seriously misrepresenting the Old Testament ideal. In fact, "the primary role of leaders is to embody righteousness and promote justice within the community," as leaders exhibit "uncompromising personal fidelity to the covenant" God had established with the nation, and "this demand for righteousness extended beyond the personal character and actions" of a leader to "a commitment to fairness toward all and special concern for the vulnerable and marginalized members of society, those

---

[31] Block, "Leader, Leadership, OT," 623.
[32] Ibid.
[33] Ibid.
[34] Ibid., 624.
[35] Ibid.

easily exploited and abused."[36] This is a critical corrective to mischaracterizations of the Old Testament teaching on male leadership. The ideal for male leadership has always involved benevolent caring for others, using one's authority not to oppress or abuse those under his care but to responsibly provide for them. This insight puts the Old Testament teaching regarding overall male leadership into proper perspective.

Implications

Our survey of the Old Testament has yielded a clear picture of male and female roles, confirming that "the offices of kingship, priesthood, judgeship, and eldership were overwhelmingly reserved for men only."[37] Echoing the truths from Genesis 1–3, the Old Testament as a whole teaches that humanity was created as a plurality of male and female but with different roles. One cannot stress the importance of this enough, because in Scripture authority isn't directly proportionate to value. That means that the king, though wielding a significant amount of authority, does not have more inherent value as a human being than, say, a farmer. As we approach the New Testament, we should keep in mind that the redemption God's people need so desperately is not redemption from male leadership. Rather, God's people need godly (male) leadership, provided ultimately in and through the Messiah. In the final analysis, therefore, the leaders of the New Testament church will pattern themselves after the true shepherd, the Messiah, as shepherds of God's people.[38]

We began our study of the Old Testament teaching on men and women in the previous chapter by focusing broadly on the creation order in Genesis 1–3. This chapter has been devoted to an investigation of how this mandate fared in the rest of the Old Testament. Men generally functioned as patriarchs, heads of households, and tribal leaders and collectively made decisions on behalf of their respective households that affected the entire community. In terms of political and religious offices, kings and priests were virtually exclusively

---

[36] Ibid., 624–25.

[37] Ibid., 626.

[38] For the biblical teaching on shepherding, see Timothy S. Laniak, *Shepherds after My Own Heart: Pastoral Traditions and Leadership in the Bible*, New Studies in Biblical Theology 20 (Downers Grove, IL: InterVarsity, 2006); Derek Tidball, *Skilful Shepherds: Explorations in Pastoral Theology*, 2nd ed. (Leicester, UK: Apollos, 1997).

male.[39] As noted, several women served in a prophetic role. Deborah also had an important role in a national crisis. The question remains whether this pattern is sustained and reaffirmed by Jesus and the early church or whether Jesus instituted a new egalitarian community. It is to this question that we now turn.

Key Resources

Block, Daniel I. "Leader, Leadership, OT." In *New Interpreter's Dictionary of the Bible.* Vol. 3, *I–Ma*, edited by Katharine Doob Sakenfeld, 620–26. Nashville: Abingdon, 2008.

———. "Marriage and Family in Ancient Israel." In *Marriage and Family in the Biblical World*, edited by Ken M. Campbell, 33–102. Downers Grove, IL: InterVarsity, 2003.

Finley, Thomas. "The Relationship of Woman and Man in the Old Testament." In *Women and Men in Ministry: A Complementary Perspective*, edited by Robert L. Saucy and Judith K. TenElshof, 49–71. Chicago: Moody, 2001.

Köstenberger, Andreas J., with David W. Jones. *God, Marriage, and Family: Rebuilding the Biblical Foundation.* 2nd ed. Wheaton, IL: Crossway, 2010. Chap. 2.

---

[39] Block, "Leader, Leadership, OT," 626, registers the interesting observation that the verb *malakh*, "to rule," occurs "with a female subject only with reference to the usurper Athaliah (2 Kgs 11:3; 2 Chr 22:12), whom neither the narrator nor the people of the land recognized as legitimate ruler."

3

What Did Jesus Do?

Gospels

He went on through cities and villages, proclaiming and bringing the good news of the kingdom of God. And the twelve were with him, and also some women.

—Luke 8:1–2a

Key Points
1. Jesus appointed twelve men to form the core leadership group for his new messianic community, the church.
2. Jesus treated women consistently with respect, dignity, and compassion and allowed them to learn from him as his disciples.
3. Jesus encouraged the participation of a few devoted women followers in his mission. These women showed their loyalty to him up to the cross and beyond.
4. Jesus affirmed the continuity of God's original design for men and women in Genesis 1–3.

In 1896 Charles Sheldon, a Congregationalist pastor in Topeka, Kansas, published a book based on a series of sermons he had preached. The title: *In His Steps: What Would Jesus Do?* In the novel, Reverend Henry Maxwell meets a homeless man who, after attending a service at his church, challenges him to live up to his Christian commitment. After the man has heard the congregation sing the song "All for Jesus" at a church prayer meeting, he wonders: Why don't more people live that way? "I suppose I don't understand," he says. "But what would Jesus do? Is that what you mean by following His steps?"[1] As the novel continues, many of the characters begin to ask themselves the question, "What would Jesus do?" as they face important decisions. As a result, they become more serious Christians and focus on the core of Christianity—the life of Jesus.

More recently, in the 1990s it became popular among Christian youth groups to wear WWJD bracelets. In 2010 a movie, *WWJD*, was released that is based on Sheldon's book. The expression, "What would Jesus do?" has led to numerous offshoots and parodies in recent years, some of them humorous. Conservatives today might ask, "What would Reagan do?" Peace advocates might put a bumper sticker on their car, sardonically asking, "Who would Jesus bomb?" Management gurus have embraced the principle as well, exhorting corporate executives to lead by example as Jesus did and to cultivate habits such as exercising "management by walking around."

Truth told, Sheldon's principle of asking the question, What would Jesus do? needs some serious qualification, if for no other reason than that there are many things Jesus did that we can never do (e.g., die on the cross for the sins of the world, perform startling miracles such as healing the sick and raising the dead). In fact, Sheldon's approach to the Christian life was one of the tributaries that led to the Social Gospel, a movement endowed with a heavy dose of theological liberalism and Christian socialism.

Nevertheless, once we've understood the centrality of the cross in salvation and our need to first and foremost repent of our sin and place our faith in Jesus as our Savior and Lord, it is hard to deny that the life of Jesus—both his teachings and his practice—should occupy a central place in our thinking and actions. As part of our biblical-theological survey on the identities and roles of men and women according to God's design, it is therefore critical to ask the question, What did Jesus do? And what did he teach on the subject? In fact, some feminists have claimed that Jesus himself was a feminist;[2] others have argued that he established an egalitarian community where leadership

---

[1] Charles M. Sheldon, *In His Steps: What Would Jesus Do?* (Alachua, FL: Bridge-Logos, 1999), 18, first published by *The Advance* (Chicago, 1867–1917) in serial form.
[2] Leonard Swidler, "Jesus Was a Feminist," *Catholic World* 212 (January 1971): 177–83. More recently, see Sarah Bessey, *Jesus Feminist: An Invitation to Revisit the Bible's View of Women* (New York: Howard, 2013).

was shared equally between women and men.[3] On the other side of the spectrum, some have countered that while Jesus was uniquely affirming of women as people and encouraged them to follow him and to learn from him, he did not radically break with the male pattern of leadership which, as we've seen, has a long pedigree in biblical history. How are we to resolve this vital question?

The New Testament picks up the biblical narrative with the four Gospels, which recount the life, ministry, death, and resurrection of Jesus. While the Gospels display a great deal of similarity, each Gospel is a literary work in its own right, and some of the Gospel writers focus on the roles of men and women more than others. Several important questions will guide our study. What do Jesus's teaching about men and women and his dealings with them contribute to the overall teaching of Scripture on the subject? Did Jesus affirm the original creation order or replace it with his own teaching? How does Jesus compare to other first-century Jewish teachers in his attitude toward women? How do Jesus's teaching and conduct relate to later New Testament teaching? Our expectation is that because the message of Scripture is unified, the practice of Jesus and the early Christians, including Paul, will ultimately be found in harmony.

In studies on the subject, the Gospels and Jesus have often been overshadowed by the statements and teachings of Paul.[4] There are relatively few evangelical treatments of the roles of men and women in Jesus and the Gospels.[5] It's always precarious when we mine data with a particular question in mind when the text being examined wasn't primarily written to answer that question. The Gospels weren't written primarily to deal with gender roles but to set forth the truth about Jesus and salvation in him. Still, we can legitimately observe some of the data that are relevant to our topic. On the whole, we'll see that the

---

[3] Elisabeth Schüssler Fiorenza, *In Memory of Her: A Feminist Theological Reconstruction of Christian Origins* (New York: Crossroad, 1983).

[4] See Jonathan Pennington, *Reading the Gospels Wisely: A Narrative and Theological Introduction* (Grand Rapids, MI: Baker Academic, 2012), who argues that the Gospels should hold a "privileged place" in interpretation (p. 230) and serve as "the guiding principle (even *regula fidei*) and lodestar for understanding and standing under all Holy Scripture" (p. 231).

[5] An exception is James Borland, "Women in the Life and Teaching of Jesus," in *Recovering Biblical Manhood and Womanhood: A Response to Biblical Feminism*, ed. John Piper and Wayne Grudem (Wheaton, IL: Crossway, 1991), 105–16. A comparable evangelical feminist work is Grant Osborne, "Women in Jesus' Ministry," *Westminster Theological Journal* 51 (1989): 259–91. Osborne's treatment of passages in which Jesus interacts with women is quite careful, but in his conclusion he at times goes beyond the evidence.

discussion in the Gospels on the subject of men's and women's roles is more indirect than in Genesis 1–3 and the New Testament letters, particularly Paul's writings. So let's continue our journey through the biblical landscape by taking a closer look at Jesus and the Gospels.

The Maleness and Humanity of Jesus Himself

Before we look at Jesus's interactions with both men and women in the Gospels, it will be important to discuss the nature of Jesus himself in terms of his humanity and his gender.[6] Scripture clearly teaches that the humanity of Jesus was essential for his mission to die on the cross for our sins. Paul writes in Romans, "For what the law was powerless to do because it was weakened by the flesh, God did by sending his own Son in the likeness of sinful flesh to be a sin offering" (Rom. 8:3 NIV). The author of the book of Hebrews writes, "Since the children have flesh and blood, he [Jesus] too shared in their humanity so that by his death he might break the power of him who holds the power of death—that is, the devil—and free those who all their lives were held in slavery by their fear of death" (Heb. 2:14–15 NIV). The author continues, "For this reason he had to be made like them, fully human in every way, in order that he might become a merciful and faithful high priest in service to God, and that he might make atonement for the sins of the people" (v. 17 NIV). Thus it is beyond dispute that Jesus must be *human* to die for our sins and bring us to God.

That said, it is also a historical fact that Jesus was incarnated not as a transgendered person or in some other generic way, but as a male. Jesus's maleness is of interest to us yet sometimes is offensive to those who see it as part of the male-centered nature of Christianity—where God is called "Father" and Jesus is the Son.[7] That their salvation depends on a male Savior's vicarious death is difficult to swallow for some. Some recent Bible translations have even gone out of their way to emphasize the humanity of Jesus and to downplay the maleness of

---

[6] See Micah Daniel Carter, "Reconsidering the Maleness of Jesus," *Journal of Biblical Manhood and Womanhood* 13 (Spring 2008): 27–41. See also the twelve reasons for Jesus's maleness, given by Bruce A. Ware, "Could Our Savior Have Been a Woman?," *Journal of Biblical Manhood and Womanhood* 2008 (Spring 2003): 33 (cited on p. 39 of Carter's essay).

[7] See appendix 1. Rosemary Radford Ruether famously asked, "Can a male savior save women?" (see the title of chap. 5 in *Sexism and God-Talk: Toward a Feminist Theology* [Boston: Beacon, 1993], 116). For an insightful study see Linda D. Peacore, *The Role of Women's Experience in Feminist Theologies of Atonement*, Princeton Theological Monograph Series (Eugene, OR: Pickwick, 2010).

Jesus, stressing that it's the former, not the latter, that is essential for salvation.

Nevertheless, the question arises whether the maleness of Jesus is really as completely irrelevant and inconsequential as is often asserted. In light of the male pattern of leadership demonstrated in the Old Testament—where patriarchs, kings, and priests were typically male—it stands to reason that it was hardly coincidental that Jesus, as the representative head of humanity and as the Davidic king, was born and walked the earth as a male. In his maleness, Jesus continues the pattern of male leadership that ranges all the way from Adam to the patriarchs, and from kings and priests to the Messiah and, as we will see, beyond to the Twelve, the Pauline circle, and elders in the New Testament church. In light of the pervasive male pattern of leadership in both Testaments, it is virtually inconceivable that Jesus might have been incarnated as a woman. And while it was Jesus's humanity, not his maleness, that was essential for our salvation, Jesus's maleness was nonetheless significant in that it underscored God's male pattern of leadership. With this, we turn our attention to men in the Gospels.

> "In his maleness, Jesus continues the pattern of male leadership that ranges all the way from Adam to the patriarchs, and from kings and priests to the Messiah and, as we will see, beyond to the Twelve, the Pauline circle, and elders in the New Testament church."

Men in the Gospels

The primary group of men mentioned in all four Gospels is Jesus's twelve apostles. Beyond this, the Gospels feature numerous other men in interaction with Jesus, as characters in Jesus's parables, and at other occasions. We'll start our discussion of men in the Gospels with a survey of the significance of the Twelve and brief character sketches of each of these men. While these character sketches don't strictly serve to advance our thesis that Scripture exhibits a pattern of male leadership, they will help us to get better acquainted with the specific men who were members of the early church's nascent leadership in training, the Twelve. After this, we'll take a look at some of the other significant men mentioned in the Gospels in various contexts and functions.

The Twelve

One of the most important aspects of Jesus's ministry was his selection and training of the Twelve, who were all men. In this, Jesus continued the pattern of male leadership which, as we've seen, originated in the Old Testament structure of the twelve tribes and was also characteristic of the offices of king and priest. The Twelve were the core group of Jesus's new messianic community, the new Israel, who would take the gospel starting in Jerusalem to the ends of the earth, in keeping with the Great Commission of the risen Christ (Acts 1:8; cf. Matt. 28:16–20). Jesus also appointed and sent out the seventy (or seventy-two; Luke 10:1). In addition, he often preached to larger audiences and was very popular with the crowds.

In contrast to the Jewish religious leaders, who misled the people in their hypocrisy and thirst for power (Matthew 23), Jesus was the model and master teacher (*rabbi*, literally "my great one"), and his followers, particularly the Twelve, were his students (*mathētai*, from *manthanō*, "to learn"). Clearly, Jesus's main purpose for the Twelve was to prepare them for roles of leadership in his messianic community after his death, resurrection, and ascension. He sought to instill in them the importance of focusing on advancing the kingdom of God; on representing him and spreading the news about him rather than being focused on themselves ("taking up his cross," Matt. 10:38; 16:24; Mark 8:34; Luke 9:23); using their positions of leadership to serve others (Matt. 18:1–5; 20:25–28; Mark 9:33–37; 10:32–45; Luke 9:46–48; John 13:1–20); and caring for those under their charge in sacrificial self-giving (John 10:28).[8]

---

[8] We are indebted for these points to the unpublished paper by Daniel I. Block, "Leadership, Leaders in the New Testament" (provided courtesy of the author). Table 3.1 essentially reproduces that in Andreas J. Köstenberger, L. Scott Kellum, and Charles L. Quarles, *The Cradle, the Cross, and the Crown: An Introduction to the New Testament* (Nashville: B&H Academic, 2009), 200–201.

Table 3.1: The Twelve

Name	Key Scriptures	Description
Simon Peter	Matt. 4:18; 16:13–17, 21–23; Luke 22:54–62; John 21:15–19	Fisherman before being called to follow Jesus; one of inner circle
Andrew	Matt. 4:18; John 1:40; 6:8; 12:22	Peter's brother; fisherman
James	Matt. 4:21; Mark 3:17; 9:2; 14:33; Acts 12:1–5	Former fisherman; John's brother; in inner circle; martyred by Herod
John	Matt. 4:21; Mark 3:17; 9:2; 14:33; John 13:23; 21:2	Former fisherman; in inner circle; "disciple Jesus loved"
Philip	John 1:43–48; 6:5–7; 12:21–22; Acts 8:4–40	Brought Nathanael to Jesus; ministry in Samaria, to Ethiopian eunuch
Bartholomew (Nathanael)	Matt. 10:3; Mark 3:18; Luke 6:14; John 1:43–49; Acts 1:13	Seen by Jesus under fig tree; calls Jesus "Son of God," "King of Israel"
Thomas	John 11:16; 14:5; 20:24–29; 21:2	Doubting Thomas; later worshiped Jesus as "my Lord and my God"
Matthew (Levi)	Matt. 9:9–13; 10:3; Mark 2:18; Luke 6:15	Former tax collector; brother of James son of Alphaeus?
James son of Alphaeus	Matt. 10:3; Mark 3:18; Luke 6:15; Acts 1:13	Brother of Matthew?
Thaddaeus (Judas son of James)	Matt. 10:3; Mark 3:18; Luke 6:16; Acts 1:13	Also known as Judas son of James; the "other Judas" (not Iscariot)

Name	Key Scriptures	Description
Simon the Zealot	Matt. 10:4; Mark 3:18; Luke 6:15; Acts 1:13	Former zealot (Jewish freedom fighter)
Judas Iscariot	Matt. 10:4; 26:14–16; 27:3–10; John 6:70–72; 12:4–6; 13:21–30; 17:12; Acts 1:16–20	The traitor; keeper of disciples' moneybag; betrayed Jesus, then hanged himself

Simon Peter. Simon Peter was the spokesman and leader of the Twelve. He and his brother Andrew were among the first disciples called by Jesus to follow him (Matt. 4:18). Both of them were Galilean fishermen. Jesus renamed Simon *petros,* "the Rock," and made the dramatic announcement that he'd build his church on Peter's confession of Jesus as the Messiah and Son of the living God (Matt. 16:13–17, 21–23). In keeping with Jesus's prediction, Peter denied knowing Jesus three times prior to the crucifixion. After the resurrection, Jesus recommissioned Peter to gospel ministry and predicted Peter's eventual martyrdom (John 21:15–19). Jesus gave Peter the "keys to the kingdom," which awarded Peter primacy in the early stages of the church's mission after Pentecost. At Pentecost, Peter preached a powerful sermon, and three thousand people were converted (Acts 2:14–41). Later, in response to a heavenly vision, he was used by God to open up the gospel to Cornelius, a Gentile (Acts 10:1–8). Peter also wrote two letters that are included in the New Testament canon (1, 2 Peter).

Andrew. Andrew, Simon Peter's brother, likewise was a Galilean fisherman (Matt. 4:18). According to John's Gospel, Andrew brought Peter to Jesus (John 1:40). Together with Philip, he's also mentioned at two other occasions in Jesus's ministry, the feeding of the five thousand and the coming of a group of Greeks to Jesus prior to the crucifixion (John 6:8; 12:22). Andrew, too, was martyred according to Christian tradition.

James. James and his brother John, the sons of Zebedee, were another pair of brothers called to follow Jesus (Matt. 4:21; Mark 3:17). Like Peter and Andrew, they were Galilean fishermen. Their father, Zebedee, had a fishing business that employed several people. James, together with his brother John and the apostle Peter, made up Jesus's inner circle, which was privileged to witness certain key events, such as the transfiguration, not witnessed by the other apostles (Mark 9:2). James was martyred by Herod, the grandson of Herod the Great, in AD 42 (Acts 12:1–5). He is not to be confused with Jesus's half-brother also named James (author of the epistle of James in the New Testament).

John. John the son of Zebedee, as mentioned, was the brother of James and a Galilean fisherman (Matt. 4:21; Mark 3:17). The author of the Gospel that bears his name, as well as of 1, 2, and 3 John and Revelation, John called himself "the disciple Jesus loved," an expression of authorial modesty (e.g., John 13:23). Love is a key theme in both the Gospel and John's letters, indicating that John never got over the fact of how much God loved him. John also penned what is arguably the most beloved verse in the entire Bible, John 3:16: "God so loved the world, that he gave his only Son, that whoever believes in him should not perish but have eternal life." According to tradition, John, who may have been the youngest member of the Twelve, lived to a ripe old age and died during the reign of the Roman Emperor Trajan (AD 98–117).

Philip and Bartholomew/Nathanael. Like Peter and Andrew, Philip was from the town of Bethsaida (John 1:43–44). According to John's Gospel, Philip brought Nathanael (possibly called Bartholomew) to Jesus, who told him that he'd seen him under a fig tree. At this, Nathanael called Jesus "Son of God" and "king of Israel" and followed him (John 1:43–48). Later, Nathanael is mentioned as one of the seven disciples who went fishing together with Peter subsequent to the crucifixion and saw the risen Jesus (John 21:2). Philip, as mentioned, is featured in conjunction with Andrew at the feeding of the five thousand and at the coming of some Greeks who wanted to see Jesus (John 6:5–7; 12:21–22). Philip's request in the upper room that Jesus show him the Father led to a memorable interchange (John 14:8–11).

Thomas. Thomas, called "the Twin" by John in his Gospel (John 11:16; 21:2), is commonly known as "Doubting Thomas." John's Gospel tells the story of how Thomas refused to believe the report by the ten other apostles (minus Judas) according to which Jesus had appeared to them in Thomas's absence. A week later, Jesus appeared to the Eleven, including Thomas, and challenged Thomas to believe, at which time he worshiped Jesus as his Lord and God (John 20:24–29). On an earlier occasion, Thomas registered a sarcastic comment when Jesus set out to raise Lazarus from the dead and later asked Jesus a question in the upper room that prompted Jesus to affirm that he was "the way, and the truth, and the life" (John 11:16; 14:5).

Matthew. Matthew (also called Levi) was a former tax collector who was called by Jesus and followed him (Matt. 9:9–13). He was also the author of the first Gospel, which has had an enormous impact on the Christian church. Like some of the other apostles, Matthew the tax collector epitomizes Jesus's ministry among the outcast and lower classes of Jewish society. Tax collectors were despised among the Jews, who viewed them as traitors because they collected taxes for the hated Roman overlords who occupied Palestine.

James son of Alphaeus, Thaddaeus, and Simon the Zealot. Comparatively little is known about these three members of the Twelve other than their consistent listing among the apostles in the apostolic lists in Matthew, Mark, Luke, and Acts (Matt. 10:3–4; Mark 3:18; Luke 6:15–16; Acts 1:13). James son of Alphaeus isn't to be confused with James son of Zebedee and brother of John. He is also not James the half-brother of Jesus, one-time head of the Jerusalem church who wrote the letter of James included in the New Testament. Thaddaeus may be the same person as Judas (not Iscariot) who asked Jesus a question in the upper room. Simon the Zealot was formerly a zealot or Jewish freedom fighter. Remarkably, he attached himself to Jesus, who took a very different approach to the Romans than the zealots did.

Judas Iscariot. Judas Iscariot was the traitor who betrayed Jesus to the Sanhedrin for thirty pieces of silver (Matt. 27:3). He was also the keeper of the moneybag and a thief who helped himself to some of its contents. He objected to Mary of Bethany's anointing of Jesus, protesting that the proceeds from the perfume she used could have been given to the poor (John 12:5–6). Jesus knew all along that Judas would betray him but chose Judas in order to fulfill Scripture (John 17:12; cf. 6:70–71; 13:1–3). After betraying Jesus, Judas was overcome by remorse and went and hanged himself (Matt. 27:3–10; see also Acts 1:16–20). He was buried in the potter's field in keeping with scriptural prediction

(Matt. 27:10). Jesus darkly remarked that it would have been better had Judas not been born (Matt. 26:24).

The Twelve: The Kind of Men They Were

What kind of men were those whom Jesus chose as his twelve apostles? What composite picture emerges from the brief character sketches of each of the members of the Twelve that we've provided? Several observations can be made. First, these men are heads of households, working and providing for their families. Several (including two pairs of brothers) are fishermen, engaging in demanding physical labor in making a living for their families. Another worked as a tax collector. Based on the biblical evidence, we can safely surmise that at least some if not most or even all of these men were heads of households, married with families (see, e.g., the references to Peter's mother-in-law in Matt. 8:14–15 and parallels; see also 1 Cor. 9:5: "Do we not have the right to take along a believing wife, as do the other apostles and the brothers of the Lord and Cephas?"). As such, they provided for their families by working in various professions. (Jesus himself, of course, worked as a carpenter, a trade he learned from his adoptive father Joseph [Mark 6:3; Matt. 13:55].)

Second, these men were doubtless diverse, not only in terms of profession but also with regard to their background, interests, and temperament. Peter's impetuous nature, as well as his raw courage, is well known. John, on the other hand, was more reflective; he may also have been considerably younger (at least he outruns Peter in their race to the empty tomb!). Thomas had a tendency to be critical, if not sarcastic. Andrew, for his part, was quite an encourager. Every time he's mentioned in John's Gospel, he's introducing someone to Jesus, most notably his brother Peter. Philip, too, encouraged Nathanael to consider Jesus's messianic claims. No wonder that Philip and Andrew seemed to like hanging out together! At least there are several occasions in John's Gospel where the two are mentioned together, such as at the feeding of the multitudes or when a group of Greeks approaches them, wanting to see Jesus. Judas Iscariot, of course, was a thief and ended up betraying Jesus into the hands of his enemies. As mentioned, we don't know a whole lot about several of the other men Jesus chose as his apostles, but clearly they were a diverse bunch.

Third (and for our present purposes, last), all of the apostles were sinners in need of a Savior. They had to learn to have faith in Jesus and to grow in their faith. As the future leaders of the church in training, they had to be fully committed to enter into Jesus's mission, to embrace it for themselves, and to make this mission their first priority, subordinating everything else in their lives to this overriding purpose: to spread the message of forgiveness of sins and salvation in Jesus, to establish his messianic community, and to advance the growth of his kingdom on earth. Under Jesus's authority, they were to lead the charge, bringing others along to join them in their mission. They were to give direction to Christ's "body" of which he continues to be the head even after his return to the Father. They were to care for Jesus's "sheep" like shepherds, providing for their spiritual needs, protecting them from doctrinal and other harm. Their leadership position was at the same time a great privilege and a grave responsibility. All but one would eventually give their lives in martyrdom. In this way, they led by example and gave eloquent expression to the all-surpassing value of allegiance to Christ and his kingdom.

The Significance of Jesus's Choice of Twelve Male Apostles

A most obvious fact, which few dispute, is that Jesus chose twelve men to be his apostles.[9] We'll discuss the theological and practical implications of this shortly. For now, it'll suffice to note that this most obvious initial observation from the Gospels of his apostles is that they are men. Jesus appointed twelve men to make up his circle of leadership in the messianic community he established. We'll look at each Gospel in detail below, but what are we to do with Jesus? Some try to present him as a proto-feminist while others reject this proposal as historically implausible. Clearly, if Jesus, as the most important figure in Christianity, pursued a particular agenda with regard to the roles of men and women in God's plan, this would be exceedingly important.[10]

---

[9] Cf. N. T. Wright, "Women's Service in the Church: The Biblical Basis," conference paper for the symposium "Men, Women and the Church," St. John's College, Durham, September 4, 2004, 5: "Among the many things that need to be said about the gospels is that we gain nothing by ignoring the fact that Jesus chose twelve male apostles." However, he goes on to say that at the cross, the men fled while the women came to the tomb first and were the first to see the risen Jesus, so they served as apostles to the apostles.
[10] Margaret's book *Jesus and the Feminists: Who Do They Say That He Is?* (Wheaton, IL: Crossway, 2008) focuses on Jesus and the Gospels as they are interpreted by various feminists, seeking to uncover and critique how various strands of feminist interpreters read and interpret the Bible. Feminists offer

To be sure, there is a significant difference between Jesus and other first-century rabbis. Jesus certainly treated women with more respect, affirming them as learners of spiritual truth and honoring them as the first witnesses to the resurrection. Yet despite the fact that he was much more positive toward women than contemporary rabbis, Jesus still chose twelve men to form the nucleus of his new messianic community, the church.[11] In terms of leadership, Jesus thus placed

various explanations for why Jesus chose twelve men. The matter is of little concern to radical feminists who take offense at Jesus's maleness and the fatherhood of God. The fact that Jesus chose twelve male apostles further confirms to them that Christianity is worthy of rejection by all feminists. Jesus and Scripture itself are seen as too patriarchal to be used by feminists.

Other, less radical "reformist" feminists approach the matter differently. In fact, ironically, their approach is diametrically opposite. In her effort to reform Scripture so it can be used by feminists, the matriarch of American feminism, Elisabeth Schüssler Fiorenza, attempts a historical reconstruction of the "Jesus community." In her book *In Memory of Her: A Feminist Theological Reconstruction of Christian Origins* (New York: Crossroad, 1983), Schüssler Fiorenza seeks to demonstrate that Jesus established a "discipleship of equals" among men and women (for a critique, see Köstenberger, *Jesus and the Feminists*, chap. 8). Her conclusion is that, contrary to the biblical witness, Jesus did *not* choose twelve men as apostles. Schüssler Fiorenza can arrive at this conclusion, which flatly contradicts the New Testament Gospels, by employing a "hermeneutic of suspicion." This hermeneutic is akin to a conspiracy theory claiming that because the Bible was written by males, the biblical writers suppressed any evidence of women leaders in the early Christian community. Viewed from such a vantage point, it is of no consequence that there is little (if any) historical evidence to support such a position. After all, males wrote Scripture in an attempt to keep women in subjection, so it's only to be expected that they would eradicate any countervailing evidence. Schüssler Fiorenza also argues that Jesus was a prophet of Sophia (wisdom personified as a female deity), a rather bizarre interpretation of Luke 7:35 ("Wisdom is justified by all her children") unsupported by any biblical texts (see her *Jesus: Miriam's Child, Sophia's Prophet: Critical Issues in Feminist Christology* [New York: Continuum, 1994]).

In addition, many reformist feminists point to neglected feminine aspects of God. They argue that Yahweh was originally a fertility goddess, again without any hard evidence to support such a claim (their primary point of reference is Prov. 8:22–31, where wisdom is *personified literarily* as a woman at God's side at creation). Strikingly, in recent years even most feminists have rejected Schüssler Fiorenza's proposal because it simply cannot be sustained historically. John H. Elliot, "Jesus Was Not an Egalitarian: A Critique of an Anachronistic and Idealist Theory," *Biblical Theology Bulletin* 32 (2002): 75–91, takes Fiorenza head on, as an egalitarian himself. He argues that his fellow feminists are guilty of anachronism and wishful thinking when they project various egalitarian ideas back onto Jesus. Kathleen Corley, a member of the Jesus Seminar, wrote a book on women and the historical Jesus in 2002 in which she argues that "the notion that Jesus established an anti-patriarchal movement or a 'discipleship of equals' is a myth posited to buttress modern Christian social engineering" (*Women and the Historical Jesus: Feminist Myths of Christian Origins* [Santa Rosa, CA: Polebridge, 2002], 1). This is rather strong language, especially coming from a fellow feminist scholar. In essence, what Corley is saying is that Schüssler Fiorenza posits her view of an egalitarian Jesus movement in order to validate her feminist agenda. But as Corley rightly notes, this does not qualify as responsible scholarly research. Other feminist scholars have been similarly critical.

As you can see, reformist feminists are rather conflicted and don't quite know what to do with Jesus. Some, like Schüssler Fiorenza, try to present him as a (proto) feminist, while others, as mentioned, reject her proposal as historically implausible. Their efforts do show the intensity of effort expended to enlist Jesus in the feminist cause. Clearly, Jesus is the most important figure in Christianity. If you could show that Jesus pursued a feminist agenda, this would make a huge difference in the debate on gender roles. In the end, however, the effort on the part of some feminists such as Fiorenza to enlist Jesus in their cause has largely been unsuccessful.

[11] Helpful resources on the Jewish and Greco-Roman background include Everett Ferguson, *Backgrounds of Early Christianity*, 3rd ed. (Grand Rapids, MI: Eerdmans, 2003); James S. Jeffers, *The Greco-Roman World of the New Testament Era: Exploring the Background of Early Christianity* (Downers Grove, IL: InterVarsity, 1999); and the *Zondervan Illustrated Bible Backgrounds Commentary*, 5 vols., ed. Clinton E. Arnold (Grand Rapids, MI: Zondervan, 2001). See also chap. 1 in Charles Ryrie, *The Role of Women in the Church*, 2nd ed. (Nashville: B&H Academic, 2011). Lynn H. Cohick, *Women in the World of the Earliest Christians: Illuminating Ancient Ways of Life* (Grand Rapids, MI: Baker Academic, 2009), is "historically engaging but not

authority into the hands of men. This is in continuity with the Old Testament pattern of male leadership where authority was vested in male kings or priests. Jesus continued this practice and called these twelve men "apostles," explicitly patterning this core group after the twelve tribes of Israel.

Did Jesus choose males only as apostles merely for pragmatic reasons? Some say that it would have been difficult for women to travel with Jesus because of feminine needs and the perceived impropriety of women traveling closely with men.[12] They suggest that Jesus chose close male followers only or primarily for pragmatic reasons such as ease of travel arrangements, not because male leadership was an essential and indispensable part of God's design for men and women.

"To be sure, there is a significant difference between Jesus and other first-century rabbis. Jesus certainly treated women with more respect, affirming them as learners of spiritual truth and honoring them as the first witnesses to the resurrection."

Though there may be a legitimate question raised here, Jesus certainly would have found a way to accommodate women traveling with him if he had really wanted to elevate women to leadership roles in his messianic community. What is more, women did in fact travel with Jesus (see Luke 8:2–3), albeit not as members of the Twelve.

So, what if Jesus knew his contemporaries weren't ready for women in leadership and so accommodated himself to the prevailing culture of the time? The obvious response is that Jesus wasn't known to compromise his convictions at all, especially when an important principle was at stake.[13] To the contrary, he was quite willing to go against cultural norms when truth was at issue. He was not known to choose the path of least resistance merely to avoid conflict. In fact, it's highly unlikely that

theologically neutral"; see the review by Benjamin L. Merkle in *Journal of Biblical Manhood and Womanhood* 16 (Spring 2011): 51–53, who notes that Cohick "consistently interprets the passages in ways that lean heavily toward egalitarianism" (p. 52, with several examples).

[12] See, e.g., Ruth A. Tucker and Walter L. Liefeld, *Daughters of the Church: Women and Ministry from New Testament Times to the Present* (Grand Rapids, MI: Baker, 1987), 46.

[13] Some might argue that slavery and women's submission are both cultural expressions that Jesus didn't formally or directly preach against, knowing that the gospel would eventually cause people to reject both. But see Robert W. Yarbrough, "Progressive and Historic: The Hermeneutics of 1 Timothy 2:9–15," in *Women in the Church*, 2nd ed., ed. Andreas J. Köstenberger and Thomas R. Schreiner (Grand Rapids, MI: Baker, 2005), 139–42, who notes that (1) neither God nor Scripture ordained slavery, while marriage and men's spiritual leadership were ordained by God; (2) slavery in Israel generally had a six-year limit, but no time limit is stated for men to continue as husbands to particular wives or as elders of churches; (3) in New Testament times, Paul advises slaves to gain their freedom if possible (1 Cor. 7:21), but he gives no such advice to wives or to people in churches with male leaders.

Jesus would have compromised merely because people weren't ready for change. He is known to have cleansed the temple in dramatic, prophetic fashion in order to challenge the abuses of the religious establishment and consistently challenged the Jewish leaders of his day in other passionate and resolute ways. If Jesus had wanted to include women leaders in his apostolic circle out of principle, he would have done so. He was the Messiah, the Son of God, God's representative to humanity. If there had been a new pattern of leadership that God wanted to establish with regard to gender roles, Jesus would have established it.

Still others assert that Jesus's choice of twelve male apostles was just a cultural thing. They draw attention to the fact that just as the Twelve were all male, they were also all Jewish. If all-male leadership is required, shouldn't Jewish leadership be required as well? However, it is not balanced logic to put the apostles' maleness and their Jewishness on the same level, because they belong in two different categories. The apostles' Jewishness is not a timeless entity but a salvation-historical phenomenon at the time of Jesus that reflects God's long-term plan for his people. According to this plan, Abraham's offspring, Jesus, who was a Jew, was to serve as a channel of blessing to all of humanity. So there is a movement from the Jews (Israel through Jesus and the apostles) to the church at large (consisting of both Jewish and non-Jewish believers). On the other hand, the biblical pattern of male leadership is constant throughout Scripture.

> "If Jesus had wanted to include women leaders in his apostolic circle out of principle, he would have done so. He was the Messiah, the Son of God, God's representative to humanity. If there had been a new pattern of leadership that God wanted to establish with regard to gender roles, Jesus would have established it."

Also, are some making too much of the distinction between apostles and disciples to find a way to exclude women from leadership? Jesus not only had male disciples but female ones as well (e.g., Luke 8:2–3: Mary Magdalene, Joanna wife of Chuza, Susanna, and many others), right? The distinction between "apostle" used for the Twelve (leaders) and "disciple" used for both male and female followers of Jesus, actually, is biblically accurate and important.[14] Though some

---

[14] Regarding Paul's use of the term *apostolos* with reference to Junia in Rom. 16:7, see the discussion in chap. 5 below.

imply that Jesus's inner circle was gender neutral, since he did have female followers, this minimizes the significance of the Twelve. It blurs the distinction between the apostles and other disciples who followed Jesus. As mentioned, the number twelve likely has symbolic significance, connecting the apostles with the twelve tribes of Israel.

"Jesus's concern to reach out to the lowly in society and his desire to elevate them and minister to them wasn't limited to women but more broadly encompassed those of other races, gender, [and] socio-economic status."

In closing, it may be helpful to note that generally the focus in the Gospels is not just on women, or gender, but on the fact that Jesus was open to people of all social classes. In Jesus's day, women unfortunately would have been grouped with people who made up the lower classes of society or otherwise lacked status such as children, the poor, or tax collectors. The Gospels make plain that Jesus didn't look down on anyone but treated all people—including women—with dignity and respect. This is so important! Jesus's concern to reach out to the lowly in society and his desire to elevate them and minister to them wasn't limited to women but more broadly encompassed those of other races, gender, socioeconomic status, and so forth.[15]

Table 3.2: Couldn't Jesus Have Chosen Women as Apostles?

1. Maybe Jesus chose only male apostles for pragmatic reasons, such as ease of travel arrangements.

2. Did Jesus accommodate himself to first-century Jewish culture because people in his day weren't ready for female apostles?

3. Isn't it just a cultural thing? Just like the Twelve were all male, they were also all Jewish. If it's required that we have all-male leaders, doesn't that mean church leaders today should all be Jewish?

4. Jesus had not only male disciples but female ones as well. The distinction between "apostle" used for the Twelve (leaders) and "disciple" used for both male and female followers of Jesus is overrated. There should be no restrictions placed on women being leaders in the church.

---

[15] Compare Paul's statement in Gal. 3:28 that in Christ there is neither Jew nor Gentile, slave nor free, male nor female, but all are one in Christ, which is a logical implication drawn from Jesus's own practice during his earthly ministry. See Andreas J. Köstenberger, "The Church according to the Gospels," in *The Community of Jesus: A Theology of the Church*, ed. Kendell H. Easley and Christopher W. Morgan (Nashville: B&H Academic, 2013), 35–63. Once this broader picture is understood, it is difficult to conceive of a compelling rationale as to why Jesus chose twelve male apostles other than to form the nucleus of his messianic community as the foundation for the leadership of the ensuing New Testament church.

Table 3.3: Probably Not. Here's Why!

> 1. The women who supported Jesus did actually accompany him on at least some of his travels. It would have been likely for Jesus to call such women "apostles" and include them among the Twelve if he had wanted to.
>
> 2. It's uncharacteristic of Jesus to bow to cultural expectations, especially if an important principle (such as male-female equality) was at stake.
>
> 3. It's not fair or accurate to put the apostles' maleness and their Jewishness on the same level, because they're two different things. The apostles' maleness reflects a constant trait. Their Jewishness reflects a particular stage of salvation history of God's plan to bless his people.
>
> 4. The apostles were distinct from the disciples and as such were identified as the core *leadership* group in Jesus's new messianic community, the nascent church. "Apostle" is in fact a technical term used in the Gospels for Jesus's core leadership group. Disciples were *followers*, but not necessarily future leaders.

Other Men in the Gospels

As we peruse the four Gospels in our Bibles, we read about a considerable number of men (and, of course, women) who are part of Jesus's story. We've already considered the Twelve, who constituted Jesus's primary focus, and have seen that they were all male in keeping with the biblical pattern of leadership. While our study of other significant male characters in the Gospels is not necessarily as relevant with regard to the question of men in leadership, it will round out the picture of men Jesus encountered during his public ministry and the kind of interactions he had with them. Essentially, these instances fall into two categories: (1) men mentioned in the narrative portions of one or more of the canonical Gospels; and (2) male characters in Jesus's parables.

Individual Men or Groups of Men in the Gospel Narratives

There are numerous male characters in the Gospel narratives that form part of Jesus's story. Jesus had many encounters with representatives of the Pharisees and the Sadducees. In some cases, the encounters were neutral or even friendly, though in many (if not most) instances they were adversarial. Jesus also faced Pontius Pilate, the Roman governor;

as well as the Jewish high priests Caiaphas and Annas toward the end of his earthly ministry.[16] In addition, Jesus met countless male individuals during the course of his three-and-a-half-year ministry (as John hyperbolically reminds us, if all of these were written down, the whole world couldn't contain the books that would need to be written; John 21:25).

In Matthew, Jesus is shown to meet several men who are in dire need of healing: a leper; a paralytic; a man with a withered hand; a man who is unable to speak; two sets of two blind men; two demon-possessed men; and an epileptic, demon-possessed boy; as well as a centurion whose son was paralyzed. Jesus healed them all. In a different type of encounter, at his transfiguration, Jesus met with Moses and Elijah, both of whom had worked major miracles in Israel's history. Mark records Jesus's meeting many of the same people, as well as an encounter with Jairus, a synagogue ruler and concerned father, whose twelve-year-old daughter had died (Jesus raised her from the dead). Luke, too, features many of the same individuals. In addition, he introduces us to Zacchaeus the tax collector, who climbs down from a tree in order to meet Jesus and to invite him to his house.

In distinction from the other Gospels, John largely carves out his own path, recounting at some length Jesus's encounters with several men (and women; see below) not featured in those Gospels. The first such encounter is that with Nicodemus, a member of the Jewish ruling council, who paid Jesus a nightly visit. Other encounters include those with an official whose son was ill; an invalid man who had been lame for thirty-eight years before he met Jesus; a man born blind (all of them healed by Jesus); and, most famously, Lazarus, who had been dead for four days and was miraculously raised from the dead by Jesus. All these amazing events revealed Jesus as the life giver, God in the flesh.

What these various encounters recorded in the Gospels show is that Jesus served these men by meeting their respective needs, whether for healing, forgiveness, or instruction. He treated them with compassion, even a memorable character such as the rich young man who

---

[16] On Jesus's dealings with the Jews and Pilate, see Andreas J. Köstenberger, "'What Is Truth?' Pilate's Question to Jesus in Its Johannine and Larger Biblical Context," in *Whatever Happened to Truth?*, ed. Andreas J. Köstenberger (Wheaton, IL: Crossway, 2005), 19–51.

wanted to follow Jesus but couldn't get himself to part with his wealth. Jesus even reached out to the hated tax collectors who were widely considered traitors, including Levi/Matthew (whom he even included among his apostles) and Zacchaeus. Not only did Jesus eventually die for people—he truly loved all the men and women whom he met during the span of his three-year public ministry on earth.

Table 3.4: Jesus's Encounters with Individual Men
(except for the Twelve) in the Gospels (Selected List)

Matthew:
Leper (8:1–4)
Centurion (8:5–13)
Two demon-possessed men (8:28–34)
Paralytic (9:1–8)
Two blind men (9:27–31; 20:29–34)
Man unable to speak (9:32–34)
Man with withered hand (12:9–14)
Moses and Elijah (17:1–8)
Epileptic demon-possessed boy (17:14–21)
Rich young man (19:16–22)

Mark:
Man with unclean spirit (1:21–28)
Leper (1:40–45)
Paralytic (2:1–12)
Man with withered hand (3:1–6)
Demon-possessed man (5:1–20)
Jairus, synagogue ruler (5:21–24, 35–43)
Deaf man (7:31–37)
Moses and Elijah (9:2–13)
Boy with unclean spirit (9:14–29)
Rich young man (10:17–33)
Blind beggar Bartimaeus (10:46–52)

Luke:
Man with unclean demon (4:31–37)
Leper (5:12–16)
Paralytic (5:17–26)
Man with withered hand (6:6–11)

Centurion (7:1–10)

Jairus (8:40–42, 49–56)

Moses and Elijah (9:28–36)

Boy with unclean spirit (9:37–43)

Man with dropsy (14:1–6)

Rich young man (18:18–30)

Blind beggar (18:36–43)

Zacchaeus (19:1–10)

John:

Nicodemus (3:1–15)

Official whose son was ill (4:46–54)

Invalid man (5:1–15)

Man born blind (9)

Lazarus (11:1–44; 12:1–8)

Male Characters in Jesus's Parables

Jesus's parables display a rich variety of both male and female characters, serving as identification figures for those who listened to them. The male characters can be grouped into several spheres of life: (1) farming, fishing, and shepherding: sower, man planting vineyard, fig tree, vinedresser, workers in vineyard, fishermen, shepherd; (2) construction, commerce, and domestic: builder of a house, man building tower, merchant, moneylender, debtors, tax collector, manager; (3) familial: father and son(s), servants; (4) public life: host, man giving banquet, king giving banquet for son's wedding, servants; (5) named figures or members of groups: Levite, Pharisee, Lazarus (poor man); (6) other: master going on a journey, traveler, priest.

The stories told by Jesus give us a fascinating glimpse into life in first-century Palestine. There are references to men as masters of the house, kings, fathers and sons, tenants, servants, messengers, doorkeepers, and banquet guests. We learn about a variety of professions held by men in Jesus's day: farming, fishing, shepherding, construction, or commerce. We hear about men throwing a feast for their son's wedding, men planting a vineyard, and men going on a journey. Clearly, today most of us no longer live in the type of agrarian society

that characterized first-century Palestine, but the occupations and activities of the men depicted by Jesus reflect a culture in which men
worked hard to provide for their own.

Table 3.5: Male Characters in Jesus's Parables

In Matthew, Mark, and Luke	
Bridegroom	Matt. 9:15; Mark 2:19–20; Luke 5:33–39
Strong man	Matt. 12:29–30; Mark 3:22–27; Luke 11:21–23
Sower	Matt. 13:1–9, 18–23; Mark 4:1–9, 13–20; Luke 8:4–8, 11–15
Man planting vineyard, tenants, servants, son	Matt. 21:33–46; Mark 12:1–12; Luke 20:9–19
Only in Matthew and Luke	
Father and son	Matt. 7:9–11; Luke 11:11–13
Builder	Matt. 7:24–27; Luke 6:47–49
Shepherd	Matt. 18:12–14; Luke 15:1–7
King, son, servants	Matt. 22:1–14; Luke 14:15–24
Master of house, thief	Matt. 24:42–44; Luke 12:39–40
Master, two kinds of servants	Matt. 24:45–51; Luke 12:42–46
Master, servants	Matt. 25:14–30; Luke 19:11–27
Only in Mark and Luke	
Man going on journey, servants, doorkeeper	Mark 13:34–37; Luke 12:35–38
Only in Matthew	
Man finding treasure	Matt. 13:44
Merchant finding pearl	Matt. 13:45–46
Fisherman	Matt. 13:47–50

Owner of a house	Matt. 13:52
King, servants	Matt. 18:23–35
Vineyard owner, workers	Matt. 20:1–16
Father, two sons	Matt. 21:28–32
Shepherd	Matt. 25:31–46
Only in Mark	
Sower	Mark 4:26–29, 30–32
Only in Luke	
Moneylender, two debtors	Luke 7:41–42
Traveler, priest, Levite, Samaritan	Luke 10:30–37
Persistent friend	Luke 11:5–8
Rich fool	Luke 12:13–21
Man planting fig tree, vinedresser	Luke 13:6–9
Host	Luke 14:7–14
Man giving banquet, servants, guests*	Luke 14:16–24
Man building tower	Luke 14:28–30
King going to war	Luke 14:31–33
Father, two sons/heirs	Luke 15:11–32
Shrewd manager	Luke 16:1–8
Rich man, Lazarus	Luke 16:19–31
Humble servant	Luke 17:7–10
Pharisee, tax collector	Luke 18:9–14

*Of those prospective guests, one excused himself, saying he had bought a field and must go see it; another said he had bought five yoke of oxen and must examine them; another said he had married a wife.

Other Teaching on Men and Women

In addition to featuring a variety of men and women in his parables, Jesus teaches on issues pertaining to men and women at various other junctures during his public ministry. At one such occasion, Jesus likened male lust to adultery (Matt. 5:28–32). At another occasion, he responded to a question addressed to him by Pharisees on the topic of adultery and divorce (Matt. 19:1–12; Mark 10:1–12; Luke 16:18). Jesus affirmed God's original design of lifelong marriage between one man and one woman and pointed out that Mosaic divorce legislation was only a concession to human hardness, not a legitimization of divorce. At yet another occasion, Jesus noted that as a result of his call to discipleship, loyalties in the natural family may be divided, setting son against father, daughter against mother, and so forth (Matt. 10:35; Luke 12:53; cf. Mic. 7:6). Once Jesus was asked if people were going to marry in the resurrection (Matt. 22:23–33; Mark 12:18-27; Luke 20:27–40). Jesus replied that in heaven, people are going to be like the angels. In this way, Jesus significantly added to our understanding of male-female identity, relationships, and roles.

Table 3.6: Jesus's Teaching Concerning Men and Women

Jesus teaches on adultery and divorce (Matt. 5:28–32; 19:1–12; Mark 10:1–12; Luke 16:18)
Daughter set against mother, etc. (Matt. 10:35; Luke 12:53)
Jesus on marriage in the resurrection (Matt. 22:23–33; Mark 12:18–27; Luke 20:27–40)

Women in the Gospels

Now that we've assessed the significance of Jesus's maleness, surveyed the members of the Twelve, discussed the significance of his selection of twelve men as apostles, and studied other men in the Gospels and male characters in Jesus's parables, we're ready to address some of the most relevant texts in the Gospels that show Jesus interacting with or teaching about women. After this, we'll look at each Gospel individually in order to delineate the particular contributions Matthew, Mark, Luke, and John make to our understanding of the big picture of the biblical theology of men's and women's roles, including regarding their service in positions of leadership. A concluding survey will attempt to tie together the various insights derived from a close study of Jesus's interaction with and teaching on women.[17]

Individual Women or Groups of Women in the Gospel Narratives (Synopsis)

The Gospels feature a considerable number of women who were grateful recipients of Jesus's healing, whether personally or of a loved one. These women include Peter's mother-in-law (Matt. 8:14–15; Mark 1:30–31; Luke 4:38–39), the widow at Nain (Luke 7:11–15), Jairus's daughter and an unnamed woman with blood flow (Matt. 9:18–26; Mark 5:22–43; Luke 8:40–56), a girl who had been possessed by a demon (Matt. 15:21–28; Mark 7:24–30), and a crippled woman (Luke 13:10–17). Jesus also included several female characters alongside male characters in his parables and taught about subjects of concern for women.[18] In addition, the Gospels record several instances where Jesus engaged in more extensive interaction with women, such as the Samaritan woman or Mary and Martha, and make reference to a group of devoted female followers of Jesus who show their loyalty all the way to the cross and beyond.

Table 3.7: Passages on Jesus and Women in the Gospels (Selected List)

Jesus and his mother at the Cana wedding (John 2:1–12)
Jesus talks with a Samaritan woman (John 4:1–42)
Jesus heals Peter's mother-in-law (Matt. 8:14–15; Mark 1:30–31; Luke 4:38–39)
Jesus raises the widow's son at Nain (Luke 7:11–15)
Jesus's family comes to take him home (Matt. 12:46–50; Mark 3:20–21, 31–35; Luke 8:19–21)
Jesus raises Jairus's daughter, heals woman with blood flow (Matt. 9:18–26; Mark 5:22–43; Luke 8:40–56)
Jesus is anointed by a sinful woman (Luke 7:36–50)
A group of women supports Jesus and the Twelve (Luke 8:2–3)
Jesus exorcises demon from a girl (Matt. 15:21–28; Mark 7:24–30)

---

[17] For more details on the tables below, see Köstenberger, *Jesus and the Feminists*, chap. 14.
[18] See the lists above.

Jesus teaches Martha an object lesson (Luke 10:38–42)

A woman calls Jesus's mother "blessed" (Luke 11:27–28)

Jesus commends the Queen of the South (Matt. 12:42; Luke 11:31)

Jesus heals a crippled woman on the Sabbath (Luke 13:10–17)

The request of the mother of the sons of Zebedee (Matt. 20:20–28; see Mark 10:35–45)

Teaching on widows and the widow's mite (Mark 12:40–44; Luke 20:47–21:4)

Pregnant, nursing mothers in the tribulation (Matt. 24:19–21; Mark 13:17–19)

Mary and Martha grieve for Lazarus (John 11:1–44)

Mary anoints Jesus (Matt. 26:6–13; Mark 14:3–9; John 12:1–8)

The wailing Jerusalem women (Luke 23:27–31)

The women near the cross (Matt. 27:55–56; Mark 15:40–41; Luke 23:49; John 19:25–27)

Mary Magdalene and others at Jesus's burial and as witnesses of the resurrection (Matt. 27:61; 28:1–11; Mark 15:47–16:8; Luke 23:55–24:12; John 20:1–18)

The Samaritan woman. Let's now take a closer look at a few of these women. In John's Gospel, we read about Jesus's conversation with a Samaritan woman (John 4:1–42). This account shows how the Samaritan woman serves as a witness to Jesus and recruits others in her village to hear his teaching. Does Jesus commission the woman for this task, and does this suggest that Jesus is formally appointing her to a leadership position in the Christian community? The narrative really only indicates that the woman bears witness to others about Jesus. This passage certainly lends support to the notion that women, like men, should passionately share their faith. At the same time, it would be anachronistic to suggest that the woman occupied a leadership position in the New Testament church, if for no other reason than that the church hadn't yet come into being at that time.

Another significant element of the story is Jesus's breaking of several social conventions in order to share the gospel with this woman. Entering into a prolonged, in-depth public conversation with a woman wasn't the norm for a first-century rabbi or any respectable Jewish male.[19]

---

[19] For primary and secondary sources, see Andreas J. Köstenberger, *John*, Baker Exegetical Commentary on the New Testament (Grand Rapids, MI: Baker, 2004), 159, who mentions that some rabbis (such as

We see the disciples at their return surprised to find Jesus in conversation with this woman (v. 27). He takes the time to speak with her since he cares for her as a person in need of salvation. The fact that she is a Samaritan suggests that Jesus isn't reaching out across only gender but also racial lines. Salvation-historical factors are likely at work as well, since Samaritans occupied a middle position between Jews and Gentiles. Jesus likely here sets the example for the early church to engage in missionary outreach in Jerusalem, Judea, Samaria, and to the ends of the earth (Acts 1:8).

Mary and Martha. While the account of the Samaritan woman is found only in John's Gospel, all four Gospels feature accounts of Jesus's interaction with Mary and Martha, two unmarried sisters who lived in Bethany just outside the city of Jerusalem (Luke 10:38–42; John 11:1–44; Matt. 26:6–13; Mark 14:3–9; John 12:1–8). The story of Jesus's conversation with Martha and her sister Mary in Luke 10:38–42, in particular, provides a fascinating glimpse into Jesus's private dealings with women. In her book *Jesus and the Feminists*, Margaret registers the following observation:

> Rather than prioritizing women's household duties, Jesus encouraged women to learn from him and become his followers. However, we must be careful not to take an instance from the Gospel narrative and invest it simplistically with normative significance. All that is said here is that Jesus rejected Martha's complaint that Mary did not help with household duties. It hardly follows that Jesus was a feminist who rejected women's managing their households and called on them to serve as pastors or elders.[20]

Jesus obviously isn't condemning Martha simply for preparing a meal (Simon's mother-in-law did so without drawing any rebuke from Jesus; see Matt. 8:14–15). Jesus certainly wasn't opposed to women staying at home and ensuring that their households are in order. It is

---

Yose ben Yohanan) "held that to talk too much to a woman, even one's own wife, was a waste of time, diverting one's attention from the study of the Torah. Potentially, this habit could grow to be a great evil, even leading to hell (*m. 'Abot* 1.5)." Other instances where Jesus talked to women in public include Luke 7:36–50; 10:38–42; and John 11:17–40.

[20] Köstenberger, *Jesus and the Feminists*, 196, quoting Stanley J. Grenz and Denise Muir Kjesbo, *Women in the Church: A Biblical Theology of Women in Ministry* (Downers Grove, IL: InterVarsity, 1995), 75, and Aída B. Spencer, *Beyond the Curse: Women Called to Ministry* (Nashville: Thomas Nelson, 1985), 60–61.

a narrative account of a conflict that historically arose between two sisters. Martha is complaining because Mary isn't helping. Jesus settles a dispute between two sisters by noting that what Mary was doing was seizing the opportunity to learn from Jesus, which showed proper discernment and right priorities.

The account illustrates Jesus's affirmation of women receiving spiritual instruction. In the Jewish culture of Jesus's day, girls were often not given the same opportunity as boys to be educated in the Scriptures.[21] Jesus is countercultural and pointedly commends Mary's desire to listen to his teaching and to learn from him. The point Luke is making is that Christianity is very open for women and individuals from every class and background to come to Jesus. Women should have access to Jesus and be able to learn from him.[22] Mary serves as a great example of a woman who is open to spiritual truth and to grow in her knowledge of the Scriptures.

"The point Luke is making is that Christianity is very open to women and individuals from every class and background to come to Jesus. Women should have access to Jesus and be able to learn from him."

Later, John records the raising of Lazarus by Jesus in an account that features Lazarus's sisters Mary and Martha (John 11:1–44). Apparently, all of them were unmarried and lived together in an extended household. In this account Lazarus has died, and his sisters are grieving. Jesus is close to the family, and they believe that if he had come earlier, he could have prevented the tragedy. Martha, significantly, utters the confession that Jesus is the Messiah and Son of God, anticipating the purpose of John's entire Gospel.[23]

Shortly before his death, Jesus visits the house of Mary and Martha again, and on that occasion Mary anoints Jesus for burial (Matt. 26:6–13; Mark 14:3–9; John 12:1–8). In the process, she breaks a bottle of expensive perfume, extravagantly "wasting" almost an entire year's worth of wages. Judas the traitor objects to Mary's actions, contending

[21] Rainer Riesner, *Jesus als Lehrer*, 3rd ed. (Tübingen: Mohr Siebeck, 1988), focuses on first-century Jewish education. Typically only boys were given the privilege of being trained in the Scriptures.
[22] At the same time, the account says nothing about Mary being a teacher or leader. Contra Wright, "Women's Service," 4, who claims that Mary here is shown to invade "the male part of the house" and that she is a student in order to be a teacher, a rabbi, herself.
[23] This is remarkable because in the other Gospels it is Peter who utters the pivotal confession. Peter issues a remarkable acknowledgment of Jesus's identity in John's Gospel as well (John 6:68–69), but Martha's statement is closer to epitomizing John's purpose; in fact, the two are identical (John 11:27; 20:31).

that the money could instead have been given to the poor. John explicitly contrasts Judas's disingenuous protest with Mary's act of service.

Unlike Judas, Mary of Bethany intuitively understood that this was a propitious moment. Jesus affirms the rightness of Mary's actions in anointing him for burial. Without fully realizing the significance of her act, Mary expressed her loyalty to Jesus, and her story continues to be told to this very day, in keeping with Jesus's prediction. Mary's example shows that Jesus loved women, and many responded to him with great devotion and unusual faith.

A Group of Women Supporters of Jesus and the Twelve

Luke alone records the presence of a devoted group of women followers supporting Jesus and the Twelve (Luke 8:2–3). There were thus at least two distinct groups surrounding and supporting Jesus: the twelve apostles and a group of women who traveled with Jesus, at least some of the time, to support him and his (male) followers in their ministry. We encounter these women again at the cross. Mary Magdalene, who later became the first witness of the resurrection, had seven demons exorcised from her by Jesus. Only three women are named in the account (Mary Magdalene, Joanna the wife of Chuza, and Susanna), but there were doubtless several others.

The account does indicate that some female followers of Jesus (such as Joanna) were apparently more prominent, being married to government or other high-ranking officials. Luke noted this most likely for apologetic purposes in an effort to show that not all Christians were members of the lower classes of society. There were many intelligent, prominent, well-connected people (including women) who placed their faith in Jesus and followed him.

These women's prominence on account of their husband's position, however, does not necessarily make them leaders in Jesus's community or in the early church. For the most part, these women were prominent because they were married to notorious individuals or government officials. Their presence with Jesus suggests that they had a genuine, deep commitment to Jesus and his cause. The present group is for all practical purposes identical to the following group of women mentioned as being near the cross and at the empty tomb subsequent to the resurrection. Women today can be greatly encouraged by this group of female disciples who were deeply devoted to Jesus's cause.

The Women Near the Cross and at the Empty Tomb, Including Mary Magdalene and Others

All four Gospels recount in varying degrees of detail the presence of a group of women at Jesus's crucifixion and burial (Matt. 27:55–56; Mark 15:40–41; Luke 23:49; John 19:25–27) and their return to the tomb in order to anoint Jesus's body after the end of the Sabbath (Matt. 27:61; 28:1–11; Mark 15:47–16:8; Luke 23:55–24:12; John 20:1–18).[24] Luke's account is especially instructive. Jesus is shown to appoint the twelve apostles at the very beginning of his Gospel while his women followers are first mentioned near the midpoint of his narrative (Luke 8:2–3). The narrative closes with everyone clustered together, including the women who had followed Jesus faithfully all the way to the cross.

It's unlikely that Jesus's first followers would have invented the account of Jesus appearing first to Mary Magdalene subsequent to his resurrection. No one seeking to validate the Christian faith would have invented a woman's testimony to Jesus's resurrection. By appearing first to a woman, the risen Jesus implicitly challenged the patriarchal culture of his day that didn't consider women as viable legal witnesses. Interestingly, John's statement at 21:14 (HCSB), "This was now the third time Jesus appeared to his disciples after he was raised from the dead," doesn't count Jesus's appearance to Mary Magdalene, most likely because she wasn't a member of the Twelve, and here "disciples" is used to denote the apostles (cf. 1 Cor. 15:3–8).

All the Gospels make clear that none of the women, similar to Jesus's male followers, expected Jesus to rise from the dead. When they went to the tomb, they were expecting to find Jesus's dead body. It was the custom for women in that culture to prepare the body for burial, and they hadn't been able to finish that task because of the Sabbath. As devoted followers of Jesus, they returned in order

---

[24] For a discussion of the women at the cross and the empty tomb, see Andreas J. Köstenberger and Justin Taylor, *The Final Days of Jesus: The Most Important Week of the Most Important Person Who Ever Lived* (Wheaton, IL: Crossway, 2014) 153, 162, 167, 177–80.

to complete that assignment within culturally prescribed norms. Mary Magdalene's devotion was rewarded by the appearance of the risen Jesus.

Female Characters in Jesus's Parables

Along with men, Jesus featured numerous women or groups of women as characters in his parables. These female characters include: the woman baking (Matt. 13:33; Luke 13:20–21); the woman who lost a coin (Luke 15:8–10); the persistent widow (Luke 18:1–8); two women grinding at a mill (Matt. 24:41; Luke 17:35); and the ten virgins (Matt. 25:1–13). In many cases, Jesus, when telling a parable, would use a male and a female character side by side, evidently so that both his male and his female listeners could better relate to his teaching. This pattern is particularly evident in Luke's Gospel (see further below). It's certainly remarkable that Jesus, in the patriarchal culture of first-century Palestine, went out of his way to teach women about the kingdom he had come to inaugurate. This shows that he genuinely sought to appeal to and attract female as well as male followers.

Table 3.8: Women in Jesus's Parables

The woman baking (Matt. 13:33; Luke 13:20–21)
The woman who lost a coin (Luke 15:8–10)
The persistent widow (Luke 18:1–8)
Two women grinding at a mill (Matt. 24:41; Luke 17:35)
The parable of the ten virgins (Matt. 25:1–13)

Passages on Women in Each Individual Gospel

Now that we've briefly surveyed some of the most important passages in the Gospels in synoptic format that feature Jesus's encounters with women, we'll look at the Gospels one at a time in order to determine their distinctive contribution to our understanding of Jesus's treatment of and teaching on women.[25]

---

[25] Margaret has included complete tables in her book *Jesus and the Feminists*, chap. 14. For this reason it will be sufficient here to limit ourselves to providing selected lists that feature the most important references to women in each of the Gospels.

Table 3.9: Selected Passages on Women in Matthew

Matthew	Woman character(s)	Description
1:3, 5, 6, 16*	Tamar, Rahab, Ruth, Bathsheba, Mary	Jesus's genealogy
1:18–25*	Mary (Joseph's perspective)	Jesus's birth
10:35	Daughter vs. mother, etc.	No peace but division
13:33*	A woman baking	Kingdom parable
15:21–28	Syrophoenician woman and daughter	Demon exorcised, faith
20:20–21	Mother of sons of Zebedee	Request on behalf of her sons
24:41*	Two women grinding at a mill	Coming of Son of Man
25:1–13*	Ten virgins	Parable on watchfulness
26:6–13	Woman at Bethany	Anointing Jesus
27:55–56	Mary Magdalene, Mary mother of James and of Joses, mother of sons of Zebedee	Watching from a distance; Had followed Jesus in Galilee
28:1–11	Mary Magdalene, other Mary	Set out to anoint Jesus's body

Only in Matthew

Matthew

Matthew's emphasis on five women in Jesus's genealogy is intriguing. What these women seem to have in common is the appearance or reality of scandal. In Mary's case, it was only the appearance of scandal related to the virgin birth. Joseph is about to divorce Mary, suspecting that she broke the betrothal, and Matthew is trying to make the point that the appearance or reality of scandal in conjunction with God's work has precedent in salvation history.

Tamar played the part of a prostitute in order to maintain her husband's name. Ruth slept beside Boaz all night, conveying the appearance, although not the reality, of scandal. Bathsheba, on the other hand, was involved in a very real, high-profile, and destructive scandal with King David. By including these five women, Matthew sets the background for Mary's virgin conception of Jesus, in keeping with the Jewish belief in the importance of patterns in history.

Other explanations have been offered for what might unify the five women, but regardless of the explanation, these commonalities have little (if anything) to do with the question of women in leadership. The reason why Matthew includes these women in Jesus's genealogy is most likely not that he has an exalted view of women but rather that he wants to provide the proper backdrop for his narration of the virgin birth of Jesus.

In the body of the Gospel, women are mentioned as characters in the narrative (Mary the mother of Jesus, Mary Magdalene) and in particular as recipients of healing (the Syrophoenician woman). On the whole, Jesus's encounters with women narrated in this Gospel show women in familiar roles as mothers and working in the domestic realm. There is no recognizable special emphasis on women.

Table 3.10: Selected Passages on Women in Mark

Mark	Woman character(s)	Description
7:24–30	Syrophoenician woman and daughter	Demon exorcized, faith
12:41–44	Poor widow	Commended for giving
14:3–9	Woman at Bethany	Anointing Jesus
15:40–41	Mary Magdalene, Mary mother of James and of Joses, Salome, and other women	Looking on from a distance at cross
16:1–8	Mary Magdalene, Mary mother of James, Salome	Set out to anoint Jesus's body

Mark

All of Mark's material on women is also found in Matthew and Luke. Mark doesn't have any special interest in women beyond the basic story line. Only the last two references in the Gospel draw attention to a group of devoted female followers of Jesus. The female characters featured in Mark's Gospel are an integral part of Jesus's story. In several cases, they approach Jesus to ask for healing, whether for themselves or a loved one (e.g., the Syrophoenician woman). Other women show noteworthy devotion, such as the woman at Bethany who anoints Jesus, the women at the cross, and the women who set out to anoint Jesus's body at the end of the Gospel.

The absence of unique material on women in Mark, on the assumption of Markan priority (the view that Mark was the first canonical Gospel to be written), may suggest that all of Mark's material on women was subsequently incorporated into the other Synoptic Gospels, Matthew and Luke. Alternatively, on the assumption of Matthean priority (Matthew wrote first), Mark didn't add any material of his own beyond what he found in Matthew. In either case, the lack of particular Markan material indicates that Mark does not show a pronounced special interest in women characters in his Gospel.

As in the case of Matthew's Gospel, there is nothing in Mark's account that strikes one as out of the ordinary. Women are shown in their customary roles as concerned, loving—and, in at least one case, scheming—mothers, and as devoted followers. Jesus heals the woman with blood flow and the daughter of Jairus and of the Syrophoenician woman and commends the poor widow. The familiar group of women is found at the cross and at the empty tomb. Mark's Gospel features an array of male and female characters who intersected with Jesus during his earthly ministry, with no necessary implications regarding the roles of men and women in leadership.

Table 3.11: Selected Passages on Women in Luke

Luke	Woman character(s)	Description
1:5–25*	Elizabeth	Birth announcement
1:26–38*	Mary	Birth announcement
1:39–56*	Mary and Elizabeth	Visit, Mary's song
1:57–58*	Elizabeth	Birth of John the Baptist
2:1–20*	Mary	Birth of Jesus
2:36–38*	Anna the prophetess	Prophesies regarding Jesus
2:39–52*	Mary	Twelve-year-old Jesus at temple
7:11–15*	Widow at Nain	Son raised from the dead
7:36–50*	Woman who had led sinful life	Earlier anointing of Jesus
8:2–3*	Mary Magdalene, Joanna wife of Chuza, Susanna, and many others	Supporting Jesus and the Twelve
10:38–42*	Mary and Martha (sisters)	Listening vs. serving
11:27–28*	Woman in the crowd	Blessed is Jesus's mother
12:53	Mother vs. daughter, etc.	Not peace, but division
13:10–13*	Woman crippled for 18 years	Healed
15:8–10*	Woman who lost a coin	Figure in parable
18:1–8*	Persistent widow	Figure in parable
21:1–4	Poor widow	Commended for giving
23:49	Women who had followed from Galilee	Watching from a distance
23:55–24:11	Mary Magdalene, Joanna, Mary mother of James, and others	Set out to anoint Jesus's body

*Only in Luke

Luke

The material in Luke significantly complements that included in Mark and Matthew. As he mentions in his preface (Luke 1:1–4), Luke used a variety of sources (most likely Mark, plus possibly a source he shared with Matthew, as well as other written accounts and oral traditions). Drawing from these materials, Luke emphasized the universal scope of Jesus's messianic ministry as Savior, healer, and teacher. Luke's Gospel stands out as giving considerable attention to women, in keeping with Luke's concern for those of low status in society, such as the poor, children, Gentiles, the disabled or sick, and tax collectors.

The birth narratives of John the Baptist and of Jesus are told from a female perspective, possibly on the basis of eyewitness accounts by Elizabeth and Mary, their mothers.[26] Luke 7:36–50 narrates a sinful woman's anointing of Jesus.[27] The group of women following Jesus from Galilee all the way to the cross serves as a significant source of eyewitness testimony as well (note the *inclusio* of eyewitness testimony, an ancient literary device indicating firsthand eyewitnesses behind a written document, in Luke 8:2–3 and 23:49).[28] Women are also quite prominent in kingdom parables. Luke thus shows far-above-average interest in women as characters in the story of Jesus. It's remarkable that Jesus created illustrations specifically for women to relate to, which implies that he treated women as potential or actual disciples.

In addition, one observes a consistent, most likely deliberate, pattern of pairing male and female characters in material unique to Luke's Gospel. There are a dozen or so pairings that can be identified in the Gospel and several more in Acts. While not necessarily indicating male-female equality with regard to leadership positions in Jesus's inner circle or the early church, this pattern does suggest, similar to Paul's reference to "no male and female" in Galatians 3:28, that the male-female distinction was immaterial with regard to salvation in

---

[26] This contrasts with Matthew's account, which reflects Joseph's perspective.

[27] Wright, "Women's Service," 4, calls this "a priestly action which Jesus accepted as such." The implications of this argument, however, are unclear: is this supposed to mean that the woman had priestly authority over Jesus?

[28] On the *inclusio* of eyewitness testimony, see Richard Bauckham, *Jesus and the Eyewitnesses: The Gospels as Eyewitness Testimony* (Grand Rapids, MI: Eerdmans, 2006), 124–47.

Jesus. The male-female pairs in Luke may include (but are not necessarily limited to) what is given in table 3.12.[29]

Table 3.12: Male-Female Pairs in Luke

Luke	Male character	Luke	Female character
1:5–23	Zechariah	1:26–56	Mary
2:25–35	Simeon	2:36–38	Anna
4:27	Naaman	4:26	Widow of Zarephath
4:31–37	Demon-possessed man	4:38–39	Peter's mother-in-law
6:13–16	The twelve apostles	8:2–3	A group of female disciples
7:11–17	Widow's son raised	8:40–56	Jairus's daughter raised
10:25–37	Teacher of the law	10:38–42	Martha and Mary
11:5–13	Persistent friend	18:1–8	Persistent widow
11:32	Men of Nineveh	11:31	Queen of Sheba
14:1–6	Man healed on Sabbath	13:10–17	Woman healed on Sabbath
19:9	Son of Abraham	13:16	Daughter of Abraham
15:3–7	Man who lost sheep	15:8–10	Woman who lost coin
13:19	Man sowing	13:21	Woman baking
24:13–35	Jesus appears to Emmaus disciples	24:1–11	Jesus appears to women

In his Gospel, Luke puts his readers more closely in touch with women such as Elizabeth and Mary by showing them their perspective as John the Baptist's or Jesus's mother. He also provides us with memorable female characters featured in Jesus's parables, such as the woman who lost a coin (balancing the references to the male shep-

---

[29] See also the male-female pairs in Acts listed in the following chapter.

herd and the father with his two sons, including the Prodigal) and the persistent widow.

Some of these pairs are more compelling than others, but even if some were eliminated, a pattern emerges that is more pronounced than what is found in the other Gospels.[30] Highlighting Jesus's appeal to both men and women may have been Luke's way of demonstrating that Christianity as a movement was attracting people from all classes and types.

Perhaps more than the other Synoptic Gospels, Luke features women as Jesus's devoted followers and disciples, most notably the group of women from Galilee as well as Mary and Martha (who are also featured in John's Gospel; see below). Nevertheless, Jesus is not shown to overturn the biblical pattern of male leadership. Of all the Gospels, Luke is most emphatic in his emphasis on Jesus's outreach to women and others of lower status in society.

Table 3.13: Selected Passages on Women in John

John	Woman character(s)	Description
2:1–11*	Jesus's mother	Wedding at Cana
2:12*	Jesus's mother	Jesus's family, Capernaum
4:1–42*	Samaritan woman	Believes in Jesus, witnesses
11:1–37*	Mary and Martha	Raising of Lazarus
12:1–8	Mary and Martha	Dinner, Mary anoints Jesus
19:25–27	Jesus's mother, mother's sister, Mary wife of Clopas, Mary Magdalene	Near the cross; Jesus ensures care of his mother
20:1–18	Mary Magdalene	Recognition scene

*Only in John

---

[30] As we'll see below, the pattern continues in the book of Acts.

John

In keeping with his pattern of selecting a limited number of significant episodes in Jesus's ministry and recounting these in greater detail, John features several accounts that include women. Examples include Jesus's mother at the Cana wedding, the Samaritan woman, and Mary and Martha at the raising of Lazarus.[31] Jesus's appearance to Mary Magdalene is also very significant.

The contrast John draws between the Samaritan woman and Nicodemus, a ruler of Israel, is most likely due not to their different genders but to the racial distinction between Jews and Samaritans so as to underscore the availability of salvation to anyone who believes (John 4:9: "Jews have no dealings with Samaritans"; cf. 12:32: "And I, when I am lifted up from the earth, will draw all [kinds of] people to myself").

The Samaritan woman is shown as an important witness to Jesus, and Mary Magdalene, significantly, is the first witness of the resurrection in the Gospel. This affirms the value of women as witnesses to the gospel story and of their calling to share their faith with others.[32] It also stands in remarkable contrast to first-century society, in which women's witness was widely disparaged.[33]

Implications

What did Jesus do? Surveying the Gospels, it is striking to see how many lives of both men and women Jesus touched and how he serves as a wonderful example of the way to treat women and men with dignity, respect, love, and compassion. We've noted how Jesus appointed and trained a core group of male followers, the Twelve, to lead his new messianic community after Jesus's physical departure from this earth. Jesus's choice of twelve men as his apostles who would form the nucleus of the leadership of the early church (Matt. 10:2–4; Mark 3:13–19; see also Eph. 2:20) is significant for the following reasons:[34]

---

[31] The account of the adulterous woman in John 7:53–8:11 is not addressed because it was likely not in John's original Gospel. See the footnotes in most English Bibles. For more details, consult Köstenberger, *John*, 245–49.

[32] E.g., Robert G. Maccini, *Her Testimony Is True: Women as Witnesses according to John*, Journal for the Study of the New Testament Supplement 125 (Sheffield: Sheffield Academic Press, 1996).

[33] E.g., Josephus, *Antiquities* iv.8.15: "But let not the testimony of women be admitted, on account of the levity and boldness of their sex."

[34] Cf. Borland, "Women in the Life and Teaching of Jesus," 111–13.

- The apostles were to be with Jesus to learn from him, to be sent out to preach the good news of the gospel, and to be trained by him personally as the future leaders of the church (Mark 3:14–15). As Jesus said, "The student is not above his teacher, but everyone who is fully trained will be like his teacher" (Luke 6:40 NIV).

- Jesus promised the apostles the teaching ministry of the Holy Spirit and the reception of special revelation, which would issue in the writing of the New Testament documents (John 14:26; 16:13–15).

- Later, when a need arose to replace Judas as twelfth apostle after Jesus's ascension, one of the requirements was that his replacement be male. Acts 1:21–22 states, "So one of the *men* [Greek *andrōn*, "males"] who have accompanied us during all the time that the Lord Jesus went in and out among us, . . . one of these *men* [implied in the Greek from verse 21] must become with us a witness to his resurrection."

- The apostles were the official leaders of the early church who continued Jesus's mission in the power of the Holy Spirit in keeping with Jesus's intentions (Acts 2:14; 5:12, 18, 40, 42; 6:2–4; 9:29; 15:2; Gal. 1:17).

- As a testimony to the permanence of male leadership in the church, the apostles will be given special positions of leadership at the end of time (Matt. 19:28; Luke 22:30) and the names of the twelve apostles will be inscribed on the foundation of the New Jerusalem (Rev. 21:14; see also Eph. 2:20).

We've also observed the considerable variety of male characters who form part of Jesus's story or who are featured in Jesus's parables.

Regarding the way in which Jesus related to women, based on our study of the relevant passages in the Gospels, we can observe the following:

- Jesus treated women consistently with respect, dignity, compassion, and kindness (e.g., Luke 7:36–50). This is characteristic of his dealings with the numerous women who approached him for help, whether on their own behalf (Luke 13:10–17) or on behalf of a loved one (Luke 7:11–15).[35]

- Jesus dealt with women honestly and straightforwardly, firmly resisting any attempts to be manipulated or otherwise swayed from truth. He didn't treat women as morally superior or inherently more virtuous because of their gender. Women are sinners just like men.[36]

- In his teaching Jesus often used women as illustrations, especially in his parables (e.g., Matt. 24:41; 25:1–13; Luke 15:8–10; 18:1–8). This indicates Jesus's desire that his message of God's kingdom resonate with women as well as men. In so doing, he made a special effort to communicate his teaching in ways that were applicable to women and to use examples that were relevant for them.

- At many occasions Jesus showed special sensitivity to women's concerns. One example of this awareness is Jesus's remark concerning the fate of pregnant women and nursing mothers at the coming tribulation (Matt. 24:19; Mark 13:17). On another occasion Jesus took the time to address the wailing Jerusalem women on his way to the cross (Luke 23:27–31).

- Women followed Jesus, often with great devotion. Luke features a group of loyal women followers who traveled with Jesus and the Twelve and supported them financially (Luke 8:2–3). The Gospels show some of these same women at the cross, the burial, and as the first witnesses of the resurrection (Luke 23:49). These women exhibit strong faith, intensity of devotion, and unusual insight regarding Jesus's true identity as the Messiah. Women had a significant part in Jesus's mission.

- Jesus taught women the Scriptures and treated them as disciples (e.g., Luke 10:38–42). This, too, is highly significant in the context of a culture where women's opportunity to learn the Scriptures was limited. It certainly serves as an encouragement for women today

---

[35] Borland (ibid., 108) writes, "Jesus showed how highly he valued women by ministering to them and meeting their needs. . . . He healed them, dialogued with them, and showed women the same care and concern He showed to men."

[36] This can be seen in Jesus's interactions with his mother (John 2:3–5; Mark 3:20–21, 31–35), the Samaritan woman (John 4:7–26), the Syrophoenician woman (Matt. 15:21–28; Mark 7:24–30), Martha and Mary (Luke 10:38–42), a woman in a crowd who called Jesus's mother blessed (Luke 11:27–28), and the mother of the sons of Zebedee (Matt. 20:20–21).

to grow spiritually, to read the Scriptures, even to go to seminary, and to learn as much as they can about the biblical teaching and to share their learning with others in appropriate ways.

• Women served as witnesses to Jesus. The Samaritan woman bore witness to her entire village (John 4:1–42). Mary Magdalene was the first to see the risen Jesus and was told to pass on the good news to his disciples (John 20:11–18). This contrasts with the generally negative Jewish attitude toward women witnesses in the first century.

• While Jesus affirmed the creation of humanity as male and female in God's image (Matt. 19:4 citing Gen. 1:27), was receptive to women's requests for help, showed great love toward women, and was genuinely interested in their spiritual welfare, he didn't elevate them to positions of leadership. This is different from his dealings with Jews and Gentiles where he clearly envisioned a future time when Gentiles would be included in the church (presumably including in leadership positions; see, e.g., Matt. 28:18–20).[37]

Table 3.14: Observations on Jesus's Treatment of Women

1. Jesus treated women consistently with respect, dignity, compassion, and kindness.
2. Jesus dealt with women honestly and straightforwardly, firmly resisting any attempts to be manipulated or otherwise swayed from truth.
3. Jesus often portrayed women alongside men in illustrations, especially in his parables.
4. Jesus showed special sensitivity to women's concerns.
5. Women followed Jesus, often with great devotion, and supported him financially, and Jesus encouraged their participation in his ministry.
6. Women served as witnesses to Jesus.
7. Jesus taught women the Scriptures and treated them as (potential or actual) disciples.
8. Jesus didn't envision a community where men and women would be equal with respect to assuming positions of leadership.

In teaching on marriage and divorce, Jesus affirmed the foundational teaching of the first two chapters of Genesis. In his choice of

---

[37]See on this Andreas J. Köstenberger and Peter T. O'Brien, *Salvation to the Ends of the Earth: A Biblical Theology of Mission*, New Studies in Biblical Theology 11 (Downers Grove, IL: InterVarsity, 2001), esp. chaps. 4–6 and 8.

twelve men as apostles, Jesus placed himself in continuity with the pattern of male leadership that can be observed from the beginning of the Bible throughout the Old Testament. At the same time, Jesus's treatment of women as disciples, witnesses, and loyal followers is truly amazing and deeply inspiring. In the next chapter, we'll take a look to see how men and women served in the early church subsequent to Jesus's ascension. We'll also look at the roles men and women played in the churches Paul planted. This will further help us to understand and apply to our own lives what it means to be a man or a woman according to God's design.

Key Resources

Arnold, Clinton E., ed. *Zondervan Illustrated Bible Backgrounds Commentary.* 5 vols. Grand Rapids, MI: Zondervan, 2001. Vols. 1 and 2 are on the Gospels.

Bauckham, Richard. *Gospel Women: Studies of the Named Women in the Gospels.* Grand Rapids, MI: Eerdmans, 2002. (Note: Read this one with particular discernment. Bauckham is a first-rate scholar, but he sometimes goes out on a limb in the conclusions he draws from the evidence.)

Borland, James. "Women in the Life and Teaching of Jesus." In *Recovering Biblical Manhood and Womanhood: A Response to Evangelical Feminism,* edited by John Piper and Wayne Grudem, 105–16. Wheaton, IL: Crossway, 1991.

Ferguson, Everett. *Backgrounds of Early Christianity.* 3rd ed. Grand Rapids, MI: Eerdmans, 2003.

Jeffers, James S. *The Greco-Roman World of the New Testament Era: Exploring the Background of Early Christianity.* Downers Grove, IL: InterVarsity, 1999.

Köstenberger, Margaret Elizabeth. *Jesus and the Feminists: Who Do They Say That He Is?* Wheaton, IL: Crossway, 2008. Chap. 14.

Osborne, Grant R. "Women in Jesus' Ministry." *Westminster Theological Journal* 51 (1989): 259–91. (Note: Osborne takes an egalitarian approach, which is apparent especially in the conclusions he draws at the end of the article.)

4

What Did the Early Church Do?

Acts

All these with one accord were devoting themselves to prayer, together with the women and Mary the mother of Jesus, and his brothers.

—Acts 1:14

Key Points

1. The pattern of male leadership, which is characteristic of the Old Testament and was perpetrated in Jesus's appointment of the Twelve, continued in the early church as exemplified by the men making up the "Pauline circle."

2. The book of Acts continues Luke's special emphasis on women, showing women's active participation in the mission of the early church in a variety of ways (praying, witnessing, good works, targets of persecution) but without any clear indication of a change in the church's approach to women in leadership.

3. The woman mentioned most prominently in Acts, Priscilla, helped her husband, Aquila, to instruct Apollos in private, which indicates her significant partnership with Aquila in ministry (but doesn't show her in a pastoral role or position of local church oversight).

4. The reference to women as well as men prophesying in Acts 2 as well as Philip's prophesying daughters illustrate how women in both Testaments prophesied in the context of the body of believers

(note, however, that "prophet" was probably not an authoritative church office).
5. The references to women in Acts indicate that women were integrally involved in the early church's witness and ministry. At the same time, there's no reference to female pastors or elders.

At the end of last summer, our family was invited to a party to kick off our son's 5th-grade year. The professionally catered party was at one of his future classmates' beautiful home. As we casually mingled with some of the other families, we got into an extended conversation with Drew, the male host. He told us about his wife Alyssa's prosperous career as well as about his son's early years, and mentioned some of the tough choices he and his wife had been faced following his son's birth. "So your wife stayed home for a while after Josh was born?" Margaret asked. "No," our host replied, "I took a couple years off work to take care of our son."

That story may seem relatively harmless and is even becoming more commonplace. However, consider the more extreme story of little Alex.[1] The night before his parents, Susan and Rob, allowed their son to wear a dress to preschool, they e-mailed parents of his classmates. "Alex," they wrote, "has been gender-fluid for a long time and identifies with superheroes as well as ballerinas." Recently, Alex had become increasingly resistant toward their ban on wearing dresses beyond dress-up time. After consulting a psychologist and parents of other children like him, they decided that the most important thing was to affirm him in who he felt he really was. The next morning, Alex went to preschool in a purple, pink, and yellow–striped dress.

These true accounts illustrate that there are people in our culture who are confused to various degrees regarding God's design for men and women or even unaware of it. Others may be aware but consciously reject it. Perhaps quite common also is the scenario in which believers try to follow Christ in other areas of their lives but are unwilling to allow him to impact their thinking and practice in the area of gender roles. However, both of the above cases must be

[1] Ruth Padawer, "What's So Bad about a Boy Who Wants to Wear a Dress?," *New York Times* (August 8, 2012).

pressed against Scripture to see how they match up with God's will in this important sphere of our lives. Now that we're almost halfway through our study, these stories reinforce the significance of what we're attempting to do in this book.

We'll be returning to matters of application later on where these kinds of matters will be addressed, but for now, in this chapter, we'll continue our journey through the landscape of Scripture by taking a closer look at men and women featured in the book of Acts. In the case of men, we'll focus our attention particularly on Paul and the so-called "Pauline circle" and discuss the significant male characters. With regard to women, we'll discuss all the female characters in the book of Acts to investigate the significant contributions of women to the life and ministry of the early church.

Men in Acts

The book of Acts features a large number of men whose lives intersect the history of the early church at one time or another. Without denying the significance of the apostles, particularly Peter, in the early portions of Acts, our survey will focus on significant members of the Pauline circle, since we already covered the Twelve in the last chapter.[2] Both the book of Acts and Paul's letters make clear that the apostle gathered around himself a circle of "faithful men," who were his co-workers and part of heading up the Pauline mission

While Paul was clearly in charge of that mission, these coworkers undergirded Paul's efforts in a variety of ways. In this, Paul continued Jesus's pattern of training a circle of followers to join in his mission and of sending them out to fulfill various ministry assignments. The Pauline circle is a somewhat amorphous group of men, not quite as clearly defined as Jesus's apostolic circle (the Twelve), however still reflective of how Jesus worked out his relationships with his followers. It includes men such as Timothy, Titus, Luke, Barnabas, John Mark, Silas (Silvanus), as well as less-known figures.[3]

---

[2] An older but still helpful basic treatment is F. F. Bruce, *The Pauline Circle* (Grand Rapids, MI: Eerdmans, 1985).

[3] In addition, see many other participants in the early church's mission, such as Trophimus (Acts 20:4; 21:29; 2 Tim. 4:20) or Tychicus (Acts 20:4; Eph. 6:21; Col. 4:7; 2 Tim. 4:12; Titus 3:12). Also a vital part of the early Christian mission were couples such as Aquila and Priscilla (Acts 18:2, 18, 26; 1 Cor. 16:19; 2 Tim. 4:19) or the lesser-known Andronicus and Junia (Rom. 16:7).

Table 4.1: The Pauline Circle

Male Character	Reference in Acts	Other New Testament References
Paul	8:1–3; 9:1–30; 11:25–26; etc.	
Timothy	16:1; 17:14–15; 18:5; 19:22; 20:4	Rom. 16:21; 1 Cor. 4:17; 16:10; 2 Cor. 1:1, 19; Phil. 1:1; 2:19; Col. 1:1; 1 Thess. 1:1; 3:2, 6; 2 Thess. 1:1; 1 Tim. 1:2, 18; 6:20; 2 Tim. 1:2; Philem. 1
Titus	Not mentioned in Acts	2 Cor. 2:13; 7:6, 13, 14; 8:6, 16, 23; 12:18; Gal. 2:1, 3; 2 Tim. 4:10; Titus 1:4
Luke	"We-passages" (e.g., Acts 16:11)	Col. 4:11, 14; 2 Tim. 4:11; Philem. 24
Barnabas	4:36; 9:27; 11:30; 12:25; 13:2, 7, 50; 14:14, 20; 15:2, 35–40	1 Cor. 9:6; Gal. 2:1, 9, 13; Col. 4:10
John Mark	2:12, 25; 15:37–39	Col. 4:10; 2 Tim. 4:11; Philem. 24
Silas (Silvanus)	15:22–40; 16:19–29; 17:4–15; 18:5	2 Cor. 1:19; 1 Thess. 1:1; 2 Thess. 1:1; 1 Pet. 5:12

Paul

We won't be able to do justice here to the stature and contribution of the apostle Paul to the mission of the early church.[4] Together with the apostle Peter, whose mission was primarily to the Jewish people, Paul was the unquestioned leader of the early church's mission to the Gentiles. The book of Acts narrates Paul's conversion (Acts 9, 22, 26), his three missionary journeys (Acts 13:1–21:17), his arrest in Jerusalem

---

[4] For a fuller treatment, see Andreas J. Köstenberger, L. Scott Kellum, and Charles L. Quarles, *The Cradle, the Cross, and the Crown: An Introduction to the New Testament* (Nashville: B&H Academic, 2009), chap. 9: "Paul: The Man and His Message." See also Andreas J. Köstenberger and Peter T. O'Brien, *Salvation to the Ends of the Earth: A Biblical Theology of Mission*, New Studies in Biblical Theology 11 (Downers Grove, IL: InterVarsity, 2001), chap. 7.

(Acts 21:27–36), his interrogation by various Roman government officials (Acts 24–26), and his journey to Rome (Acts 27–28). When the risen Christ appeared to Paul on the road to Damascus, Paul (still called Saul) was on his way to persecute Christians there. His encounter with Christ turned the church's number-one nemesis into its most fervent propagator.

Over the years, Paul built up a network of what many have called "the Pauline circle," men and couples such as Aquila and Priscilla (possibly Andronicus and Junia, Rom. 16:7) who worked together in the cause of Christ and the gospel. In his preaching of the gospel, Paul adamantly insisted that salvation is by grace through faith apart from any good works a person might perform (e.g., Rom. 3:21–31). The issue came to the fore in the Judaizing controversy, which was dealt with by the church collectively and decisively at the Jerusalem Council in about AD 50 (Acts 15). The ruling opened the door wide for the mission headed up by Paul to the "ends of the earth," all the way to Rome, the capital of the empire, and beyond Rome possibly to Spain (Rom. 15:23–24).

Paul had unquestionable authority due to his status as apostle, though he acknowledges that he wasn't originally one of the Twelve and that he was "the least of the apostles" (1 Cor. 15:9) because he'd once persecuted the church. At the same time, he fiercely defended his apostolic ministry (see, e.g., 2 Corinthians 10–13) and regularly invoked his status as apostle at the opening of his letters. Trained by the Jewish rabbi Gamaliel (Acts 22:3), Paul had a keen theological mind that God put to use in the thirteen letters Paul wrote that are included in the New Testament (which means Paul is responsible for almost half of the twenty-seven New Testament writings). Paul's contribution is thus monumental not only owing to the churches he planted but also due to the abiding value of his letters in Scripture.

Timothy

Timothy had a special place in Paul's heart. The apostle met his foremost disciple first in Lystra in modern-day Turkey, which was part of the Roman province of Galatia (Acts 16:1; it is possible that they had met earlier; Acts 14:8–20; cf. 2 Tim. 3:10–11). Timothy was the son of a Gentile father and a Jewish mother, a believer who was taught the Scriptures from an early age (2 Tim. 1:5; 3:15). Apparently, he was quite young when he joined Paul in his ministry, because even fifteen years later Paul could still urge him not to let anyone despise his youth (1 Tim. 4:12).

Upon the recommendation of his local congregation, Timothy came alongside Paul on the apostle's second missionary journey and participated in the preaching of the gospel in Macedonia and Achaia (Acts 16:2; 17:14–15; 18:5). He was with Paul during the majority of his ministry in the city of Ephesus (Acts 19:22), journeyed with him from Ephesus to Macedonia, to Corinth, back to Macedonia, and to Asia Minor (Acts 20:1–6); and also was with the apostle during his first imprisonment (Phil. 1:1; Col. 1:1; Philem. 1). Timothy served as Paul's messenger on at least three occasions prior to being assigned to set things in order in the church of Ephesus (1 Tim. 1:3): to Thessalonica (c. AD 50); to Corinth (AD 53–54); and to Philippi (c. AD 60–62).

Timothy was Paul's coworker (Rom. 16:21; 1 Cor. 16:10; Phil. 2:22; 1 Thess. 3:2) and had a vital part in his ministry. He was associated with Paul in the writing of several of his letters (1 and 2 Thessalonians, 2 Corinthians, Philippians, Colossians, and Philemon; see esp. Phil. 2:19–22; cf. 1 Cor. 16:10). The author of Hebrews mentions Timothy's own imprisonment at an unknown date and occasion (13:23). Timothy's mixed Jewish-Gentile heritage made him an ideal person to preach the gospel in a Jewish-Hellenistic environment.

Titus

While Titus was not as close an associate of Paul's as Timothy, he, too, was a trusted coworker of the apostle. Paul took Titus with him when he went to discuss the gospel with the leaders of the Jerusalem church (Gal. 2:1–3). Unlike Timothy who, as mentioned, was of mixed Jewish-Gentile descent, Titus was a Gentile. When he converted to Christianity, Titus was not compelled to be circumcised, which Paul used to illustrate the nature of his gospel as being by grace alone through faith alone (Gal. 2:3–5). While he isn't mentioned in the book of Acts, Titus repeatedly surfaces in Paul's letters as belonging to the Pauline circle;

in particular, he had a sensitive assignment to deliver Paul's "sorrowful letter" to the church in Corinth confronting the Corinthians with tolerating sin (2 Cor. 2:12–13; 7:5–6; 8:6).

Paul's letter to Titus finds him on the island of Crete, where he is to take care of some unfinished business, specifically that of appointing elders in every church in a still relatively young set of local congregations (Titus 1:5). In the ancient world, Cretan culture was known for its immorality, and so Titus's assignment wasn't an easy one. As with his two letters to Timothy, Paul wrote the epistle to Titus to encourage his apostolic delegate to complete the assignment he was given by his apostolic mentor. Later, Paul wants Titus to meet him in Nicopolis (Titus 3:12). After this, Paul reports that Titus had gone to Dalmatia (modern-day Albania and part of former Yugoslavia) in the Roman province of Illyricum (2 Tim. 4:10; Rom. 15:19). He thus continued to labor as Paul's ally in bringing the gospel to the ends of the earth.

Luke

Luke, the "beloved physician" (Col. 4:14), and most likely a Gentile ("most likely" because there is no explicit reference to him as a Gentile anywhere in the New Testament), was a dedicated layman who served the gospel exceedingly well in his day. His contributions are both significant and strategic. As an author, he contributed as much as 25 percent of the entire New Testament (in terms of word length) by writing his two-volume work Luke-Acts, a defense of the innocence of Christianity as a movement in light of the charges brought against it by its (mostly) Jewish opponents. In this way, Luke provided an important apologetic for the Christian faith in the Greco-Roman world. His Gospel and the book of Acts are overtly addressed to Theophilus, apparently a Roman government official, who most likely served as his literary patron (Luke 1:3; Acts 1:1). Second, Luke joined Paul on several of his missionary journeys. At times, Luke stayed behind in a certain location and then rejoined Paul on subsequent travels: in Philippi, Miletus, and Caesarea. The we-passages in the book of Acts in table 4.2 provide information regarding their joint travels.

In his Gospel, Luke eloquently narrates the fulfillment of God's promises to Old Testament Israel in the Messiah, Jesus. He notes that Jesus, whose ancestry is traced all the way back to Adam (not merely Abraham as in Matthew), came, not only to the people of Israel, but also so that his gospel of salvation could be proclaimed to the ends of the earth, reaching Gentiles as well as Jews. Luke himself was not an eyewitness of Jesus's ministry, but in compiling his own Gospel he performed his research by accessing many accounts of those who were.

Table 4.2: The "We-Passages" in Acts

Reference in Acts	Journeys and Locations	Event
16:8–17	Troas to Philippi	Ministry in Philippi
20:5–15	Philippi to Troas to Miletus	On way to Jerusalem
21:1–18	Miletus to Jerusalem via Caesarea	On way to Jerusalem
27:1–28:16	Caesarea to Rome	All the way to Rome

Paul's First Missionary Journey (Acts 13:4–14:26)

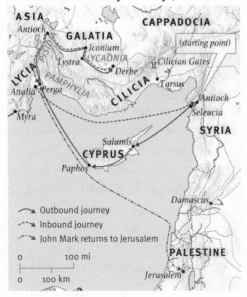

Paul's Second Missionary Journey (Acts 15:36–18:22)

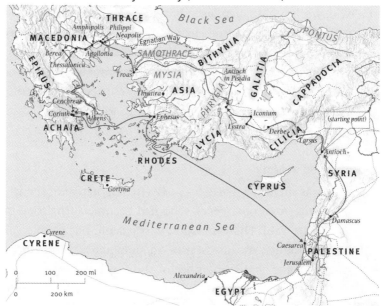

Paul's Third Missionary Journey (Acts 18:22–21:17)

Luke is an excellent example of a well-educated member of the church who, while a physician, used his education to further the cause of Christ. His dedication to Paul personally and to the gospel was so great that Paul, at the end of his life, when most others had deserted him or gone off on their various ministry assignments, could write, "Demas, in love with this present world, has deserted me and gone to Thessalonica. Crescens has gone to Galatia, Titus to Dalmatia. *Luke alone is with me*" (2 Tim. 4:10–11).

Barnabas and John Mark

The book of Acts mentions Barnabas, a Levite and native of the island of Cyprus (off the coast of Greece), who had become a Christian even before the apostle Paul. His real name was Joseph, but people called him "Barnabas" (which means "son of encouragement"), a tribute to the selfless character of this member of the Pauline mission. In one such act of selflessness, Barnabas sold a field he owned and brought the money to the apostles (Acts 4:36–37). Later, in another selfless act, Barnabas took Paul, who had recently been converted, to the apostles, who were afraid of Paul because they were aware of Paul's previous persecution of Christians and distrusted reports of his conversion: "But Barnabas took him [Paul] and brought him to the apostles and declared to them how on the road [to Damascus] he had seen the Lord, who spoke to him, and how at Damascus he had preached boldly in the name of Jesus" (Acts 9:27). This was a vital connection for Barnabas to make. Later, in the days of the Roman emperor Claudius, the elders of the church sent a relief offering to Jewish believers in Judea by the hand of Barnabas and Paul, an indication of the trust the church leaders placed in Barnabas, who at that time was the senior partner in the ministry, which may be suggested by the fact that he is mentioned first in the narrative (Acts 11:27–30; cf. Gal. 2:9).

Barnabas also was the uncle of John Mark, who most likely hailed from the capital city of Jerusalem and would later write the second Gospel. Apparently, the early church met in the upper room of his mother Mary's house (Acts 12:12; cf. 1:14). In Mark's case, too, Barnabas proved to be an encourager. Barnabas and Paul first brought John Mark along with them after they had completed their mission in Jerusalem

(Acts 12:25). John Mark joined Paul and Barnabas on their first missionary journey but didn't last long. Before the trip really got underway, Luke tersely reports that "John [Mark] left them [i.e., Paul and Barnabas] and returned to Jerusalem" (Acts 13:13).

While Paul and Barnabas continue on their journey and evangelize much of the province of Galatia, John Mark fades from the narrative until he becomes the occasion of a "sharp disagreement" between Paul and Barnabas. Barnabas wants to take his nephew with them on their follow-up second missionary journey to Galatia, while Paul refuses. Barnabas takes Mark with him, sailing off to Cyprus (neither of them is heard from again in the book of Acts), while Paul takes Silas along on his second journey, strengthening the churches he and Barnabas had previously planted (Acts 15:36–40). Later, Barnabas's commitment to Mark pays off when Paul writes to Timothy, "Get Mark and bring him with you, for he is very useful to me for ministry" (2 Tim. 4:11). This is a moving tribute to Barnabas's continued encouragement of Mark who obviously had a change of heart. Peter also mentions Mark in his first epistle, which finds both of them in Rome (1 Pet. 5:13), the location where Mark likely also wrote his Gospel (according to tradition, as Peter's spokesman). Like Luke, Mark thus made an invaluable contribution to the church and to the Christian canon.

Whenever we see Barnabas in the Bible, he selflessly and sacrificially encourages others, whether John Mark or the apostle Paul or the local fellowship of believers. By exercising his spiritual gift of encouragement, Barnabas made a vital contribution to the mission of the early church and was a valuable member of the Pauline circle.

Silas (Silvanus)

Silas (called "Silvanus" in Paul's letters) was a Roman citizen and Jewish-Christian prophet (Acts 15:32) chosen by Paul to accompany him on his second missionary journey. Luke calls him a "leading [man] among the brothers" (v. 22) who joins Paul in delivering the all-important letter to the churches communicating the decisions made at the Jerusalem Council. As mentioned, when Paul and Barnabas cannot reach an agreement on whether to take John Mark with them on their second missionary journey, Paul chose Silas (v. 40). Shortly thereafter, however, Paul connects with Timothy and asks him to join his group as well, and it appears that over time, Timothy became the more prominent coworker of Paul. Nevertheless, it is Paul and Silas who are imprisoned in Philippi and are instrumental in the conversion of the Philippian jailer when they pray and sing hymns to God while the other prisoners listen (Acts 16:19–29).

Silas continues to be a vital part of Paul's mission. In Thessalonica, they persuade many to convert to Christ (Acts 17:4; see also 1 Thess. 1:1; 2 Thess. 1:1), and the local believers send Paul and Silas away by night to Berea to temporary safety (Acts 17:10). When they meet opposition there as well, the local believers in Berea send Paul off to sea while Silas and Timothy remain. When Paul arrives in Athens, he sends word to both of them to join him as soon as possible (vv. 14–15). Later, they rejoin him in Corinth (Acts 18:5; cf. 2 Cor. 1:19). Peter, too, used Silas either to carry his first epistle to its destination or as a secretary (1 Pet. 5:12), indicating that at that time Silas had made his way to Rome, the empire's capital (see the designation "Babylon," a code word for Rome, in 1 Pet. 5:13).

While not as widely known as Timothy, Titus, Luke, Barnabas, or Mark, Silas also made a very significant contribution to the early Christian mission. A close associate of Paul starting from the aftermath of the Jerusalem Council, Silas is well regarded by his fellow believers in the church and has the honor of being closely associated with Paul throughout the remainder of his ministry. Like the other members of the Pauline circle, Silas was very devoted to Paul personally and willing to endure persecution and suffering so that the preaching of the gospel could continue throughout the Roman Empire "to the ends of the earth."

Women in Acts

In the New Testament canon, the book of Acts immediately follows the Gospels because Luke and Acts are essentially a two-volume work by the same author. As we'd expect, Acts continues Luke's special emphasis on women, emphasizing how they were included as active participants in the church. There are several women mentioned throughout Paul's letters that correspond to places and ministries mentioned in Acts.

We'll discuss these at this point in our study before we look at specific teaching texts in the letters of Paul in the next chapter.

Table 4.3: Women in Acts

Reference in Acts	Information Given
1:14	Women including Mary in the upper room
2:17–18	Sons and daughters will prophesy
5:1–11	Ananias and Sapphira lie to the Holy Spirit
6:1–6	Hellenistic widows cared for by first deacons
8:3; 9:2	Women as well as men persecuted
9:36–43	Dorcas raised to life by Peter, known for good works, helping the poor
12:12	Mary the mother of John Mark
16:1	Mother of Timothy
16:13–15	Lydia and the women by the river
17:4	Prominent believing women in Thessalonica
18:2, 18, 26	Priscilla wife of Aquila, together with her husband instructs Apollos
21:5	Disciples, wives, and children
21:9	Philip's prophesying daughters

Women in the Upper Room (Acts 1:14)

Luke writes that various women, including Mary, were gathered in the upper room with Jesus's other disciples in the interim between Christ's ascension and Pentecost (see also on Acts 12:12 below). This group of women, presumably some of the same women who were at the cross and the empty tomb, were part of the group of early committed believers.[5] Again, we see here how women were an integral part of

---

[5] This verse doesn't say anything about leadership but rather pertains to membership and participation in the group of early believers in Jesus.

the community of faith who participated in sacrificial service, prayer, fellowship, and worship.

Peter's Quotation of Joel's Prophecy (Acts 2:17–18)

When Peter is preaching at Pentecost, he cites a prophecy from Joel 2:28–32 to the effect that on the future day of the Lord, when God would pour out his Spirit on all humanity, their sons and daughters would prophesy. First Corinthians 11 also talks about women prophesying. In the present passage, Peter is focusing on the outpouring of the Spirit on all of humanity, both male and female, with the result that both men and women are given utterances from the Spirit.[6] There is no gender division in experiencing the Spirit, here in terms of prophesying.

Sapphira (Acts 5:1–11)

Acts 5 provides a negative example of how Sapphira conspires with her husband to lie to the Holy Spirit and to pretend to give the entire price of the sale of their land while keeping back a portion for themselves. They both die due to God's severe judgment. Fortunately, not everyone who lies dies! Many of the events in Acts are recorded by Luke to emphasize how unusual the occurrences were, not because they happened every day or were the norm for ministry. Also, we see here that the consequences of sin apply to both genders: same sin, same consequence.

The Care for Widows in the Early Church (Acts 6:1–6)

This account records how the Hellenistic widows were being neglected in the regular distribution of food. The early church solved the problem by appointing seven men to oversee the fair administration of this ministry. Here we see that widows were recognized as a separate group in the early church who relied on the church to support them if they had no other family to take the place of their husband's financial and other support of them. The church made sure to take care of these valued and dedicated women servants of God.

---

[6] It's interesting to see how this plays itself out in Paul's thinking in terms of authority in 1 Corinthians 11–14 (see the next chap.). See also the discussion of Philip's prophesying daughters in Acts 21:9 below.

The care for widows has a long pedigree in ancient Israel. This ethos of caring for the poor and unprotected is well summarized by James: "Religion that is pure and undefiled before God, the Father, is this: to visit orphans and widows in their affliction, and to keep oneself unstained from the world" (James 1:27). Jesus repeatedly reached out to widows or commended them, such as in the well-known case of the widow's mite. Seeing that this widow put two small copper coins into the offering box at the temple, Jesus remarked, "Truly, I tell you, this poor widow has put in more than all of them. For they all contributed out of their abundance, but she out of her poverty put in all she had to live on" (Luke 21:1–4; cf. Mark 12:41–44).[7] Later in the book of Acts, Peter, at the occasion of raising Dorcas from the dead, gave special attention to widows (Acts 9:39, 41).

Paul, likewise, makes repeated reference to the church's care of widows, even establishing criteria for what made such women eligible for church support (1 Tim. 5:3–16).[8] He urges, "But if a widow has children or grandchildren, let them first learn to show godliness to their own household and to make some return to their parents, for this is pleasing in the sight of God. . . . But if anyone does not provide for his relatives, and especially for members of his household, he has denied the faith and is worse than an unbeliever" (vv. 4, 8). The obvious implication is that we today must likewise care for our parents in their old age.

Men and Women Persecuted (Acts 8:3; 9:2)

This passage is another instance of Luke's characteristic pattern of pairing male and female characters. Luke is careful to note that faith-

---

[7] While Matthew and John do not mention widows, Luke has a special interest in them. He observes that Anna the prophetess was a widow until age eighty-four (2:37); records Jesus's reference to the many widows in the days of Elijah, including the widow of Zarephath in Sidon (4:25–26); recounts Jesus's raising of the widow's son at Nain, one of only three such raisings in all four Gospels combined (7:11–17); includes Jesus's parable of the persistent widow (18:1–8); and recounts Jesus's denunciation of the scribes "who devour widows' houses" and will be subject to more severe judgment (20:47).

[8] Criteria for what makes a widow a "true" widow (i.e., one who is eligible for church support) include: (1) no relatives to provide for her ("left all alone," v. 5); (2) godliness: has set her hope on God, praying day and night (v. 5); (3) at least sixty years of age (v. 9); (4) a reputation for good works: has brought up children, has shown hospitality, has helped meet needs of fellow believers, has cared for the afflicted (v. 10). While these guidelines are eminently sensible, it would seem appropriate to adapt them to life in our culture today, where many seniors enjoy social security and other benefits and where life expectancy is considerably higher than in the ancient world. The church's responsibility to care for widows remains; specifics may vary (such as the sixty-year age limit).

ful servants, both men and women, were dragged off and imprisoned. This highlights the severity and universality of the persecution and the fact that women, too, were being persecuted. If they hadn't been actively involved in the ministry of the church, they in all probability wouldn't have been persecuted.[9] The depth of their involvement in Jesus's mission likely consisted of a deep commitment to him and a vibrant sharing of their faith. Because of their significant involvement, they were recognized as threats to the Jewish religious authorities.

Dorcas (Tabitha) (Acts 9:36–43)

The account in Acts 9 describes how Peter raised Dorcas, a much loved disciple, to life after she had become ill and died. Dorcas was known in the area to have consistently engaged in a variety of good works and to have helped the poor. Upon her death, the disciples immediately contacted Peter to come to Joppa (modern-day Jaffa, part of Tel Aviv) where she had died. The appreciation and affection that the disciples had for her were palpable, and their actions reveal the commitment and unity that colaboring in the gospel must have engendered.

The good works Dorcas was known for were characteristic marks of the piety of disciples in the early church. Even as many other women have done over the centuries, and women can do today, this woman showed her Christian commitment by practical acts of Christian charity. The fact that she's identified in Scripture specifically as a disciple reveals that she was known as a dutiful follower of Jesus. Her good works were not praiseworthy in and of themselves, but in her following of the Lord Jesus, she expressed her faith.

What an inspiring woman!

Mary the Mother of John Mark (Acts 12:12)

This brief mention of Mary the mother of John Mark tells of her provision of her house as a meeting place for members of the early church. Women or couples hosting a church meeting in their house were a

[9] N. T. Wright, "Women's Service in the Church: The Biblical Basis," conference paper for the symposium "Men, Women and the Church," St. John's College, Durham, September 4, 2004, p. 6, takes the matter one step further, arguing that women's persecution in Acts "only makes sense if the women, too, are seen as leaders, influential figures within the community." Maybe so, but not necessarily. Does history really bear out that only leaders are persecuted?

common phenomenon in the early church. We can see this in Paul's writings. Nympha (Col. 4:15), Lydia (Acts 16:40), Priscilla and Aquila (Rom. 16:5; 1 Cor. 16:19), as well as Philemon and Apphia (Philem. 1–2) had churches meeting in their homes. This form of sacrificial hospitality where women and couples opened up their homes for Christian meetings was of great value and service to the body of Christ. This kind of ministry and service can continue to be helpful in today's churches in the form of home groups if not actual church meetings.[10]

The Mother of Timothy (Acts 16:1)

Timothy's mother, Eunice, was a Jewish believer and serves as an example of a Christian who, with the help of her mother (Timothy's grandmother Lois), raised Timothy according to scriptural teaching and in the faith, even though her husband (whose name is unknown) might not have been a believer (Acts 16:1 says Timothy was the son of a Jewish woman, but his father was a Greek and therefore possibly an unbelieving Gentile). Mothers and grandmothers, like Eunice and Lois, have an important role in the spiritual development of their children and grandchildren, especially if the men in their life fail to accept responsibility for nurturing their offspring in the faith.

Paul later came along and replaced the father figure in Timothy's life. In his final letter to Timothy, Paul wrote, "I am reminded of your sincere faith, a faith that dwelt first in your grandmother Lois and your mother Eunice and now, I am sure, dwells in you as well" (2 Tim. 1:5). He urged Timothy, "But as for you, continue in what you have learned and have firmly believed, knowing from whom you learned it and how from childhood you have been acquainted with the sacred writings, which are able to make you wise for salvation through faith in Christ Jesus. All Scripture is breathed out by God and profitable . . . , that the man of God may be complete, equipped for every good work" (2 Tim. 3:14–17). In this way, Paul paid tribute to the formative influence of Timothy's mother and grandmother in his early years and highlighted the importance of passing on Scripture and one's faith to the next generation.

---

[10] It is sometimes argued that this implies that the women were pastors or leaders of those churches, but this is an argument from silence, or at least an improper inference, with little actual evidence to support such a claim.

Eunice's and Lois's examples ought to be a huge encouragement for women whose husbands are unbelievers or not spiritual leaders in the home, as well as for single mothers. Imagine what would have happened if Timothy's mother had given up rather than persevering in teaching her son the Scriptures! In due course, God provided the male role model Timothy needed: "You, however, have followed my teaching, my conduct, my aim in life, my faith, my patience, my love, my steadfastness, my persecutions and sufferings" (vv. 10–11). Over time, Timothy developed into a godly example for other young men (1 Tim. 4:12) and became a strategic and trusted leader in the church (Heb. 13:23 even mentions Timothy's release from imprisonment).

Lydia and the Women by the River (Acts 16:13–15)

The women by the river, most notably Lydia, were the first converts in Greece during Paul's missionary work. The Acts narrative mentions that Paul, on the Sabbath, went outside the gate to the riverside where some women were praying. Apparently, Lydia was particularly receptive to Paul's message and believed and was baptized, together with her household (presumably including household slaves).

Lydia was a businesswoman, a purple cloth dealer from Thyatira, one of the churches also mentioned in the book of Revelation. She was a very enterprising and presumably unmarried woman who also functioned as a benefactress to the church. Benefactresses were unmarried women of means who used their wealth to support the cause of Christian mission in the tradition of the women in Luke 8:2–3 who supported the ministry of Jesus and the apostles. Another New Testament example of a benefactress is Phoebe (Rom. 16:2).

Lydia also excelled in hospitality. After her baptism, she prevailed upon Paul and his coworkers to come to her house (Acts 16:15). The book of Acts then recounts how Paul and Silas were thrown into jail, where they sang praises to God when a major earthquake struck. In God's providence, this was used to lead the Philippian jailer and his household to faith. After their release, Paul and Silas visit Lydia and "the brothers," presumably believers who met at Lydia's house (v. 40), and after encouraging them, departed.

Lydia serves as an example of a highly energetic, God-fearing, unmarried businesswoman who used her resources to further the gospel ministry. Rather than deplore the lack of a husband, she used her talents in her chosen profession and was apparently quite successful. Unmarried women such as Lydia have plenty of opportunities to get involved in ministry themselves and to support others in ministry by way of giving, exercising hospitality, praying, and encouraging other believers in the local church.

Prominent Believing Women (Acts 17:4)

In this account, Luke mentions that not a few prominent (the ESV has "leading") women believed from the synagogue in Thessalonica. Later in the chapter, Luke mentions that among the few who believed Paul's message in Athens was "a woman named Damaris" (Acts 17:34). Most likely, Luke includes this kind of information to impress on Theophilus, his literary patron (most likely a Roman government official), the fact that Christianity was not just for the simple-minded or lower class. It should be remembered, however, that in many cases, these women weren't prominent in their own right but because of the status their husbands held in society (see Luke 8:2–3, which mentions Joanna, the wife of Chuza, Herod's household manager; and Susanna). Also, the prominence of these women pertained to the society in which they lived and didn't necessarily carry over to particular leadership roles in the church.

Women such as these serve as examples in two ways: first, in submission to unbelieving authorities, and, second, in courage. It would have been easy for them to rebel against their husbands or to disrespect them because of their lack of faith and spiritual leadership. By submitting to them despite their lack of faith, simply because they were in a position of authority over them, these women showed Christlike submission to the order God instituted for marriage. At the same time, they serve as examples of courage. Rather than blindly follow their husbands in a culture where women were expected to take on the religion of the head of the household, they responded to the gospel. Peter talks about situations such as these in his first letter (1 Pet. 3:1–6), where he urges such women to win their husbands over to the faith through their godly example without a word. Similarly, Paul writes,

"If any woman has a husband who is an unbeliever, . . . the unbelieving husband is made holy because of his wife" (1 Cor. 7:13–14).

Priscilla (Acts 18:2, 18, 26)

Priscilla was the wife of a man named Aquila, both of whom were friends of Paul in Corinth and later traveled with him to Ephesus.[11] In Acts 18:2 Luke introduces the reader to the couple by referring to them as "Aquila and Priscilla." Later on in the same chapter, in reverse order, they are described as instructing Apollos in their home: "He [Apollos] began to speak boldly in the synagogue, but when *Priscilla and Aquila* heard him, they took him and explained to him the way of God more accurately" (v. 26).

Why the order "Priscilla and Aquila"? One scholar thinks Priscilla was "the brains of the operation"![12] What the text does say is that the couple invited Apollos into their home and instructed him in a private setting.[13] The two worked in tandem, serving as an example of a married couple engaged in full-time bivocational ministry of tent making and serving the church across the first-century Mediterranean world. Over time, they moved from Rome to Corinth, from there to Ephesus, then back to Rome, and finally back to Ephesus.[14] This dynamic duo always seemed to be where the action was.

Perhaps most important is the fact that the instruction of Apollos took place in a private setting. The narrative doesn't warrant the conclusion from Priscilla's involvement in teaching Apollos that Paul and the larger church allowed women to teach in a public setting.[15] All that can safely be said is that women may instruct someone privately in conjunction with their husband. Priscilla serves an example of a woman who was spiritually astute and gifted in teaching and used

[11] See further the discussion of Priscilla and Aquila below.
[12] James D. G. Dunn, *Romans 9–16*, Word Biblical Commentary (Dallas: Word, 1988), 892. We'll come back to this below in our discussion of women in the Pauline mission.
[13] For an interesting study see Dan Wallace, "Did Priscilla 'Teach' Apollos? An Examination of the Meaning of ἐκτίθημι in Acts 18:26" (http://bible.org/article/did-priscilla-teach-apollos-examination-meaning-acts-1826). Wallace concludes that the instruction wasn't primarily, or even secondarily, exhortation oriented in nature. It was a historical-doctrinal explanation of the Christian faith. Further, it was done in private and by both Priscilla and Aquila. Priscilla apparently didn't perform the same ministry as Apollos.
[14] See table 4.8 below.
[15] Contra authors such as Lynn H. Cohick (*Women in the World of the Earliest Christians: Illuminating Ancient Ways of Life* [Grand Rapids, MI: Baker Academic, 2009], 224), who calls Priscilla "the teacher" simply because she's shown to instruct Apollos with her husband, Aquila.

her gift to impact others. We'll return to this remarkable woman again later in this chapter.

Disciples, Wives, and Children (Acts 21:5)

This is an example in Acts where Luke states explicitly that the disciples were with their wives and children as they escorted Paul out of the city. By this reference, Luke highlights the participation of women and children in the life of the early church. The brief passing reference shows that the Christian faith was a family affair, impacting entire families. Even where men were the leaders and left their families for short-term missionary endeavors, their wives and children were drawn into the life of faith and the Christian witness that was borne and often suffered persecution as a result.

Philip's Prophesying Daughters (Acts 21:9)

Almost incidentally, Luke mentions that Philip had four unmarried daughters who prophesied. This fits very nicely with what we saw in Peter's quotation from Joel 2:28–32 in Acts 2:17–18 concerning the outpouring of God's Spirit on all believers with the result that their sons and daughters would prophesy. In Old Testament times, God's Spirit would occasionally descend on a leader, such as David, but now he has come to live in every true believer.

Table 4.4: Male-Female Pairs in Acts

Acts	Male Character(s)	Acts	Female Character(s)
1:13	The Eleven	1:14	The women, Mary mother of Jesus
5:1–6	Ananias	5:7–11	Sapphira
9:32–35	Aeneas	9:36–43	Dorcas (Tabitha)
16:25–40	Philippian jailer	16:11–15	Lydia
17:34	Dionysius the Areopagite	17:34	Damaris
25:13	Agrippa	25:13	Bernice

The issue of New Testament prophecy is fascinating, and the question arises as to whether there may be a difference between Old and New Testament prophecy. In the Old Testament, prophets are God's spokespersons who communicate his Word to his people Israel. In the New Testament, prophecy is a spiritual gift that is subject to apostolic authority and evaluation by the leadership of the church.[16]

In the case of Philip's daughters, the reference is fairly incidental, and we're not given many specifics. The first readers of Acts would most likely have read the reference to Philip's daughters in light of Peter's quotation of Joel in Acts 2:17–18, which shows this prophecy being fulfilled in the early church. As mentioned above, the passage shows that men and women participate in the life of the Spirit both in the days of the early church and in the church age.

Summary

Joel's prophecy as quoted by Peter at Pentecost has now come to fulfillment: the Spirit has been poured out on men and women alike. In the days following Pentecost, women were an integral part of the life of the early church. They were disciples; they were known for their hospitality and good works; they participated in prayer, worship, and witness; and, like men, were persecuted and suffered for their faith. One observes that there's an increased emphasis on the participation of women in the believing community in the book of Acts.

At the same time, we see in the early church a continuation of the pattern of male leadership that is found in the Old Testament and in Jesus's ministry. This is evident particularly in the apostles' leadership in the establishment of the early church and the mission to the

---

[16] In the early church, a prophet might prophesy several times; in one instance, the prophecy might be found to be from the Spirit while at another time it might be found as originating with the prophet rather than being Spirit-induced. The prophet would not be stoned as a false prophet, but his or her prophecy would be declared genuine or inauthentic. The emphasis seems to shift from the *person* of the prophet in the OT to the *actual prophetic utterance* in the NT. This seems indicated by the NT teaching on prophecy, esp. in 1 Corinthians 12–14. See D. A. Carson, *Showing the Spirit: A Theological Exposition of 1 Corinthians 12–14* (Grand Rapids, MI: Baker, 1996). See also Wayne Grudem, "Prophecy—Yes, But Teaching—No: Paul's Consistent Advocacy of Women's Participation without Governing Authority," *Journal of the Evangelical Theological Society* 30 (1987): 11–23. But since women as well as men are shown to prophesy in both Testaments, any such distinction between the role of OT and NT prophets and prophecy is ultimately immaterial for the primary thesis of this book. The main insight regarding prophecy is that the authoritative function of prophecy doesn't rest in an institutionalized office but in the utterance as the word of God itself. See the discussion in Thomas Schreiner, "An Interpretation of 1 Timothy 2:9–15: A Dialogue with Scholarship," in *Women in the Church*, 2nd ed., ed. Andreas J. Köstenberger and Thomas R. Schreiner (Grand Rapids, MI: Baker, 2005), 102.

Gentiles and also in the Pauline circle. No female pastors or elders are mentioned in the book of Acts. Priscilla's joint ministry with her husband indicates significant and important ministry but not necessarily a public leadership role.

We conclude that the book of Acts presents women and men in gospel partnership and women as active participants in the church's life and witness, with men in roles of overall leadership in local churches and in overseeing missionary outreach. The elders appointed in all the churches were male (Acts 14:23; 20:17–35). This was in keeping with the culture of the times and consistent with God's original design for men and women as affirmed and practiced also by the Lord Jesus during his earthly ministry.

Men and Women in Paul's Churches

Building on our survey of the various men and women mentioned in the book of Acts, we can now proceed with our study of the men and women mentioned by name in Paul's letters.[17] Will the picture be consistent with the one painted by Luke in Acts? We'll have to be careful, because some have overplayed the authority exercised by women in the Bible and have accentuated the leadership dimension of a given woman in some individual cases in an effort to build a biblical basis for a claim that positions of leadership should be fully open to women today.[18] For this reason it'll be important for us to be guided by the evidence and to exercise appropriate interpretive restraint.

Most of the available scholarship on this topic has focused on Paul's explicit teaching on women's roles, while less attention has been given to references to individual women in his writings. Focusing primarily on teaching passages is in keeping with sound interpretive procedure. However, it is nonetheless important to explore how Paul's mention of the activities of men and women in his mission and in the churches to which he wrote supports what he taught explicitly. This raises the

---

[17] For further details and discussion see Andreas's article "Women in the Pauline Mission," in *The Gospel to the Nations: Perspectives on Paul's Mission*, ed. Peter Bolt and Mark Thompson (Downers Grove, IL: InterVarsity, 2000), 221–48.

[18] Wendy Cotter, "Women's Authority Roles in Paul's Churches: Countercultural or Conventional?," *Novum Testamentum* 36 (1994): 350–72, discusses many of these women and argues that they exercised authority in the early church, but see Andreas's review in *CBMW News* 1, no. 4 (1996): 14, http://www.biblicalfoundations.org/wp-content/uploads/2012/01/11-CBMW-Women-and-Early-Church-Authority.pdf.

important question, was Paul consistent in his teaching and in the way in which the churches he planted actually functioned? Let's find out.

Men in Paul's Churches

Since we've already discussed the major members of the Pauline circle, it won't be necessary to go over the same territory again. It's clear that the nucleus of Paul's missionary leadership team was composed of "faithful men" (2 Tim. 2:2) who were closely associated with the apostle in his gospel preaching and planting of new local congregations. In many cases, they also served as his apostolic delegates, appointing leaders in local churches and engaging in a ministry of preaching and teaching. The other men mentioned in table 4.5 round out the picture of male leadership in the mission of the early church.

Table 4.5: Men in Paul's Churches (Selected List)

Epistle	Names of Men	Information Provided
1 Corinthians	Gaius (1:14; cf. Rom. 16:23)	From Achaia (Corinth); baptized by Paul, his host
Romans	Andronicus (16:7)	A noted missionary, together with his wife Junia
	Urbanus (16:9)	"Coworker in Christ"
	Apelles (16:10)	Approved in Christ
	Herodion (16:11)	Paul's "kinsman"
	Narcissus (16:11)	Church meets at his house
	Rufus (16:13)	"Chosen in the Lord"
	Sosipater (16:21)	One of Paul's "kinsmen"
	Tertius (16:22)	Paul's amanuensis for writing Romans
	Quartus (16:23)	"The brother"
Philippians	Epaphroditus (2:25; 4:18)	Coworker of Paul from Philippi

Epistle	Names of Men	Information Provided
	Clement (4:2–3)	Coworker of Paul
Colossians	Epaphras (1:7; 4:12; cf. Philem. 23)	Most likely the founder of the church at Colossae
	Justus (4:10–11)	Jewish coworker of Paul, Jesus called "Justus"
	Luke (4:14)	Accompanied Paul on parts of missionary journeys
	Archippus (4:17; cf. Philem. 2)	Urged to fulfill his ministry
Philemon	Philemon (1)	Church meets at his house (wife's name Apphia)
	Demas (24; cf. Col. 4:11; 2 Tim. 4:10	Coworker of Paul who later deserted him
Titus	Titus (1:4)	Coworker of Paul; apostolic delegate to Crete
	Artemas (3:12)	Coworker of Paul
	Zenas (3:13)	"The lawyer"
1 Timothy	Timothy (1:2)	Paul's apostolic delegate to Ephesus
2 Timothy	Timothy (1:2)	Paul's foremost disciple who carried on his legacy
	Pudens, Linus (4:21)	Sent greetings to Timothy through Paul

Women in Paul's Churches

Each prominent woman mentioned by Paul will be focused on individually in an effort to understand her role in the early church. We'll also explore any helpful information we are given in relation to these particular women. How they're described is particularly important because we're primarily dealing with passing references or passages that provide a limited amount of information. As mentioned, this calls for observing women's roles as they truly were, neither overplaying nor underplaying them. We'll consider these women chronologically in order to get a sense of how the ministry of men and women in the early church unfolded throughout Paul's ministry. Overall, there are nineteen references to named women in Paul's letters and eighty-eight references to named men. Once multiple instances are eliminated, we find mentions of fifty-five men and seventeen women (a ratio of about 3:1).

Table 4.6: Women in Paul's Churches

Epistle	Names of Women	Information Provided
Galatians	None mentioned	
1 Thessalonians	None mentioned	
2 Thessalonians	None mentioned	
1 Corinthians	Chloe (1:11)	Some "from Chloe"
	Priscilla (16:19)	Church at her house
2 Corinthians	None mentioned	
Romans	Phoebe (16:1)	"Our sister," servant/deacon of church in Cenchrea, benefactress/patroness
	Priscilla (16:3)	Fellow worker (with Aquila); church at their house
	Mary (16:6)	"Has worked hard for you"
	Junia (?) (16:7)	"Well known to the *apostoloi*" (with Andronicus)
	Tryphaena and Tryphosa (16:12)	"Workers in the Lord"
	Persis (16:12)	Another woman who "has worked hard in the Lord"
	Rufus's mother (16:13)	"Who has been a mother to me as well"
	Julia (16:15)	None

Epistle	Names of Women	Information Provided
	Nereus's sister (16:15)	None
	Olympas (16:15)	None
Ephesians	None mentioned	
Philippians	Euodia and Syntyche (4:2)	Coworkers, "contended at my side in the cause of the gospel"
Colossians	Nympha (4:15)	"The church in her house"
Philemon	Apphia	"Our sister" (cf. Rom 16:1); church at her house (with Philemon)
1 Timothy	None mentioned	
2 Timothy	Priscilla (4:19)	None
	Claudia (4:21)	None
Titus	None mentioned	

Chloe (1 Cor. 1:11). No women are mentioned specifically in Galatians and 1–2 Thessalonians. The first time Paul refers to a woman by name is 1 Corinthians 1:11, where he mentions some from Chloe's household. In this reference, the apostle isn't focusing directly on Chloe but on those who were from her household, most likely members of her extended household or related to her in some other way. We know very little about this woman because this is the only time she is mentioned in all of Scripture. In the context of 1 Corinthians, it's difficult to know what to do with such an incidental reference. We know that this report from members of Chloe's household is part of the reason that Paul wrote the letter itself to the church. We don't know where Paul met up with the members of Chloe's household. It may even have been an incidental encounter, but it appears that she was known by the readers by the way Paul speaks of her without reference to any accompanying details about her. We don't have any other information.

We can't even be sure Chloe was a Christian or a church member. She was probably unmarried, because there is no mention of a male head of household, and well-off, perhaps a businesswoman, because she had a household attached to her. It's possible that while conducting business in Corinth, Chloe and her household became aware of divisions in the Corinthian church and reported this to Paul when they returned to Ephesus. There's not enough evidence to draw any firm conclusions about women's roles from this brief reference to Chloe.

Priscilla (Prisca; 1 Cor. 16:19; Rom. 16:3; 2 Tim. 4:19). Priscilla and Aquila were already known as strategic partners with Paul in his mission in multiple locations. They hosted house churches (1 Cor. 16:19; Rom. 16:3)—in fact, it seems that wherever this couple went, they had a church meeting in their home—taught people such as Apollos, and risked their necks for Paul and the gospel. They're a couple that clearly operated in tandem. Apart from the three times she is mentioned in Acts, Priscilla is mentioned together with her husband by the short form "Prisca" in 1 Corinthians 16:19; Romans 16:3, and 2 Timothy 4:19.

The variation in the order of their names is paralleled in Acts with Paul and Barnabas. Sometimes they're described as "Barnabas and Paul," while at other times they're referred to as "Paul and Barnabas."[19] It is hard to make a case that the order of names reflects authority. The variation could simply be stylistic or incidental. The theory that Priscilla is mentioned first in some cases because she was in charge is but one possibility. Likewise, when Aquila is mentioned first, this doesn't mean that he was the pastor of the church or exercised local church authority.

Table 4.7: References to Priscilla (Prisca) and Aquila in the New Testament

New Testament Reference	Order
Acts 18:2	Aquila and Priscilla
Acts 18:18	Priscilla and Aquila
Acts 18:26	Priscilla and Aquila

---

[19] Barnabas and Saul/Paul: 11:30; 12:25; 13:1, 2, 7; 14:12, 14; 15:12, 25; Paul and Barnabas: 13:43, 46, 50; 15:2, 22, 35.

New Testament Reference	Order
1 Cor. 16:19	Aquila and Prisca (i.e., Priscilla)
Rom. 16:3	Prisca and Aquila
2 Tim. 4:19	Prisca and Aquila

Table 4.8: Movement of Priscilla and Aquila in New Testament Times

1. Rome	Expelled by Claudius's edict in AD 42 (Acts 18:2)
2. Corinth	Met Paul (Acts 18:18; 1 Cor. 16:19)
3. Ephesus	Instructed Apollos (Acts 18:26)
4. Rome	Moved back to Rome after Claudius's death (Rom. 16:3–5)
5. Ephesus	Back to Ephesus (2 Tim. 4:19)

After 1 Corinthians 16:19, Priscilla is next mentioned in Romans 16:3, where Paul sends greetings to Priscilla and Aquila, his coworkers in Christ Jesus and the church that meets in their home. Some have drawn attention to the description of this couple as Paul's "coworkers" and argued that since Paul was an apostle, Priscilla and her husband were apostles as well. However, the term "coworkers" simply indicates partnership in ministry (cf. Phil. 1:27; 4:3). How many people were really like Paul, with his level of apostolic authority? Priscilla and Aquila are the first in a long list of people to whom Paul sends greetings in Rome, which may show their prominence but doesn't necessarily put them on the same level as Paul in terms of authority of apostleship. The final reference to Priscilla in the New Testament is found in 2 Timothy 4:19. Paul is writing from Rome to Ephesus, and apparently Priscilla and Aquila are back in Ephesus (cf. Acts 18:26).

Clearly, Priscilla and Aquila are an inspiring example of a couple who were completely committed to propagating the mission of the church through church planting in strategic urban centers throughout the Greco-Roman world. The way in which they supported themselves, were willing to accompany Paul on some of his travels and partner with him, and hosted house churches wherever they went is a powerful example of a marriage completely surrendered to the larger goal of reaching the world for Christ. They are also an example of a passionate and dedicated partnership in the gospel, giving sacrificially of themselves in ministry to leaders such as Apollos and being vitally involved in establishing new churches as part of the Pauline circle.

Phoebe (Rom. 16:1–2). Over half of the women mentioned in Paul's letters are found in Romans 16, and the vast majority of them are not referenced elsewhere in Paul's writings or the rest of the New Testament. Without this chapter, the list of women would shrink to half a dozen or so names. The Roman congregation was a church that Paul didn't plant and hadn't previously visited; however, he had hoped to connect with them and raise support to engage in further missionary work in Spain (Rom. 15:19). It was possibly in order to establish a connection that Paul mentioned the many people he knew in the church who could vouch for him.[20]

The first woman mentioned in Romans 16 is Phoebe: "I commend to you our sister Phoebe, a *servant* of the church at Cenchrea, that you may welcome her in the Lord in a way worthy of the saints, and help her in whatever she may need from you, for she has been a *patron* [the NIV has "benefactor"] of many and of myself as well" (Rom. 16:1–2). First, Phoebe was a servant (*diakonos*) of the church in Cenchrea. Second, she was a benefactress or patroness (*prostatis*), as those women were sometimes called. Third, she was most likely the individual who carried the letter from Corinth to Rome. Just think of what would have happened if she'd lost the letter! Her role as letter carrier indicates that she was fully trusted by Paul and her church.

Phoebe was clearly a woman of some importance and stature. She was probably unmarried, because no husband is mentioned. Many of the prominent women in the early church were widows. Wives typically outlived their husbands, didn't remarry, and inherited their husband's estate. They were therefore in a position to engage in a variety of good deeds by opening their home to a church or to individuals such as Paul or other itinerant preachers. This is what the term "benefactress" (*prostatis*) most likely means here. We don't know for

---

[20] The references to individuals at the end of Romans aren't there so much because of the importance of the individuals themselves but in order to establish rapport with the church in Rome.

sure, but Phoebe may have been a well-to-do widow. If so, she serves as a wonderful example of a woman who used her home and financial means to provide hospitality and support the preaching of the gospel in tangible ways.

In addition, some argue that Phoebe was likely "in charge of the charitable work of the church."[21] According to this view, she was the benevolence director of the church at Cenchrea. However, this conclusion goes beyond the evidence. Phoebe clearly engaged in good works, but there's no evidence that she was in charge of her church's benevolence. Others argue that patronesses were essentially leaders and heads of households.[22] One writer even calls her "President Phoebe"![23] This conclusion seems far-fetched, especially since the proposal is supported by a questionable use of background information regarding the role of priestesses in goddess worship in Greek religion.[24] Most likely, *prostatis* conveys the idea of "helper."[25]

Phoebe is also called "our sister," so she was clearly a fellow Christian. With regard to her designation as a *diakonos*, even many non-feminist commentators argue that the term here should likely be understood as "deaconess."[26] This is supported by the fact that "servant" would be an unlikely expression to use since there seems to be a more technical nature to *diakonos*, especially in connection with a specific church. It seems that Phoebe held a particular office in that church. Theologically, there would be no good reason for Phoebe not to serve in that role as long as the role of deaconess was not an

---

[21] Ben Witherington, *Women in the Earliest Churches* (Cambridge, UK: Cambridge University Press, 1988), 114.

[22] Craig S. Keener, *Paul, Women, and Wives: Marriage and Women's Ministry in the Letters of Paul* (Grand Rapids, MI: Baker Academic, 1992).

[23] Ray R. Shultz, "A Case for 'President' Phoebe in Romans 16:2," *Lutheran Theological Journal* 24 (1990): 124–27. For a helpful critique, see Esther Yue L. Ng, "Phoebe as *Prostatis*," *Trinity Journal* 25NS (2004): 4–6.

[24] The questionable use of background information is a common interpretive fallacy. See appendix 3.

[25] See Thomas R. Schreiner, "The Valuable Ministries of Women in the Context of Male Leadership: A Survey of Old and New Testament Examples and Teaching," in *Recovering Biblical Manhood and Womanhood: A Response to Biblical Feminism*, ed. John Piper and Wayne Grudem (Wheaton, IL: Crossway, 1991), 211–27. There may also be a play on words involving "help" and "helper": "*Help* her in whatever she may need from you, for she has been a *helper* of many and of myself as well." See also Thomas Schreiner, review of Philip Payne, *Man and Woman, One in Christ*, in *Journal of Biblical Manhood and Womanhood* 15 (Spring 2010): 35, where Schreiner concurs that Phoebe served as deacon but contends that she didn't serve as elder and convincingly rebuts the argument advanced by Payne that Phoebe served as Paul's leader (*prostatis*). See further the article by Ng, "Phoebe as *Prostatis*," and the interaction in notes above and below.

[26] See the commentaries on Romans by Douglas J. Moo, *The Epistle to the Romans*, New International Commentary on the New Testament (Grand Rapids, MI: Eerdmans, 1996), 913–14; and Thomas R. Schreiner, *Romans*, Baker Exegetical Commentary on the New Testament (Grand Rapids, MI: Baker, 1998), 787–88 (see also the previous note).

authoritative or teaching role. When you compare the qualifications for elders and deacons in 1 Timothy, for example, one element that's conspicuously absent from the qualifications for deacons is the ability to teach. Likewise, any reference to the exercise of authority is absent.

Phoebe's role as a benefactress indicates that she was a woman of some means (though to call her "wealthy" may exceed the evidence) who opened up her home, supported Christian ministry, and on occasion provided financial assistance (though it is far from certain whether she was Paul's patron and supported him financially).[27] Her role of carrying the letter indicates that she was trustworthy. She was clearly an important person in the church who served significantly in many ways. She must have been of sufficient means to travel from Corinth to Rome. Keep in mind that all these references are incidental. This is the only place where Phoebe is mentioned in the New Testament. Paul wanted to commend this dear woman so that the Christians in Rome would receive and help her in any way they could.

Mary, Tryphaena and Tryphosa, and Persis (Rom. 16:6, 12). The next person mentioned in Romans 16 is Mary: "Greet Mary, who has worked hard for you." We don't know anything about Mary other than her hard work, but she must have been sufficiently significant to be mentioned specifically by Paul. The same word is applied to Tryphaena and Tryphosa, women who also worked hard in the Lord (v. 12). Some people think the latter two women may have been sisters because it was common to assign children names from the same Greek root word. Their names mean "soft" and "delicate," respectively. Romans 16:12 also mentions Persis, "who has worked hard in the Lord." Persis means "Persian woman" and was a typical Greek slave name. Hard work may imply a variety of good works, which were a hallmark of committed, mature, pious women in the first century. Mary, Tryphaena and Tryphosa, and Persis all serve as examples of women who worked hard in

---

[27]See Ng, "Phoebe as *Prostatis*," 8–9, who, citing Paul's words in 2 Cor. 11:9–10 ("And when I was with you and was in need, I did not burden anyone. . . . So I refrained and will refrain from burdening you in any way"), maintains that "it is doubtful that Paul depended on Phoebe for money" (note that Cenchrea was near Corinth). Ng also notes that Phoebe is not mentioned at all in Acts, which, while admittedly an argument from silence, "would be very strange indeed if Phoebe had been an influential benefactor in the life of Paul" (p. 12). Ng further observes that it would have been "very unusual in Greco-Roman letter writing for one to recommend somebody superior to oneself in social standing" (ibid., with further references). She concludes that Phoebe was conceivably "a woman of some wealth, but she was probably not a member of the upper social class, nor extremely wealthy and influential" (p. 13).

the ministry. Sometimes we forget that ministry is hard work. Being involved in ministry may not always be convenient, but it may benefit those who need to hear the gospel or to have a critical need met.

Junia (Rom. 16:7). In Romans 16:7 Paul writes, "Greet Andronicus and Junia, my kinsmen and my fellow prisoners." Some contend that the evidence is inconclusive as to whether Junia was a man or a woman, perhaps even favoring the thesis that this person was a man.[28] However, there seems to be sufficient evidence to conclude with a high degree of confidence that this was a lady named Junia. Junia is a Latin name transcribed into Greek. There is no record of Junias, the male version of the name, ever being used. The name occurs only in its feminine form Junia. Unless more evidence surfaces, we should conclude that Junia is a woman.

Junia is mentioned along with Andronicus, very likely a couple like Priscilla and Aquila. Paul describes both Andronicus and Junia as his kinsmen. This may mean fellow Jews but could also just mean friends or close associates. He also calls Andronicus and Junia "fellow prisoners," which could refer to some unknown imprisonment or indicate that Paul is using the phrase metaphorically, with the latter perhaps being more probable.

Paul continues, "They are well known to the apostles, and they were in Christ before me" (v. 7b; some translations have "among the apostles"). There is a certain amount of debate as to what the adjective *episēmoi* ("well known" or "outstanding") means, and what is meant by "apostles" (*apostolos*). The interpretation of the passage also depends on whether the Greek preposition *en* should be translated as "to" or "among." Two leading English translations render the passage as "well known to the apostles" (ESV; footnote: "or messengers") or "outstanding among [footnote: "or esteemed by"] the apostles" (NIV). The former translation suggests that the two weren't apostles themselves but only known to the apostles,[29] while the latter rendering indicates that they were particularly prominent apostles (or whatever "apostle" is taken to mean here).

How are we to resolve this variation? The first question pertains to whether the couple is included among the apostles or distinct from

---

[28] Piper and Grudem, *Recovering Biblical Manhood and Womanhood*, 79–80.
[29] See Michael H. Burer and Daniel B. Wallace, "Was Junia Really an Apostle? A Re-examination of Rom 16.7," *New Testament Studies* 47 (2001): 76–91.

them. The second question concerns whether they were "outstanding" or "well known." Regarding the first question, if Andronicus and Junia were included among the apostles, would this rank them among the most prominent apostles? This doesn't seem likely because the two are mentioned only here in the New Testament. Quite evidently, they were not among the most widely known *apostoloi*.

With regard to the meaning of *apostolos*, there are at least four different options. First, in secular Greek the expression simply indicated a messenger, and the related verb conveyed the sense "to send." Second, in the Gospels, in conjunction with Jesus's ministry, the term began to be used in a technical sense to refer to the twelve apostles.[30] Third, there were other people called *apostoloi* in the early church, but not many. Paul, Barnabas, and Matthias, the replacement for Judas, are among these. Fourth, there are instances of the use of *apostolos* in a broader sense with reference to church planters or missionaries. This broader usage is found beyond the apostolic era, in which the church was established on the foundation of the apostles and prophets (Eph. 2:20) who had been eyewitnesses (Acts 1:21–22).[31] This represents the range of meaning for *apostolos* in the New Testament. The meaning of the term in each usage must be determined by the surrounding context. The only way to know which of those four different possibilities applies is to look at the context and parallel passages, weigh the possibilities, and make a decision.

In the particular case of Romans 16:7, all things being equal, part of the adjudication depends on how one translates the adjective *episēmoi* ("well known" or "outstanding") and the preposition *en* ("to" or "among"). If an interpreter opts for "well known," it's unlikely that the couple was on par with the original twelve apostles. The decision is more significant if Andronicus and Junia were apostles in the more technical sense. They were clearly not members of the Twelve. Could they have been on the level of Paul, Barnabas, or Matthias? This is pos-

---

[30] In the upper room at the Lord's Supper, Matthew and Mark mention that the Twelve were with Jesus while Luke says that the "apostles" were with him. It seems clear that Luke, at least, viewed "apostle" as a technical term for the Twelve.

[31] This fourth sense of the word may be in view with the spiritual gifts mentioned in Eph. 4:11, where it is stated that God gave the church *apostles*, prophets, evangelists, and shepherd teachers. There are also a few times in the NT where *apostolos* is used in the broader sense of the word as messenger or someone who was sent on an errand by someone else.

sible, but it's more likely that, like Priscilla and Aquila, they were an outstanding missionary couple. Most likely, Andronicus and Junia are part of an emerging group of people who participated in Paul's mission and planted churches. It's also noteworthy that Junia isn't mentioned by herself but along with her husband.

In all probability, then, Andronicus and Junia were a distinguished missionary couple. This doesn't mean that Junia occupied a position of leadership on her own in the church. The reference indicates the noble calling for a woman to be a missionary wife and to serve in cross-cultural ministry alongside her husband. Those who, neglecting Andronicus, contend that Junia was a full-blown apostle holding a prominent position of authority in the early church seem to exceed the evidence.[32] More likely, *apostolos* was used in the broader sense of "missionary," the more customary usage of the word by the time Romans was written, and Junia's ministry was with other women, for "the wife can have access to the women's areas, which would not be generally accessible to the husband."[33]

We've already commented on the strategic importance and vital contribution of couples and families to the propagation of the gospel when discussing the example of Priscilla and Aquila above. In all likelihood, Andronicus and Junia were another such couple that distinguished themselves through dedicated missionary service. While families sometimes don't have the same flexibility as single men or women, they are nonetheless indispensable for the church's outreach and mission. We'll say more about the importance of men and women partnering on mission for God in the concluding chapter on application. For now, it must suffice for us to point out that there are few things as powerful in the propagation of the gospel as a marriage and family completely dedicated to the service of God.[34]

The mother of Rufus and Julia (Rom. 16:13, 15). No additional information is given about these women. Mark 15:21 mentions a Simon from Cyrene, the father of Alexander and Rufus, who was compelled to bear

---

[32] See, e.g., Cohick, *Women in the World of the Earliest Christians*, 216, who claims that Junia was counted as one of the apostles, inferring from this that she was "an authoritative figure in the community."

[33] Ernst Käsemann, *Commentary on Romans* (Grand Rapids, MI: Eerdmans, 1980), 413, cited by Schreiner, review of Payne, *Man and Woman, One in Christ*, 35.

[34] See esp. Christopher Ash, *Marriage: Sex in the Service of God* (Leicester, UK: Inter-Varsity, 2003).

Jesus's cross for a time. If there's a connection, the mother of Rufus would be Simon's wife, but this is uncertain.

Euodia and Syntyche (Phil. 4:2–3). Ephesians doesn't contain any references to women by name, while Philippians includes Paul's exhortation to two specific women. Paul writes, "I entreat Euodia and I entreat Syntyche to agree in the Lord. Yes, I ask you also, true companion, help these women, who have labored side by side with me in the gospel together with Clement and the rest of my fellow workers, whose names are in the book of life" (Phil. 4:2–3). Euodia and Syntyche are mentioned as having contended (Greek *synathleō*) with Paul in the cause of the gospel. The same expression is used in Philippians 1:27 with reference to the entire congregation at Philippi.[35] These women are part of a congregation that in its entirety contended with Paul in the cause of the gospel.

What's more, Euodia and Syntyche are also called Paul's "fellow workers" (Greek *synergoi*). The entire Philippian church is described as partners in the gospel (Phil. 1:5). Some argue that these two women are important and influential church leaders. However, it's illegitimate to infer teaching or leading authority from the description of the women as Paul's fellow workers. They were clearly women who had a running dispute with each other that was affecting the whole church. It was probably embarrassing for them to be addressed directly by Paul, but he obviously thought it was necessary. Paul handles a thorny situation with kindness by positively describing these women even though he's addressing a problem. They were partners with him in ministry but not necessarily in official positions of authority.

The example of Euodia and Syntyche is both encouraging and convicting. On the positive side, we have here two women (most likely unmarried) who had a vital part in the ministry of their local church. They labored side by side with Paul and suffered for the gospel. They were right in the thick of things and serve as a source of inspiration particularly for unmarried women today to make an important contribution to the ministry of the gospel in and through their local church. At the same time, these two women also serve as a warning. Even for those who contribute significantly to the church's ministry, it is important to maintain a stance of humility and not to get caught

---

[35] These are the only two places where the word "labored together" occurs in the New Testament.

up in ourselves and in promoting our own interests and ambitions so as not to get entangled in personal vendettas or petty arguments. Apparently, these two women temporarily succumbed to this temptation. We need to make sure we do not.

Nympha, Apphia, and Claudia (Col. 4:15; 2 Tim. 4:21). Paul mentions a few other women in his letters, such as Nympha, Apphia "our sister" (possibly Philemon's wife), and Claudia. We already mentioned, when discussing Mary the mother of (John) Mark in Acts 12:12, the phenomenon of women having churches meeting in their homes. Apart from this, Paul provides no further information about any of these women.

Implications

The book of Acts continues the male pattern of leadership that we found in the Old Testament and in Jesus's ministry.[36] The Pauline circle, consisting of men such as Timothy, Titus, Barnabas, John Mark, and Luke, while not as narrowly circumscribed as the Twelve, continues to show that the leadership of the early church's mission was given to particular qualified and selected men. At the same time, we see in Acts that women were active participants in the early Christian mission in a variety of ways. Women took part in prayer meetings, engaged in a variety of good works, served as benefactresses or patronesses, were the targets of persecution, possibly served as deaconesses, and ministered alongside their husbands.

Interpreting narrative references to men and women is a delicate task. This is true especially because, as we've seen, such incidental references may not contain sufficient evidence to render a confident judgment as to the exact role a person had. For this reason it's important methodologically to supplement one's study of narrative passages with an investigation of passages that are explicitly designed to instruct believers in the churches on the subject at hand. The following two chapters will therefore explore Paul's teaching on male-female roles in the family and in the church. After this, we'll look at relevant portions in the General Epistles and the book of Revelation.

---

[36] The assertion by Wright, "Women's Service," 5, that "we find so many women in positions of leadership, initiative and responsibility in the early church" doesn't accurately represent the actual evidence from the Gospels, the book of Acts, and the NT letters.

Key Resources

Bock, Darrell L. *Acts*. Baker Exegetical Commentary on the New Testament. Grand Rapids, MI: Baker, 2007.

———. *A Theology of Luke and Acts: God's Promised Program, Realized for All Nations*. Biblical Theology of the New Testament. Grand Rapids, MI: Zondervan, 2012.

Bruce, F. F. *The Pauline Circle*. Grand Rapids, MI: Eerdmans, 1985.

Köstenberger, Andreas J. "Women in the Pauline Mission." In *The Gospel to the Nations: Perspectives on Paul's Mission*, edited by Peter Bolt and Mark Thompson, 221–48. Downers Grove, IL: InterVarsity, 2000. http://www.biblicalfoundations.org.

Schnabel, Eckhard. *Acts*. Zondervan Exegetical Commentary on the New Testament. Grand Rapids, MI: Zondervan, 2012.

5

Paul's Message to the Churches

First Ten Letters

> There is neither Jew nor Greek, there is neither slave nor free, there is no male and female, for you are all one in Christ Jesus.
>
> —Galatians 3:28

> And we all, with unveiled face, beholding the glory of the Lord, are being transformed into the same image from one degree of glory to another. For this comes from the Lord who is the Spirit.
>
> —2 Corinthians 3:18

> Wives, submit to your own husbands, as to the Lord. For the husband is the head of the wife even as Christ is the head of the church, his body, and is himself its Savior. . . . Husbands, love your wives, as Christ loved the church and gave himself up for her.
>
> —Ephesians 5:22–25

Key Points

1. Galatians 3:28 teaches that it doesn't matter whether a person is a Jew or a Gentile, a slave or a free person, or a man or a woman when it comes to salvation and thus church membership. The passage doesn't address the question of church leadership roles, much less the equality of men and women in this regard.

2. First Corinthians 11:2–16 teaches that women may participate in praying and prophesying in church under male spiritual leadership and authority. While the principle of headship and submission is abiding, the cultural expression of submission to authority (such as first-century head coverings) may vary.

3. First Corinthians 14:33b–36 most likely teaches that women shouldn't participate in the authoritative function of evaluating prophecy in settings of public worship.

4. Ephesians 5:21–32 calls on wives to submit to their husbands and on husbands to love their wives. The word for "head" (*kephalē*) conveys the sense of "authority" rather than "source." The earlier use of *kephalē* in Ephesians clearly supports an authoritative sense. Rather than teaching mutual submission, the passage suggests that the submission in view in marriage is from one group to another (wives to husbands; also children to parents, slaves to masters).

It's hard to overstate the importance of the creation story for Paul's theology. When, in Galatians 3:28, the apostle states that in Christ there is "no male and female," the creation story resonates in the background (cf. Gen. 1:27). Later in the same letter, Paul writes that "neither circumcision counts for anything, nor uncircumcision, but a new creation" (Gal. 6:15). In 1 Corinthians 11, when explaining his rationale for why the women in Corinth should pray with their head covered, he writes, "For a man ought not to cover his head, since he is the image and glory of God, but woman is the glory of man. For man was not made from woman, but woman from man. Neither was man created for woman, but woman for man" (1 Cor. 11:7–9). Again, the creation narrative clearly shines through and forms the basis for Paul's theologizing with regard to the identities and roles of man and woman.

In his second letter to the Corinthians, the apostle affirms, "Therefore, if anyone is in Christ, he is a new creation" (2 Cor. 5:17). Remarkably, though, in this life this new creation still includes distinct male-female identities and roles. This is suggested already by the fact that, as we've just seen, Paul in 1 Corinthians, and later in Ephesians, still affirms specific male and female roles, writing several years after asserting in his letter to the Galatians that with regard to salvation in Christ there is no male and female. In Ephesians, too, after calling on wives to submit to their husbands and on husbands to love their wives, Paul cites the creation narrative: "Therefore a man shall leave his father and mother and hold fast to his wife, and the two shall become one flesh" (Eph. 5:31, citing Gen. 2:24). Quite clearly, for Paul God's original creation design for the man and the woman is still in effect for believers today and has in no way been set aside.

As we continue our quest to discern the biblical teaching on what it means to be a man or a woman according to God's design, we need to remember, therefore, that the New Testament teaching on male and female identities and roles is firmly grounded in the creation narrative. And while Paul and the other New Testament writers apply these foundational passages to Christian men and women in the church, they do not fundamentally change God's original design but rather develop it and extend it in a way that is faithful to the Old Testament teaching. God's image, they claim, which was imprinted on humanity as male and female in the beginning, and which was distorted at the fall, is now, in Christ, being restored to its original beauty, wisdom, goodness, and glory. God's original design does not need to be improved; it needs only to be restored, like an ancient masterpiece that has lost some of its beautiful original colors to the ravages of time.

Table 5.1: Paul's New Creation Theology

Passage in Paul	Content	Genesis Background
Gal. 3:28	Humanity created as male and female	Gen. 1:27
Gal. 6:15	New creation in Christ	Genesis 1–2
1 Cor. 11:7–9	Image/glory of God; woman made from/for man	Genesis 1–2
2 Cor. 5:17	New creation in Christ	Genesis 1–2
Eph. 5:31	One-flesh union of husband and wife	Gen. 2:24

With these important foundational considerations in mind, we're now ready to continue on our journey to see how Paul in his writings contributes to our understanding of the biblical theology of manhood and womanhood. We'll proceed in chronological order of writing. In this chapter, we'll look at four Pauline passages that have featured prominently in the debate on men's and women's roles in the church because they are the main passages discussing the issue: (1) Galatians 3:28, where Paul teaches that in Christ there is neither male nor female but all are one in Christ; (2) 1 Corinthians 11:2–16, where the apostle discusses head coverings as a sign of women's submission to male authority in the church; (3) 1 Corinthians 14:33b–36, which deals with the evaluation of prophecies; and (4) Ephesians 5:21–33, the foremost passage on marriage in Paul's writings and in the New Testament where Paul speaks of husbands' headship and wives' submission.

Male-Female Unity in Christ (Gal. 3:28)

Is Galatians 3:28 lodging a claim for undifferentiated gender equality as some have maintained? Is this the high point of the Bible's teaching on gender roles, and should every other passage, including 1 Timothy 2:12, be subordinated to Paul's affirmation in Galatians 3:28 that in Christ there's no male and female? Have all gender role distinctions been abolished in Christ? Does Galatians 3:28 even address the topic of male and female roles in the home and/or in the church? In what follows, we'll address these questions and attempt to determine how the affirmation in Galatians 3:28, that in Christ there is no male and female but all are one in Christ, relates to the biblical pattern of male leadership that we've already identified in Scripture (Old Testament, Jesus's teaching and practice, life and mission of the early church).

Galatians 3:28 reads, "There is neither Jew nor Greek, there is neither slave nor free, there is no male and female, for you are all one in Christ Jesus." Before focusing on this verse, it'll be instructive to address the usual question raised, since at first reading this passage seems to be saying that women are to be considered equal to men in every respect. Is it true, as some have suggested, that Galatians 3:28 is the "most socially explosive statement in the New Testament"[1] that calls for the obliteration of all gender roles in the home, the church,

---

[1] Klyne Snodgrass, "Galatians 3:28—Conundrum or Solution?," in *Women, Authority, and the Bible*, ed. Alvera Mickelsen (Downers Grove, IL: InterVarsity, 1986), 161.

and society?[2] If so, the change in women's status indicated here would require a change in role! In this view, it seems as if Christ has ushered in a new era of mutuality, equality, and freedom in contrast to the old era, which was a time of subordination and submission.

All of these thoughts are interesting and worthy of consideration, but let's not get ahead of ourselves. Many things changed with redemption in Christ, but not everything changed. The cross achieved several important benefits, such as the substitutionary atonement (Christ's death on the cross in our place) and our justification (the declaration that we're now right with God—not guilty—in Jesus Christ). However, as those redeemed by Christ, isn't it rather that we're now enabled to live out the roles God has given to us in the first place, aided by the Spirit who dwells within us? Isn't it true that God's original plan for marriage has been reaffirmed by Christ and is still valid in the church age? In the matter of gender roles, isn't it more likely that the New Testament exhibits essential continuity rather than radical discontinuity with the Old Testament?[3] Let's now explore these issues in light of the historical context of the letter.

Background

Galatians is the first letter Paul wrote that's included in the New Testament.[4] It was most likely written shortly before the Jerusalem Council (around AD 50), where grace and law were debated in determining necessary requirements for admission into the church (cf. Acts 15). Apparently, Paul had previously confronted Peter, expressing concern that Peter had been intimidated by certain Judaizers (Jewish false teachers) who claimed that Gentiles must undergo circumcision before they could be accepted into the church (Gal. 2:11–21). For Paul, the matter struck at the very heart of the gospel, because if church membership could be attained by circumcision or other external means, why

---

[2] Ibid., 175, 178. Similarly, Richard Longenecker maintains, "The most forthright statement on social ethics in all the New Testament is found in Galatians 3:28." Richard N. Longenecker, *New Testament Social Ethics for Today* (Grand Rapids, MI: Eerdmans, 1984), 30.

[3] See N. T. Wright, "Women's Service in the Church: The Biblical Basis," conference paper for the symposium "Men, Women and the Church," St. John's College, Durham, September 4, 2004, 3: "So does Paul mean that in Christ the created order itself is undone? . . . No. Paul is a theologian of new creation, and it is always the renewal and reaffirmation of the existing creation, never its denial."

[4] For a thorough discussion of the circumstances surrounding the writing of Galatians, see Andreas J. Köstenberger, L. Scott Kellum, and Charles L. Quarles, *The Cradle, the Cross, and the Crown: An Introduction to the New Testament* (Nashville: B&H Academic, 2009), chap. 10.

did Jesus still have to die on the cross (Gal. 6:12–16)? Salvation and church membership were a matter of grace, not of keeping the Old Testament law.

One, Not Equal, in Christ:
The Meaning of the Greek Word *Hen* ("One")

Now that we understand what the issues are and what the relevant historical background is, we're in a better position to take a closer look at the text itself. The first pertinent question relates to the meaning of the important word translated "one" in our passage. Lexically, it's important to realize that the Greek word *hen* used in the verse means "one" rather than "equal" (see, e.g., Mark 10:8; John 10:30; Rom. 12:5).[5] Paul could have used another Greek word, *isos* ("equal"), if he'd wanted to focus on unfettered male-female equality, but that's not the expression he chose to use. Instead, he employed the term *hen*, "one," to convey the notion of *unity*. There's no known example of *hen* anywhere in Greek literature being used in the place of *isos*. Also, there's no English translation that renders *hen* as "equal" in our passage (i.e., "all are equal in Christ"). For these reasons, we conclude that Paul's actual purpose in Galatians 3:28 is to teach racial, socioeconomic, and gender unity in Christ. The various groups in the church—Jew and Gentile, slave and free, male and female—while remaining distinct (i.e., not equal or literally the same), are unified (i.e., figuratively one) in Christ.

Paul's point to his original readers was that in the New Testament church, it was God's will, in Christ, to break down the barriers that divided people. Are Jews, then, no longer going to be Jews? No, but they're now united with others who are different from them ethnically by virtue of their common faith in Christ. Economic differences remain in the church as well; the Bible doesn't teach a Christian "communism" where church members are compelled to donate all personal property to their local church.[6] Likewise, there'll still be men and women; salvation in Christ doesn't magically remove all gender differences. As we've seen, the Greek word *hen* is used of diverse rather than

---

[5] Richard Hove, *Equality in Christ? Galatians 3:28 and the Gender Dispute* (Wheaton, IL: Crossway, 1999), provides a rigorous lexical discussion.
[6] Where believers in the early church sold their property and "laid it at the apostles' feet" (Acts 4:32–35), they did so voluntarily rather than under compulsion.

identical objects, and the emphasis in Galatians 3:28 is on unity rather than undifferentiated equality in Christ—the respective elements in each of the three pairs aren't one and the same in every respect. Applied to gender, therefore, the phrase "one in Christ" means that men and women are united in the church on the basis of their common salvation by grace through faith. Conversely, it doesn't mean that all male-female role distinctions are abolished. Succinctly put, Paul's topic in Galatians 3:28 is not church leadership; it's church membership.

Galatians 3:28 Read in the Context of Galatians 3

Contextually in Galatians, as mentioned, Paul was arguing against the Judaizers, who apparently taught, in effect, that Gentiles must be circumcised in order to join the church in order to keep the Jewish law. How, then, are we to interpret Paul's response to this teaching in the immediate context of our passage in Galatians 3? A close reading of our passage yields the important observation that, structurally, Galatians 3:28 is set in parallel with 3:26.

In order to understand what Paul means in verse 28 when he says that we are all "one in Christ," we'll therefore do well to consult the parallel verse 26. That verse, for its part, indicates that being "one in Christ" means that we're all sons and daughters of God in Jesus Christ. This observation, too, suggests that Paul is here focusing on unity in diversity rather than equality. When we put our faith in Christ, whether we're male or female, the result isn't that we're all becoming the same but that we're all united in the church in the midst of our continuing diversity.

Table 5.2: Parallel Statements in Galatians 3:26 and 28

Gal. 3:26	"for <u>in Christ Jesus</u> you are all sons of God, **through faith**"
Gal. 3:28	"there is **no male and female**, for *you are all one <u>in Christ Jesus</u>*"

What's more, the male-female pair is only one of three pairings in the passage, the other two being Jew/Greek and slave/free. If all male-female differences were obliterated, consistency would seem to demand that the same would be true with those other two groups as well. However, ethnic Israel continues in existence, and while Gentiles are to be allowed into the church on equal footing with Jews (Paul's primary point in Galatians), Paul is not saying they should be absorbed into the church in such a way that the two groups lose all of their ethnic distinctiveness. The same is true regarding work relationships. Slaves (in Paul's day) must still submit to their masters—though, of course, subsequent history has witnessed the abolition of slavery—or they may soon find themselves looking for a new job![7] Paul isn't calling for the removal of all authority and submission in the workplace. He's rather pointing out how faith in Christ spiritually levels the playing field. At the same time, he didn't seek to eradicate all male-female roles or attempt to alter God's original design for men and women.

In Galatians 3:28, then, Paul is not arguing that we're equal—the same—in Christ, but rather that we're all one in Christ—united. Paul is emphasizing that there's no difference in terms of church membership (the primary issue in Galatians). His message to the Galatians, and to the Judaizers in his day, is that salvation isn't by grace plus works of the law such as circumcision—the abiding message of the gospel. Correspondingly, Paul contends in Galatians 3:16 that Genesis 12:7 pointed not to Abraham's many offspring but "to one . . . who is Christ." Abraham was not merely the prototypical Jew; he was, more importantly, the prototypical believer. What's more, while Abraham practiced circumcision, God had issued his promise, that the righteous will be saved by faith, to Abraham prior to circumcision. This is a very Jewish argument—required because Paul's opponents were Jewish—and Paul uses several Old Testament passages to support his point (including Gen. 15:6 and Deut. 21:23).

Contextually, therefore, Galatians 3:28b, "For you are all one in Christ Jesus," refers back to the divine promise made to Abraham of which all believers—not merely Jews—are heirs (see v. 29). To sum up Paul's main argument in its original context, therefore, whether

---

[7]Note in this regard that the slave-free distinction resulted from the fall while the male-female difference predates the fall. Both Jesus and Paul ground God's design for male and female in the created order (Matt. 19:4–6; 1 Cor. 11:8–9; 1 Tim. 2:13) while the Bible never derives slavery from the created order. See on this the insightful discussion in Robert W. Yarbrough, "Progressive and Historic: The Hermeneutics of 1 Timothy 2:9–15," in *Women in the Church*, 2nd ed., ed. Andreas J. Köstenberger and Thomas R. Schreiner (Grand Rapids, MI: Baker, 2005), 139–42.

Jew or Gentile, slave or free, male or female, all are recipients of God's promises to Abraham through faith in Christ.[8] In the book of Galatians, Paul is primarily focused on the first pair: Jew/Gentile. He then extends his argument from ethnicity to relationships in the workplace and to gender (each individual's relationship to God). Notice, by the way, that in the parallel in 1 Corinthians 12:13, "For in one Spirit we were all baptized into one body—Jews or Greeks, slaves or free—and all were made to drink of one Spirit," there's no mention of the male-female pair at all! This further suggests that Paul's primary focus wasn't on gender.

Relationship between the Couplets Jew-Gentile, Slave-Free, Male-Female

Now that we've studied Galatians 3:28 in context, let's take a closer look at the three couplets Jew-Gentile, slave-free, and male-female. Richard Hove, in his important study of this verse, *Equality in Christ?*, makes the following helpful points. First, the three couplets need to be interpreted together, although they're not the same: the slave-free distinction resulted from the fall, while the Jew-Gentile distinction did not. For this reason, Hove avers, it's illegitimate to conclude that male headship and female submission are merely a result of the fall. Each couplet is related to the fall in a unique way with no observable common pattern:

> It appears that the three categories differ in nature, and that accordingly the social implementations for them are not the same. Whereas slavery, as a social institution created by sinful men, can and should be abolished, and the Jew/Gentile distinction, which retains its validity as a purely ethnic reality, has been transcended through the reconciliation accomplished by Christ (Eph. 2:14–16), the male/female distinction, unlike the other two, has its roots in creation itself and continues to have significance in the realm of redemption.[9]

---

[8] For an excellent recent study of Gal. 3:26–29 explaining the text in context and discussing its contemporary application, see Thomas R. Schreiner, *Galatians*, Zondervan Exegetical Commentary on the New Testament (Grand Rapids, MI: Zondervan, 2010), 253–61.

[9] Ronald Y. K. Fung, "Ministry in the New Testament," in *The Church in the Bible and the World*, ed. D. A. Carson (Grand Rapids, MI: Baker, 1987), 184.

Second, we should interpret each of the couplets in light of the reason Paul himself gives for their negation. There's no more Jew-Greek, slave-free, or male-female because all are one in Christ. As mentioned, Galatians 3:28 is framed by the phrase "you are all sons [and daughters] of God" (v. 26) and by the statement that "you are Abraham's offspring, heirs according to the promise" (v. 29). Galatians 3:28 is part of a larger argument in which Paul contends that the blessings of being united with Christ obtain regardless of race, socioeconomic status, or gender. This interpretation best situates the couplets in the flow of chapters 3 and 4 of Galatians and in the context of the entire book.

Summary

Paul is arguing in Galatians that Genesis, rightly interpreted, teaches that righteousness comes through faith, not through circumcision or other marks of Jewish ethnic identity. Galatians 3:28 declares the universal availability of salvation and the inclusion of all genuine believers among the people of God. While Paul's primary point in Galatians 3:28 is spiritual, the passage does have social implications.[10] With regard to race, the church should be characterized by racial unity rather than segregation. With regard to socioeconomic status, the church should not discriminate on the basis of a person's lack of material wealth. With regard to gender, women ought not to be treated as second-class church members or as inferior in value to men. Yet rather than trying to make everyone the same, we can celebrate our diversity because we know that it won't threaten our unity. What's more, in our diverse roles we must treat each other with humility, respect, and dignity.

That said, Galatians 3:28 says nothing about the specific roles of men and women in the church. As Tom Wright candidly notes, "The first thing to say is fairly obvious but needs saying anyway. Galatians 3 is not about ministry."[11] As mentioned, the passage is about church membership, not leadership. Regarding the latter issue, 1 Timothy 2:12 is more directly relevant. The supposed axiomatic verse of Galatians 3:28 therefore cannot be legitimately used to argue for equal male-

---

[10] For more discussion of the social implications, see Hove, *Equality in Christ*, 143–48.
[11] Wright, "Women's Service," 3.

female participation in roles of church leadership because the passage doesn't address the roles of men and women in the church at all, whether directly or indirectly. At the same time, there are other passages in Paul's writings that clearly *do* address the issue of male-female roles in the home and in the church, including the question of who's eligible for church offices involving teaching or oversight authority. We'll take a look at those passages later on in this chapter and also in the following chapter.

To conclude, "The biblical evidence for androcentric administrative structures in both Old and New Testaments is consistent and unequivocal. Paul's declaration in Gal 3:28 . . . relates primarily to how people relate to God, both in their salvation and in their sanctification. If he had intended hereby to address administrative structures, it is remarkable that in his actions in the book of Acts and in his letters he did not act or teach like one out to change the system."[12] As we've seen, Paul's focus in Galatians 3:28 in the context of his argument in the entire letter is on how people relate to God as believers, not on male-female roles or church leadership. As we also saw in the previous chapter, nothing in the book of Acts suggests that Paul sought to redefine the way in which men and women serve in the church's administrative structures. With this, let's look at several other passages in Paul's writings that have a potential bearing on our subject.

Head Coverings and Submission to Authority (1 Cor. 11:2–16)

Paul most likely wrote 1 Corinthians in AD 53 or 54 from Ephesus.[13] Two events prompted the writing of the letter: (1) a report from Chloe's people that there were divisions in the church (1 Cor. 1:11), which prompted Paul's response in 1 Corinthians 1–6 (esp. chaps. 1–4); and (2) a written letter sent from some in the Corinthian church to the apostle requesting clarification and adjudication on some matters that had arisen in the church and that called for Paul's input and direction (1 Cor. 16:17). Paul takes up those matters in the second half of his letter starting in chapter 7 ("Now concerning the matters you wrote about,"

---

[12] Daniel I. Block, "Leader, Leadership, OT," in *New Interpreter's Dictionary of the Bible*, vol. 3: *I–Ma*, ed. Katharine Doob Sakenfeld (Nashville: Abingdon, 2008).

[13] For a thorough discussion of the circumstances surrounding the writing of 1 Corinthians, see Köstenberger, Kellum, and Quarles, *The Cradle, the Cross, and the Crown*, chap. 12.

v. 1). He first addresses the question of the appropriateness of single-ness (chap. 7), then the question of eating food sacrificed to idols in the context of the larger issue of Christian liberty (chaps. 8–10), and after this turns his attention to the matter of head coverings.

Meaning of the Word *Kephalē* ("Head")

At the outset of our study of 1 Corinthians 11:2–16, it'll be helpful to say something about the issue of headship and the meaning of the Greek word *kephalē* ("head"). This word will also be important in our discus-sion of Ephesians 5:21–32 below. Some recent interpreters, such as Catherine Kroeger, have claimed that the word *kephalē* doesn't convey the sense of authority but rather that of source.[14] Kroeger has adduced a small handful out of several thousand extant references in ancient Greek literature where *kephalē* may possibly indicate source, such as in the phrase "the *kephalē* of a river" where the headwaters are the source of the water further downstream. However, the problem with this kind of lexical work is that it has little relevance to the biblical contexts where the word *kephalē* is used with reference to human relationships. While there's a range in the type of authority the term conveys, the meaning "source" for *kephalē* in the New Testament, therefore, is at best a secondary option, with the sense of "authority" being primary.

In fact, Kroeger's proposal has been subjected to extensive criti-cal examination and has largely been found wanting.[15] What's more,

---

[14]Catherine Clark Kroeger, "Appendix 3: The Classical Concept of Head as 'Source,'" in *Equal to Serve, Women and Men in the Church and Home*, ed. Gretchen Gaebelein Hull (Old Tappan, NJ: Revell, 1987), 267–83. See also Wright, "Women's Service," 8, who, after acknowledging that Paul in 1 Corinthians 11 at times uses *kephalē* in a metaphorical sense and sometimes literally, goes on to state that Paul in verse 3 "is referring not to 'headship' in the sense of sovereignty, but to 'headship' in the sense of 'source,' like the *kephalē* of the woman in 1 Corinthians 11 and the reference to the husband as the head of his wife in Ephesians 5 "where it relates of course to husband and wife and where a different point is being made." Wright contends that Paul "was freer than we sometimes imagine to modify his own metaphors accord-ing to various contexts." However, there's an obvious connection between the reference to the man as the *kephalē* of the woman in 1 Corinthians 11 and the reference to the husband as the head of his wife in Ephesians 5 that can't easily be set aside by claiming the senses of the same word are different and the message is different owing to different contexts. More likely, Paul, who wrote both 1 Corinthians and Ephesians, consistently affirmed male headship in the church as well as in the home, as we attempt to show in this and the following chapter.

[15]See, e.g., Wayne Grudem, "Does *Kephalē* ('Head') Mean 'Source' or 'Authority Over' in Greek Lit-erature? A Survey of 2,336 Examples," *Trinity Journal* 6NS (1985): 38–59; "The Meaning of *Kephalē*: A Response to Recent Studies," *Trinity Journal* 11NS (1990): 3–72; "The Meaning of *Kephalē* ('Head'): An Examination of New Evidence, Real and Alleged," *Journal of the Evangelical Theological Society* 44 (2001): 25–65. Grudem studied over two thousand uses of *kephalē* in extrabiblical Greek literature, demon-strating that the expression conveys the notion of *authority* in the vast majority of its occurrences. See also Joseph A. Fitzmyer, "*Kephalē* in 1 Corinthians 11:3," *Interpretation* 47 (1993): 52–59; "Another Look at *Kephalē* in 1 Corinthians 11:3," *New Testament Studies* 35 (1989): 503–11; and Thomas Schreiner, review

with regard to the contextual interpretation of the word *kephalē* in its major New Testament occurrences, it's hardly necessary to resort to wide-ranging extrabiblical lexical analysis. Much closer at hand, a careful study of the contexts of 1 Corinthians 11 and Ephesians 5 in those letters themselves clearly and consistently yields the sense of authority ("head"), while "source" seems strangely foreign to the context. First Corinthians 11:10 explicitly uses the language of authority (Greek *exousia*), and in Ephesians *kephalē* is used throughout the book to denote authority (Eph. 1:22; 4:15; 5:23 [twice]). In Ephesians 1:22, for example, Paul's message is not that Jesus is the source of demons but that he's in a position of authority over them and that everything will ultimately be subjected to Jesus's authority and control. For this reason, it's not absolutely necessary to study the myriads of uses of *kephalē* in extrabiblical Greek literature; the case for *kephalē* meaning "source" in 1 Corinthians and Ephesians already falls short in light of the consistent usage of *kephalē* in these letters.

In the interpretation of 1 Corinthians 11:2–16, as mentioned, the meaning of *kephalē* is the first major issue to address and adjudicate. As we've seen, *kephalē* denotes first and foremost the notion of authority ("head") rather than source. This is further supported by logical reasoning and common sense. On a literal level, the head is the location of the human brain and the place where people reason, make decisions, and control the body. From this literal referent—the head as the command and control center directing a human being's thoughts and actions—it's a small and natural step to the figurative sense of "head" as denoting authority. That said, it's of course true that one of the functions of the head is to provide nurture and support to the rest of the body, so it's not always necessary to choose between the two options. Nurture, support, provision, and protection are all a part of headship, exercised properly, but not to the exclusion of the exercise of authority.[16]

---

of Philip Payne, *Man and Woman, One in Christ*, in *Journal of Biblical Manhood and Womanhood* 15 (Spring 2010): 36–38.

[16] The failure to acknowledge this is the major weakness of Jim and Sarah Sumner, *Just How Married Do You Want to Be?*, who claim that "oneness" is central to the Pauline head/body metaphor while implausibly denying any meaningful distinction between the respective roles of head and body, and in particular the authority implied in the NT use of the word *head*. See the review by Denny Burk in *Journal of Biblical Manhood and Womanhood* 16 (Fall 2011): 51–57, which includes an excellent survey of the Pauline instances of the word *kephalē* (pp. 53–55).

Timeless Principles and Cultural Application

What types of appeal, then, does Paul use in our passage? To answer this question, it'll be helpful to understand the issue he was dealing with. Apparently, there was some confusion in the Corinthian church with regard to head coverings, whatever their precise nature. Some women didn't wear them and thus gave the impression that they were nonsubmissive to male authority. In addressing this particular, occasional issue, Paul enunciates several important universal principles. Some scholars tend to read the entire passage as merely cultural in import, but a natural reading of the passage reveals several unmistakable abiding principles in 1 Corinthians 11:2–16 that shouldn't be easily dismissed, especially since, as we'll see, they are grounded in God's creation order.

One fact that makes this passage difficult to interpret is that Paul combines several types of appeal in the rationale for his instructions: creation order, common sense, and cultural convention.[17] It's important to discern at what point Paul is stating a timeless principle and at what point he's conveying a cultural expression of that principle. An example may help here, the account of the foot washing in John 13:1–20 and its modern application. In the original context, Jesus, shortly before the crucifixion, washes his disciples' feet and then tells his followers that they ought to follow his example. The question arises, should Jesus's disciples literally wash each other's feet in any and every culture, or is it sufficient to derive from the story the general need to relate to fellow believers in a disposition of humility and service and to express this attitude in whatever cultural mode is appropriate?

The example of John 13 illustrates that at times it's difficult to separate on mere textual grounds what's normative from what's merely cultural. Taken at face value, there's little in the passage itself to suggest that Jesus's command is culturally relative. To the contrary, Jesus's command to his disciples to wash each other's feet is expressed in categorical, universal terms ("Do you understand what I have done to you? . . . If I then, your Lord and Teacher, have washed your feet,

---

[17] See the table below. See also Claire Smith, *God's Good Design: What the Bible Really Says about Men and Women* (Kingsford, Australia: Matthias Media, 2012), 70–76, citing Mary Kassian, *Women, Creation, and the Fall* (Wheaton, IL: Crossway, 1990), 97–100.

you also ought to wash one another's feet. For I have given you an example, that you also should do just as I have done to you," John 13:12–15). Nevertheless, the reader of Scripture must discern the obvious cultural dimension of the passage and distinguish between the underlying generic principle and its original and subsequent cultural expressions. Washing feet makes sense in a context where men wore sandals and walked long distances. It was customary for a person upon the arrival at their destination to be greeted at the door by a slave who washed their feet so they didn't get their food dirty. In today's context where most of us drive everywhere we go, it'd be rather strange if we were met at the door of a friend's house by a slave (or anyone!) offering to wash our feet.

Against the backdrop of the analogy of John 13, we can readily understand that the same interpretive procedure applies to 1 Corinthians 11. Like the foot washing, women's wearing of head coverings is clearly a cultural practice that only communicates the underlying principle it's seeking to convey—proper submission to authority—in cultures where women wear head coverings to indicate their submissive stance. The wearing of a head covering is merely the external sign; the real purpose and meaning is the need for proper God-instituted authority and for appropriate submission to that authority. This calls for a submissive spirit, whether expressed by the wearing of a head covering or some other gesture (a possible partial parallel in Western culture today may be a woman's taking her husband's last name). Paul took the matter seriously, not because of the particular manner of its cultural expression but because of the underlying principle at stake. In the Corinthian context, Paul contended that if believers didn't follow the cultural convention, they were rebelling against the underlying timeless principle.

Verses 2–3. In verse 2 Paul begins his discussion by praising the Corinthians for remembering him and his instructions. In verse 3 he raises a new topic that has to do with headship, not just figuratively but literally. In the present passage, there's clearly a symbolic correspondence between figurative headship and what women literally wore on their heads. The principle of headship, as mentioned, is abiding, but how this principle is expressed at any particular place and time depends on the culture. There's no point in perpetrating a custom that no longer communicates the abiding principle in a culture different from the context in which a command was first given. Thomas Schreiner rightly argues that whatever those women wore on their heads as a symbol of authority would not communicate in our culture what it conveyed in first-century Corinth.[18]

Table 5.3: Paul's Types of Appeal in 1 Corinthians 11:2–16

Verse(s) in 1 Corinthians 11	Type of Appeal
2	Tradition
3	Theology (the nature of God): the head of Christ is God
4–7	Nature/contemporary practice: head coverings, hair length
8–9	Creation order: woman created *from* and *for* the man (Genesis 2)
10	Angels (delighting in God's order, present at church's worship?)
11–12	Nature/logic (balancing truth, conciliation): man born of woman
13–16	Nature/contemporary practice: head coverings, hair length

In enunciating the general principle underlying his instructions, Paul provides an analogy between the husband-wife (or male-female) relationship and that of God/Christ and Christ/man: "But I want you to understand that the head of every man is Christ, the head of a wife is her husband, and the head of Christ is God" (1 Cor. 11:3).[19] It should be noted that some deny that Christ is subordinate to God the Father,

[18] Thomas R. Schreiner, "Head Coverings, Prophecies, and the Trinity: 1 Corinthians 11:2–16," in *Recovering Biblical Manhood and Womanhood: A Response to Biblical Feminism*, ed. John Piper and Wayne Grudem (Wheaton, IL: Crossway, 1991), 124–39, provides a detailed discussion of this passage.
[19] In his discussion of the passage, Michael F. Bird (*Bourgeois Babes, Bossy Wives, and Bobby Haircuts: A Case for Gender Equality in Ministry*, Fresh Perspectives on Women in Ministry [Grand Rapids, MI: Zondervan, 2014], n.p.) contends that the order of the couplets (Christ/man, then husband/wife, and finally God/Christ) "does not lend itself to a hierarchy from the Father at the top with women at the bottom." Later in the same paragraph, he acknowledges that "there is indeed a hierarchy of relations between the persons mentioned in the various couplets" but that this needs to be understood in light of the gospel

but this seems to be clearly taught in the present passage. What's more, later on in the same letter, Paul writes, "When all things are subjected to him, then the Son himself will also be subjected to him who put all things in subjection under him, that God may be all in all" (1 Cor. 15:28). The latter passage indicates that there's a sense in which Christ will submit to God the Father even at the end of time without compromising his unity with the Father in his essential being. Clearly, the Son's submission to the Father doesn't entail any personal inferiority on his part, so there's likewise no reason why the woman's submission to the man should indicate any inferiority of person.

Verses 4–7. Verses 4–7, then, get into hairstyles. What's the argument here?[20] The head covering has to do with authority, shame, and dishonor.[21] There was apparently some dilution of gender differences conveyed by men wearing their hair long and women wearing their hair short (vv. 5–6). Paul wants women to wear head coverings because this reflects the intended relationship and roles of men and women toward each other. Paul's argument here should be understood in light of Genesis 1–2. Creation in God's image doesn't remove the role distinctions between men and women. The man received the command not to eat from the Tree of the Knowledge of Good and Evil directly from God while the woman received the command through the man. There's a difference in terms of relationship and immediacy. The man honors God by being properly submitted to him while the woman honors God by being properly submitted to her husband (similar to the way in which an employee reports to a manager while the manager reports directly to the CEO of the company).[22] This pattern was instituted not because of any intrinsic

---

where Paul affirms mutuality, reciprocity, and the value of others. However, this is a rather confusing way of putting things and seems to amount to special pleading.
[20] For an interesting background study, see Bruce Winter, *Roman Wives, Roman Widows: The Appearance of New Women and the Pauline Communities* (Grand Rapids, MI: Eerdmans, 2003), who argues that beginning in the first century AD, across the Roman Empire a new kind of woman emerged whose provocative dress and sometimes promiscuous lifestyle stood in stark contrast to the decorum of the traditional married woman. The presence of this new kind of woman was also felt in the early church where Christian wives and widows were urged to emulate neither her dress code nor her way of life.
[21] Shame and honor were important cultural dynamics in first-century culture (see further the discussion of 1 Cor. 14:33b–36 below). They are still significant in many cultures today. For relevant bibliographical references, see John J. Pilch, "Honor and Shame," *Oxford Bibliographies*, http://www.oxford bibliographies.com/view/document/obo-9780195393361/obo-9780195393361-0077.xml (accessed June 28, 2013).
[22] Obviously, this analogy breaks down when pressed too far. We're not suggesting that conducting a marriage is the same as working for a company, nor are we proposing that a wife "report" to her hus-

merit on the man's part. It was simply God's way of designing the male-female relationship.

Verses 8–9. In verses 8–9 Paul again echoes Genesis 2, contending that the woman's purpose is essentially oriented toward the man. Rather than arguing that authority and submission are completely interchangeable, Paul affirms the difference and distinctness of male and female in the creation order and the divine purpose for the man and the woman. This renders the position problematic that male headship is merely a result of the fall, because it sets Paul's words in the present passage in conflict with God's created order. Also, it becomes clear that 1 Timothy 2:9–15 is not the only passage that supports a continuing distinction between male and female roles. Rather, as we've seen, not only 1 Corinthians 11 but in fact the entire sweep of the biblical theology of manhood and womanhood supports such an understanding.

In the present passage, Paul first addresses the issue in terms of human tradition and identifies female head coverings as the cultural expression of the abiding principle of women's submission to male authority. He then proceeds to discuss the deeper principle of headship, even invoking the analogy of Trinitarian relationships. In this regard, Paul adduces the wearing of head coverings as an appropriate cultural expression of that deeper principle. Then he grounds this practice in God's purpose in creating man and woman. Again, note that Paul grounds the principle of headship in God's original creation, not the fall. This clearly contradicts the common proposal that male headship is solely a result of the fall.

Verse 10. In verse 10 Paul adds that the symbol or sign of authority women ought to wear on their heads is required also "because of the angels." It's hard to know how to understand this rather oblique reference. Fortunately, the precise identification of the nature of this reference isn't essential to understanding the broader teaching on headship and submission in this passage. The verse requires a certain degree of reading between the lines. What would the Corinthian believers have understood by the reference to the angels? That's hard to know. It's possible that Paul here refers to angels who observe our worship

---

band the way he reports to his boss at work. If we practiced that kind of marriage, we probably wouldn't still be married. Still, there is an analogy in terms of direct vs. indirect submission to authority.

and delight in seeing the order of creation maintained.[23] There's also a sense in which the angels are spectators watching the progression of history and the restoration of all things under Christ's authority.

Verses 11–12. In verses 11–12 Paul affirms the interdependence of men and women in order to balance his previous affirmation of the man's authority over woman in verses 8–9. Both men and women, as those made in the image of God, were created to partner together in fulfilling God's creation mandate of multiplying and subduing the earth. Paul's affirmation here is not that there is no human authority or need for submission but that, in the end, all people are under God's rule. This implies that men must not be proud or arrogant about their God-given position of leadership but should exercise it in humility and for the benefit of others.

Verses 13–16. In verses 13–15 Paul adduces an argument from nature, while verse 16 indicates that some in the Corinthian church were inclined to argue about Paul's teaching concerning the importance of head coverings. In response, Paul states that if anyone is contentious, he (Paul) has only been presenting what is the custom in all the churches. This final appeal adds to the creation order argument and the natural commonsense reasoning used by Paul. Just in case the readers weren't persuaded by his earlier pleas, he urges them to agree because there was no other custom in Paul's day. The wearing of head coverings was established practice among the churches and conveyed the important principle of proper submission to God-ordained authority.

But what was the head covering? Was it women's hair? If so, did the Corinthian women wear their hair loose and flowing down their backs? Thomas Schreiner rejects this possibility and instead suggests that the head covering consisted of some sort of shawl (though not a veil or a hat).[24] Most likely, women did wear some sort of physical object upon their heads in addition to their hair. This is still common today in some cultures. In any case, the main principle isn't materially affected by the exact nature of the head covering. If women fail to give tangible expression of their submission to (male) authority, they may be perceived as nonsubmissive.

---

[23] Cf. Schreiner, "Head Coverings, Prophecies, and the Trinity," 136.
[24] Ibid., 126.

The issue of head coverings was only one of many problems in the Corinthian church. We know that the church was divided into different factions (chaps. 1–4). The Corinthians had questions about the legitimacy (or even superiority) of singleness and eating food sacrificed to idols, and the list goes on and on. Many of the issues Paul addresses have to do with authority. With regard to spiritual gifts, Paul contends that God isn't a God of disorder but of peace and stipulates that everything should be done with decency and in order (1 Cor. 14:40; cf. 14:9). Paul isn't merely concerned with female submission to male authority but also with proper submission to ecclesiastical and civil authority. This was an important part of God's creation order and brought honor to God.

Summary

In 1 Corinthians 11:2–6 Paul addresses yet another issue brought to his attention by some in the Corinthian church. Apparently, some women refused to wear a head covering, which in that culture conveyed submission to male authority. These women's refusal to wear "[a symbol of] authority on their head" thus was likely perceived as lack of submission. In response, Paul affirmed that head coverings should be worn, both because this was in keeping with common practice and because a more abiding principle was at stake: proper submission to God's created order.

Paul's teaching in 1 Corinthians 11 is perfectly congruent with the male pattern of leadership identified in the Old Testament as well as in the Gospels and Acts. In the present instance, Paul urges female submission to male authority in the church yet with active female participation in worship.[25] Women are to worship and pray at the church's worship gatherings yet in such a way that they express their submission to male leadership in the church. This provides a powerful example of humanity as created male and female with differences in role as persons created by God for a distinctive purpose.

---

[25] Wright, "Women's Service," 6–9, reduces the message of 1 Corinthians 11 to men and women "celebrating the genders God has given them." He argues for equality but not identity, affirming differences between the ministries of men and women within an egalitarian framework. However, while this may be part of Paul's message (v. 11), this construal hardly does justice to the consistent references to male authority throughout the passage (see esp. vv. 3, 7–10).

Weighing of Prophecy (1 Cor. 14:33b–36)

The next passage relevant to our discussion of male-female relationships is found a few chapters later in 1 Corinthians 14. After addressing the need for love (chap. 13) and the proper exercise of spiritual gifts in the church in general and of the gift of prophecy in particular (1 Cor. 14:1–33a), Paul concludes his discussion as follows:

> As in all the churches of the saints, the women should keep silent in the churches. For they are not permitted to speak, but should be in submission, as the Law also says. If there is anything they desire to learn, let them ask their husbands at home. For it is shameful for a woman to speak in church. Or was it from you that the word of God came? Or are you the only ones it has reached? (vv. 33b–36)

Paul's statement is rather startling and could easily be taken as insensitive (or worse), so we must be careful to discern his underlying intent.[26]

Admittedly, taken out of context Paul's words, "It is shameful for a woman to speak in church," sound repugnant. As David Garland explains, however, "shameful behavior" is relative to a given cultural context.[27] He elaborates, "The situation that best fits the adjective 'shameful' is one in which wives defy convention by publicly embarrassing their husbands through their speaking."[28] Specifically, "in the context, it is likely that Paul imagines a wife joining in the process of weighing what is being said during the congregational scrutiny of prophecy (14:29). . . . By doing so, they compromise their husband's authority over them and appear to undermine the good order of the household."[29] As in 1 Corinthians 11, the subject is prophecy. In context, Paul's command for women to refrain from speaking most likely concerns the evaluation of prophecies that had been uttered.

As we saw, 1 Corinthians 11 makes clear that women were in fact

---

[26] Some, such as Gordon Fee and Philip Payne, argue that 1 Cor. 14:34–35 wasn't part of the original text but represents a later interpolation. But see the recent study by Adam D. Hensley, "σιγάω, λαλέω and ὑποτάσσω in 1 Corinthians 14:34 in Their Literary and Rhetorical Context," *Journal of the Evangelical Theological Society* 55 (2012): 343–64, who convincingly responds to this claim. See also the similar critique by Schreiner, review of Payne, *Man and Woman, One in Christ*, 38–40.

[27] David E. Garland, *1 Corinthians*, Baker Exegetical Commentary on the New Testament (Grand Rapids, MI: Baker, 2003), 668.

[28] Ibid.

[29] Ibid.

prophesying in the church in Corinth, so there's no reason to think that Paul is prohibiting the act of prophesying itself. Rather, he's now moved on in his argument to address proper decorum in the evaluation of prophecy. In this regard, D. A. Carson contends, similar to Garland above, that "women, of course, may participate in such prophesying; . . . they may *not* participate in the oral weighing of such prophecies. . . . In that connection, they are not allowed to speak."[30] The prohibition obtained because the evaluation of prophecy was an authoritative function which within the framework articulated in 1 Corinthians 11 ought to be reserved for men. First Corinthians 14:33b–36 thus provides another specific application of the underlying abiding principle Paul discussed in 1 Corinthians 11:2–16.

Headship and Submission in Marriage (Eph. 5:21–33)

We turn now to one of the most important passages on our subject in the entire New Testament, Paul's words to husbands and wives in Ephesians 5:21–33. Paul wrote this letter to the church at Ephesus, a major city in the province of Asia Minor where he had spent three years establishing the church (see Acts 20:31). At the same time, the lack of personal references or greetings suggests that Ephesians is a circular letter intended to be read more widely by churches in the larger region. This underscores the broad applicability of its contents.[31] The teaching of Ephesians 5:21–6:9 is given in the form of a house table, a set of instructions issued to the members of a household in the Greco-Roman world, in which instructions were given first to the person in submission and then to the person in authority: wives/husbands (Eph. 5:22–33); children/parents (Eph. 6:1–4); and slaves/masters (Eph. 6:5–9).

In order to understand Ephesians 5:21–33 more fully, it'll be essential to study the passage in the context of the entire letter.[32] This will

---

[30] D. A. Carson, "'Silent in the Churches': On the Role of Women in 1 Corinthians 14:33b–36," in *Recovering Biblical Manhood and Womanhood*, 151.

[31] For a more detailed survey of the book of Ephesians, including its historical setting, literary aspects, and theological themes, see Köstenberger, Kellum, and Quarles, *The Cradle, the Cross, and the Crown*, chap. 14. For helpful discussions of the ancient background of Eph. 5:21–33, see Clinton E. Arnold, *Ephesians*, Exegetical Commentary on the New Testament (Grand Rapids, MI: Zondervan, 2010), 369–79, "In Depth: The Instructions to Family Members in Ephesians in Light of Ancient Household Codes"; and "In Depth: The Role of Wives in Roman-Era Ephesus and Western Asia Minor" (with further bibliographic references).

[32] Cf. Köstenberger with Jones, *God, Marriage, and Family*, 55–62.

require that we look at Paul's teaching on marriage against the larger backdrop of the message of Ephesians as a whole rather than simply looking at Ephesians 5:21–33 in isolation from the rest of the book, proof-texting, as it were, or engaging in mere topical study. As we'll see, this careful study of Paul's teaching on marriage in the context of the entire letter will yield rich insights that have the potential of revolutionizing our view of God's design for marriage and male-female relationships.

In the opening chapter of the book, Paul articulates God's larger plan for the ages which sets the framework within which God's plan for marriage is to be understood. Ephesians 1:9–10 and 21 are particularly important for rightly understanding Ephesians 5:21–33. Ephesians 1:9–10 presents God's overarching purpose in Christ as follows: "making known to us the mystery of his will, according to his purpose, which he set forth in Christ as a plan for the fullness of time, to bring all things back together again under Christ as the head, things in heaven and things on earth" (AT).[33] This may be the key verse in all of Ephesians and serves as Paul's thesis statement, the validity of which he seeks to demonstrate in the remainder of the letter. According to Paul, God's end-time goal is to bring everything back together again under the headship of Christ, and marriage under the husband's headship is an important part of God's overarching program.

Later in the same chapter, verse 21 makes clear that Christ is over every angelic or human authority—similar to Jesus's affirmation, "All authority in heaven and on earth has been given to me," in the Great Commission (Matt. 28:18)—and that God has subjected everything to his authority, having appointed him as the head (*kephalē*). At the present time, there are multiple authorities, but on the last day there'll be only one, the Lord Jesus Christ. He holds the position of ultimate authority and is head over all. These instances of *kephalē* terminology in chapter 1 set the stage for Paul's use of *kephalē* later on in the book, particularly in his description of the husband's headship in relation to his wife in Ephesians 5:21–33. Significantly, the latter passage needs to be understood in the larger context of Paul's affirmation in chapter 1

---

[33] The ESV translates the phrase "to unite all things in him," but this translation, while not necessarily inaccurate, obscures the fact that the underlying Greek word of "unite" is *anakephalaioō*, the first instance of *kephalē* vocabulary in the book.

that Christ is head over all and that one day all of creation will rightly acknowledge his authority.

Does the Bible Teach Mutual Submission?

Now that we've set the larger framework for understanding Paul's teaching on marriage in Ephesians 5:21–33, we're ready to look at this passage in greater detail. Paul's words, with their teaching on the husband's headship and the need for wives to submit to their husbands, pose a major difficulty for those who deny that Scripture teaches distinct and nonreversible male-female roles. How, then, are those interpreters able to reconcile Paul's teaching in the present passage with their belief that Scripture teaches undifferentiated male-female equality? The answer, in essence, is that at least some of these interpreters tend to interpret Paul's injunction in Ephesians 5:21 in terms of mutual submission. They acknowledge that Paul calls on wives to submit to their husbands but contend that husbands, too, in the same way must submit to their wives. Thus all believers should submit "to one another out of reverence for Christ." On the surface, this may appear to follow from a plain reading of Ephesians 5:21. A closer look reveals, however, that only a reading of Ephesians 5:21 in isolation from the rest of the letter and the verses that follow can yield such an erroneous conclusion.

Wayne Grudem, in a careful study, analyzes the "one another" language in the New Testament in general and in Ephesians in particular.[34] He concludes that "one another" denotes actions that are reciprocal but not necessarily mutual in the sense that both parties are called to do the exact same thing. For example, when Paul exhorts all Christians to forgive one another, this doesn't necessarily mean that in a given instance the roles of the sinning and the offended party are identical. To the contrary, one person sins against the other, and the other person is sinned against. Forgiving one another in such an instance involves the offending party asking for forgiveness and the offended party extending forgiveness to the person who sinned against them. An even more compelling example is a reference in the book of Revelation to people slaying one another (Rev. 6:4). Clearly, these people don't all kill each

---

[34] Wayne Grudem, "The Myth of Mutual Submission," *CBMW News* 1 (Fall 1996): 1, 3–4.

other at exactly the same time, but rather some are doing the killing while others are getting killed. Roles aren't identical but rather reciprocal in a broader sense.

What's the application of this insight to Ephesians 5:21? It's that Paul's command for husbands and wives to submit to each other doesn't necessarily imply identity of roles or mutual submission. Rather, Paul's injunction is for wives to submit to their husbands—note that husbands are never called to submit to their wives—and for husbands to be on the receiving end of their wives' submission (note also that the parallel in Col. 3:18 refers only to the wives' submission of husbands; no word of mutual submission here). Husbands, for their part, are later in the passage called to love their wives as Christ loved the church— certainly a tall order but not identical to wives' role of submitting to their husbands as the church submits to Christ. What's more, clearly Christ and the church don't practice mutual submission in terms of identical role assignments. The church submits to Christ, and Christ is the head over the church, exercising authority over it in a loving, self-sacrificial way.

Mutual submission in the sense of interchangeability of roles also doesn't work in the larger context of Ephesians 5:21, where Paul moves from wives to children to slaves, calling each group to submit to its respective authorities. Clearly, mutual submission is not a realistic option in the case of the two other kinds of relationships in view, that of child-parent and that of slave-master. How would it work for children and parents, or for slaves and masters, to practice mutual submission? In such a scenario, would children and parents discipline each other if one group (say, the parents) was disobedient? If no one's in a position of authority, the entire edifice begins to crumble. However, consistency would seem to demand that we interpret the first pair (wives/husbands) in the same way as the two following pairs (children/ parents, slaves/masters).

Admittedly, the word used for children's submission to parents is a different Greek word (*hypakouō*)[35] than that employed for wives' submission to their husbands. This seems to indicate a different type of

---

[35]Though note that the same word is used for Sarah submitting to Abraham in 1 Pet. 3:6. In fact, both *hypotassō* (1 Pet. 3:5) and *hypakouō* (1 Pet. 3:6) are used in that passage, apparently interchangeably.

submission, at least by degree, but it doesn't negate the fact that the word used for wives submitting to their husbands likewise conveys subordination to a person in authority (*hypotassō*). Similarly, it seems highly unlikely that Paul would have enjoined slaves and masters to practice mutual submission in a first-century context. Even in our twenty-first-century context, it would be highly uncommon, to say the least, for employers and employees to practice mutual submission. More likely, Paul first sets down the overarching principle—submission to authority—and then specifies that in each of the three types of relationship he adduces, one group should submit to the authority of the other: wives to husbands, children to parents, and slaves to masters.[36]

The biblical message of submission is deeply countercultural and incompatible with the deep-seated egalitarianism, with its individualism and emphasis on personal freedom and inalienable personal rights pervading our culture. Countercultural positions call for courage. Submission is generally stereotyped and caricatured in our culture and given a very negative connotation. This is the case even though submission is found everywhere in our culture. Our lives are full of instances in which we are called to practice submission: our employers, the Internal Revenue Service, the police, and other local and federal authorities. Unfortunately, there's also a pervasive negative attitude toward these institutions (in part, this is related to the abuse of authority; in other cases, it's a function of our human sinfulness and reluctance to submit to anyone). At best, cultural dispositions toward authority tend toward ambivalence. People are resigned to the fact that you can't live with authority very well, but you can't very well live without it either. To adapt Winston Churchill's adage concerning democracy, authority may be the worst part of human relationships except all the other forms of relating that have been tried.[37] Nevertheless, it's important to understand that opposition to wives' submission in marriage, while at times exegetically grounded, often stems not from a biblical lack of clarity but from powerful cultural forces.

---

[36] This, as mentioned, doesn't mean that these three relationships are the same in every respect. It's only a matter of common sense that a marriage relationship is different from a parent-child or employer-employee relationship. But the "submission to authority" principle obtains in each.
[37] The actual quote is, "It has been said that democracy is the worst form of government except all the others that have been tried."

Ephesians 5:21–33 Read in Context

We've already seen that the purpose statement in Ephesians 1:9–10 establishes the overall framework for Paul's teaching on marriage in chapter 5. Ephesians 1:9–10 is one of at least three passages that are absolutely vital for understanding the full import of Ephesians 5:21–33. The other two passages are Ephesians 5:18 and Ephesians 6:10–18. These three passages inform the larger, immediately preceding, and immediately following context of Ephesians 5:21–33. In order to get a full-orbed view, we'll briefly recapitulate the comments on Ephesians 1:9–10 above and then proceed to a succinct presentation of Ephesians 5:18 and Ephesians 6:10–18 so that we can place Ephesians 5:21–33 in its immediate context in the book of Ephesians as a whole.[38]

Ephesians 1:9–10. Put succinctly, Ephesians 1:9–10 indicates that headship and submission are part of God's purpose of restoring all things under Christ's headship in the present age with a view toward the age to come. Christ is the head, and under his headship there is proper order—reflective of God's original design—in the marriage relationship. Christ's headship is to be emulated in marriage by the two marriage partners in the context of their respective, complementary roles.

Ephesians 5:18. Instead of beginning the investigation of Ephesians 5:21–33 with verse 21, the discussion should begin with verse 18. The original Greek lacks punctuation so that verse 21 is connected to the command to be filled with the Spirit in verse 18 by way of a participle (*hypotassomenoi,* "submitting"). The HCSB gives a hint of this by marking all of Ephesians 5:19–21 as poetry. The entire passage flows from the command in verse 18 to be filled with the Spirit. Paul's command to submit to husbands is addressed to Spirit-filled wives, and the command to love wives as Christ loved the church is addressed to Spirit-filled husbands. If the husband and wife are not Spirit-filled, they won't be able to live out their marriage relationship in the way God intended. Even if husband and wife agree with the rightness of the command directed to them, without the Spirit's empowerment they

---

[38] For a careful study of Eph. 5:21–33, see Arnold, *Ephesians,* 363–410. See also George W. Knight III, "Husbands and Wives as Analogues of Christ and the Church: Ephesians 5:21–33 and Colossians 3:18–19," in *Recovering Biblical Manhood and Womanhood,* 165–78.

won't be able to obey it from the heart. The imperative in verse 18 to "be filled with the Spirit" is fleshed out in corporate worship and in proper submission in various relationships (wives/husbands, children/parents, slaves/masters).

"Paul's command to submit to husbands is addressed to Spirit-filled wives, and the command to love wives as Christ loved the church is addressed to Spirit-filled husbands. If the husband and wife are not Spirit-filled, they won't be able to live out their marriage relationship in the way God intended."

Ephesians 6:10–18. Following Paul's instructions concerning submission, the apostle in verses 10–18 calls on believers to put on the full armor of God, reminding them that their battle is not against flesh and blood but spiritual in nature. Paul's injunction here shouldn't be read in isolation from his immediately preceding comments regarding marriage, parenting, and behavior in the workplace, because Paul's discussion of these relationships and his remarks regarding spiritual warfare are closely related. Should people put on the armor of God as isolated individuals? No, they should do so as wives, husbands, parents, children, slaves, or masters.

Believers' enemy is not their spouse, their parents, or their employer, or any other human being. Ever since the Serpent approached Eve in the garden and she and Adam succumbed to temptation, marriage relationships are perennially lived out in the context of spiritual warfare.[39] Because Satan wages war against God's plan for marriage and the family, Christ's Spirit-filled disciples must put on the full armor of God so as to be properly protected against the Devil's assaults.

As we go about living our lives in keeping with the roles God has assigned to us, whether husband or wife, father or mother, child, employer or employee, we must habitually and persistently put on this spiritual frame of mind in light of actual spiritual realities (cf. 2 Cor. 10:3–5). This mind-set, our passage seems to insist, includes a joyful and willing acknowledgment of God's sovereign design of relationships, an order that is founded on the principle of proper submission to authority—not, as mentioned, as an end in itself, but as a means to an end: the glory of God the creator and of our loving head, the Lord Jesus Christ.

---

[39] See the discussion of the Genesis fall narrative in chap. 1 above.

Application

It's hard for a man to tell a woman that she needs to submit, because it seems as if the man is trying to impose this pattern upon the woman. Nevertheless, Scripture clearly teaches that wives should submit to their husbands. Biblical submission is not a harsh thing, nor is it something the man has to earn or deserves. Rather, his role of authority is sovereignly assigned to the man by God. Scripture never particularly defends the ideas of submission and authority; it just presents these realities as the way things are in God's created order. As mentioned, however, much of American society is highly ambivalent toward the notion of authority. There's a grudging acknowledgment that authority is necessary in the form of government, police, or teachers, but it's often viewed as a necessary evil. As Christians, we can joyfully affirm that authority, as God created it, is a good thing. This is how God has structured the world because he is a God of order. Submission and authority aren't just part of the male-female relationship; they're found throughout all of God's creation.

The opening chapter of the book of Genesis sets forth God's order in creation. God separates and assigns different domains, boundaries, and habitats to every part of his creation. Many in our culture are committed to a different kind of order, egalitarianism, in which equality serves as a non-

"As Christians, we can joyfully affirm that authority, as God created it, is a good thing. This is how God has structured the world because he is a God of order. Submission and authority aren't just part of the male-female relationship; they're found throughout all of God's creation."

negotiable bedrock principle. Unfortunately, however, this egalitarian principle militates against God's foundational principle of order in the form of authority and submission. At the same time, God's order doesn't give those in authority—whether husbands, parents, or the government—the right to exercise their God-given authority in an arbitrary or God-dishonoring manner. Scripture doesn't frame human relationships in terms of rights but in terms of God's created order.

By contrast, in much of our cultural discourse, the language of "rights" has replaced the language of order if not morality. Evangelical and other feminists typically eschew the notion of hierarchy, which is understandable if all forms of human authority are understood in

188 God's Design for Man and Woman

top-down, military-style command-and-obey terms. But, as we've seen, this stereotype is unfortunately misleading, unduly simplistic, and biblically unwarranted. While authority can be (and, in this sinful world, often is) abused, Scripture presents authority not only as a fact of life but also as a pervasive and integral part of God's creation. In fact, as our study of Ephesians 5 has shown, the submission of wives to husbands is but one small part of a much bigger picture, God's full-orbed creation order in and through the Lord Jesus Christ.[40]

What's more, while the man's headship in the home and the church entails authority, Scripture presents this authority within the context of a husband's or male church leader's *care and responsibility*. Husbands are to love their wives and care for them (Eph. 5:25–30). Elders are to exercise their leadership in a way that's "not domineering over those in your charge, but being examples to the flock" (1 Pet. 5:3), in keeping with Jesus's words that leadership ought to be defined primarily as service and sacrifice for others (Mark 10:45; see also vv. 42–43).

Yet balance is important here. Servant leadership is biblical, but not leadership that is drained of all notions of authority.[41] Consider, for example, the following passages of Scripture: "Obey your leaders and

---

[40] See, e.g., the subtitle of the standard egalitarian work *Discovering Biblical Equality: Complementarity without Hierarchy*, ed. Ronald W. Pierce and Rebecca Merrill Groothuis (Downers Grove, IL: InterVarsity, 2004). Regarding the phrase "submit in everything," see the study by Steven R. Tracy, "What Does 'Submit in Everything' Really Mean? The Nature and Scope of Marital Submission," *Trinity Journal* 29NS (2008): 267–312. On pp. 306–12, Tracy suggests these Bible-based limits to submission. A wife must not submit to her husband when obedience to him would (1) violate a biblical principle (not just a direct biblical statement); (2) compromise her relationship with Christ; (3) violate her conscience; (4) compromise the care, nurture, and protection of her children; and (5) enable (facilitate) her husband's sin. In addition, (6) a wife must not submit to physical, sexual, or emotional abuse. However, see the review by Heath Lambert in *Journal of Biblical Manhood and Womanhood* 15, no. 1 (2010): 285–312; and the strong cautions registered by Clinton E. Arnold, *Ephesians*, Zondervan Exegetical Commentary on the New Testament (Grand Rapids, MI: Zondervan, 2010), 403, who says with regard to Tracy's third criterion that what a wife may determine to be a "violation of her conscience" may in fact be "a matter of her own personal preference or even a manifestation of her own self-centeredness."

[41] This is insufficiently recognized by William and Aída Spencer and Steve and Celestia Tracy, *Marriage at the Crossroads: Couples in Conversation about Discipleship, Gender Roles, Decision Making, and Intimacy* (Downers Grove, IL: InterVarsity, 2009). While one would expect the Spencers, as egalitarians, to espouse mutual submission, the Tracys, too, while claiming to be more traditional (calling themselves "soft complementarians"), unfortunately drain male leadership in marriage of all meaningful authority, saying they believe only in an "authority of love." See the review by Heath Lambert in *Journal of Biblical Manhood and Womanhood* 18 (Spring 2013): 36–38.

An even more extreme position is advocated by Alan G. Padgett, *As Christ Submits to the Church: A Biblical Understanding of Leadership and Mutual Submission* (Grand Rapids, MI: Baker Academic, 2011), who advances the notion, contradicted by Eph. 5:24 ("Now *as the church submits to Christ*, so also wives should submit in everything to their husbands"), that Christ submits to the church. Padgett argues that the term "submit" (*hypotassō*) in the NT almost always refers to "mutual submission." However, it's widely recognized that the term means "to take a subordinate role in relation to another." See the review by Denny Burk, *Journal of Biblical Manhood and Womanhood* 17 (Fall 2012): 50–52.

submit to them, for they are keeping watch over your souls, as those who will have to give an account" (Heb. 13:17). Leaders are accountable, but they have real authority to which others are called to submit: "Respect those who labor among you and are over you in the Lord and admonish you" (1 Thess. 5:12). Elders are to "rule well"; if they do, they are worthy of special honor (1 Tim. 5:17; cf. 1 Tim. 3:4–5). God's design exhibits admirable balance that we must strive to emulate.

Table 5.4: New Testament References to the Authority of Church Leaders (Selected List)

"Respect those who . . . are over you."	1 Thess. 5:12
"Let the elders who rule well be considered worthy of double honor."	1 Tim. 5:17
"Obey your leaders and submit to them."	Heb. 13:17

Table 5.5: New Testament References to the Care and Responsibility of Church Leaders (Selected List)

"For even the Son of Man came not to be served but to serve, and to give his life as a ransom for many."	Mark 10:45
"Pay careful attention to yourselves and to all the flock, in which the Holy Spirit has made you overseers, to care for the church of God."	Acts 20:28
"Shepherd the flock of God . . . exercising oversight."	1 Pet. 5:2

As we've seen, the teaching of Ephesians 5:21–6:9 is given in the form of a "house table," instructions addressed to the particular members of a given household in which guidelines were first issued to the person in submission and after this to those in authority: wives/husbands, children/parents, and slaves/masters. Neither wives and husbands, nor children and parents, nor slaves and masters are to practice "mutual submission." Rather, wives should submit to their husbands, while the latter are to love their wives (Eph. 5:25–29). Thus marital roles are complementary but not interchangeable.

We've also seen that the claims that the word for "head" (*kephalē*) denotes source rather than authority and that Ephesians 5:21 and the following verses should be understood in terms of "mutual submission" lack adequate biblical support. The use of *kephalē* in Ephesians 1:21–22 indicates that Jesus has authority over angels and demons, not merely that he's their source, and Ephesians 5:22–23 makes clear that the submission in marriage Paul has in view is from one group (wives) to another (husbands).

Implications

In this chapter, we've engaged in a study of some of the most important passages in Paul's writings regarding God's design for men and women, both with regard to their inclusion in the church and with regard to male-female identity and roles. We've seen that Galatians 3:28, with its emphasis on male-female unity in the church on the common ground of our salvation in Christ, is exceedingly important in establishing parity with regard to church membership but that the passage doesn't address the question of male or female participation in roles of church leadership.

First Corinthians 11:2–16 and 14:33b–36, on the other hand, did contribute to our understanding of Paul's teaching on men's and women's roles in the church by setting forth God's creation order entailing male leadership and female submission to male authority in the church. Ephesians 5:21–33, then, was shown to extend this principle also to the marriage relationship. In fact, we've seen that the husband-wife relationship is part of a much larger purpose, that is, reestablishing proper lines of authority in all of God's creation under the ultimate authority of the Lord Jesus Christ.

Now that we've completed our study of the first ten letters Paul wrote, we're over two-thirds through our study of Paul's teaching on the roles of men and women. It remains for us to scrutinize several relevant passages to our subject in the last three letters Paul wrote, the so-called Pastoral Epistles. So far, Paul's teaching has turned out to be in perfect harmony with the pattern of male leadership found in the Old Testament, Jesus's teaching and practice, and the life of the early church. Will it be borne out also by his teaching in the letters to Timothy and Titus?

Key Resources

Carson, D. A. "'Silent in the Churches': On the Role of Women in 1 Corinthians 14:33b–36." In *Recovering Biblical Manhood and Womanhood: A Response to Evangelical Feminism*, edited by John Piper and Wayne Grudem, 140–53. Wheaton, IL: Crossway, 1991.

Grudem, Wayne. "Does *kephalē* ('Head') Mean 'Source' or 'Authority Over' in Greek Literature? A Survey of 2,336 Examples." *Trinity Journal* 6NS (1985): 38–59.

———. "Wives Like Sarah, and the Husbands Who Honor Them: 1 Peter 3:1–7." In *Recovering Biblical Manhood and Womanhood: A Response to Evangelical Feminism*, edited by John Piper and Wayne Grudem, 194–208. Wheaton, IL: Crossway, 1991.

Hove, Richard. *Equality in Christ? Galatians 3:28 and the Gender Dispute*. Wheaton, IL: Crossway, 1999.

Knight, George W., III. "Husbands and Wives as Analogues of Christ and the Church: Ephesians 5:21–33 and Colossians 3:18–19." In *Recovering Biblical Manhood and Womanhood: A Response to Evangelical Feminism*, edited by John Piper and Wayne Grudem, 165–78. Wheaton, IL: Crossway, 1991.

Köstenberger, Andreas J., with David W. Jones. *God, Marriage, and Family: Rebuilding the Biblical Foundation*. 2nd ed. Wheaton, IL: Crossway, 2010. Chap. 3.

Ng, Esther Yue L. "Phoebe as *Prostatis*." *Trinity Journal* 25NS (2004): 3–13.

Schreiner, Thomas R. "Head Coverings, Prophecies, and the Trinity: 1 Corinthians 11:2–16." In *Recovering Biblical Manhood and Womanhood: A Response to Evangelical Feminism*, edited by John Piper and Wayne Grudem, 124–39. Wheaton, IL: Crossway, 1991.

6

Paul's Legacy

Letters to Timothy and Titus

> I do not permit a woman to teach or to exercise authority over a man. . . . Therefore an overseer must be above reproach, the husband of one wife . . .
>
> —1 Timothy 2:12; 3:2

> Train the young women to love their husbands and children, to be self-controlled, pure, working at home, kind, and submissive to their own husbands, that the word of God may not be reviled.
>
> —Titus 2:4–5

Key Points

1. First Timothy 2:12 indicates that Paul didn't allow women to serve as elders or overseers, including pastor-teachers, in local churches.
2. In 1 Timothy 2:15, "saved" likely doesn't refer to salvation in our traditional, religious sense but rather to spiritual preservation, and "childbearing" most likely refers to a woman's broader domestic sphere, so a woman is understood to be protected spiritually by committing herself and living out her role in the family and domestic sphere.
3. The "one-wife husband" requirement of church leaders in 1 Timothy 3:2 and 12 and Titus 1:6 refers to marital faithfulness and isn't directly aimed at addressing single, divorced, or polygamous candidates for elder, so candidates for church office must be examined as to their present faithfulness in marriage.

4. First Timothy 3:11 may refer to female deacons, a nonteaching, non-authoritative, servant role, which the early church likely practiced (e.g., Phoebe); if so, women are biblically permitted to serve as deaconesses. Since this is a servant role, churches are free to encourage qualified women in this regard without compromising scriptural guidelines for male leadership.
5. Titus 2:3–5 contains instructions for older women in the church to train and mentor young women, particularly in their relationship to their husbands, children, and role in the home.

Imagine yourself planting a new church. You're committed to following the Bible in everything you do in your church. You want everyone to feel welcome, though you're persuaded from Scripture that the true church of Christ is made up only of those who have repented of their sin, placed their trust in Christ, and been born again by the Spirit (Rom. 8:9; 1 Cor. 12:13). You also believe that Scripture teaches plurality of local church leadership in the form of a team of pastors or elders and allows for (though does not demand) a group of deacons to help with meeting a variety of congregational needs. But what, you wonder, should be done about the roles of pastor, elder, and deacon in your new church? Should only men occupy these roles, in keeping with the biblical teaching that men are to serve as leaders in their natural households? Or should the default assumption be that men and women are equally eligible for such roles?

Good questions. No sitting on the fence possible here.

In our study thus far, we've endeavored to trace the biblical theology of manhood and womanhood through Scripture. We've tried to get a sense of the biblical teaching in its totality by looking at relevant passages in the Old Testament, the Gospels, the book of Acts, and several passages in Paul's first ten letters where the apostle discusses male-female identity and roles. In particular, we saw that interpreting Ephesians 5 within the context of the entire letter clarifies Paul's teaching on submission and headship. Christ is the ultimate head, and everything in this universe is in the process of being placed under his headship once again. Christians at the present time embody Christ's headship by exercising authority as Christ does and by submitting to authority as the church does.

In this chapter, we'll continue our journey by looking at the primary passages in the letters to Timothy and Titus that relate directly to our subject.[1] We'll single out the following six passages for closer attention: (1) 1 Timothy 2:12, where Paul addresses the issue of women teaching or having authority over men in the church; (2) 1 Timothy 2:15, which speaks to women's God-given family and domestic responsibilities; (3) 1 Timothy 3:2 and 12, stipulating that church leaders be faithful husbands; (4) 1 Timothy 3:4–5, requiring that church leaders manage their own households well; (5) 1 Timothy 3:11, which in the context of establishing qualifications for office holders in the church provides instructions on women deacons or deacons' wives; and (6) Titus 2:3–5, which addresses the need for older women in the church to train young women.

Should Women Teach or Have Authority in the Church? (1 Tim. 2:12)

In the context of establishing qualifications for church leaders (see 1 Timothy 3), Paul writes to Timothy, "I do not permit a woman to teach or to exercise authority over a man; rather, she is to remain quiet" (1 Tim. 2:12).[2] First Timothy 2:9–15 poses a difficulty for those who argue for undifferentiated male-female roles in the church on biblical grounds. Nevertheless, the argument that Scripture teaches male-female differences in role (particularly with regard to church leadership) is regularly challenged or ignored in the general culture. In our culture, a person doesn't have to work very hard to convince people of the egalitarian viewpoint because, by and large, many in the Western world are already predisposed toward this view.

The burden, it appears, is largely to show why the church ought not to go the way of the general culture. Increasingly, those advocat-

---

[1] In the following discussion, we'll assume the Pauline authorship of the letters to Timothy and Titus. For a recent scholarly defense, see Eckhard J. Schnabel, "Paul, Timothy, and Titus: The Assumption of a Pseudonymous Author and of Pseudonymous Recipients in the Light of Literary, Theological, and Historical Evidence," in *Do Historical Matters Matter to Faith?*, ed. J. K. Hoffmeier and D. R. Magary (Wheaton, IL: Crossway, 2012), 383–403. See also Andreas J. Köstenberger, L. Scott Kellum, and Charles L. Quarles, *The Cradle, the Cross, and the Crown: An Introduction to the New Testament* (Nashville: B&H Academic, 2009), 639–42 (with further bibliographic references).

[2] Andreas has dealt with this passage in more detail in his article "The Crux of the Matter: Paul's Pastoral Pronouncements Regarding Women's Roles in 1 Timothy 2:9–15," *Faith and Mission* 14 (1997): 24–48 (repr. as chap. 12 in Andreas J. Köstenberger, *Studies in John and Gender: A Decade of Scholarship*, Studies in Biblical Literature [New York: Peter Lang, 2001]), http://www.biblicalfoundations.org/wp-content/uploads/2012/01/09-Crux.pdf (accessed June 28, 2013).

ing God-given, male-female role distinctions are portrayed as behind the times. In fact, the growing rejection of the biblical teaching on male-female relationships in our culture may increasingly turn into persecution for which believers ought to brace themselves, because the biblical texts won't change. Those affirming male-female role distinctions may increasingly be caricatured as dogmatic, intolerant individuals who are out to suppress and oppress women. Such believers ought not to be afraid or forced to apologize for what the Bible teaches regarding God's design for human relationships as they understand it.

Today, some evangelicals in the church claim to use the same approach to hermeneutics as careful Bible students while arriving at diametrically opposite interpretations. However, their claim that they've discovered undifferentiated male-female equality in Scripture apart from the influence of feminism on the general culture is curious. Demonstrably, the rise of egalitarian interpretation follows the surge of feminism in the larger culture.[3] Let's remember that a study on a topic such as ours can hardly be neutral. It takes place in a cultural environment that has a profound impact on discussions in the church. This may explain why a passage that seems fairly innocuous at the outset has become the bone of considerable contention in recent years.

The Framework for Interpreting 1 Timothy 2:12

Paul most likely wrote 1 Timothy between his two Roman imprisonments. The first one was a light imprisonment, resembling a house arrest; the second one was severe and eventually issued in his martyrdom. This was a window of opportunity in which the aging apostle labored to prepare the church for his departure. He had left Timothy in Ephesus, where he'd invested three years planting the church, to deal with false teachers, establish qualifications for church leaders, remove sinning elders, teach sound doctrine, and serve as a model of godliness for the believers there. In Acts 19 we read about Paul preaching the gospel for two years daily in the hall of Tyrannus and the Lord performing extraordinary miracles through the hands of the apostle.

---

[3] See Robert W. Yarbrough, "Progressive and Historic: The Hermeneutics of 1 Timothy 2:9–15," in *Women in the Church*, 2nd ed., ed. Andreas J. Köstenberger and Thomas R. Schreiner (Grand Rapids, MI: Baker, 2005), 133–39.

We also hear of some who burned their magic books (worth fifty thousand pieces of silver!), as well as of Demetrius, a silversmith who made silver shrines of Artemis (whose temple was a major landmark in the city), who stirred up a riot against Paul that the Asiarchs (rulers of the city) deflected with some difficulty. Clearly, planting a church in Ephesus was no easy task, and Paul no doubt kept a close eye on the church after he left the city.[4]

Cultural Background: First-Century Ephesus

Let's now take a look at the relevant ancient background for Paul's first letter to Timothy. S. M. Baugh has conducted a thorough survey of first-century Ephesus based on ancient inscriptions and other data.[5] The city had a natural harbor and a royal road up the Maeander River valley, both of which made it an ideal place for commerce and trade. Some myths had it that the mysterious female Amazons had founded the city, which some have cited as evidence for Ephesus's alleged feminist character. The Ephesians themselves, however, ascribed founding the city to a Greek male hero named Androclus. Politically, the city's life was controlled by monarchs, tyrants, satraps, proconsuls, and bureaucrats, but never by radical democrats. Thus "Ephesus never adopted an egalitarian democratic ideology that would necessitate feminism or, minimally, the inclusion of women in public offices."[6]

In Paul's day, the city's political climate was Roman, not feminist. The Roman emperor Augustus inaugurated a golden age of peace and prosperity that lasted two centuries. Augustus himself stopped at Ephesus after vanquishing his foes at the battle of Actium (31 BC), confirming the city as provincial capital. With a population of about one hundred thousand, the city was poised to become one of the largest and most prominent cities in the whole empire. Baugh proceeds to survey first-century Ephesus's political institutions, showing that even though women had some public roles, "leadership in the political and social spheres was solidly in the hands of exclusively male

---

[4] For more information on the background to 1 Timothy, see Köstenberger, Kellum, and Quarles, *The Cradle, the Cross, and the Crown*, chap. 15.
[5] S. M. Baugh, "A Foreign World: Ephesus in the First Century," in *Women in the Church*, 13–38.
[6] Ibid., 17.

198 God's Design for Man and Woman

institutions."[7] The religious climate was dominated by the Artemis cult, centered in the Artemisium, the largest building in the Greek world (four times larger than the Athenian Parthenon). Nevertheless, the cult hierarchy of Artemis Ephesia was controlled by the male political establishment. Baugh also shows that Artemis was not a fertility goddess or mother deity who sponsored the religious or social superiority of Ephesian women.

Was Paul Addressing First-Century Feminism?

Was there anything special about the specific historical location of Ephesus in the first century in support of arguments that Paul is addressing here a unique situation? As we've seen, S. M. Baugh shows on the basis of extensive research, including a plethora of first-century AD inscriptions from the area, that Ephesus was a typical society in the ancient world.[8] There was little (if anything) unique or particularly feminist about first-century Ephesus. Inscriptions would typically acknowledge rulers, city officials, or donors and would be found on buildings and various other places. Baugh shows that there was nothing about first-century Ephesus that would have required Paul to address a particular problem there that wouldn't have been present also in many of the other major cities in the Greco-Roman world of the first century.[9]

Some claim that Ephesus was uniquely proto-feminist in light of the fact that goddess worship was practiced there in the form of the Artemis cult.[10] However, the argument that the presence of goddess worship in the ancient world inexorably leads to female leadership in society just doesn't hold up. Just because men worshiped a female goddess doesn't mean that women ruled their society. The so-called

---

[7] Ibid., 18.

[8] Ibid. See also Steven M. Baugh, "1 Timothy," in Jeffrey A. D. Weima and Steven M. Baugh, *1 and 2 Thessalonians, 1 and 2 Timothy, Titus*, Zondervan Illustrated Bible Backgrounds Commentary, vol. 3, ed. Clinton E. Arnold (Grand Rapids, MI: Zondervan, 2001), 444–77.

[9] Contra N. T. Wright, "Women's Service in the Church: The Biblical Basis," conference paper for the symposium "Men, Women and the Church," St. John's College, Durham, September 4, 2004, 11, who points to the Artemis cult with its goddess worship and female priestesses and claims that Paul's message is "that women must have the space and leisure to study and learn in their own way, not in order that they may muscle in and take over the leadership as in the Artemis-cult." However, not only does this insufficiently recognize the first-century Ephesian evidence set forth by Baugh (see esp. "Foreign World," 20–23); it also contradicts Paul's statement in verses 13–14 linking his prohibition in verse 12 to the order of creation and the scenario at the fall (see further below).

[10] Richard C. Kroeger and Catherine C. Kroeger, *I Suffer Not a Woman: Rethinking 1 Timothy 2:11–15 in Light of Ancient Evidence* (Grand Rapids, MI: Baker, 1992).

feminist Ephesus of the first century is more a twenty- or twenty-first-century myth than a first-century reality. Also, Paul wasn't actually addressing the general culture in 1 Timothy 2:12. This is seen in the fact that he grounds his argument in creation order prior to the fall as well as in the fall itself rather than in perceived abuses or aberrations in the general culture.

Was Paul Addressing First-Century Gnosticism?

Others say that Paul was merely addressing an early form of Gnosticism in our passage, again arguing that 1 Timothy 2:12 is directed merely to correct some kind of false teaching. Right at the outset, however, we need to be careful here because it's been shown conclusively that full-orbed Gnosticism, the first major Christian heresy, didn't emerge until the second century AD.[11] At the same time, the kind of spirit-body dualism that was part of full-blown Gnosticism was certainly already present in the first century. We may see traces of this kind of thinking in 1 Corinthians 7:1, for example, where apparently some believed that it was preferable for a man not to have sexual relations with a woman.

We also know that some in Timothy's day were forbidding marriage and requiring abstinence from certain kinds of food so that Paul had to encourage Timothy to teach people in his church that marriage and eating were things "that God created to be received with thanksgiving by those who believe and know the truth" (1 Tim. 4:3). At the end of the letter, Timothy is told to "avoid the irreverent babble and contradictions of what is falsely called 'knowledge,' for by professing it some have swerved from the faith" (1 Tim. 6:20–21). Paul's comment that women "will be saved through childbearing" might also represent an attempt at correcting some who disparaged women's childbearing role for similar reasons.

Relevance

Where does this leave us with regard to 1 Timothy 2? While it can at times be helpful to read between the lines, we'll want to be careful

---

[11] The classic work is Edwin M. Yamauchi, *Pre-Christian Gnosticism: A Survey of Proposed Evidences* (Grand Rapids, MI: Eerdmans, 1973). More recently, see Carl B. Smith II, *No Longer Jews: The Search for Gnostic Origins* (Peabody, MA: Hendrickson, 2004).

not to substitute an unstated possible background for what is stated explicitly in the text. This is especially true since what Paul says here about women dressing modestly, learning quietly with all submissiveness, and submitting to male authority in the church is amply corroborated by Pauline and New Testament teaching elsewhere (see, e.g., 1 Cor. 11:2–16; 14:33b–36; Eph. 5:21–33; 1 Pet. 3:1–7). In other words, writings addressed to Corinth or Rome contain the same injunctions to women as Paul's first letter to Timothy, which makes it less likely that 1 Timothy 2 is some kind of special teaching.

What's more, Paul's explicit rationale doesn't engage any Gnostic or other unique circumstance in first-century Ephesus but makes reference to God's original creation of the man and the woman as well as to the scenario at the fall where the woman acted apart from her God-given partner and leader. It's also hard to see how Paul in this present passage would prohibit women from teaching or exercising authority over men in the church in response to Gnosticism, because Gnosticism, for its part, took a fairly negative stance toward women.[12] It doesn't make sense that Paul would counter the negative Gnostic view of women with a prohibition of women teaching or exercising authority over men.

The Genre of the Letters to Timothy and Titus

After taking a look at the ancient background, we now need to consider briefly the genre of 1 Timothy. The letters to Timothy and Titus, including 1 Timothy, were written by Paul toward the end of the apostolic period at a juncture when Paul was trying to prepare the church for the period subsequent to the apostolic era (the so-called sub-apostolic or patristic period). In other words, these letters anticipate the passing of the baton from Paul to other leaders such as Timothy, and the apostle is seeking to provide the church with an abiding pattern of organization and leadership that those who come after him can follow. It's very hard to argue that these letters are merely occasional. If you want to look

---

[12] The second-century AD Gnostic *Gospel of Thomas*, for example, closes with the following words: "Simon Peter said to him, 'Let Mary leave us, for women are not worthy of life.' Jesus said, 'I myself shall lead her in order to make her male, so that she too may become a living spirit resembling you males. For every woman who will make herself male will enter the kingdom of heaven'" (114). Translation from James M. Robinson, ed., *The Nag Hammadi Library* (rev. ed., San Francisco: HarperCollins, 1990).

anywhere in the New Testament, the letters to Timothy and Titus are the place to look for normative instructions for church life.

Nevertheless, some contend that 1 Timothy 2:12 is just like 1 Corinthians 11:2–16 where female head coverings were a mere cultural issue. Similarly, because of changes in society and education the passage is not binding for the church today and Paul is simply sharing his opinion. There are several problems with this argument. In 1 Corinthians 11:2–16, female head coverings may have been a cultural expression, but the principle on which this cultural expression is based—submission to authority—transcended the original occasion. In 1 Timothy 2:12, the abiding principle that is taught can't be separated from any culturally limited application simply because nothing cultural is mentioned.[13] Teaching and exercising authority aren't merely cultural activities. There's also no qualitative difference between people teaching or exercising authority in the church in the first century and in the twenty-first century. For this reason, it won't work to argue for a distinction between a general principle and a culturally limited expression of the principle in 1 Timothy 2:12. Rather, a norm of male leadership that is abiding and transcends culture is taught here. This is consistent with the biblical pattern exhibited throughout both Testaments. Paul made clear that the principle of male leadership wasn't merely his personal opinion when grounding it in creation order and in the scenario at the fall.

Purpose, Structure, and Rationale

What was Paul's purpose for writing 1 Timothy? At the beginning of the letter, Paul writes in verses 3–4: "As I urged you when I was going to Macedonia, remain at Ephesus so that you may charge certain persons not to teach any different doctrine, nor to devote themselves to myths and endless genealogies, which promote speculations rather than the stewardship from God that is by faith."[14] Later, he writes in 1 Timothy 3:14–15, "I hope to come to you soon, but I am writing

---

[13] See Benjamin L. Merkle, "Paul's Arguments from Creation in 1 Corinthians 11:8–9 and 1 Timothy 2:13–14: An Apparent Inconsistency Answered," *Journal of the Evangelical Theological Society* 49 (2006): 527–48.

[14] Interestingly, the Greek word behind the phrase "to teach different doctrine" is *heterodidaskaleō*, not the word used by Paul in 1 Tim. 2:12 (*didaskō*). This is the appropriate Greek word to indicate false teaching (*heteros* means "other" and gives the entire word a negative connotation), which shows that Paul knew the negative word for teaching and used it prior to 1 Tim. 2:12 in the same letter.

these things to you so that, if I delay, you may know how one ought to behave in the household of God, which is the church of the living God, a pillar and buttress of the truth." Thus we see that Paul pursues a dual purpose: (1) dealing with false teachers; and (2) providing general instructions regarding proper conduct in the church. In fact, it seems that Paul oscillates between these two purposes throughout the letter (see table 6.1).

Table 6.1: Purpose and Structure of 1 Timothy

Unit	Purpose Statement	Main Concern
1:1–2		Introduction
1:3–20	1:3–4	Dealing with false teachers
2:1–3:16	**3:14–15**	**Conduct in God's household (incl. 2:9–15)**
4:1–5		Dealing with false teachers
4:6–6:2a		Conduct in God's household
6:2b–10		Dealing with false teachers
6:11–21		Conclusion

Paul's dual purpose. Paul's initial purpose, as indicated in 1 Timothy 1:3–4, is dealing with false teachers. After acknowledging in 1 Timothy 1:12–17 that he himself once had been an opponent and persecutor of the church, Paul specifically names two *men* who were false teachers threatening the church in Ephesus, Hymenaeus and Alexander (v. 20). Hymenaeus is mentioned again in 2 Timothy 2:17, where he is charged with deviating from the truth by claiming that the resurrection had already taken place, overturning the faith of some (in effect, he was denying the reality of a future resurrection).[15]

First Timothy 2:1 then starts a new section in which Paul broadens the scope of his teaching to provide instructions for people's general

---

[15] There is an element of truth in the fact that the resurrection had already taken place physically in Christ and spiritually for believers (Eph. 2:6), but these false teachers were taking these realities to an undue extreme, denying the reality of the future, end-time resurrection.

conduct in the church (most notably, qualifications for church leaders such as elders and deacons; 1 Tim. 3:1–12). The beginning of a
new unit is indicated by the specific wording with which Paul begins
the chapter: "First of all, then." This unit ends with the above-cited
purpose statement in 1 Timothy 3:14–15 and reaches all the way to
1 Timothy 3:16, concluding with an apparent hymn called the "Mystery
of Godliness."

The content of chapters 2 and 3 suggests that these chapters are
broader in orientation and concerned with more than simply rebutting
false teachers. Otherwise, to be consistent, one would have to argue that
everything in these chapters was written to combat false teaching—the
command to pray for those in authority would imply some said not to
pray for them; instructions that church leaders not be drunkards and
that they exercise hospitality meant some were actually teaching that
church leaders should be drunkards and shouldn't exercise hospitality.
This seems hard to believe. More likely, Paul doesn't say everything in
these chapters in response to false teaching but instructs Timothy more
broadly concerning people's proper conduct in the church.

In 1 Timothy 4:1, then, Paul starts another section in which he returns to the topic of false teachers. These heretics apparently prohib-
ited marriage and demanded abstinence from certain foods (v. 3). Paul's
response is that "everything created by God is good, and nothing is to
be rejected if it is received with thanksgiving" (v. 4). After this, Paul
seems to return to more general instructions regarding people's conduct in the church, including Timothy's own example (1 Tim. 4:6–5:2),
caring for widows (1 Tim. 5:3–16), dealing with elders (1 Tim. 5:17–25),
and slaves' respectful behavior toward their masters (1 Tim. 6:1–2). One
final section on dealing with false teachers (1 Tim. 6:3–10) is followed
by a concluding charge, benediction, and greeting (1 Tim. 6:11–21).

Relevance for interpreting 1 Timothy 2:12. With regard to the interpretation of 1 Timothy 2:12, some argue that dealing with false teachers was
Paul's sole purpose in writing 1 Timothy and thus interpret 1 Timothy 2:12 as narrowly concerned to prohibit women from teaching
false doctrine in the Ephesian church.[16] However, structurally, Paul's

[16] Gordon D. Fee, *1 and 2 Timothy, Titus*, New International Biblical Commentary on the New Testament
(Peabody, MA: Hendrickson, 1988); "Issues in Evangelical Hermeneutics, Part III: The Great Watershed—
Intentionality and Particularity/Eternality: 1 Timothy 2:8–15 as a Test Case," *Crux* 26 (1990): 31–37;

instructions in 1 Timothy 2–3 seem to point in the opposite direction. As we've seen, 1 Timothy 2:12 is part of a section in the letter that includes instructions to "the household of God," "the church of the living God," "a pillar and buttress of truth" (1 Tim. 3:14–15), which is relevant for people "in every place" (1 Tim. 2:8), not merely first-century Ephesus. Paul's appeal to creation order with Adam and Eve in verse 13 also gives the passage a universal sense.

Not only does the interpretation of 1 Timothy 2:12 as narrowly prohibiting women false teachers square poorly with the structure of the letter, but it also should be noted that, on a historical level, all the named false teachers in the Pastoral Epistles are actually men.[17] Women are typically presented as victims of false teaching in the Pastorals, not teachers, such as in cases where Paul addresses the problem of false teachers infiltrating households and taking advantage of vulnerable women (2 Tim. 3:6; see also 1 Tim. 5:11–15). Add to this the fact that Eve is explicitly presented as a victim of deception in the immediate context (i.e., 1 Tim. 2:14) rather than as someone who propagated false teaching herself. In fact, Eve is virtually never presented in Jewish literature as a false teacher. The argument that Paul is concerned with false women teachers deceiving the men in the Ephesian congregation thus doesn't fit the broader context of the Pastorals where men are presented as the false teachers, women as the victims, and Eve as the prime victim of deception.

Summary

An overview of the purpose and structure of the letter has revealed that 1 Timothy 2:12 is most likely broader in scope than merely prohibiting false teaching by women. Paul's dual purpose as indicated by the structure of the letter as well as the portrayal of male false teachers and women as victims of false teaching render it highly unlikely that everything Paul writes to Timothy relates only to first-century Ephesus.

"Reflections on Church Order in the Pastoral Epistles, with Further Reflections on the Hermeneutics of *Ad Hoc* Documents," *Journal of the Evangelical Theological Society* 28 (1985): 141–51. See the interaction with Fee in Andreas J. Köstenberger, "'Biblical Hermeneutics: Basic Principles and Questions of Gender' by Roger Nicole and 'Hermeneutics and the Gender Debate' by Gordon D. Fee," *Journal of Biblical Manhood and Womanhood* 10 (Spring 2005): 88–95; and "1–2 Timothy, Titus," in *Ephesians–Philemon*, vol. 12, The Expositor's Bible Commentary, ed. Tremper Longman III and David E. Garland, rev. ed. (Grand Rapids, MI: Zondervan, 2005), 504 and elsewhere.

[17] E.g., Hymenaeus and Alexander (1 Tim. 1:20); Hymenaeus and Philetus (2 Tim. 2:17).

More likely, in chapters 2 and 3 Paul is issuing directives as to how people should conduct themselves in God's household, the church, in any age. Note also that in 1 Timothy 2:8 Paul gives instructions to men "in every place," which suggests that his injunctions in the rest of the chapter likewise apply to people everywhere. Doubtless the qualifications for church leaders in chapter 3 extend beyond Ephesus because Paul gives similar instructions to Titus who was on the island of Crete (see Titus 1:6–9).

Table 6.2: Framework for Interpreting 1 Timothy 2:12

Background	Ephesus was a typical Greco-Roman city, not uniquely proto-feminist
Genre	Letter from the apostle Paul to Timothy, his apostolic delegate (Pastoral Epistle)
Purpose	(1) Dealing with false teachers; (2) abiding instructions for church conduct

Interpreting 1 Timothy 2:12 in Context

Verses 9–10

Let's now explore 1 Timothy 2:12 in context, using 1 Timothy 2:9–10 as our obvious starting point, where Paul moves from addressing men (v. 8) to discussing women in the church: "Likewise also that women should adorn themselves in respectable apparel, with modesty and self-control, not with braided hair and gold or pearls or costly attire, but with what is proper for women who profess godliness—with good works." It's evident that what Paul writes in these verses isn't limited in application to Ephesus, because these types of instructions are repeated elsewhere in the New Testament (cf., e.g., 1 Pet. 3:3–4).

Thomas Schreiner sums up the issue well: "The text does not rule out all wearing of jewelry by women but forbids ostentation and luxury in adornment."[18] In essence, Paul speaks out here "against seductive and enticing clothing," a concern that is at least as relevant today as it

---

[18] Thomas Schreiner, "An Interpretation of 1 Timothy 2:9–15: A Dialogue with Scholarship," in *Women in the Church*, 95.

was in the first century.[19] While the specific type of clothing, jewelry, or hairstyle may vary from culture to culture, there are moral issues such as women's modesty and self-control at stake that transcend any one culture. Schreiner discerns two abiding principles in this passage: (1) no extravagant and ostentatious adornment; (2) no clothing that is seductive and enticing.[20]

Verses 11–12

Verses 11 and 12 must be read together as referring to appropriate conduct for men and women in the public assembly of the church gathered for worship. The positive instruction in verse 11 is for women to learn quietly and in full submission, while the negative instruction in verse 12 is for them not to teach or have authority over men. Just as Paul's instructions in verses 9–10 were directed toward all women, not merely wives, he uses generic language, "a woman," in verse 11, and in verse 14 calls Eve "the woman." The generic language throughout the passage, as well as the fact that no husbands are mentioned in these verses, strongly suggests that Paul's instructions in verses 9–15 apply to all women generically, whether married or not, in the context of the public assembly gathered for worship, rather than merely to husbands and wives in a family setting.[21]

Moving on to the interpretation of the important verse 12, you won't be surprised to learn that virtually every word in verse 12 as conventionally translated has been disputed, and doubt has been cast on the natural—and traditional—reading of the passage from every conceivable angle.[22] To start with, first, some say the first-person verb ("I") means this is just Paul's personal opinion.[23] In the overall context of the letter (1 Tim. 1:1: "Paul, an apostle . . . to Timothy"), however, the passage is part of Paul's apostolic command that he conveys to Timothy rather than merely one man's private, nonbinding view as to the way in which men and women should relate to each other in the church.[24]

---

[19] Ibid.
[20] Ibid.
[21] Schreiner (ibid., 97) concurs that the expression *gynē* "is generic and all women are included."
[22] For a thorough discussion of the various interpretive issues, see ibid., who writes, "Virtually every word in verses 11–12 is disputed."
[23] See the discussion in ibid., 100.
[24] Compare, e.g., the way the chapter opens: "First of all, then, I urge that supplications . . . be made for all people" (1 Tim. 2:1). While in the first-person singular ("I urge"), Paul issues a command rather

Second, some take the verb "do not permit" to suggest that Paul may not have allowed women to teach or have authority over a man at the time of writing but that he held open the possibility that he may change his mind and allow them to do so in the future, especially if they receive proper training.[25] But the present-tense form "do not permit" shouldn't be construed to limit the applicability of Paul's injunction to the present time as if the apostle were only to say, "I am not currently permitting"; "I do not permit" is atemporal, denoting a general principle valid for all time.

Third, in a similar vein, it's suggested—primarily on the grounds that "permit" is not in the form of an imperative—that Paul here merely expresses his preference for women not to teach or have authority over men in the church. Again, this suggestion is highly implausible. More likely, Paul's statement is akin to a categorical no, an apostolic prohibition. True, the statement is in the indicative rather than the imperative, but if someone in authority says, "I don't want you to do this," the statement functions as an imperative even if, grammatically speaking, it's not in the form of one.[26]

Fourth, as mentioned, some say "woman" should be translated "wife" because the Greek word *gynē* can mean either, so that Paul is only telling wives but not women in general not to teach their husbands.[27] It's true that the word can mean "woman" or "wife," but the context of our passage makes clear that here all women, not merely married ones, are in view. In verses 8–9, Paul addresses the proper dress of all women, not just wives, and in verse 14, he calls Eve "the woman." Even though Adam and Eve were a married couple, they also represented male and female humanity, so Paul is referring to Eve here as representative of all women. Otherwise, Paul would be saying that only wives but not unmarried women should be modest in their

---

than merely voicing his private, personal opinion. Or see verses 8–9, leading right up to our passage: "I desire then that in every place the men should pray . . . likewise also that women should adorn themselves in respectable apparel, with modesty and self-control" (1 Tim. 2:8–9). Again, the first-person singular verb "I desire" conveys Paul's apostolic directives to Timothy, not a mere wish or suggestion.

[25] See the discussion in Schreiner, "An Interpretation of 1 Timothy 2:9–15," 99–100.

[26] See ibid., 99.

[27] See, e.g., Gordon P. Hugenberger, "Women in Church Office: Hermeneutics of Exegesis? A Survey of Approaches to 1 Tim 2:8–15," *Journal of the Evangelical Theological Society* 35 (1992): 341–60, esp. 350–60, who adduces parallels between 1 Pet. 3:1–7 and 1 Tim. 2:8–15 to make his case. While we do not concur with Hugenberger's argument, we do appreciate his helpful cautions regarding various background reconstructions on pp. 348–50 of his article.

clothing. This, of course, is hardly the case, because Paul would have wanted all women, whether married or unmarried, to dress modestly. Also, 1 Timothy 2 isn't part of a house table that might have been directed exclusively or primarily to wives.

Fifth, some argue that "to teach or have authority" shouldn't be taken to imply that Paul prohibits women from teaching in general but that he merely doesn't want them to teach error or heresy, giving the word commonly translated "to have authority" (*authenteō*) a negative connotation and subordinating it to the word "teach" (*didaskō*). They claim that there was a specific problem with false teaching at Ephesus that Paul didn't want women to perpetrate. Several important word studies have contributed to our better understanding of the meaning of the word *authenteō*.[28] The word is found only here in the New Testament and is also rare in extrabiblical writings, occurring only twice in Greek literature prior to 1 Timothy 2:12. Arguably, this is an insufficient data base for adjudicating the matter on the basis of word study alone, even though some have inappropriately used this data to establish a negative connotation for the word *authenteō*.

Sixth, in a related point, some, as mentioned, recast the relationship between the terms "to teach" and "to have authority" in a way that subordinates women's exercise of authority to a certain manner of teaching, as if Paul were only prohibiting negative teaching or spreading false doctrine. However, there are several problems with this proposal. Most important, it stumbles over the fact that the Greek word *oude* ("or") is a coordinating rather than subordinating conjunction, that is, joins two activities side by side ("not . . . to teach or to exercise authority") rather than conveying a single command ("not teach falsely"). Clearly, the two activities of teaching and exercising authority are related to each other in some way (most likely, teaching is one way in which church leaders exercise authority). While related, the two activities remain nonetheless distinct, however, and should both have the same force (positive or negative) according to typical ancient usage. Most likely, *authenteō* has no negative connotation here because within the phrase "do not permit to teach or to exercise authority,"

---

[28] See esp. the chapter by Henry Scott Baldwin, "An Important Word: *Authenteō* in 1 Timothy 2:12," in *Women in the Church*, 39–51. See also Albert Wolters, "A Semantic Study of *authentēs* and Its Derivatives," *Journal for Biblical Manhood and Womanhood* 11, no. 1 (2006): 46–65.

"to teach" is almost certainly positive.[29] Thus 1 Timothy 2:12 turns out to mean what it says in most English translations: "I do not permit a woman to teach or to exercise authority over a man."[30]

Seventh, some propose that the reason for Paul's prohibition is merely cultural, whether because women weren't well educated in ancient times or for some other reason.[31] In today's culture, they claim, women can go to seminary, and once they're properly trained, there's no problem with them serving as pastor.[32] However, this cultural argu-

---

[29] The conjunction linking "to teach" and "to have authority" (*oude*, "or") indicates that the two activities, while related, are not identical. While teaching does involve the exercise of authority, there are other ways a person may exercise authority apart from teaching (e.g., participate in important decision making). Most likely, Paul implies in 1 Tim. 3:2 and 5:17 that all elders should be able to teach but that not all will focus on preaching and teaching; some will devote themselves primarily to giving general oversight to the church. If so, teaching is the most obvious and important way in which authority is exercised in the church because of the importance of sound doctrine (cf. Titus 1:9), but in 1 Tim. 2:12 Paul expands the prohibition beyond teaching to include even more broadly the exercise of authority over men in the church.

In a previous study, Andreas examined the uses of *oude* ("or") joining two infinitives in the NT and extrabiblical literature and discovered an interesting pattern of usage ("A Complex Sentence: The Syntax of 1 Timothy 2:12," in *Women in the Church*, 53–84). The term always joins two words or ideas that are either both positive or both negative but never alternating positive and negative expressions. So even if there is uncertainty regarding the exact meaning of *authenteō* in our passage, since the word is used in conjunction with the term *didaskō* ("to teach"), which almost certainly carries a positive connotation here and elsewhere in the Pastorals (1 Tim. 4:11; 6:2; 2 Tim. 2:2), it follows that *authenteō*, likewise, should be understood positively. Paul isn't prohibiting women from teaching because such an activity would have been in and of itself improper (i.e., false teaching) but because formal public teaching, like the exercise of authority in the church, was to be reserved for men in keeping with God's original design.

The results of Andreas's study have been widely accepted by a wide variety of scholars (see ibid., 74–84). Philip B. Payne, "1 Tim 2.12 and the Use of *oude* to Combine Two Elements to Express a Single Idea," *New Testament Studies* 54 (2008): 235–53, however, has countered that only ninety-one of the one hundred examples Andreas has adduced in the above-mentioned study are accurate. Andreas has responded to this critique in detail and has shown that the nine counterexamples Payne gives do indeed conform to the pattern of "all positive or all negative" but never "positive linked with negative": Andreas J. Köstenberger, "The Syntax of 1 Timothy 2:12: A Rejoinder to Philip B. Payne," *Journal for Biblical Manhood and Womanhood* 14 (2009): 37–40. See also Thomas Schreiner, review of Philip B. Payne, *Man and Woman, One in Christ*, in *Journal of Biblical Manhood and Womanhood* 15, no. 1 (Spring 2010): 43–44 (the entire review on pp. 33–46 is excellent and well worth reading).

[30] See, e.g., the ESV and the NASB (the HCSB similarly translates "have authority," as does the NLT). Note, however, that the 2011 NIV changed the original NIV rendering ("have authority") to "assume authority" (in fact, this rendering was already previously introduced in an update of the TNIV). It's unclear, however, where in the word *authentein* (present infinitive) the translators find the incipient (i.e., someone starting to do something) meaning "assume authority" (in the sense of "take up" authority), since this sense is usually conveyed by the aorist, not the present tense, and there in the indicative, not the infinitive, especially since to our knowledge no new lexical data has surfaced in recent years that would seem to warrant such a change in translation (not to mention the fact that the new rendering potentially disregards the common pattern of the conjunction *oude*, which commonly joins two verbs that are either both positive or both negative in meaning; see on this the essay mentioned in the previous note). For discussions, see Andreas J. Köstenberger and David A. Croteau, eds., *Which Bible Translation Should I Use? A Comparison of 4 Major Recent Versions* (Nashville: B&H Academic, 2012). See also the critique by Denny Burk, "The Translation of Gender Terminology in the 2011 NIV," in *Journal of Biblical Manhood and Womanhood* 16 (Spring 2011): 20–22 (including his reference to Andreas's study on 1 Timothy 2:12 that the 2011 NIV inadequately considers).

[31] See the discussion in Schreiner, "Interpretation of 1 Timothy 2:9–15," 108–10.

[32] Regarding the argument that Paul's injunction for women to learn in verse 11 implies permission to teach later, see Schreiner, "Interpretation of 1 Timothy 2:9–15," 97–98. Schreiner points out that Paul explicitly prohibits women from teaching in verse 12 and Paul's focus in verse 11 is not on women learning as such but on the *manner* in which women should learn: quietly and in submission.

ment runs into the stubborn fact that Paul's explicit rationale for his prohibition in 1 Timothy 2:13–14 says nothing about any such cultural limitations. Instead, Paul avers that the man's priority in creation indicates primacy of authority and that the woman's priority in the fall further reinforces the rightness of this God-given pattern. Paul isn't grounding his prohibition of women teaching or having authority over men in the church in their inability to obtain equal access to education but in the creation order and the scenario at the fall.

Table 6.3: The Disputed Meaning of 1 Timothy 2:12

Word/Phrase in 1 Tim. 2:12	Disputed Meaning
"I"	Is Paul merely stating his personal opinion or preference?
"Do not permit"	Is Paul only currently opposed but may change his mind later?
"A woman"	Does Paul's prohibition merely pertain to wives?
"To teach"	Is only *false* teaching in view, not teaching in general?
"Or"	Is Paul's concern that women not teach in a domineering way?
"To have/exercise authority"	Does Paul not want women to usurp men's authority?
"Over a man"	Do Paul's words relate only to husbands?

Verses 13–14

Verses 13 and 14 provide the dual rationale for Paul's instruction in verses 11–12. They're connected to verse 12 by the common conjunction "for" (*gar*). Most likely, this conjunction serves to give the causal rationale for the preceding statement.[33] It's sometimes argued that

---

[33] See, e.g., Schreiner, "Interpretation of 1 Timothy 2:9–15," 105 (listing scholars who oppose a causal *gar* on p. 222n156), who points out that when Paul issues a command elsewhere in the Pastorals, *gar* almost always gives the *reason* for the command (1 Tim. 4:7–8, 16; 5:4, 11, 15, 18; 2 Tim. 1:6–7; 2:7, 16; 3:5–6,

verses 13 and 14 simply provide illustrations, but even if that were the case, it wouldn't weaken the relationship between verse 12 and verses 13–14 or the substance of what verses 13–14 are actually saying.

In verse 13 Paul argues that because Adam was created first, creation order indicates that authority rests with Adam, as flows plainly from a natural reading of Genesis 2. Paul is referring to creation order not merely as a self-evident truth but adduces this foundational passage as compelling evidence from the authoritative Hebrew Scriptures. According to Paul, priority in creation entails primacy with regard to the exercise of authority in the church. Creation order comes prior to the fall, so Paul's argument concerning the male church leaders' authority and women's submission is not a result of the fall (cf. 1 Cor. 11:3). This refutes one of the central planks in the argument that authority is inherently improper and merely the result of the fall. Authority is good if exercised properly and predates the fall.

Paul doesn't stop with creation order but, in good rabbinic fashion, provides a second reason from the Genesis narrative that involves the fall: "And Adam was not deceived, but the woman was deceived and became a transgressor" (v. 14). This second reason is harder to understand.[34] Was Adam not also deceived? In verses 13–14, Paul is simply reading the Genesis narrative and registering some basic observations. The Serpent approached and deceived the woman, not the man. Why did the Serpent approach the woman when the man was in charge and had received both the direct mandate to cultivate the garden and the direct prohibition from God concerning the Tree of the Knowledge of Good and Evil? Paul reminds his readers what happened historically when the woman acted apart from the man, leading him into disobedience, rather than the man fulfilling his role and leading the woman.

Summary

Paul's argument, then, is twofold: women ought not to teach or exercise authority over a man because, first, Adam was created first,

---

9–10; 4:11, 15; Titus 3:1–3, 9, 12). See also David K. Huttar, "Causal *Gar* in 1 Timothy 2:13: A Response to Linda L. Belleville," *Journal for Biblical Manhood and Womanhood* 11, no. 1 (2006): 30–33.

[34] For a thorough discussion, see Schreiner, "Interpretation of 1 Timothy 2:9–15," 111–15.

then Eve (the man's priority in creation); and, second, the woman was deceived first, then the man (the woman's priority at the fall). Because of God's creation order (Adam-Eve) and because of the negative consequences that ensued when the first man and the first woman subverted that creation order (Eve-Adam), Paul urges that men, rather than women, teach and exercise authority in the church.

The obvious application is that Paul doesn't allow women to serve as elders or overseers, including as pastor-teachers (cf. 1 Tim. 3:2; 5:17). This injunction, in turn, is entirely consistent with the biblical pattern of male leadership that we have identified throughout the Scriptures in our investigation thus far. Paul's argument in 1 Timothy 2:9–15 culminates in verse 15, which is perhaps even more difficult to interpret than verse 12 and has confounded interpreters for centuries.

Women's Focus on Their Domestic and Familial Role (1 Tim. 2:15)

"Yet she will be saved through childbearing—if they continue in faith and love and holiness, with self-control." There have been at least seven different interpretations of this verse throughout church history.[35] The messianic view, for example, relates verse 15 to Mary the mother of Jesus and argues that women will be saved by "the" birth, that is, the birth of Christ.[36] This interpretation seems unlikely, however, because *men*, too, are saved by the Messiah, and salvation is not so much by Jesus's *birth* as by his substitutionary death on the *cross*. The interpretation is also unlikely because there's little contextual indication that justifies importing a reference to Mary into an otherwise rather generic context. Rather, in the flow of the passage, verse 14 refers to "the woman" generically, moving past Eve, Mary, or any particular woman. Others argue that women's physical preservation through childbirth is

---

[35] See Andreas J. Köstenberger, "Ascertaining Women's God-Ordained Roles: An Interpretation of 1 Timothy 2:15," *Bulletin of Biblical Research* 7 (1997): 107–44, for various views and a fuller presentation of the following material. For a more accessible summary, see "Saved through Childbearing? A Fresh Look at 1 Timothy 2:15 Points to Protection from Satan's Deception," *CBMW News* 2, no. 4 (1997): 1–6. Among others, Köstenberger is followed by Claire Smith, *God's Good Design: What the Bible Really Says about Men and Women* (Kingsford, Australia: Matthias Media, 2012), 37–40.

[36] See, e.g., Aída B. Spencer, "Eve at Ephesus," *Journal of the Evangelical Theological Society* 17 (1974): 220. But as Andreas notes in "Ascertaining Women's God-Ordained Roles," 118, "The presence of the definite article in the original Greek merely indicates the *generic nature* of childbirth rather than pointing to a *specific birth* of a child" (emphasis added).

in view, but this is unlikely as well given that some very godly women died while giving birth over the course of history.[37]

On the whole, the dynamic of the passage seems to be that Paul is trying to end up on a positive note after having issued a prohibition in verse 12 against women teaching or exercising authority over men in the church. In verse 15 he instead focuses on the positive function of childbearing and women's continuation in faith, love, and holiness. The opening chapters of Genesis, likewise, highlighted the important role of procreation and childbearing in fulfilling God's creation mandate for man and woman to multiply and subdue the earth and serve as God's representative rulers over the earth (Gen. 1:26–28). Paul is here applying Genesis 1–3 to the New Testament church. Rather than introducing new teaching, the apostle is extending God's original design for men and women to the life of the church, redirecting the aspirations of women from teaching and exercising authority over men in the church to the domestic, familial realm.

What Does "Childbearing" Mean?

The Greek word for *childbearing* (*teknogonia*) is relatively rare in the New Testament. This makes the parallel in 1 Timothy 5:14–15 all the more important: "Therefore, I want younger widows to get married, bear children, keep house, and give the enemy no occasion for reproach; for some have already turned aside to follow Satan" (NASB). In that close parallel passage, Paul is specifically applying his earlier reference to women and childbearing in 1 Timothy 2:15 to young widows and places childbearing within the larger context of marriage and managing a household. The woman's fulfillment of her domestic function also serves an important apologetic role in not giving the adversary any room for reproach and aims at protecting women, keeping them from turning aside to follow Satan.

In light of this parallel, "childbearing" in 1 Timothy 2:15 is likely shorthand for women's involvement in the domestic sphere. Some historical background information may be helpful at this point. In 1 Timothy 4:3 Paul mentions that some in his day were actually rejecting marriage altogether. Paul, on the other hand, is contending that

---

[37] See further note 40.

marriage is good—even though some in his day denied this—because God created it that way. Using 1 Timothy 4:3 to interpret 1 Timothy 2:15 (following the Reformation principle of "Scripture interpreting Scripture"), it's reasonable to assume that some viewed childbearing as inferior, just as they viewed marriage as inferior. If so, Paul may be saying here that childbearing is not to be despised but is a noble calling. Even in Paul's day, therefore, albeit for different reasons than those of some modern feminists, some were arguing that childbearing was unspiritual.

In summary, Paul is likely using childbearing as a figure of speech commonly known as "synecdoche" where a part is used to describe the whole. Here "childbearing" is likely referring to the whole complex of marriage, childbearing, and a woman's domestic calling.

What Does "Saved" Mean?

The Greek word for *saved* (*sōzō*) is more difficult to interpret in this context than *childbearing*. Usually in the Bible, the expression refers to religious salvation from sin through believing the gospel (e.g., Eph. 2:8: "For by grace you have been *saved* through faith"). This immediately raises the question, are women saved by childbearing or by faith in Christ? Most interpreters are astute enough to realize that salvation is not by works, and on the face of it, salvation by childbearing would be salvation by works. Some conclude that the future tense of *sōzō* in 1 Timothy 2:15 indicates final rather than present salvation. It's unclear, however, whether this sufficiently alleviates the difficulty. Salvation is still through faith in Christ rather than works, whether in the present or the future. Thomas Schreiner advocates the future salvation view and interprets 1 Timothy 2:15 as referring to sanctification, the process of growth in holiness subsequent to conversion until Christ's return.[38] If so, "saved" would be referring to the process of women working out their salvation, not the basis of their salvation.

When all is said and done, 1 Timothy 2:15 remains a difficult verse that eludes scholarly consensus. The verse is an example of the fact that Paul doesn't always spell things out in as much explicit detail as we would have liked him to do (see 2 Pet. 3:15–16). In light of the

---

[38] Schreiner, "Interpretation of 1 Timothy 2:9–15," 118–19.

complexity of the verse, the lack of scholarly consensus, and the difficulty of making sense of Paul's intended meaning when using the common definition of *sōzō*, we're led to explore alternate possibilities. In so doing, we discover that while "saved" is the most common meaning for *sōzō* in Paul's writing, it isn't the only possible one. As with all words, there's a range of meaning associated with the term, and the expression may also refer to physical healing (as frequently in the Gospels) or more generically to rescue from any kind of danger (specified in the context). In secular Greek, the term usually referred to rescue from danger, while Christians narrowed the scope of reference to rescue from the danger of sin and eternal suffering in hell. While religious salvation thus became the predominant sense of *sōzō* in New Testament times, however, Christians didn't always use the term in this narrow sense, occasionally still employing it in a broader sense to refer to rescue from a danger other than sin or damnation in hell.

As an example of this broader sense of *sōzō* in the New Testament, in fact in the same letter as 1 Timothy 2:15, take 1 Timothy 4:16, where Paul urges Timothy, "Pay close attention to yourself and to your teaching; persevere in these things, for as you do this you will *sōzō* [variously translated "save," "ensure salvation," or "preserve"] both for yourself and for those who hear you" (NASB). Now it seems beyond dispute that Timothy won't literally save his hearers; it's Jesus who saves them. But Timothy is charged with protecting the people in his congregation from falling into doctrinal and practical error. His responsibility is to pay close attention to his doctrine and his teaching so as to help protect and spiritually preserve those under his charge.

In this possible parallel passage, 1 Timothy 4:16, therefore, just a few verses later in the same letter, *sōzō* seems to indicate spiritual protection or preservation rather than actual salvation from sin. Arguably, this sense of *sōzō* also works better in seeking to apprehend Paul's intended meaning in 1 Timothy 2:15, especially when keeping in mind Scripture's teaching on the nature of salvation elsewhere. In fact, the preservation theme is pervasive in the Pastoral Epistles.[39] Paul is calling on Timothy to help preserve his hearers from doctrinal error by paying careful attention to his way of life and to his doctrine.

---

[39] See Köstenberger, Kellum, and Quarles, *The Cradle, the Cross, and the Crown*, 661–62.

Applied to 1 Timothy 2:15, then, Paul's teaching there seems to be that women will be spiritually preserved if they devote themselves to their God-given role in the domestic and familial sphere. In this way, women will be kept safe and out of trouble. This fits the rationale introduced with Eve in verse 14. The woman was deceived because she stepped out of her God-given role (and thus outside of her husband's protective care), which rendered her vulnerable to deception. If so, Paul seems to be answering the question, how can women avoid repeating Eve's mistake that resulted in such dire consequences? His answer: They can do so by remaining within their God-given sphere and by devoting themselves to proper activity within that domain.

From what danger does the woman need protection? The answer is satanic deception, which in its essence challenges the veracity of God's Word, casts doubts on the Creator's goodness, and promotes dissatisfaction with the role God has assigned. This led to Satan's own fall, and now the Devil is trying to spread his discontent to humanity. "You can do better than abiding by God's design and submitting to the man," the Devil whispers into the woman's ears. "Assert your independence; you deserve it; don't let anyone tell you what to do." Sadly, the first woman succumbed to Satan's implicit reasoning that she deserved better than God's design for her and for the man and fell into sin. Dissatisfaction with her God-given role in relation to her husband is thus an important entailment of the woman's transgression and rebellion against God.

One final observation is that the word *sōzō* in 1 Timothy 2:15 is in the passive voice. (In my Greek classes, I [Andreas] sometimes call this a "diabolical passive," with Satan serving as the implied agent, in analogy to the well-known phenomenon of the "divine passage," which has God as the implied agent.) The context of Eve's deception by Satan indicates that she will be preserved or saved from Satan's deception. Satan doesn't need to be explicitly mentioned here because everyone knows that according to Genesis 3 it was Satan who deceived the woman (see also the above-mentioned parallel 1 Timothy 5:14–15, which makes Satan explicit).[40]

---

[40] An alternative view has been presented by Moyer Hubbard, "Kept Safe through Childbearing: Maternal Mortality, Justification by Faith, and the Social Setting of 1 Timothy 2:15," *Journal of the Evangelical Theological Society* 55 (2012): 743–62, who argues that "the social-historical context of high maternal

Summary and Relevance

In light of these observations, Paul's rationale in 1 Timothy 2:15 can be paraphrased as follows. Humanity fell into sin when the woman stepped out of her God-ordained sphere and was deceived by Satan's temptation. Women can avoid the first woman's misstep and be preserved (i.e., be kept safe spiritually) from Satan's deception if, unlike Eve, they devote themselves to their God-ordained domestic sphere (caring for their husband and children and managing their household). The shift in subject from third singular ("she") to third plural ("they") in verse 15 may signal a shift from women to men and women jointly. If so, we can discern a creation-fall-restoration pattern in verses 13–15: Adam was created first (creation, v. 13); the woman (Eve) was deceived (fall, v. 14); the woman is called back to her original childbearing function, and both the man and the woman (or just women) are called to continue in faith, love, holiness, and self-control (v. 15). This closely follows the Genesis narrative recounting Adam's creation prior to the woman's (Gen. 2:5–25), the woman's deception (Gen. 3:1–13), and the divine pronouncement of consequences on the woman and the man (Gen. 3:14–19).

With regard to the contemporary scene, contrary to what some in the culture tell women, the allure of "realizing your potential" and "authenticating your existence" will lead women away from God's original creation design for women. If the above interpretation is at least approximately on target, radical feminism perpetrates the Devil's lie of telling women that their God-given role of childbearing and coming alongside their husband in marriage isn't good enough so they must assert their independence and carve out an autonomous identity.

mortality, together with the line of thought in this passage (Eve's transgression → safety in childbirth), [and] the semantic range of σῴζω as defined by the phrase attached to the word all combine to make Paul's meaning in 1 Tim 2:15 quite clear: God will be faithful to those who are faithful, and he will keep you safe even through this harrowing ordeal of childbirth." However, while we agree that *sōzō* refers to nonspiritual deliverance, we're concerned that Hubbard makes too little of the crucial spiritual preservation theme in the Pastorals that extends beyond mere physical preservation. Also, Hubbard's argument that *teknogonia* isn't used elsewhere in the NT with a broader meaning unduly minimizes the crucial parallel 1 Tim. 5:14. Contrary to Hubbard, the synecdoche is obvious enough in the context because it refers to Eve's spiritual deception, which sets up the reference to women's spiritual (not merely physical) deliverance. It's true that usually the preposition *ek* indicates that from which people are saved, but there's no reason why an author couldn't choose to imply this rather than making it explicit. Also, even if this were the only place where *teknogonia* is used as a synecdoche in the available literature, there still wouldn't seem to be any good reason why Paul couldn't have done so here. Finally, contrary to Hubbard, we're not expanding the semantic domain of *teknogonia* but merely understanding Paul's use in terms of the literary device of synecdoche.

In Paul's day, 1 Timothy 4:1–3 makes clear that people had departed from the faith and followed the teaching of demons, including the forsaking of marriage. This rebellion against God's creation design is implied in 1 Timothy 2:14 and made explicit in 1 Timothy 5:15, where Paul identifies Satan as the motivating force behind the false teachers. The scenario adduced by Paul eerily rings true in a day when "traditional" marriage is called, by many, merely one of multiple alternative lifestyle choices, cohabitation and births out of wedlock are on the rise, and promiscuity in all its forms is increasingly widespread.

Some people today use the negative rhetoric of "confining women to the home." This is a pejorative way of putting things. The scriptural position is not that wives are confined to the home but that they impact the world through being based in the home (see, e.g., the "excellent wife" in Prov. 31:10–31). There is certainly a danger for some men today to use this biblical teaching in a harsh way to "put women in their place." A harsh approach to the issue, however, differs from the biblical one.[41] Working in the home is in no way a death sentence; it can be a liberating reality. In fact, being based in the home makes a woman's family her positive center of gravity. Take our own marriage as an example. For me (Andreas), engaging in scholarship is pursuing my academic calling. For Margaret, to write a book together like this one is a nice extra because her center of gravity is our home and our family. She enjoys helping other women find fulfillment in embracing and living out God's design, but the moment there's a potential question as to where she should focus her attention, her priority is her family and the home. In this way, Margaret instinctively agrees that God's design is good and wise and serves not to confine or restrict her but to help her find true fulfillment.

Returning to 1 Timothy 2:12 once more, Paul's point is not that women mustn't teach at all but that they shouldn't teach men in a public church setting. Women are free biblically to teach women (Titus 2:3–6) and children. We live in a day when egalitarianism has become such a large part of our culture that we need to make a determined effort to present the positive aspects of the Bible's teaching on women's

---

[41] On the distinction between fundamentalism and evangelicalism, see the discussion in appendix 3.

roles once again which, if heeded, can have a liberating rather than debilitating effect.[42]

We conclude that in 1 Timothy 2:15 *sōzō* most likely doesn't refer to religious salvation but to spiritual preservation from falling into error (specifically, Satan's deception). "Childbearing" refers to the broader domestic sphere, not merely giving birth to children but also devotion to a woman's husband and family. While not everyone agrees, this understanding makes best sense of the context and coheres most closely with Paul's teaching in the letters to Timothy and Titus and elsewhere. Admittedly, this interpretation will be difficult to explain to others because most English translations render *sōzō* as "save" in 1 Timothy 2:15. The interpretation will also not be popular with some feminists because it in effect places radical feminism in a trajectory with Satan's deception of the woman in the very beginning.

The Requirement for Church Leaders to Be Faithful Husbands (1 Tim. 3:2)

We've seen that Paul doesn't allow women to teach or have authority in the church over men (1 Tim. 2:12). Who, then, is eligible to serve as church leader? The answer: spiritually qualified men. Paul stipulates, "Therefore an overseer must be above reproach, the husband of one wife [*mias gynaikos andra*], sober-minded, self-controlled, respectable, hospitable, able to teach" (1 Tim. 3:2). In our day, and in any day, there is a great need for godly male leadership. Sadly, men often succumb to temptation, fail to lead, or are weakened or intimidated by the aggressive stance taken by a culture pervaded by elements of feminism and saturated by egalitarianism.

While it isn't necessary here to cover all the qualifications enunciated in this passage and the parallel in Titus, it'll be helpful to focus briefly on the *mias gynaikos andra* requirement for church leaders in 1 Timothy 3:2 to find out what kind of man can legitimately serve in leadership.[43] Whatever the phrase means, the passage clearly refers to a husband and can't legitimately be interpreted to mean "faithful wife."

---

[42] See, e.g., Rebecca Jones, *Does Christianity Squash Women? A Christian Looks at Womanhood* (Nashville: B&H, 2005).

[43] See also the parallel requirement in Titus 1:6 and the similar requirement for deacons in 1 Tim. 3:12.

This is yet another piece of evidence indicating that Paul envisioned *men* in roles of church leadership and positions of authority.[44]

There's some question as to the most likely interpretation of the Greek phrase literally translated "husband of one wife" (*mias gynaikos andra*). While, analogous to the word for "woman" or "wife" (*gynē*), the word *anēr* can mean "husband" or "man," it's clear that in the present passage it means "husband" because it's used in conjunction with the word for "wife." Over the course of church history, at least five major interpretations of that expression have been set forth. As we'll see, the first four of these views take the word "one" literally as referring to one rather than zero, two, or more wives. The fifth and final interpretation interprets the phrase idiomatically as referring to a candidate's marital faithfulness.

No Single Men?

The first interpretation holds that the phrase refers to one wife as opposed to no wives and that church leaders must not be single men. This would most likely have disqualified Paul—I say "most likely" because some scholars believe Paul was actually married at some point and subsequently widowed—and probably Timothy as well. While it's highly probable that Paul assumes most candidates for overseer are going to be married—hence the present stipulation—it's far less certain that being married is actually a requirement to serve as elder or overseer.

This is the case especially since Paul in 1 Corinthians 7 acknowledges the gift of celibacy and notes that it enables a believer who chooses to remain unmarried to serve in a more unencumbered manner than those who must fulfill their marital and familial obligations. For this and other reasons, it's highly unlikely that Paul, by stipulating that candidates for the office of elder be *mias gynaikos andra*, seeks to exclude unmarried men from serving in this capacity. It's an indication of the implausibility of this interpretation that very few interpreters actually take this view today. Single men are therefore potentially to serve as church leaders.

---

[44] Note also the close proximity of 1 Tim. 3:2 to 1 Tim. 2:12, especially since there were no chapter divisions when Paul wrote the letter.

No Divorced Men?

The second interpretation takes the phrase to exclude divorced men. Again, however, this view is rather unlikely for several reasons. To begin with, there would have been easier, more straightforward ways for Paul to make this point if this had been his intent. "Husband of one wife" (*mias gynaikos andra*) would have been an exceedingly awkward way for Paul to rule out a divorced man from serving as elder or deacon. Note that divorce is never mentioned in the letters to Timothy and Titus, and while arguments from silence are notoriously precarious, in conjunction with the other reasons given, this shows at least that divorce may not have been a very pressing concern for Paul as he wrote the letter.

As mentioned, this interpretation, too, takes the word "one" literally. Anyone who is divorced is currently not the husband of *any* wife and so fails literally to fulfill the "husband of *one* wife" requirement. In light of the traditional belief that divorced people shouldn't serve as church leaders, it may be tempting to adduce 1 Timothy 3:2 in support of such a view. However, it's less than certain that Paul intended to exclude divorced men from holding that particular church office here. It's therefore possible that divorced men may be considered, especially if they've been victims of their wife's unfaithfulness or if their divorce occurred prior to conversion, though other biblical and practical factors would need to be considered as well.

No Remarried Widowers?

The third interpretation argues that the phrase prohibits widowers who have remarried. You may be surprised to learn that this was the virtual consensus view in the early church and of the church fathers. A remarried man was (or had been) literally the husband of two wives—his deceased wife and his current wife—as opposed to only one wife total. Thus a literal reading of the phrase *mias gynaikos andra* once again may seem to exclude remarried widowers.

However, the question arises as to what would morally be wrong with a widower getting remarried. Nowhere in Scripture does there seem to be any moral objection to such a practice. Elsewhere, Paul encourages widows to get remarried, and he would not likely have counseled people to do something that he elsewhere viewed as problematic.

This is a good example of an instance where the church fathers were almost certainly universally wrong.

No Polygamists?

The fourth interpretation holds that Paul is excluding polygamists, stipulating that a candidate for elder must have only one wife as opposed to multiple wives simultaneously as would be the case with polygamy (or, to be technical, polygyny). In theory, this is certainly a possible interpretation of Paul's statement. What makes the interpretation unlikely, however, is the fact that polygamy was virtually unknown among first-century Jews. This is a good example of how background research can help show us the plausibility (or lack thereof) of a particular interpretation. Even in the larger Greco-Roman world, polygamy was relatively rare. It was far more common for Greek and Roman men to be married to one wife and at the same time, however, to have one or several mistresses (i.e., concubinage).[45]

Faithfulness in Marriage?

This leads us to the fifth and final interpretation, which holds that the phrase stipulates that a prospective elder be faithful to his wife.[46] This would thus exclude those men who had concubines or engaged in illicit sexual relationships with other women outside of marriage. In this case, the interpretive gloss would be "faithful husband" (or "one-wife-type-of-husband"). In support of this interpretation is the close parallel in 1 Timothy 5:9, which states, "Let a widow be enrolled if she is not less than sixty years of age, *having been the wife of one husband.*" The Greek contains the mirror image, in female terms, of the phrase in 1 Timothy 3:2. Is Paul's requirement that the widow must have been faithful to her husband while he was still living (original NIV) or that she was the wife of only one husband (most other translations)? But what if she was married twice and widowed twice? Paul, in that same passage, encourages young widows to remarry. If 1 Timothy 5:9 indi-

---

[45] See S. M. Baugh in Weima and Baugh, *1 and 2 Thessalonians, 1 and 2 Timothy, Titus,* 501–2, who notes that rather than polygamy, concubinage—the practice of husbands having mistresses while continuing in their marriage—was much more common. In some cultures, this same practice does not carry a moral stigma today.

[46] See Sidney Page, "Marital Expectations of Church Leaders in the Pastoral Epistles," *Journal for the Study of the New Testament* 50 (1993): 105–20.

cates one husband, Paul would be penalizing older widows for having followed his advice to young widows! This strongly supports the idea that the phrase is referring to marital faithfulness and not the numerical total of spouses (whether at one time or successively). I believe the original NIV got it right in 1 Timothy 5:9 but unfortunately failed to be consistent and did not translate 1 Timothy 3:2 accordingly. Fortunately, the updated NIV has now remedied this deficiency.

An intriguing piece of background information from the ancient world lends further support to this interpretation: tombstones bearing the phrase "one husband" engraved on them. Apparently, the phrase "faithful wife" was a common idiom to indicate marital fidelity in the Greco-Roman world.[47] The question was not the (successive) number of husbands (in case of widowhood), but a woman's marital faithfulness. It's also interesting to note that Paul is focusing on the moral character traits of church leaders. Faithfulness to one's wife fits this list better than if Paul were excluding divorced or remarried men (regardless of the circumstances of their divorce or remarriage). If it weren't for 1 Timothy 5:9, which is fairly compelling evidence, other interpretations may be possible, but it doesn't seem likely that Paul intended to exclude divorced or unmarried men from church office in this passage. This doesn't necessarily mean that divorced men should hold the office of elder or deacon; it only means that 1 Timothy 3:2, 12 or Titus 1:6 can't be legitimately used to make such a case. Passages that have a more likely bearing on such matters are the requirements that a candidate for office be above reproach (1 Tim. 3:2; cf. Titus 1:6, 7) and have a good reputation with outsiders (1 Tim. 3:7).

Relevance

The phrase *mias gynaikos andra* refers to marital faithfulness and isn't directly addressing the issues of singleness, divorce, or polygamy. If Paul's desire was to stipulate marital faithfulness, translating *mias gynaikos andra* as "husband of one wife" doesn't communicate the original meaning very effectively, since the phrase "husband of one wife" has no currency in our culture (outside of church circles). Literal

---

[47]See M. Lightman and W. Zeisel, "Univira: An Example of Continuity and Change in Roman Society," *Church History* 46 (1977): 19–32, cited in Köstenberger, "1–2 Timothy, Titus," 524.

translations (such as the NASB) are unhelpful in our understanding in cases where translators fail to recognize that a given phrase represents an idiom and translate it word for word instead. Not every idiom can or should be translated into another language word for word, and it appears that *mias gynaikos andra* is a case in point. Most likely, then, the fifth and final interpretive option—which reflects broad consensus and has been adopted by translations such as the updated NIV ("faithful to his wife")—is correct and Paul has marital faithfulness in view.

> "Qualifications for church leaders don't present an ideal of perfection but set a standard of spiritual and moral maturity. I've heard Don Carson make the point more than once that what is most remarkable about the qualifications for church leadership enunciated by Paul is that they are so unremarkable."

What, then, does "husband of one wife" mean? It certainly means faithfulness to the elder candidate's present wife. Faithfulness is demonstrated over time, but it may not always be appropriate to apply Paul's injunction retroactively to a candidate's distant past. The important question is, does a man currently exhibit faithfulness? If the Bible permits divorce in exceptional cases—the "exception clause" in Matthew 19 referring to sexual marital unfaithfulness and the "Pauline privilege" in 1 Corinthians 7 pertaining to the abandonment of a marriage by the unbelieving spouse—there would seem to be no *a priori* reason to prohibit such men from serving.[48] In some cases, the man may have been the victim of his wife's unfaithfulness. Qualifications for church leaders don't present an ideal of perfection but set a standard of spiritual and moral maturity. I've heard Don Carson make the point more than once that what is most remarkable about the qualifications for church leadership enunciated by Paul is that they are so unremarkable.[49]

The Requirement for Church Leaders to Manage Their Own Households Well (1 Tim. 3:4–5)

"He must manage his own household well, with all dignity keeping his children submissive, for if someone does not know how to man-

---

[48] On divorce and remarriage, see chap. 11 in Andreas J. Köstenberger with David W. Jones, *God, Marriage, and Family: Rebuilding the Biblical Foundation*, 2nd ed. (Wheaton, IL: Crossway, 2010).

[49] See, e.g., D. A. Carson, "Defining Elders," http://sites.silaspartners.com/partner/Article_Display_Page /0,,PTID314526_CHID598014_CIID2157886,00.html: "In some respects, the list is remarkable for being unremarkable."

age his own household, how will he care for God's church?" A further requirement for church leadership is that such men must manage or rule (*proistēmi*) their households well. The Greek word *proistēmi* clearly communicates the notion of authority, and "manage" doesn't quite capture the idea of a head of household and his position of authority. It's exactly the same word translated in 1 Timothy 5:17 as "Let the elders who *rule* well . . ." Paul is here drawing a parallel between an elder's and a husband's authority. In the Jewish and Greco-Roman context, there was a strong sense of male authority in the household. Having his children under control reveals another aspect of this authority. How can a man take care of God's household, the church, if he cannot manage and govern his own natural household? Paul's logic is utterly compelling. Unfortunately, however, Paul's words are not always heeded in the church today, and men whose family life and marriage aren't sufficiently established to warrant appointment to such a responsible position, in that they're too young or lack life experience and spiritual maturity, are regularly appointed to serve.

Women Deacons or Deacons' Wives? (1 Tim. 3:11)

Following the instructions in 1 Timothy 3:1–7 regarding candidates for the office of overseer, which is reserved biblically for men (implied, as mentioned, by the requirement that an elder be a "faithful husband," Greek *anēr*), Paul proceeds to delineate qualifications for a second office, that of deacon, in verses 8–13. We won't look at the qualifications for male deacons in detail here since Andreas has done so elsewhere[50] and since these are not disputed. The passage starts with "Deacons likewise" and calls for such men to be "dignified, not double-tongued, not addicted to much wine, not greedy for dishonest gain." Also, "they must hold the mystery of the faith with a clear conscience" and first be tested if they prove blameless (vv. 8–10).

This is followed by this stipulation: "Their wives [or better: women; the Greek word is *gynaikas*] likewise must be dignified, not slanderers, but sober-minded, faithful in all things." Translations of this verse differ. The women mentioned are related to the male deacons mentioned

---

[50] See Köstenberger, "1–2 Timothy, Titus," 527–30.

in verses 8–10 and 12 in some way, whether by being married to them or by being deaconesses in their own right. The 2011 NIV includes the notation "possibly deacons' wives or women who are deacons" in a footnote. There's some discussion over how to translate *gynaikos* in this passage, with some choosing a neutral option and simply translating the word as "women." Most translations seem to prefer "deacons' wives," though most versions include both options, one in the text and the other in a footnote.

The broader context, as mentioned, indicates that 1 Timothy 3:1–7 deals with male elders. We'll return to this shortly, but notice that there's complete silence with regard to any requirements for elders' wives. The transition in verse 8, as noted, then says, "Deacons likewise." This almost certainly indicates a second church office in addition to the first office of elders. First, there are elders, and then there are deacons. This is perfectly consistent with Paul's mention of "overseers [a synonym for elders] and deacons" in Philippians 1:1. When the interpreter arrives at 1 Timothy 3:11, the verse begins with, "Their wives likewise." This opening, as we'll develop further below, seems to suggest that Paul is moving on to a distinct group here who hold a church office as well.

Paul gives some qualifications for male deacons in 1 Timothy 3:8–10, which we've already briefly listed. Verse 11 then refers to women, while verse 12 reverts to men. Verse 11, addressing women, doesn't stipulate any marriage or family qualifications. The significance of this fact is hard to determine, however, because arguments from silence are notoriously difficult to sustain. It may be that Paul isn't adding a family-related qualification because he didn't necessarily expect these women to be married (in which case they might be unmarried deaconesses). This would fit the pattern of unmarried older women—including mature widows—serving in the early church (e.g., Phoebe).

Why does Paul use language that leaves the expression ambiguous, at least for interpreters today? Couldn't he have made clear whether he was referring to deacons' wives or women deacons? Interestingly, at the time of writing there was no Greek word to describe women deacons. In Romans 16 Paul uses the male form *diakonos* to refer to Phoebe, almost certainly because there was no feminine form such as the term *diakonissa*, which developed later. Thus Paul's options were limited, and he couldn't have used the feminine word *deaconess* because this form wasn't (yet) in use.

Relevance

The interpretation of 1 Timothy 3:11 as referring to female deacons is sometimes contested because in some traditions the office of deacon conveys a ruling function reserved only for men. Scripture itself doesn't associate a ruling function with deacons. It's important to realize that some churches don't conceive of the ministry of deacons in line with biblical terminology. They apply the word *deacon* to men who function for all practical purposes as elders. What's more, many churches actually ordain deacons; in such cases, those who believe that it wouldn't be appropriate to ordain women will naturally be opposed to women deacons, even if this office doesn't entail the exercise of authority.

These various traditions add further complexity to the issue. Our traditions and practices are powerful presuppositions that we bring to the text. However, if we understand what Paul is clearly saying, that serving as a deacon isn't a ruling or teaching function, it becomes clear that even if the women in 1 Timothy 3:11 were deacons, this wouldn't conflict with Paul's teaching elsewhere that women ought not to serve in authoritative church offices (cf. 1 Tim. 2:12). In fact, many conservative commentators favor a reference to women deacons in Romans 16 and 1 Timothy 3:11 because they don't see the office of deacon to involve the exercise of authority.[51]

Arguments for Deaconesses

There are at least four exegetical arguments that support female deacons from the biblical text.[52]

1) Lack of qualifications for elders' wives. As mentioned, no qualifications are given for elders' wives. If verse 11 were to refer to deacons' wives rather than female deacons, the question arises why Paul stipulates

---

[51] Examples include Douglas J. Moo and Thomas R. Schreiner; see discussion above.
[52] See the excellent article by Jennifer H. Stiefel, "Women Deacons in 1 Timothy: A Linguistic and Literary Look at 'Women Likewise . . .' (1 Tim 3.11)," *New Testament Studies* 41, no. 3 (1995): 442–57.

qualifications for deacons' wives but not elders' wives, especially since elder is a higher office than deacon. We haven't come across a satisfactory explanation for the omission of qualifications for elders' wives if it were to be assumed that 1 Timothy 3:11 provides qualifications for deacons' wives. This favors taking this passage to refer to deaconesses.

2) *"Likewise."* The word "likewise" in verse 11 (*"Gynai* [women, i.e., women deacons or wives of deacons] likewise, . . .") seems to indicate a group that is distinct from the male deacons mentioned in 1 Timothy 3:8–10 and significant in their own right (cf. the transition between vv. 7 and 8: "Deacons likewise"). This, too, seems to suggest that Paul is moving on in verse 11 to a new group of office holders, deaconesses, as opposed to continuing to talk about deacons and their wives.

3) *Absence of possessive pronoun "their."* Normally when there's a reference to wives in the New Testament, there's a possessive pronoun (such as "their" wives) indicating the way in which these women are related to their husbands, but there is no possessive pronoun in the Greek text here. Some English translations (such as the ESV) add the possessive pronoun even though it's absent from the original Greek, which amounts to an indirect concession that such a pronoun would be required to make sense of the text on the assumption that deacons' wives are in view.

4) *Lack of family qualifications.* As mentioned, there are no family qualifications in verse 11. One possible explanation is that if women deacons are in view, they weren't necessarily expected to be married. As noted above, many older women in the early church were widowed and functioned as benefactresses and patronesses, an activity that involved benevolence and a variety of good works. The list of qualifications for a woman to be put on the list of widows is every bit as stringent as the qualifications for deacons. First Timothy 3:11 seems to be referring to a church office, but is deacon's wife a church office?

Some churches today think by appointing a couple jointly as deacons, they avoid the difficulty, but in so doing they discriminate against unmarried women who might otherwise be qualified. Also, some deacons' wives may not be qualified to serve or even be believers though their husbands are. Titus provides a possible indication of the service of women deacons when Paul instructs Titus to have the older women instruct and mentor the younger women rather than for Titus to instruct them directly (Titus 2:3–6).[53]

Relevance

The decision on how to interpret 1 Timothy 3:11 isn't primarily a matter of logic or preference. The question is, rather, did women serve in the early church as deacons or didn't they? If a church has no elders and only functions with deacons, it'll be difficult to install women deacons, and there's no biblical mandate to have women deacons (or any deacons). Biblically, the deacon's role is a nonteaching, nonauthoritative servant role. If deacons function in a church in a ruling capacity, the pervasive biblical pattern of male leadership would seem to render it impermissible to appoint women deacons. If the deacon ministry is construed as servant ministry, however, there seems to be no good reason why women shouldn't be appointed to such a role.

Paul is clearly talking about two offices. Elders are to be male (faithful husbands), while deacons could potentially include both men and women. The text isn't entirely conclusive but on balance seems to favor women deacons. The burden of proof thus lies with those who would deny the possibility of female deacons serving in a nonauthoritative, nonteaching role. Those who believe that, biblically, women shouldn't serve in authoritative church offices should make it especially clear that they are very much for women being involved in active ministry. Allowing women to serve as deaconesses seems to be a great way to affirm women in ministry, even in publicly recognized and appointed type of ministry in the church. It's very important that we actively promote women's service in the kind of ministry that is scripturally appropriate and that we publicly recognize them for doing so.

There seems to be no biblical reason why women couldn't serve as servants (deacons), and be officially recognized as such. Often churches recognize men for their service but not women. This is unfortunate, because women are every bit as worthy of recognition and affirmation as men are. This neglect also serves to reinforce the notion that those

---

[53] There's another reference to women deacons from Pliny the Younger, a governor under the Roman emperor Trajan around AD 110. In one of his letters to Trajan, he mentions two Christian deaconesses (Lat. *ministrae*; *Epist.* 10.96.8). This is indirect but helpful evidence from shortly after the apostolic period.

who recognize biblical role distinctions between men and women aren't sufficiently open to the contribution women can make in a congregation. There seems to have been little progress or movement over the past decade or two in this regard. Though some pastors seem afraid to teach on this subject because they don't want to be perceived as liberal or moderate, practically it's often easier to institute a biblical pattern of ministry in newly planted churches than to try to change traditional church structures in established churches.

The Need for Older Women to Train Young Women (Titus 2:3–5)

"Older women likewise are to be reverent in behavior, not slanderers or slaves to much wine. They are to teach what is good, and so train the young women to love their husbands and children, to be self-controlled, pure, working at home, kind, and submissive to their own husbands, that the word of God may not be reviled" (Titus 2:3–5). Discussing Titus 2 is an appropriate way to conclude our investigation of Scripture and transition to practical matters. In Titus 2:2, we find a list of qualifications for older men, followed by a transition to older women in verse 3 with the word "likewise." Paul first gives some characteristics of older women and then in verse 4 elaborates on their purpose. Women ought to cultivate certain virtues not just for the sake of these virtues themselves, but so that they'll be in a position to pass those on to the next generation of mothers and wives and so prepare them for God's calling on them as women. This passage relates the message from God to women in a way equivalent to the message to men in 2 Timothy 2:2, where Paul instructs Timothy, "And what you have heard from me in the presence of many witnesses entrust to faithful men who will be able to teach others also."

The Church as the Family of God

Paul's teaching regarding older women instructing younger women is based on an understanding of the church as the family of God. It's in the family where this kind of mentoring naturally should take place: from fathers to sons and from mothers to daughters. The family of God, however, steps in to provide spiritually for the needs especially of those who grew up with non-Christian or spiritually immature parents. By God's grace and enabling, the mature women of the church should rise up and accept responsibility as spiritual mothers and mentor the younger women. There's sadly a limited supply of older women who aren't only spiritually and practically ready to do this but who are also willing to expend themselves in service to young women. Titus 2 doesn't paint a picture of older people retiring and, say, moving to the beach to play golf, but of their continuing in active participation in God's family.

Characteristics of Older Women

The characteristics for older women are provided in Titus 2:3. They are to be reverent in the way they live and not to be slanderers (*diabolos*; cf. 1 Tim. 3:11). The reference to reverence recalls the description of the virtuous woman: "A woman who fears the LORD is to be praised" (Prov. 31:30). With regard to slander, we see that the word *diabolos* is the same as that used for the Devil.

> "By God's grace and enabling, the mature women of the church should rise up and accept responsibility as spiritual mothers and mentor the younger women. There's sadly a limited supply of older women who aren't only spiritually and practically ready to do this but who are also willing to expend themselves in service to young women."

This makes clear that to slander is to speak in a way that is characteristic of the Devil. This is therefore much to be abhorred! Older women are also not to be addicted to much wine. Such women may not have a problem with addiction to alcohol, but there may be other areas of possible addiction that they might need to address, such as self-control in eating or various other forms of dependence.

Training Young Women

After this, Paul provides a list of the "good things" that the older women are to teach the younger women. This is an interesting list! Why does the apostle mention these particular items? One thing we know is that the letter was addressed to people on the island of Crete, a very immoral society (Titus 1:12). In that kind of environment and its immoral surroundings, it must have been a challenge to find any spiritually mature people to appoint as leaders. Older women here are instructed to "train" young women. The idea here is to teach, and thus train, the young women.

The Greek word translated "train" (*sōphronizō*) indicates that older women are "to impart to the young women a sound mind," and thus "train" is a better translation than "encourage," as the word is sometimes rendered.[54] There may also be the idea of thinking of oneself and one's role in a way that's appropriate (cf. Rom. 12:3: "For by the grace given to me I say to everyone among you not to think of himself more highly than he ought to think, but to think with sober judgment [*sōphronein*]"). The word also often implies that a person is controlled by one's mind rather than emotions or impulses, that is, that he or she is sensible and exercises self-control.[55]

It's also interesting to note that there's no comparative component here. The text does not refer to "young*er*" women (even though some translations put it this way), but rather the Greek has "young" women. Mainly in view are those who are young in age and are therefore less experienced as wives and mothers.

In the church, then, our focus should be to build Christian character into the lives of our youth and young women heading toward and beginning their lives as wives and mothers. Though it's true that we're to encourage all women of lesser maturity to grow in their faith, the emphasis here isn't on these women in general but specifically on young women. There are also important implications for mothers of young daughters who need spiritual and practical guidance as they prepare for a life of service as wives, mothers, and managers of their homes.

Seven Characteristics to Impart

There are seven characteristics that older women are to pass on to young women, three pairs of two traits each and a final seventh one.

Love for husband and children. The first pair of characteristics indicates that older women should train young women to be lovers of their husbands (*philandros*; literally, "husband lovers") and children (*philoteknos*;

---

[54] There's another word for "encourage," *parakaleō*, which Paul could have used.
[55] As is required of church leaders (1 Tim. 3:2; Titus 1:8; cf. 2 Tim. 1:7; Titus 2:2). Another associated notion is that of living a reasonable, modest, and restrained life consisting in the renunciation of worldly passions in light of Christ's return (Titus 2:12–13). See *Exegetical Dictionary of the New Testament*, vol. 3, ed. Horst Balz and Gerhard Schneider (Grand Rapids, MI: Eerdmans, 1993), 330.

literally, "children lovers"). Sometimes in a marriage, these priorities need to be evaluated. The higher priority here appears for young women first to be lovers of their husbands and then second to be lovers of their children. Does this love of husband and children, then, not come naturally for women? It appears that in some ways, at least, young women need to be taught to express this love in practical ways. What does it mean to love your husband or to love your children, and how do we do this in concrete terms? It's older women who are expected to have this kind of knowledge, most likely because of their greater experience in these areas.

Self-control and purity. The next pair of characteristics focuses on Christian character in terms of self-control and purity. Self-control is a recurring theme in Titus and is part of the instructions for each category of people listed in this chapter (older men, older women, younger men; Titus 2:2, 5, 6). This attribute goes beyond the idea of not losing one's temper to a disciplined lifestyle generally with proper priorities in view. Purity in a young woman's life includes faithfulness to her husband and purity in her character and personal life, and toward her children, just as Jesus pronounced a blessing on those who are "pure in heart" (Matt. 5:8).

Busy at home and kind. The third pair of characteristics focuses on being busy at home and being kind. This emphasizes the domestic sphere of activity as central for the woman. It means that she devotes her energies to running her household and managing her home. The question usually arises as to whether the woman has the freedom to work outside the home. The choice of the couple here is a matter of their hearts, and their decision should probably center on whether the woman's and the man's God-ordained roles are compromised. There may be situations in which the woman's role may also be compromised by her excessive work inside the home or by her serving in the church or other volunteer activities beyond what is reasonable or appropriate. A woman's stage of life may also play into this decision in that a woman at a particular juncture may have more time to serve or work in ways that a young, married woman with several children may not. Temporary or even permanent crisis situations, such as health or financial difficulties, may require a woman to focus on matters outside her home for a time, and even though this isn't ideal, it's a fact of life in the fallen world in which we live. Couples must work through these situations, committing them to the Lord, who will be faithful to provide for all their needs (though not necessarily all their wants!). In the ancient world, the woman partnered with her husband in managing slaves and overseeing the extended household. The emphasis on kindness indicates that the woman wasn't to be irritable or hostile, but to have a good-natured disposition toward others inside and outside the household.

Husbands should provide adequately for the wives in their homes, investing in household tools and all that is necessary for the woman to make the house a haven of support and ministry to their family and those to whom God calls them to minister. It's part of the husband's role to give his wife the supplies and support she needs to do her job well and to build and protect this environment in whatever way possible. Proverbs 31:10–31 provides a great example of a woman who lived out her role to the fullest. Her home was a wonderful place to thrive and impact the world. If there's a negative stereotype associated with work in the home, churches may actually pull people away from their appropriate center in the home. The church should seek ways to strengthen families since the home is also a powerful center and springboard for ministry. If you look at the ministry of the early church in the book of Acts, you'll find that ministry often flowed from the homes of individual believers.

Submissive to husband. Finally, the seventh characteristic involves wives' submission to their husbands (and thus the list begins and ends with wives' relationship to their husbands). Paul stipulates that wives are to be "submissive to their own husbands" (Titus 2:5). As in the case of Ephesians 5, this doesn't communicate a sense of mutual submission as some contend, so that we see here again that it's the wife who is to be in submission to her husband and not vice versa. The woman is also not taught here to be submissive to anyone else's husband (except, of course, in a general sense as a regular church member to her pastor). Her focus is to be on her own husband. How are older women to train the young women in this? No specifics are given, but such training could involve personal modeling, counsel, and explicit teaching.

Implications

In this chapter, we've studied some of the most important passages on male-female roles in the church, including leadership roles. We've seen that 1 Timothy 2:12, in keeping with God's original design, limits the role of elder or overseer to men (cf. the "faithful husband" requirement for elders in 1 Tim. 3:2 and Titus 1:6). This continues the pattern of male leadership throughout Scripture from beginning to end. Women, for their part, rather than engage in public authoritative roles, are primarily called to serve in the domestic and familial spheres (1 Tim. 2:15). They are, however, most likely eligible to serve as deaconesses, which does not involve any ruling or authoritative dimension (1 Tim. 3:11). They also may train young women in the faith (Titus 2:3–5). In this way, Paul's teaching stands in perfect continuity with Old Testament teaching.

In our culture, we're progressively seeing more wives working outside the home while some husbands stay at home for a variety of reasons. There are situations in which a wife can make more money than her husband or in which the couple has chosen to work out their marriage in this way because this is their preference. In other cases, the husband may be lazy or may even misuse his position of authority. Whatever the reason, it's important for families to look to Scripture to learn and to stand by their biblical convictions regarding God's design of them. Men need to come to realize that they should act out their leadership role in a loving, sacrificial, and humble way and work to provide for and protect their families, while women should focus their energy on the domestic sphere. God's creation order is certainly not arbitrary, and living out his design will result in blessing those who follow it.

Key Resources

Köstenberger, Andreas J. "1–2 Timothy, Titus." In *Ephesians–Philemon*, 487–625. Vol. 12, *The Expositor's Bible Commentary*, edited by Tremper Longman III and David E. Garland. Rev. ed. Grand Rapids, MI: Zondervan, 2005.

———. "Ascertaining Women's God-Ordained Roles: An Interpretation of 1 Timothy 2:15." *Bulletin of Biblical Research* 7 (1997): 107–44. See also the summary "Saved through Childbearing? A Fresh Look at 1 Timothy

2:15 Points to Protection from Satan's Deception." *CBMW News* 2, no. 4 (1997): 1–6.

———. "A Complex Sentence: The Syntax of 1 Timothy 2:12." In *Women in the Church*, edited by Andreas J. Köstenberger and Thomas R. Schreiner, 53–84. 2nd ed. Grand Rapids, MI: Baker, 2005.

———. "The Crux of the Matter: Paul's Pastoral Pronouncements Regarding Women's Roles in 1 Timothy 2:9–15." *Faith and Mission* 14 (1997): 24–48.

———. *The Letters to Timothy and Titus*. Biblical Theology for Christian Proclamation. Nashville, TN: Broadman, forthcoming.

Köstenberger, Andreas, J., with David W. Jones. *God, Marriage, and Family: Rebuilding the Biblical Foundation*. 2nd ed. Wheaton, IL: Crossway, 2010. Chap. 12.

Moo, Douglas J. "What Does It Mean Not to Teach or Have Authority Over Men?: 1 Timothy 2:11–15." In *Recovering Biblical Manhood and Womanhood: A Response to Evangelical Feminism*, edited by John Piper and Wayne Grudem, 179–93. Wheaton, IL: Crossway, 1991.

Schreiner, Thomas. "An Interpretation of 1 Timothy 2:9–15: A Dialogue with Scholarship." In *Women in the Church*, edited by Andreas J. Köstenberger and Thomas R. Schreiner, 85–120. 2nd ed. Grand Rapids, MI: Baker, 2005.

Stiefel, Jennifer H. "Women Deacons in 1 Timothy: A Linguistic and Literary Look at 'Women Likewise . . .' (1 Tim 3.11)." *New Testament Studies* 41, no. 3 (1995): 442–57.

Weima, Jeffrey A. D., and Steven M. Baugh. *1 and 2 Thessalonians, 1 and 2 Timothy, Titus*. Vol. 3, Zondervan Illustrated Bible Backgrounds Commentary, edited by Clinton E. Arnold. Grand Rapids, MI: Zondervan, 2001.

Yarbrough, Robert W. "*Progressive and* Historic: The Hermeneutics of 1 Timothy 2:9–15." In *Women in the Church*, edited by Andreas J. Köstenberger and Thomas R. Schreiner, 121–48. 2nd ed. Grand Rapids, MI: Baker, 2005.

7

The Rest of the Story

Other New Testament Teaching

Likewise, husbands, live with your wives in an understanding way, showing honor to the woman as the weaker vessel, since they are heirs with you of the grace of life, so that your prayers may not be hindered.

—1 Peter 3:7

And he carried me away in the Spirit to a great, high mountain, and showed me the holy city Jerusalem coming down out of heaven from God, having the glory of God. . . . It had a great, high wall, with twelve gates, and at the gates twelve angels, and on the gates the names of the twelve tribes of the sons of Israel. . . . And the wall of the city had twelve foundations, and on them were the twelve names of the twelve apostles of the Lamb.

—Revelation 21:10–14

Key Points

1. Hebrews presents Jesus, the Son, in continuity with male leaders in Old Testament history such as Moses, Joshua, or the high priests. Two women, Sarah and Rahab, are included along with prominent Old Testament male characters in the "Hall of Faith" in chapter 11 because they trusted God's promise.
2. James, similar to Hebrews, uses Old Testament characters as examples, whether men such as Abraham, Job, and Elijah or women

---

such as Rahab. The continued use of the term "elders" (*presbyteroi*) for male leaders in James 5:14 indicates continuity between Old Testament Israel and the New Testament church.

3. First Peter 3:1–7 makes clear that the principles of submission and authority discussed by Paul were held broadly by the earliest Christians, including Peter. First Peter 5 confirms the pattern of a plurality of male elders, who are also called shepherds and overseers.
4. Second Peter draws an explicit connection between the Old Testament prophets and the New Testament apostles, showing God's continual plan in revealing himself through his appointed spokesmen.
5. John's first epistle opens with a reference to apostolic eyewitness testimony (all apostles, i.e., the Twelve, were male). The church leaders mentioned in 3 John are all male (such as Gaius, Demetrius).
6. The author of 2 and 3 John—the apostle John—refers to himself as "the elder" (conveying advanced age as well as authority), while the recipient churches are metaphorically called "the elect lady" and her children, personifying the church as a woman without implications as to the gender of church leaders.
7. The book of Revelation affirms the pattern of male leadership in both Testaments by symbolically linking the heads of the twelve tribes of Israel and the twelve apostles. Israel, the unbelieving world, and the church are all symbolically depicted as women, drawing on the images of a woman giving birth and of a bride joyfully submitting to her husband.

Paul Harvey Aurant (1918–2009), better known simply as Paul Harvey, was an American broadcaster for the ABC radio network. From the 1950s to the 1990s, Harvey's programs, including the famous *The Rest of the Story*, reached almost 25 million people a week. His news program was carried by twelve hundred radio stations, three hundred newspapers, and four hundred military stations. His *New York Times* obituary remembers him for "his own trademarks: a hypnotic timbre, extended pauses for effect, heart-warming tales of average Americans and folksy observations that evoked the heartland, family values and the old-fashioned plain talk one heard around the dinner table on Sunday."[1]

---

[1] Robert D. McFadden, "Paul Harvey, Homespun Radio Voice of Middle America, Is Dead at 90," *New York Times*, March 2, 2009.

Harvey's radio program *The Rest of the Story* premiered on May 10, 1976. Written by his son Paul Jr., the series rapidly grew to six broadcasts a week and continued for thirty-three years until Harvey's death in 2009. The program invariably started with the announcement, "Hello Americans, I'm Paul Harvey. You know what the news is. In a minute, you're going to hear . . . the rest of the story." Well, in this book, we've come a long way. We started back in Genesis and made our way through the remainder of the Old Testament, meeting a series of patriarchs, kings, priests, and prophets along the way. Then, in the New Testament, we studied Jesus and the early church, as well as the writings of Paul. Now, it's time for . . . the rest of the story.

Most discussions of the roles of men and women according to Scripture focus on the teaching of the apostle Paul. In addition, people may look at gender roles in the Old Testament—particularly, notable women such as Deborah or Esther (neither of whom can legitimately be used as examples of women in positions of authority; see chap. 2 above)—as well as consider Jesus's approach to women and the practice of the early church according to Acts (see chaps. 3–4). Very seldom do interpreters consider the possible contribution of the General Epistles or of the book of Revelation to the question at hand. The reason for this is that most of the teaching on gender roles is found in the above-mentioned documents. Also, the majority of works on men and women doesn't use a biblical-theological approach.

While understandable, this focus on the major biblical voices and the neglect of what might be considered minor voices (i.e., the General Epistles and Revelation) is unfortunate, because, as we'll see, a study of these latter writings yields some fruitful and unexpected returns. Therefore, while little that has been said in the preceding chapters breaks new ground (though hopefully the biblical-theological approach adds an important dimension in tying together the material from various portions of the canon), the present chapter explores territory that has previously been inadequately considered. However, the General Epistles and Revelation do contribute to our understanding of the biblical teaching on the roles of men and women according to God's design. Do these authors concur with previous writers? Let's find out.

Jesus, God's Son and High Priest of the New Covenant (Hebrews)

The main focus of the book of Hebrews is squarely *Jesus*, in whom God revealed himself "in these last days" and through whom God provided definitive atonement for the sins of his people (Heb. 1:1–4).[2] The author compares Jesus with both Moses and Joshua. Moses was faithful as a servant, while Jesus was faithful as a son (Heb. 3:1–6). Joshua gave people temporary rest by leading them into the Promised Land; Jesus will give them permanent rest (Hebrews 4). In this, the author erects and affirms a salvation-historical structure in God's program of revelation and redemption that presents Jesus as the culmination of God's previous work in and through Moses and Joshua, particularly at the exodus where God delivered the Israelites from bondage in Egypt.

The author also presents Jesus as the great high priest of his people. In order to represent his people before God, Jesus had to be human yet without sin (Heb. 2:10–18). As high priest, he also had to be male. Again, the author draws a contrast between the Levitical priesthood, which was limited in scope, and Jesus's priesthood, harking back to the priesthood of Melchizedek, which was eternal (Heb. 4:14–5:11; 7; cf. Ps. 110:4). As this kind of high priest, Jesus instituted a new covenant that was not subject to the limitations of the old covenant but was sealed by Jesus's own blood shed on the cross (Hebrews 8–10; cf. Jer. 31:31–34). In all of this, Jesus's maleness is essential in continuing the Old Testament pattern of male leadership, which included such leaders as Moses, Joshua, and the high priest. As we saw in chapters 2 and 3, according to this pattern of male leadership, ultimate authority for leading God's people was consistently given to men.

The so-called Hall of Faith in Hebrews 11 provides a stellar survey of faith in the Old Testament, presenting an entire "cloud of witnesses" that can encourage believers until this very day as we run the marathon of faith (v. 1), though ultimately we are to look to Jesus, "the founder and perfecter of our faith" (Heb. 12:2). Those who exercised commendable faith in the Old Testament and are selected by the author for special mention and/or commentary are listed in table 7.1.

---

[2] On the significance of the maleness of Jesus in God's redemptive plan see chap. 3 above.

Table 7.1: The Hall of Faith (Hebrews 11)

Old Testament Character	Reference in Hebrews 11
Abel	v. 4
Enoch	v. 5
Noah	v. 7
Abraham	vv. 8–10, 17–19
Sarah*	v. 11
Isaac	v. 20
Jacob	v. 21
Joseph	v. 22
Moses	vv. 23–28
Rahab*	v. 31
Gideon	v. 32
Barak	v. 32
Samson	v. 32
Jepthah	v. 32
David	v. 32
Samuel	v. 32
The prophets	v. 32

female characters

The two Old Testament figures that receive the most attention are Abraham and Moses (six verses each); no other character is mentioned in more than one verse. This appropriately acknowledges that they were the main leaders of Israel in Old Testament times (though it appears that the author has run out of time by the time he gets to David—the entire letter may originally have been a series of sermons—

and so is able to make only cursory reference to him).[3] The only two references to women in this chapter are to Sarah and Rahab. In Sarah's case, the author highlights her faith in trusting God's promise of a son in her old age (graciously overlooking Sarah's incredulous laughter when she received the news). In Rahab's case, he notes her friendly welcome to the spies scouting out the Promised Land.

Though Sarah and Rahab are mentioned prominently in that they're listed with men such as Abraham and Moses, these women are not singled out so much because they were female or because they were women leaders; instead, the references are salvation-historical and refer specifically to their exercise of faith. Both Sarah and Rahab were part of the history of God's people, part of the biblical story line, whether in giving birth to God's promised son, Isaac, or in helping Israel take possession of the land God had promised. In their exercise of faith, these two women take their place among the ranks of those in Old Testament times who had trusted God and his promises, which included many of the male leaders of Israel.

One also notes that women such as Deborah, Miriam, and Huldah are not mentioned (though Barak is; see Heb. 11:32), though the author obviously needed to be selective, and it's hard to speculate as to why certain other men or women weren't included. Similar to what was said above regarding the author's references to Moses, Joshua, and the Levitical priesthood, the Old Testament "Hall of Faith" in Hebrews 11 continues to affirm and faithfully reflect the pattern of male leadership in Old Testament Israel.

In the final chapter, the author urges his readers to honor marriage and to keep the marriage bed undefiled (Heb. 13:4), that is, to keep marriage free from adultery or other forms of sexual immorality. This, of course, tells us nothing about leadership roles but testifies to the author's high view of marriage. The author also enjoins his audience to obey their leaders (v. 17; Greek *hēgoumenois*) and later asks them to greet their leaders (v. 24; the same Greek word is used). Note that both references are plural. One surmises that these leaders were male (this is implicit in the masculine forms used). Intriguingly, the book also

---

[3] Cf. Matt. 1:1–18, which divides Jesus's genealogy into fourteen generations, with Abraham and David being the main figures.

includes a passing reference to the release of Timothy (a member of the Pauline circle) from an otherwise unknown imprisonment (v. 23).

Old Testament Characters as Examples of "Justification by Works," Patience in Suffering, Prayer in Faith (James)

James, the author of the New Testament book that bears his name, was the half-brother of Jesus (Matt. 13:55) and the leader of the church in Jerusalem (Acts 15). He was known as "James the Just" and was executed by the Romans in AD 62.[4] In his letter, James addresses a variety of issues that need attention in the church(es) to which he writes, such as the need for impartiality in dealing with wealthy and poor people in the congregation (James 2:1–7).

There's little in this letter that's relevant for our study of male-female identity, relationships, and roles. At one point, James stresses that faith must show itself in action, contending that people aren't justified by sheer faith unaccompanied by works but that, rightly understood, justification is by works (James 2:14–26).[5] In this context, James adduces both Abraham and Rahab as examples of those in the Old Testament who were justified by works: Abraham by offering up Isaac, and Rahab by protecting the spies. Both a male and a female example are given.

In chapter 5 James cites two additional male examples, Job and Elijah: Job as an example of patience in suffering, and Elijah as an example of a righteous man whose prayer of faith was effective. In highlighting some of these examples, James is similar to the author of Hebrews, especially in his "Hall of Faith" in chapter 11, which we've already discussed. Both authors seek to commend Old Testament characters who exercised faith and other godly virtues to their readers.

The most relevant passage for the question of gender in church leadership may be the reference to "the elders of the church" (*tous presbyterous tēs ekklēsias*) in James 5:14—which would have been male in keeping with universal Jewish practice—in the context of ministering

---

[4] For introductory information on James and the other NT books treated in this chapter, see Andreas J. Köstenberger, L. Scott Kellum, and Charles L. Quarles, *The Cradle, the Cross, and the Crown: An Introduction to the New Testament* (Nashville: B&H Academic, 2009), chaps. 16–20.
[5] Though note that while there is an apparent tension here with Paul's teaching of justification by grace apart from works, James and Paul are not really at odds with one another, because Paul, too, affirms the need for works as an expression of faith (see, e.g., Eph. 2:8–10).

to an ill church member. This shows the continuity between the Old Testament leadership pattern in Israel in which male elders were in charge of individual households and the congregation at large and the New Testament headship of husbands and groups of male elders in local churches.

Wives Submit to Unbelieving Husbands, Husbands Honor Wives as Weaker Vessels and Fellow Heirs Of Life, Elders Exercise Oversight as Examples to the Flock (1 Peter)

Peter sends his first letter to the "elect exiles" scattered across multiple provinces (1 Pet. 1:1). Throughout his letter, he emphasizes that these believers are "sojourners and exiles" (1 Pet. 2:11) whose true home is heaven and whose role in this life is to be witnesses to the unbelieving world around them. This witness includes giving a defense to anyone who asks regarding believers' hope (1 Pet. 3:15), but it also means proper submission to authorities even if that involves suffering. This is a practical expression of one's faith and of putting God and the gospel first. It's also Christlike because just as Christ suffered for us, so believers in a sense suffer for others in order to bring them to God (1 Pet. 2:21–25; 3:18).

Peter's Instructions to Wives and Husbands

The most important passage on male-female relationships in Peter's writings is found in 1 Peter 3:1–7. The passage, addressed to wives and husbands, is part of a household code or "house table" where an author addresses the different members of the ancient household, often including slaves as well.[6] Peter begins his instructions by writing, "Likewise, wives," continuing his instructions to believers to "be subject for the Lord's sake to every human institution," starting in 2:13. Christian citizens must submit (*hypotassō*) to governing authorities (vv. 13–17), Christian servants to masters (vv. 18–21), and Christian wives

---

[6] Helpful treatments of the passage include Wayne Grudem, "Wives Like Sarah, and the Husbands Who Honor Them: 1 Peter 3:1–7," in *Recovering Biblical Manhood and Womanhood: A Response to Biblical Feminism*, ed. John Piper and Wayne Grudem (Wheaton, IL: Crossway, 1991), 194–208; J. Ramsey Michaels, *1 Peter*, Word Biblical Commentary 49 (Waco, TX: Word, 1988), 154–72; and Peter H. Davids, *The First Epistle of Peter*, New International Commentary on the New Testament (Grand Rapids, MI: Eerdmans, 1990), 114–23.

to husbands (3:1–7). As we saw in our study of Ephesians 5, the word *submit* means "to subordinate" or to place oneself deliberately, voluntarily, and consciously under someone else's authority.

So we can see that it wasn't just Paul who taught headship and submission in the marriage and family relationship, but Peter as well. In fact, Peter's teaching is even more remarkable because he calls even wives of unbelieving husbands to submit to them. This continues Peter's earlier teaching in the letter that submission, in fact, is good and right in God's sight even when it involves suffering (1 Pet. 2:19–20).[7] The ultimate example of unjust suffering, as mentioned, is none other than Jesus Christ himself, who "continued entrusting himself to him who judges justly" (vv. 21–25; cf. 4:19). The purpose and result of Christ's suffering was "to bring us to God" (1 Pet. 3:18). Similarly, wives ought to submit to their unbelieving husbands so that "they may be won without a word by the conduct of their wives, when they see your respectful and pure conduct" (vv. 1b–2).

The idea of the wife submitting "without a word" is certainly not prohibiting the wife from sharing the gospel with her husband but is drawing attention to the persuasive power of a life lived in godliness and submission to God and in submission and respect for the husband. So Peter is not saying here that a wife married to an unbelieving husband should never use words; rather, that the husband won't be won primarily by his wife's words but by her respectful, submissive, and godly behavior. In verses 3–4 Peter elaborates on the type of woman that will commend the gospel: a woman whose primary focus is not external adornment but "the hidden person of the heart with the imperishable beauty of a gentle and quiet spirit" (cf. 1 Tim. 2:9–10).[8] This is contrary to what might be expected in a society where external beauty and charm are the norm in getting the attention of a man.[9]

In 1 Peter 3:5, Peter is extending his teaching on wifely submission

---

[7] There are obviously limits to Christian wives' submission to unbelieving husbands when it comes to physical abuse, though they are called to endure suffering that inevitably arises from their husbands' disobedience to the Word. On abuse, see Claire Smith, *God's Good Design: What the Bible Really Says about Men and Women* (Kingsford, Australia: Matthias Media, 2012), 181–94.

[8] See the discussion of 1 Tim. 2:9–10 in the previous chapter.

[9] See also Prov. 31:30: "Charm is deceitful, and beauty is vain, but a woman who fears the LORD is to be praised."

also to marriages in which both partners are believers, writing about holy women who hoped in God in the past just as Sarah submitted to Abraham. Peter even draws attention to the fact that Sarah called her husband "lord" (Gen. 18:12) and obeyed him (*hypakouō*, a stronger word than *hypotassō*).[10] Reading Genesis, we see that Abraham wasn't always the perfect husband (though he did cook!).[11] Neither was Sarah always the perfect wife![12] Nevertheless, Peter here upholds her as an example of wifely submission.[13]

Only one verse is devoted to husbands, perhaps because Peter's primary topic is submission to unjust authorities and suffering for the glory of God. Nevertheless, Peter does give them instructions as well to balance out the house table. Specifically, husbands are commanded to "live with your wives in an understanding way, showing honor to the woman as the weaker vessel, since they are heirs with you of the grace of life, so that your prayers may not be hindered" (1 Pet. 3:7). Peter admirably balances women's status as weaker vessels with their status as fellow heirs of salvation: men and women share in God's blessings in Christ while being different and unique creatures in keeping with God's creative design.

We may share a few brief observations. First, the Greek word for "your wives" is *gynaikeios*, literally "the feminine" or "female" (or even "femininity," the term's sole occurrence in the New Testament). This may draw special attention to the feminine makeup of a woman in contrast to a man. The command "live in an understanding way" renders the more literal "live in accordance with knowledge" (Greek *gnōsis*), which in context is further explained by the immediately following phrase "as the weaker vessel" ("vessel" [Greek *skeuos*] is a common metaphor for "person," perhaps with reference to her physical makeup). What husbands primarily need to understand, Peter seems to be saying, is that, as feminine beings, wives are in some sense weaker

---

[10] Does that mean that Christian wives today should address their husbands as "lord" or "master" as Rachel Held Evans seems to imply? (*A Year of Biblical Womanhood: How a Liberated Woman Found Herself Sitting on Her Roof, Covering Her Head, and Calling Her Husband "Master"* [Nashville: Thomas Nelson, 2012]). No. It means that they should respect their husbands and submit to them in the Lord, mindful that Christ himself is the head of the church (cf. Eph. 5:21–24).

[11] See, e.g., Gen. 18:6–8.

[12] See, e.g., Gen. 16:1–6.

[13] At one point, Abraham failed to exercise his God-given role of leadership. In Gen. 16:2, the inspired writer says that "Abram *listened to the voice of* Sarai," which eerily mimics the words used when Adam was judged subsequent to the fall in Gen. 3:17 ("Because *you have listened to the voice of* your wife").

(more fragile? more delicate?) and treat them with gentleness and sensitivity (see also Col. 3:19; cf. 3:21).[14]

The obvious question arises: weaker in what sense?[15] Peter is likely referring to women holistically. Some suggest the reference may be to physical weakness,[16] or to weakness in lacking authority,[17] but Peter may not have compartmentalized women into separate components of their being (physical body, emotions, intellect, etc.). Women certainly aren't weaker than men intellectually or spiritually (they are "fellow heirs"), though they might lack strength in that they were created from and for the man (Gen. 2:18–23; cf. 1 Cor. 11:8–9) and thus have a need for the man's leadership and depend on him to provide this leadership for them.[18] Regardless of the exact meaning of the phrase "weaker vessel," Peter does seem to hint at a role distinction between husband and wife. Also, "weaker vessel" is a positive identification of a woman's role of which she should not in any way be ashamed.[19]

As if Peter can sense the import of these kinds of questions, he proceeds to add a second, balancing command. Men are to show honor to women (now switching to the plural) because they are fellow heirs of the grace of life.[20] In what ways should husbands honor their wives? In the original cultural context, such honor may have been suggested by the following:

A husband's tenderness, affection, kindness, understanding of his wife's feelings, attention to her sexual needs, giving her children,

[14] Wayne Grudem, *1 Peter*, Tyndale New Testament Commentary (Grand Rapids, MI: Eerdmans, 1988), 143, is perhaps a bit too broad when he says, "The knowledge Peter intends here may include any knowledge that would be beneficial to the husband-wife relationship."
[15] Note that the notion is not unique in Paul. For example, Plato wrote in the fourth century BC, "The woman is weaker than the man" (*Rep.* 5.455E). A papyrus dated to AD 55 speaks of "womanly weakness" (*gynaikeian astheneian*; P.Oxy.II 0261); see Bernard Pyle Grenfell and Arthur Suffidge Hunt, *The Oxyrhynchus Papyri* (London: Egypt Exploration Fund, 1898–1922), 2.231.
[16] See, e.g., the church father Jerome. See Jonathan Yates, "Weaker Vessels and Hindered Prayers: 1 Peter 3:7 in Jerome and Augustine," *Augustiniana* 54 (2004): 245.
[17] See, e.g., Susan T. Foh, *Women and the Word of God* (Grand Rapids, MI: Maker, 1979), 204.
[18] At the same time, as Paul makes clear, men and women need each other (1 Cor. 11:11–12).
[19] Some people ignore this verse because they're fearful that it may challenge women's sense of worth. In actual fact, this is not a negative but a positive reference to the way in which a woman was made. In the relationship with her husband, she finds protection, comfort, peace, and security, as she was purposefully made to be interdependent with the man and live out her role as his suitable helper. She is weaker in the sense of being created from the man and for the man, needing him in marriage for fulfillment. Others choose to ignore this verse because it seems difficult for them to continue to advocate a view of women's unqualified equality with men when she is called "weaker." However, it is virtually impossible to recast the meaning of the word here. Whatever "weaker" means, it doesn't mean "stronger" or "equal," as these people might want to redefine the meaning of the term.
[20] The word translated "show" renders the Greek word *aponemō*, which occurs only here in the NT. The expression "fellow heirs" is found elsewhere in the NT only in Rom. 8:17; Eph. 3:6; and Heb. 11:9.

protection of her sexual purity, insuring a mutual communion that respects the common advantage of husband and wife, his delegation to her the charge (*cura*) of the household . . . speaking well to and of his wife publicly, and his certification in his will that his wife had been a good spouse.[21]

A husband can also honor his wife by sexual fidelity. According to Aristotle,

> Now a virtuous wife is best honored when she sees that her husband is faithful to her, and has no preference for another woman; but before all others loves and trusts her and holds her as his own. . . . Now to a wife nothing is of more value, nothing more rightfully her own, than honored and faithful partnership with her husband. Wherefore it befits not a man of sound mind to bestow his person promiscuously, or have random intercourse with women; for otherwise the base-born will share in the rights of his lawful children, and his wife will be robbed of her honor due, and shame be attached to his sons.[22]

The expression "heirs with you" is reminiscent of earlier passages in the letter that place believers' present suffering in the context of their eternal destiny (e.g., 1 Pet. 1:3–9). Both men and women who believe in Christ are heirs of eternal salvation and will one day spend eternity with him in heaven (v. 4; cf. Gal. 3:28–29). In this passage, then, Peter warns husbands that unless they treat their wives with sensitivity as to their feminine makeup, their (or the couple's) prayers will be hindered (cf. vv. 11–12; 1 Cor. 7:5; James 5:16).[23] Husbands, therefore, should be considerate toward their wives, mindful that (1) their wives are created in such a way that they depend on a godly male leader; (2) their wives are fellow heirs of eternal life; and (3) otherwise their prayers will be rendered ineffective.

Peter's Instructions to Elders

In terms of church leadership, the most important reference in Peter's first epistle is 5:1–5:

---

[21] Barth L. Campbell, *Honor, Shame, and the Rhetoric of 1 Peter*, Society of Biblical Literature Dissertation Series 160 (Atlanta: Scholars Press, 1998), 164.

[22] *Oec.* 3.2. I am grateful to Chuck Bumgardner for bringing this and the previous reference to my attention.

[23] Gk. *egkoptō* (lit. "cut out"); cf. Acts 24:4; Rom. 15:22; Gal. 5:7; 1 Thess. 2:18.

So I exhort the elders among you, as a fellow elder and a witness of the sufferings of Christ, as well as a partaker in the glory that is going to be revealed: shepherd the flock of God that is among you, exercising oversight, not under compulsion, but willingly, as God would have you; not for shameful gain, but eagerly; not domineering over those in your charge, but being examples to the flock. And when the chief Shepherd appears, you will receive the unfading crown of glory. Likewise, you who are younger, be subject to the elders. (1 Pet. 5:1–5a)

Remarkably, in a short span of verses Peter uses all three New Testament terms for church leaders, whether in noun or verb form: (1) elder (Greek *presbyteros*, masculine); (2) shepherd (*poimainō*); and (3) overseer (*episkopeō*), clearly indicating that these terms are used in conjunction with one another.[24] It's elders who shepherd and exercise oversight. Just like Peter, these other elders would have been male, consistent with previous New Testament teaching and in keeping with Old Testament precedent.[25]

Note also that both Silvanus (Silas) and (John) Mark are mentioned, both members of the Pauline circle but both also working in conjunction with Peter (vv. 12, 13). Silvanus was either Peter's secretary or (perhaps more likely) the letter carrier,[26] while Mark (whom Peter calls his spiritual "son") joins Peter in sending greetings from Rome (called "Babylon," v. 13). This continues to paint the picture of the early Christians as a close-knit network of believers and churches. It also confirms the conclusion gained from reading the book of Acts and Paul's letters that the early Christian mission was spearheaded by male leaders such as Paul, Peter, Silas, Mark, and others.[27]

The Apostles, Old Testament Prophets, and False Teachers (2 Peter)

Peter's second epistle was written primarily to combat false teachers who denied the prospect of Jesus's second coming, saying, "Where is

---

[24] See also 1 Pet. 2:25, where "shepherd" (*poimēn*) and "overseer" (*episkopos*) are used in parallel fashion.
[25] See the comments on James 5:14 above.
[26] See the discussion in Köstenberger, Kellum, and Quarles, *The Cradle, the Cross, and the Crown*, 731–32, esp. p. 731n22, with reference to D. A. Carson and Douglas J. Moo, *An Introduction to the New Testament*, 2nd ed. (Grand Rapids, MI: Zondervan, 2005), 645.
[27] See the discussion of the "Pauline circle" in chap. 4 above.

the promise of his coming? For ever since the fathers fell asleep, all things are continuing as they were from the beginning of creation" (2 Pet. 3:4). It appears that these false teachers claimed that ever since creation, God had not intervened in human affairs. As Peter pointed out, however, these people overlooked the fact that God had punished humanity by way of a universal flood, as the Scriptures indicate (Genesis 6–8), and thus denied the authority of God's Word. Peter also argued that the apparent delay in the second coming is not due to God's unreliability or unfaithfulness to his promise but is so that people are given every opportunity to repent. Also, Peter noted, "with the Lord one day is as a thousand years, and a thousand years as one day" (2 Pet. 3:8).

Against this backdrop, Peter testifies that he had *already* seen Jesus's glory at his first coming when Peter and some of his fellow apostles had witnessed the Transfiguration (2 Pet. 1:17; cf. Matt. 17:5; Mark 9:7; Luke 9:35). For this reason, Peter maintains, the apostles "did *not* follow cleverly devised myths [as the false teachers charged] when we made known to you the power and coming of our Lord Jesus Christ, but we were eyewitnesses of his majesty" (2 Pet. 1:16). The apostles (i.e., the Twelve, who were all male) were authorized and authoritative eyewitnesses. For this reason, their message regarding the reality and certainty of Jesus's coming was firm. In this way, the apostles' testimony further confirmed the reliability of the message of the Old Testament prophets, which had its origin not in the prophet's own imagination but in the revelation of God himself (2 Pet. 1:19–21).

In Peter's second epistle, we see therefore the connection between the Old Testament writing prophets—who provided the foundational revelation of God, especially regarding the coming of the Messiah—and the New Testament apostles, who built on this message and proclaimed the salvation made available through the Messiah's first coming and the expectation of Jesus's second coming at the end of time. Note that all four major Old Testament prophets (Isaiah, Jeremiah, Ezekiel, and Daniel) were male, and all twelve minor prophets were male as well.[28] All of this shows the continuity between the Testaments, which jointly testify to the biblical pattern of male leadership. Apparently, this pat-

---

[28] Contra Preston Kavanagh, *Huldah: The Prophet Who Wrote Hebrew Scripture* (Eugene, OR: Pickwick, 2012), who argues, on highly speculative grounds, that Huldah was "significantly involved" with Daniel, Ezra-Nehemiah, Chronicles, Proverbs, and Psalms (p. 77).

tern also extends to the way in which God's revelation was mediated through the authoritative, inspired Scriptures.

The Apostolic Testimony and Hospitality to Traveling Teachers (1–3 John)

1 John

John's first epistle starts with an opening reference to the apostolic eyewitness testimony to Jesus: "That which was from the beginning, which we have heard, which we have seen with our eyes, which we looked upon and have touched with our hands, concerning the word of life" (1 John 1:1; cf. John 15:27). As we saw in chapters 3 and 4 above, these apostles—the Twelve—were male, both in Jesus's original appointment and again when a replacement for Judas was sought.

A latter passage in the letter, 1 John 2:12–14, records John's instructions to "little children," "fathers," and "young men." This may refer to those who are younger in the faith ("little children") or all church members in the first instance and in the second and third instances to older believers ("fathers") or newer believers ("young men"). The references to fathers and young men may reflect the fact that men are heads of households and thus the ones primarily addressed.[29]

2–3 John

Both 2 and 3 John identify the author as "the elder" (probably combining the notions of a person's authority and that person's advanced age), almost certainly a reference to the apostle John.[30] As we've seen repeatedly already, "elder" is part of the pattern of male leadership in both Testaments (there are no female "elders"). Second John mentions an "elect lady and her children" (2 John 1; cf. v. 5) as well as the children of her "elect sister" (2 John 13). Most likely, the reference is to a mother church and one or several daughter churches.[31] This

---

[29] See, e.g., Robert W. Yarbrough, *1–3 John*, Baker Exegetical Commentary on the New Testament (Grand Rapids, MI: Baker, 2008), 116–24. See esp. p. 116, where Yarbrough quotes another source as saying, "the cornerstone of the patriarchal and patrilineal social edifice [was] the father." Yarbrough calls a man's twenties a period of "high energy, idealistic vision, willingness for conflict when necessary, and great potential for service" (p. 117). See also Yarbrough's discussion of those who call John's teaching here unduly androcentric (i.e., male-centered) (p. 117–18).
[30] See ibid., 329–31.
[31] Ibid., 333–34.

says nothing about the sex of the leaders of these churches, so it'd be improper to infer from the female designations that women served as pastors of those churches. In 3 John, the author mentions three men: (1) the beloved Gaius, a local pastor (v. 1); (2) Diotrephes, a dictatorial pastor who apparently refused to welcome itinerant teachers and put those who did out of the church (vv. 9–10); and (3) Demetrius, most likely the carrier of the letter (v. 12).[32] These church leaders mentioned in 3 John are all male.

False Teachers in Keeping with Predictions of the Apostles (Jude)

Interestingly, Jude tells his readers that his original intent was to write a positive letter regarding their common salvation, but instead he found it necessary to write to them in order to urge them to contend for "the faith that was once for all delivered to the saints" because "certain people" had "crept in unnoticed" who long ago were marked for condemnation, "ungodly people who pervert the grace of our God into sensuality and deny our only Master and Lord, Jesus Christ" (Jude 3–4).

There's little in Jude's letter that sheds any additional light on the question of church leadership. The only relevant reference is that to "the predictions of the apostles of our Lord Jesus Christ" in verse 17, which once again draws attention to the important place of the apostles in the New Testament church.[33] Jude's point here is that the presence of these false teachers validated the apostles' prediction that the rise of false teachers should be expected as a sign of "the last time" (v. 17). This prediction is not recorded elsewhere in the New Testament and is found only here in Jude's letter.

The Twelve Apostles, The Twenty-Four Elders, and the Messiah's Return (Revelation)

With this, we've arrived at the final book of the Bible in our biblical-theological survey. We saw God's design for man and woman in the

---

[32] For details, see ibid., 363–81.
[33] See discussion above. For details on Jude 17, see Richard J. Bauckham, *Jude, 2 Peter*, Word Biblical Commentary 50 (Waco, TX: Word, 1883), 102–7.

first book of Scripture, the book of Genesis. God designed humanity as male and female, in his image, that is, as his representatives charged with multiplying and subduing the earth for God. God made the man first, conveying that ultimate responsibility rests with him, and then fashioned the woman from the man and for the man, denoting the woman's orientation toward the man and her dependence on the man for his leadership. We also saw how the fall brought not only physical death as a consequence of the man's and the woman's sin but also distorted the male-female relationship, injecting into it a constant struggle for control. Nevertheless, the remainder of the Old Testament presents a continual pattern of male leadership exhibited in patriarchs, kings, and priests. This pattern of male leadership continues throughout Jesus's ministry and through the ministry of the early church, including in local church government, through male elders.

The book of Revelation provides the closing bookend of the biblical canon, in many ways showing the manner in which the eternal state restores God's design for the original creation and climactically fulfills it. The last two chapters of the book depict humanity in the new heaven and the new earth, now not in a garden—the garden of Eden—but in a city, the New Jerusalem. In keeping with God's covenant promises, God will once again dwell with redeemed humanity: "He will dwell with them, and they will be his people, and God himself will be with them as their God" (Rev. 21:3). There'll be no more death, no more suffering, and no more pain, "for the former things have passed away" (v. 4; cf. 2 Cor. 5:17). This, of course, will be the experience of men and women alike, in perfect harmony and eternal bliss.

In the fourth and final vision of the book, John is carried away in the Spirit to a high mountain where he's shown the glorious holy city, Jerusalem, the gates of which are inscribed with the names of the twelve tribes of the sons of Israel and on whose foundations are written the names of the twelve apostles of the Lamb (vv. 12, 14; cf. Eph. 2:20).[34] This indicates the affirmation of the continual biblical pattern of male leadership in both Testaments, with the twelve male apostles

[34] For background, see Grant R. Osborne, *Revelation*, Baker Exegetical Commentary on the New Testament (Grand Rapids, MI: Baker, 2002), 749–52 (though Osborne believes the twenty-four elders are angelic beings and not to be identified with the group made up of the heads of the twelve tribes and the twelve apostles; see ibid., 228–30).

254 **God's Design for Man and Woman**

serving as the New Testament equivalent of the male heads of the twelve tribes of Israel. It also affirms the intentional and corresponding nature of these two groups.[35] The two groups—most likely identical to the "twenty-four elders" mentioned earlier in the book (Rev. 4:4, 10)—also symbolize the unity of Old and New Testament believers. The church, for her part, is symbolized as a bride, "the wife of the Lamb," who longs for the coming of her bridegroom, the second coming of the Lord Jesus Christ (Rev. 21:9; 22:17). This female symbolism, too, is in keeping with previous depictions of the church in feminine terms (see, e.g., 2 John 1; in terms of role, see Eph. 5:24).

Earlier visions are of (1) the ascended, glorified Christ giving his seven letters to the seven churches (Rev. 1:9–22); (2) scenes of heavenly worship and seals, bowls, and trumpets of divine judgment on unbelievers (chaps. 4–16); and (3) Christ's one-thousand-year reign (the millennium) and final judgment of unbelievers and of Satan at Christ's second coming (17:1–21:8). In chapter 12, the seer witnesses a "great sign" in heaven, "a woman clothed with the sun, with the moon under her feet, and on her head a crown of twelve stars," pregnant and crying out in birth pains and the agony of giving birth (vv. 1–2). The woman most likely symbolizes Israel giving birth to the Jewish Messiah.[36] Another sign appears, a "great red dragon, with seven heads and ten horns, and on his heads seven diadems" (v. 3). When the woman gives birth to a male child, the dragon seeks to devour it, but the child is caught up with God and transported to his throne, while the woman flees into the wilderness, symbolizing persecution (see further vv. 13–17).[37]

Later, the unbelieving world is symbolized by "the great prostitute," who is seated on many waters and with whom the earth's rulers have committed sexual immorality (17:1–2). The woman is shown as adorned with all kinds of fine jewelry, but she's "drunk with the blood of the saints, the blood of the martyrs of Jesus" (v. 6). In the original historical context, the seven hills on which the woman is seated point to Rome, the capital of the mighty Roman Empire (vv. 9–11), though

---

[35] See the discussion of Jesus's choice of twelve male apostles in chap. 3 above.

[36] For details, see Osborne, *Revelation*, 456–58.

[37] See ibid., 458: "The emphasis here is on the woman as the persecuted church (the messianic woes)." For a discussion of the entire passage (Rev. 12:1–17), see ibid., 452–86.

Rome, in turn, is a type of all the major empires over history who have set themselves against God's people and have persecuted them. As mentioned, the church, too, is symbolized by a woman, the bride and wife of the Lamb, particularly at the marriage supper of the Lamb, at which a great multitude cries out, "Hallelujah! For the Lord our God the Almighty reigns. Let us rejoice and exult and give him the glory, for the marriage of the Lamb has come, and his Bride has made herself ready" (19:6–7).

We see, therefore, that Israel, the unbelieving world, and the church are all symbolized by women in this highly symbolic book: (1) a woman clothed with sun, moon, and stars; (2) the great prostitute; and (3) the bride of the Lamb. This is similar to the personification of wisdom and folly as women, as well as the character of the adulterous woman, in the book of Proverbs. It would be improper to infer from the symbolic representation of Israel and the church as women in Revelation what gender ought to be serving as pastors or elders in local churches. As we saw at the outset of our study of Revelation, the book strongly affirms the consistent biblical pattern of male leadership, ranging from the heads of the twelve tribes to the twelve apostles. Also, a woman is a fitting symbol for Israel since women by nature and in keeping with God's design give birth. The symbolism of the church as the bride of Christ, as mentioned, is fitting in that the church is called to submit to Christ as its head just as wives are called to submit to their husbands (cf. Eph. 5:22–24).

Implications

So now you know the rest of the story. This concludes our brief theological survey of the biblical teaching on God's design for man and woman. Our investigation has shown how there's a very consistent and unified picture of manhood and womanhood from the beginning of creation to the structure and ordering of families in the church while we wait expectantly for Christ's return. Men and women are joint expressions of the divine image yet different in role.[38] The biblical theology of manhood and womanhood exhibits a clear pattern of male

---

[38] See on this the essay by Steven B. Cowan, "The Metaphysics of Subordination: A Response to Rebecca Merrill Groothuis," *Journal of Biblical Manhood and Womanhood* 14 (Spring 2009): 43–53.

leadership from Genesis through Revelation. The biblical-theological survey doesn't depend on one or two isolated texts but rests on the firm foundation of the unified, coherent, and consistent scriptural witness. We'll tie our findings together in the concluding chapter and explore how we can apply what we've learned in the context of our contemporary culture, which is in considerable ferment with regard to men's and women's roles.

Key Resources

Bauckham, Richard J. *Jude, 2 Peter*. Vol. 50, Word Biblical Commentary. Waco, TX: Word, 1983.

Grudem, Wayne. "Women Like Sarah, and the Husbands Who Honor Them (1 Peter 3:1–7)." In *Recovering Biblical Manhood and Womanhood: A Response to Evangelical Feminism*, edited by John Piper and Wayne Grudem, 194–208. Wheaton, IL: Crossway, 1991.

Köstenberger, Andreas J., L. Scott Kellum, and Charles L. Quarles. *The Cradle, the Cross, and the Crown: An Introduction to the New Testament*. Nashville: B&H Academic, 2009.

Michaels, J. Ramsey. *1 Peter*. Vol. 49, Word Biblical Commentary. Waco, TX: Word, 1988.

O'Brien, Peter T. *The Letter to the Hebrews*. Pillar New Testament Commentary. Grand Rapids, MI: Eerdmans, 2010.

Osborne, Grant R. *Revelation*. Baker Exegetical Commentary on the New Testament. Grand Rapids, MI: Baker, 2002.

Yarbrough, Robert W. *1–3 John*. Baker Exegetical Commentary on the New Testament. Grand Rapids, MI: Baker, 2008.

8

God's Design Lived Out Today

But be doers of the word, and not hearers only, deceiving yourselves. For if anyone is a hearer of the word and not a doer, he is like a man who looks intently at his natural face in a mirror. For he looks at himself and goes away and at once forgets what he was like. But the one who looks into the perfect law, the law of liberty, and perseveres, being no hearer who forgets but a doer who acts, he will be blessed in his doing.

—James 1:22–25

Key Points

1. Men and women are created in God's image to be partners on mission for God. Scripture consistently reveals a pattern of male leadership in the home and the church. Women are complementary partners, confidants, and advisors.
2. Application of the biblical teaching on this topic is sometimes complex and involves a process of understanding the text through: (1) identifying the intended meaning of the author for the original recipients; (2) identifying the specificity of the teaching in the original context; (3) establishing a universal timeless principle, if possible; and (4) determining a specific contemporary application in light of four components: cultural, personal, circumstantial, and ethical.
3. The household or family of God is the pattern for the church to emulate, in which believers are related to one another spiritually as members of the same family, and male-female roles are to be lived out in the context of natural families.

4. Church leaders should strive to equip families to be worshiping communities that provide a context for the intentional ministries of mentoring and discipleship in the church. Mature men should disciple younger men, and mature women should invest in younger women.

5. Single believers, like those who are married, are called to live out their male or female identity in their natural family ties and in the local church, the spiritual "family of God."

6. Biblical roles and activities of men include worshiper, disciple, witness, husband, father, leader, provider, and protector. Qualified men may also serve as elder or deacon.

7. Biblical roles and activities of women include worshiper, disciple, witness, wife, and mother. Qualified women may also serve as deaconess.

8. True masculinity and femininity are grounded in a man's or woman's underlying God-given purpose and roles. We should be careful to avoid stereotypes of masculinity and femininity that owe more to cultural perceptions than to biblical guidelines.

We've come a long way in our understanding of God's design for men and women by going through Scripture from beginning to end. We've seen in the story the Bible weaves about the creation and life of human beings that there's a continuing thread pertaining to God's plan for man and woman. This plan is beautiful, consistent, and good. We've observed that God made humanity male and female in his image, and that he created the man first and then the woman to partner in domesticating the earth and filling it with godly offspring. Creating humanity male and female in his likeness, God sovereignly designed a relationship in which the man is given ultimate responsibility and the woman is placed alongside him as his suitable partner and helper and pronounced it "very good." This original pattern, which preceded the fall and the corruption of God's original design, is reiterated by the New Testament writers, who describe the restoration of the husband-wife relationship under Christ's overall authority. Because of the curse, these roles are now difficult, if not impossible, to live out apart from God's enablement through the Holy Spirit.

The Bible clearly describes the scenario at the fall, when Satan appealed to the woman's sense of independence and enticed her to break God's command. She acted outside the authority of her husband *and* her Creator, and the man followed her lead, listening to her rather than God's voice, and humanity plunged into sin. Since then, humankind has stood in need of redemption, and both the man and the woman face the consequences of rebelling against God. The difficulty we face now is that the woman typically finds within herself a tendency to subvert the man's leadership and to wrest authority from him in order to seize control. The man, for his part, finds within himself a tendency to treat his wife harshly or to retreat into passivity, abdicating his God-assigned leadership. The man's work in providing for his family is rendered more difficult, as is the woman's labor in childbearing, hitting right at the center of her God-given domain, her family and home.

Throughout the Old Testament period, we saw the pervasive effects of the curse on male-female relationships, including this constant struggle for control, and aberrations from God's design for marriage and family as seen in polygamy, adultery, divorce, and homosexuality. We also saw that the biblical pattern of male leadership continued to be upheld in the form of kings and priests. Prophets were mostly male (including all the writing prophets), though a few (such as Deborah or Huldah) were women. However, prophets had no institutional authority in and of themselves.

Turning to the New Testament, we witnessed how Jesus, while holding women in the highest regard, didn't overturn the original husband-and-wife relationship but affirmed it throughout his ministry. He encouraged men and women to learn from him and taught them the Scriptures. He received women's support along with men's. He regularly healed women as he did men and used illustrations of both men and women in his parables, relating directly to each group. He reached out to men as well as women and affirmed them in numerous other ways. At the same time, he appointed only men as apostles and continued to perpetrate the pattern of male leadership characteristic of God's original design and in ancient Israel.

Paul, for his part, similarly encouraged both men and women. He referred to women in various ministries in his letters and ardently

260 God's Design for Man and Woman

encouraged them to participate in the gospel mission. At the same time, he taught that men should serve as elders and pastors in churches. He makes clear that the results of the fall are still with us but can be overcome in the power of the Spirit. In Christ, believers are once again given the ability to be restored to God's original design for man and woman.

In Ephesians, Paul painted a beautiful picture of the ideal of a husband's loving, sacrificial leadership and a wife's respectful submission. In fulfillment of God's original vision, the two—husband and wife—are to become one. A believing husband and wife can again be unified in purpose and mission as they seek to live out their roles for the glory of their Creator and for their own good. We also learn that the same pattern that governs the marriage relationship applies to the church, God's household, where qualified men are to serve as leaders and women are to willingly submit to and support male leadership, participating as advisors, supporters, and encouragers as the Lord leads, and in ministry to women and children. The General Epistles and Revelation complete the picture presented in Scripture.

God's will is for man and woman to work together harmoniously in fulfilling his divine mandate through their God-given roles. They are to fill the earth and subdue it, and as members of the body of Christ they are to take part in Christ's commission to make disciples of all the nations. In the local church, too, harmony and humility are to characterize both men and women as they exercise their spiritual gifts for the common good. Women who are gifted in the areas of teaching or administration should exercise these gifts fully within God-established parameters, respecting the pattern of male leadership God instituted. At the same time, Paul reminds us that men and women are dependent on each other. The leadership and authority given to men ought to be one of example and of sacrificial, self-giving love. Women's advice, support, and participation are essential in the gospel mission. The intelligence or the teaching or administrative ability of men or women isn't determinative in God's assigning of men's and women's roles. It's simply a matter of his sovereign discretion and deliberate design.

It's interesting that Jesus and Paul didn't merely refer to the Old

Testament leadership structures of kings and priests but went back all the way to Adam (see, e.g., Matt. 19:5–6; 1 Cor. 11:8–9; Eph. 5:31; 1 Tim. 2:12–14; cf. Rom. 5:12–14). According to the book of Revelation, Jesus is the King of all kings, and in the book of Hebrews Jesus is said to have fulfilled the Old Testament priesthood and sacrificial system. Other New Testament writers make clear that all believers are now, in a sense, priests (see, e.g., 1 Pet. 2:9). However, this fulfillment of the kingly and priestly roles in Christ doesn't mark a shift from male leadership to egalitarian gender roles, nor is there clear scriptural evidence to support such an assertion. By rooting their teaching in God's creation of Adam, Jesus and Paul show that the principle of male leadership is more foundational to humanity than temporary structures such as the monarchy or the priesthood. Thus, kingship and priesthood, as well as the husband's role in the home and elders in the New Testament church, all serve as tangible expressions of the divine design of male leadership established at creation.

Table 8.1: New Testament References to Genesis 1–3

Genesis	New Testament References	Description
1:27	Matt. 19:4 // Mark 10:6; Gal. 3:28	Creation of humanity as male and female
2:7, 22	1 Cor. 11:8–9; 1 Tim. 2:13	Creation of man first, then woman
2:18, 20	1 Cor. 11:9	Creation of woman for the man
2:21–23	1 Cor. 11:8	Creation of woman from the man
2:24	Matt. 19:5 // Mark 10:7–8; 1 Cor. 6:16; Eph. 5:31	Man, woman become one flesh in marriage
3:2–6, 13	2 Cor. 11:3; 1 Tim. 2:14	Deception of Eve by Satan at the fall
3:16	1 Tim. 2:15	Fall ensues in struggle for control

Table 8.2: The Biblical Pattern of Male Leadership

Adam (Genesis 1–3)	Kings and Priests (Old Testament)	Christian Husbands and Elders (Gospels; Ephesians 5; 1 Timothy 2)
	The Biblical Pattern of Male Leadership	

Application

We've surveyed the scriptural teaching on our topic and briefly summarized our major findings. We've connected the dots in a way that is both coherent and consistent. But if we stop there—if we know what Scripture teaches on a particular subject but then fail to do it—our efforts have been in vain.

Now how do we apply what we've learned in this book? In order to do this, we need to talk about the ins and outs of application. For those who consider Scripture authoritative, affirmations of the truth and commands given in it are binding. We're not at liberty to make decisions that conflict with or disregard the biblical teaching. For example, the Bible issues clear instructions on divorce, and though we may find ourselves in marital difficulty, we must do everything we can to sustain the marriage, balancing all the relevant concerns appropriately.[1] We're also given other normative (permanent) principles in Scripture to adhere to. At the same time, it's not always easy to take what Scripture says and just "do it."

Application invariably involves some hard work and thought. As we mature in our Christian walk, this discernment in decision making becomes increasingly second nature (1 Cor. 2:16). This happens as we get to know God better and experience his work in our lives and in the lives of those around us. In beginning to think this through, we need to go through four essential steps as we process the biblical teaching and determine how to live in a godly way.[2] First, it helps to know what

---

[1] For more detail on this see Andreas J. Köstenberger with David W. Jones, *God, Marriage, and Family: Rebuilding the Biblical Foundation*, 2nd ed. (Wheaton, IL: Crossway, 2010), chap. 11 and the appendix on pp. 275–88.

[2] For more details, see Andreas Köstenberger and Richard D. Patterson, *Invitation to Biblical Interpretation: Exploring the Hermeneutical Triad of History, Literature, and Theology* (Grand Rapids, MI: Kregel, 2011), 784–95, esp. "Complications," 786–89, and "Guidelines for Application," 790–95, which include: (1) determine the intended purpose of the author; (2) assess the level of specificity of the original passage; (3) identify cross-cultural principles; and (4) find appropriate specific applications.

the intention of the author is in writing a given passage to the original recipients. Second, we need to assess whether the passage is specific to the original context or whether it directly applies to us today. Third, if it doesn't directly apply to us, is there a timeless principle that we can derive? Fourth, we need to find an appropriate, specific application to our lives today. This fourth step isn't always easy, so we need to spend a little more time discussing it, specifically as it relates to our roles as men and women. As noted, at least four elements come into play: cultural, personal, circumstantial, and ethical.

The first thing to remember, as we said, is that, in most cases, Scripture is either directly applicable or provides us with timeless principles.[3] In any case, application is inevitably cultural. As we choose to live out God's design for men and women, we must do so in the context of the culture in which we live. And culture is rarely neutral! Either it reflects biblical principles in some way (out of tradition or previous Christian influence on the cultural customs and laws of the land), or it has moved away from scriptural norms (due to the influence of other prevailing ways of thinking, feminism being but one example; see appendix 1), or it's somewhere in between. As we live out God's design for men and women, we'll be called to discern the larger societal values and worldviews in relation to which we have to make decisions (many of which have also impacted the church) and in some cases make choices that go against the grain of the prevailing cultural expectations.

Second, there's also an important personal dimension in applying scriptural teaching in our lives. As believers, we have the indwelling Holy Spirit guiding us, forming in us the mind of Christ, transforming our thinking, our values, even our affections (Rom. 12:1–2). If you're married, you can pray with genuine openness that the Spirit will guide you and your spouse in the decisions you'll be called to make together, and some of them may be genuinely complex. Making lists of what is appropriate for women or men to do or not to do in the home or church, in light of biblical teaching on gender issues,

---

[3] Of course, there are different interpretive rules for different genres, and special caution applies to narrative portions of Scripture where application is often indirect. For detailed discussion, see the respective chapters on interpreting the different biblical genres in Köstenberger and Patterson, *Invitation to Biblical Interpretation*.

has some limitations. Should the wife work outside the home? If so, how many hours? Should the husband take on a second, part-time job? How about your lifestyle expectations in light of biblical values? Should you downsize so that you can focus on being the man or woman God wants you to be? If you're single, does God want you to get married? If so, how will he guide you, and whom will you marry? The answers to these questions aren't always easy, and there's an inescapably personal dimension to making these kinds of decisions as an individual or couple. The Spirit will guide you (if you let him), and he will certainly do so in a way that's in keeping with the principles God has revealed in his Word.

Third, there are circumstantial factors that may play into your decision making as you live out the roles God has designed for you. We're referring here to the availability of unique choices or options a person may have in a given matter. They occur within your culture yet aren't defined by that culture but, rather, transcend it. Circumstantial factors differ from cultural issues in that they simply are the condition in which you find yourself at a given time in your life, the raw material out of which you must shape your God-honoring responses as you live for and follow the Lord. Such circumstantial factors are the flip side of personal factors in decision making. The emphasis is on the resources, opportunities, training, skills, and abilities (or lack thereof) that may lead you and your spouse to choose differently from another couple. What house you choose to buy and how you set up your home for family life and worship is dependent on several circumstances, such as how much money you have, your respective backgrounds, and your personal tastes and preferences. Adopting a child will be feasible only if the opportunity presents itself, financial resources are available, and a couple has the capacity to accommodate the addition to their family. In such cases, you should prayerfully seek the Lord's guidance both individually and as a couple.

The ethical part of decision making relates to the cultural, personal, and circumstantial aspects but involves the consideration of what the overall, morally superior of a complex set of choices might be. When a clear and direct application of Scripture is impossible, what's the best course of action? For instance, when a spouse is terminally ill or a couple has incurred large debt because of a lavish lifestyle of which they may have now repented, how will they live out male leadership in the context of male-female partnership? There may be times when a woman may need to work to support her family, at least temporarily, contrary to what might be her God-given role in her family in an ideal situation. If the husband is led by the Lord to go to college or graduate school for several years to train for a profession, should his wife go to work to support him financially so no debt is incurred? Or should he go to school part-time and take on a part-time job or ministry position that provides a certain amount of income? Should the whole family sacrifice and trust the Lord to provide as they follow his leading? In this case, they may live below the living standard they're used to. What about a combination of some of these options?

There's no substitute for thinking through these complicated issues personally and prayerfully, expecting the Spirit to guide you and your family in your unique, individual circumstances. At the same time, let's remember that we live in a sin-stained world, that we also have a sinful nature within us, and that we face continual spiritual warfare from the outside! We'll have to deal with all of these factors as we seek to live wisely and circumspectly in this world in the power of Christ (Eph. 5:15; Col. 4:5). In fact, wisdom is the key to making God-honoring decisions in all areas of life, including questions having to do with our male-female identity. The book of Proverbs calls on us to seek wisdom no matter the cost. It's not that wisdom is hard to find. The Bible says the fear of God is the beginning of wisdom (Prov. 1:7) and that God desires us to grow in the wisdom he alone is able to supply, in keeping with his own character and the way he set up the world, including human relationships. In fact, Jesus is our wisdom (1 Cor. 1:30). As we grow in him, we will also grow in wisdom and in our ability to make wise decisions that honor God and are good for us.

As we attempt to build up the body in this crucial area, we should make every effort to refrain from judging others for making decisions that are different from what we might choose to do if we were in their place. To begin with, we may not be aware of the unique circumstances and complex factors that affect other people's decision making. Also, as all of us live and grow in Christ, we're at different stages of maturity and ability to apply these truths. We need to be sensitive to these elements as we try to encourage one another in love to be obedient in living out our God-given roles. At the same time, however, as mentioned, we must not forget the parameters set in Scripture of God's original design as it is being restored by the power of the Spirit in Christ, and in this regard we should encourage the fainthearted and help the weak (1 Thess. 5:14). Wisdom is best sought and attained in community: "In an abundance of counselors there is safety" (Prov. 11:14). Let's make sure we build each other up rather than tear others down.

Men and Women Together on Mission for God

Now that we've reflected briefly on the complexity of applying the teaching of Scripture on God's design for men and women on a personal level, let's talk about some practical ways in which men and women can embark together on mission for God. Let's also discuss briefly what it means for the church to be the family or household of God. Let's then consider what churches can do to help and strengthen families and to help men and women as individuals live out their God-given roles. Along with this, let's take up several other important application issues, such as: What if I'm single? or: What about women in the workplace or in political office? We may not always have the final answer to all these questions, and there'll be times when, as mentioned, the application of biblical principles isn't as straightforward as we might like it to be. In those cases, we affirm embracing God's design and asking the Holy Spirit to conform us to this design, no matter the circumstances in which we find ourselves.

Partners Together in God's Mission

Men and women are to work in tandem to fulfill God's divine mandate through their God-given roles. In the power of his Spirit, they're to fill the earth and subdue it, and as members of the body of Christ (Rom. 12:4–8; 1 Corinthians 12–14; Eph. 4:11–17; 5:30) they're called to exercise their spiritual gifts and take part in Christ's commission to make disciples of all nations. In the local church, men and women are to exercise their spiritual gifts humbly and harmoniously for the common good. In keeping with God's design, qualified men should lead, and women should exercise their gifts within divinely established parameters.

How, then, should we specifically live out God's design for man and woman, and how should churches support and strengthen families in order to do this?[4] How should this amazing, beautiful, and consistent plan of God that gradually surfaced on the previous pages be clearly impressed upon the church? How can men be encouraged to be spiritual leaders and Christlike husbands in the home and women be taught how to love their husbands and children and to actively minister in the church body in a variety of ways? Contrary to those churches that shy away from even talking about men's and women's roles, this needs to be a central core of the teaching of the church.

Men and Women in the Family of God

As we move into practical suggestions on applying the biblical teaching on men's and women's roles, take a moment to reflect on the fact that the Bible pictures the church itself as the household or family of God (1 Tim. 3:4–5, 12, 14–15; 5:1–2; Titus 2:1–5). Paul draws an important connection between a man's handling of his natural family and his qualification to oversee the affairs of the church in the role of elder (1 Tim. 3:4–5).[5] What is more, in keeping with the household metaphor, Paul tells believers to relate to older people in the church as their fathers and mothers in Christ and to members of the same age or younger as brothers and sisters (1 Tim. 5:1–2; cf. Titus 2:1–8). This is also consistent with Jesus's teaching that all those who do his Father's will are his brothers and sisters (e.g., Mark 3:31–35; Luke 11:27–28).

As we've seen, Paul encourages older women to train young women as mothers would their daughters in the natural household, encouraging them to love their husband and children, to be working at home, and to be submissive to their own husbands (Titus 2:3–5; cf. 1 Tim. 2:15; 5:14). The same is true for older men in the church in relation to younger men who need to be grounded in the Word of God and learn to overcome the Evil One (e.g., 1 John 2:12–14). The family or

---

[4] Some of the material below is based on Köstenberger with Jones, *God, Marriage, and Family*, chap. 13. Used by permission.
[5] See ibid., chap. 12.

household model underscores that the church is built upon the model of the natural household as its spiritual equivalent. This has important implications for the way in which God wants the church to function. Accordingly, we might set up our men's and women's ministries to reflect these emphases rather than seeing them as "my time away from the kids." Ironically, society will teach children as young as preschool about sexuality and family roles while the church may limit its input to a session or study on dating and purity. Rather, young men and women should, from an early age, be learning alongside the older and wiser generation what it means to be a man or a woman, so that they may increasingly catch a vision of what God wants to do in their own lives in this regard. "Whoever walks with the wise becomes wise, but the companion of fools will suffer harm" (Prov. 13:20).

Paul's teaching on older believers in the faith mentoring the younger generation builds on a long trajectory in both Testaments. In ancient Israel, parents (and in particular fathers) were called to train the younger generation in the faith (Deut. 6:1–6; 11:18–21; see also Pss. 78:1–8; 145:4–7). The Old and New Testaments feature several significant mentoring relationships, including Moses and Joshua; Elijah and Elisha; Jesus and the Twelve; and Paul and Timothy. The church must be encouraged to recover the lost art of mentoring and of passing on the faith to the next generation of men and women. So not only should God's design for men and women be implemented in natural marriages and families, but believers in the church should be ordered and function in a similar way.

Table 8.3: Mentoring Relationships in Scripture

Scripture Passage	Mentoring Relationship or Teaching
Deuteronomy (e.g., 6:1–6; 11:18–21)	Parents training children in the faith
Deuteronomy/Joshua	Moses and Joshua
1 Kings 19; 2 Kings 2	Elijah and Elisha
Psalms (e.g., 78:1–8; 145:4–7)	One generation leaving a legacy for the next

Scripture Passage	Mentoring Relationship or Teaching
Jeremiah	Jeremiah and Baruch
Gospels	Jesus and the Twelve
Acts (early stages)	Barnabas and Paul
1–2 Timothy	Paul and Timothy
2 Tim. 2:2	Paul to Timothy to faithful men to others
Titus	Paul and Titus
Titus 2	Older women teaching young women

The Church's Ministry to Men and Women

What can church leaders do to design ministry that encourages men and women to live out their lives together on mission for God and spiritually function as the family of God? Due to the centrality of the family in God's plan from the beginning, the church should do everything it can to strengthen men and women in their natural families. Pastors and church leaders should make it their goal to teach the true biblical roles of husband and wife and God's plan for them to establish a family. The various forms of communicating truths to the body should be employed through preaching, role modeling, mentoring, premarital counseling, and other ways, especially to young couples but also to all other members of the church. As such, it will encourage existing marriages and families to bear witness to God's goodness, wisdom, and faithfulness to the surrounding culture.

Also, the church should be deliberate in patterning itself after God's plan for the natural household in which the older, mature generation trains and disciples the younger members, recognizing that some may be called to remain unmarried for the sake of God's kingdom. Nevertheless, these unmarried church members should be integrated fully into the life of the church. As is fitting for God's household and family, church leaders in particular should model healthy family relationships (1 Tim. 3:4–5). Church leaders should strive to equip families in the church to be worshiping communities, embodying on the micro level what the church ought to reflect on the macro level as the "household of God" (v. 15).[6]

Churches should be intentional in their approach to mentoring and discipleship, reaching out to everyone regardless of their stage of life, race, or socioeconomic background, not only to certain kinds of people in keeping with the demographic makeup of the majority of church members. Unfortunately, in many of our churches we've failed to affirm the husband's leadership in the home and the father's central role in the family. As a result, the church has at times joined forces with the unbelieving world to weaken marriages and families yet further. As the church fails to affirm, nurture, and encourage biblical roles for male-female relationships and to incorporate singles into the family structure, it weakens the mission of the church. Unintentionally, it may also set up further structures that weaken the family through an emphasis on age- or peer-oriented ministry (though there's obviously nothing wrong or unbiblical about ministering specifically and intentionally to certain demographic groups). Families are often separated the moment they walk through the church doors, each going to their own age-related class for the duration they're at church, and singles and seniors are isolated from children and youth. Wisdom is needed in order to meet the challenge of balancing the meeting of needs of church members at certain ages or stages of life with integrating them into the church body as a whole.

In strengthening marriages and families as a vital part of the church's mission, we should be regularly asking ourselves: What can we do to grow people's understanding of, commitment to, and actual practice of God's design for men and women? Simply put, church leaders and members should deliberately and vocally affirm the man's leadership in the home and church and in the same way should encourage women in their roles as wives and mothers. Men who sorely need encouragement to be spiritual leaders will begin to be stabilized, and many women who need a fresh perspective on their roles will be supported in the countercultural lifestyle of submitting to their

---

[6] For a helpful study, see Vern S. Poythress, *The Church as a Family: Why Male Leadership in the Family Requires Male Leadership in the Church as Well* (Wheaton, IL: Council on Biblical Manhood and Womanhood, 1990).

husbands (or preparing for marriage and supporting others in these God-ordained roles). In a world that treats this role largely with derision, intentional and deliberate action is necessary. Inter- or multi-generational ministry will also be helpful in unifying the church and will prevent unnecessary segmentation of the church into disjunctive, isolated individual units. It'll build on the natural affinity group of the extended family and lead to a more natural and meaningful ministry of mentoring and outreach.

In so doing, it should be kept in mind that, according to the New Testament, people become members of God's family through personal repentance and faith in the Lord Jesus Christ. The true church is thus made up of regenerate, born-again believers in Christ. Believers, therefore, are called to love and care for each other as natural brothers and sisters would. Thus they act toward non-flesh-and-blood relatives as if they were related, because, spiritually speaking, they are, united in their common faith in Jesus Christ. This is the family that is primary in the Scriptures. It's believers that we are most effectively teaching to live out these roles that God has given. It's not primarily natural kinship that unites us, but faith. Because of that shared faith, we worship together, pray together, study the Scriptures together, and minister together. In this new family, in a miraculous way, we love total strangers (though they don't stay strangers for long!) as if they were our fathers and mothers and sisters and brothers—because in Christ, they are, and we have more in common with them than we do with our natural relatives who don't necessarily share the same faith. Nevertheless, to the extent that it is possible, we should try to minister from the natural family and develop it into a worshiping, serving community.

It also may be that within each of our families, sadly, some may not be believers. Things may not always go as we want or hope. We should remember that Jesus, in the context of his call to discipleship, said: "Do not think that I have come to bring peace to the earth. I have not come to bring peace, but a sword. For I have come to set a man against his father, and a daughter against her mother, and a daughter-in-law against her mother-in-law. And a person's enemies will be those of his own household" (Matt. 10:34–35; Luke 12:53; cf. Mic. 7:6).

Making disciples according to the Great Commission should include an overt emphasis on equipping Christian men to practice their Christian faith in their homes as spiritual leaders of worship, Scripture reading, and so forth, rather than focusing exclusively on individual, personal growth. Likewise, discipleship for women should include training as instructed in Titus 2:3–5 where the older women teach the young women "to love their husbands and children, to be self-controlled, pure, working at home, kind, and submissive to their own husbands." Rather than conceiving of discipleship primarily or even exclusively in individualistic terms, it'll be important to view growing in one's faith and spiritual maturity in the context of one's family and the larger Christian community. In keeping with this, families should be encouraged to serve together, to grow together, and to engage in missions together as far as this is possible. Let's be careful to counteract the tendency to compartmentalize churches into men's ministry, women's ministry, singles ministry, youth ministry, children's ministry, and so on. We should be careful to avoid the kind of mind-set that thinks that simply by setting up each of those ministries we've succeeded in setting up a church that optimally facilitates the discipleship and mentoring of all of its members.

If this approach were to be adopted as ministry philosophy by the leaders and practiced on a church-wide basis, a greater meeting of needs and ministry might ensue. Much of this ministry might be more effective taking place in mature people's homes and families rather than merely by way of special, optional programs such as marriage seminars or discipleship classes on marriage and the family. These kinds of classes that take place in classrooms outside of natural life settings have some value but often lack long-term effectiveness in terms of passionate life-on-life involvement. Church events and various conferences and programs shouldn't be viewed as a substitute for a core of relational ministry in the discipling of men and women to pass on the faith and to make passionate disciples who honor God's plan for biblical manhood and womanhood.

Every aspect of the church should be oriented toward people in their family contexts with the acknowledgment of the added complexity that true family is the family of God. Those of our own household may not be receptive to godly influence and may require much grace and careful guidance not to upset the balance of the work of God in our families. We should not overlook those from broken or unusual situations, those—believers and unbelievers alike—whose lives have been marred by the shattering pain of poverty, divorce, or dysfunction. Our churches and homes can offer a taste of God's healing touch as we express love, acceptance, and hope. Just by living out our family roles—albeit imperfectly—others can begin to gain a vision for what Christ can do in their own lives. With godly families as the backbone of the congregation, those who are currently (or permanently) un-married can be drawn into a family context and make for healing for those recovering from broken relationships. This will likely result in hope, guidance, and protection for those, whether young and unmar-ried or previously married, who long for loving and nurturing family relationships.

If You're Single

Getting connected with family in the church as a single or single-again (through being widowed or divorced), whether young or old, rich or poor, is an important part of connecting and belonging in the church. Some, however, may still feel deficient in some way. "Do unmarried people reflect God's image the same way married people do?" they may ask. "How can I live out many of the principles enunciated in this book since I'm not currently a husband or father, wife or mother?" Andreas has addressed singleness in an entire chapter in his book *God, Marriage, and Family*, so for a fuller answer, please refer to the treatment in that volume.[7]

In short, our response is that *every* person is created in God's image and reflects masculinity or femininity just by being male or female, though it is true that those who aren't married are limited in the way in which they can physically fulfill God's creation mandate to multiply and manage the earth for him. At the same time, they're part of the fabric of human relationships in which they're called to love others, forgive or be forgiven, and exercise or submit to authority. They're

[7]Chap. 9. See also the bibliography on pp. 304–6; and Carolyn McCulley, "When You Don't Have a Better Half: Encouraging Biblical Roles as a Single Woman," *Journal for Biblical Manhood and Womanhood* 11, no. 2 (2006): 69–75.

still male and female and as such are called to express their God-given masculinity or femininity in keeping with their personality, temperament, interests, and life situation.

Single women and men can live out their masculinity and femininity through an expression of their design in their respective nurturing or leading relationships in families as well as in the church at large. There are many ways a man or woman can be deliberate in doing this. Some examples may include the Lord's leading them to be a big brother or sister to an orphaned or abandoned child in the context of the church. A woman may use her home to provide hospitality and to nurture other, younger women under the leadership of the church. A man may partner with other mature men to lead a group in sharing their faith or on a mission trip or serving in the church. He may also aspire to lead men in a Bible study, be an elder, or even be a pastor.

Biblical Roles and Activities of Men

Now that we've talked about various considerations and different ways in which the church as a whole can encourage men and women to live out their biblical roles within the context of the family, let's zero in specifically on the significant roles of men and women in living out God's design. All men are called to be spiritual leaders in their homes. This means they must be spiritually mature or else accept guidance from mature men until they are able to lead others to faith and to help their family grow in their faith.

Men also need to be in accountability relationships with other men who are spiritually more mature than they are and to partner with other men of similar maturity in pouring into younger men. And all of these men are to be ultimately submitted to the Lord Jesus Christ himself as they live out their roles.

Some Significant Male Roles

Specifically, men are to be worshipers, disciples, witnesses, husbands and fathers, leaders, providers, and protectors. As they grow in their faith, they will also get more involved in mentoring and training men; further develop their spiritual gifts and exercise hospitality; participate more actively in public worship; teach men, women, and children; and in some cases serve as elder or deacon. As a foundation for living out their roles as husbands and fathers, men should follow the Lord Jesus Christ. Humbling themselves to learn from God and to submit to his authority and his lordship in their own life will provide the source and power for their mission. If they aren't first and foremost disciples—learners—themselves, they won't have much to teach to their children.

Men may feel under great pressure at times as providers and leaders. Without God, living out all their roles adequately, or even with excellence, is virtually impossible. It's a high calling to be ultimately held accountable for all that occurs in their family (and in the case of elders, the church). It is at this point that men must learn to trust God to provide for all their needs and to seek first God's kingdom and his righteousness (Matt. 6:33), and God *will* provide everything they need. Their primary goal in life should be to serve God with all their heart and to care adequately for their family by his strength, guidance, and enablement. God is faithful, and he will enable them to be faithful as they put their trust in him. God has also provided the church to be a source of support and accountability in all of their important tasks.

In light of all this, they should aim to excel as husbands and fathers. It'll more than likely happen that men outgrow the initial wonder of being a newlywed or a new father. Men might gradually get drawn disproportionately into their work or various hobbies, whether golfing, fishing, or watching sports on television. Even ministry can become an obsession. However, as they continually, by God's grace, seek to nurture their wives and children, both physically and spiritually, God will provide. As husbands, they should love their wives, be faithful to them, and be sensitive rather than harsh with them. As fathers, they should be consistent in the discipline and instruction of their children, in love and for their own good. They should draw their entire family into God's mission in and through their lives—both as a family and individually. They should also be aware of the spiritual warfare that is a constant reality and encourage all the members of their family to put on the full armor of God (see Eph. 6:10–18).

As men mature in their faith, and as they prove themselves in the way in which they manage their own household (1 Tim. 3:4–5), they may aspire to serve in a leadership role in their local church. Whether or not they'll be chosen to serve in a leadership capacity in their church, all men should strive to meet the qualifications for church leaders set forth in Paul's letters to Timothy and Titus. Most of these qualifications are relevant for all men in terms of maturing in the faith. Men should also be committed and consistent in their witness to their faith in Christ to others and to be faithful in worshiping God in the company of others. If they strive to obey the Great Commission ("Go therefore and make disciples of all nations") and to follow the great commandments ("Love the Lord your God with all your heart, and love your neighbor as yourself"), they will do well. Such a man's wife and children will be blessed to have this kind of husband, father, and godly example.

"In keeping with God's original design, as restored in the Lord Jesus Christ, a true man . . . [will] provide for, protect, and lead responsibly those entrusted to his charge."

True Masculinity

What, then, does it mean for a man to be a man? By making him male, God has built into the man a masculinity that is very different from the femininity designed for women. In our culture, masculinity is often defined by external traits: a man rides a motorcycle or a pickup truck; goes fishing or golfing; is loud, aggressive, and boisterous; hangs out with his buddies; likes NASCAR and fast cars; and so on. Is this really what it means to be a man? Those activities may be limited expressions of masculinity in our particular culture, but being male goes a lot deeper than that.[8] In keeping with God's original design, as restored in the Lord Jesus Christ, a true man, as rooted in his essential, God-given identity, will reflect characteristics of his design as a man in his concern to provide for, protect, and lead responsibly those entrusted to his charge.

In this way, true and mature masculinity will be grounded in a man's underlying God-given purpose and expressed in his God-given roles. He will, with courage, conviction, and faithfulness, be seen as a

[8] See, e.g., Kevin DeYoung, "Play the Man," *Journal of Biblical Manhood and Womanhood* 16 (Fall 2011): 12–13: "I know conservatives want to push back the tide of feminism and fight against the emasculation of men in our culture, but offering stereotypes is not the way to do it. It is not fair to say, without qualification, 'Real men hunt and fish. Real men like football. Real men watch ultimate fighting. Real men love *Braveheart*. Real men change the oil and chop firewood.'"

man who engages in activities and tasks that are in keeping with his masculine identity. He will not only "hang out with the guys" but bond with other men in various ways to accomplish God-given purposes. He will mentor his sons and others in what it truly means to be a man and leader. He will take godly, energetic initiative in leading his family and nurture and provide for his wife and children. He will exercise his spiritual gifts in humility and submission in the context of the local church. In all this, he will model proper respect for authority and will discipline his ambitions and drives, physical and otherwise, in order to honor God in all of his life. If the body of Christ is functioning properly, he'll receive the respect from his wife, his family, and other people in the church that God has designed for him, and there won't be a void or need to seek significance in any way from empty, boisterous, and wasteful external pursuits to express his manhood.

Table 8.4: Male Leadership throughout Scripture

Adam's headship over the human race
The patriarchs
Moses and Joshua
The judges
Samuel
Saul, David, Solomon, and the kings in the northern and southern kingdoms
The Levitical priesthood
The Old Testament prophets, including the major and minor prophets
Jesus
The Twelve including Peter
The Pauline circle
The twenty-four elders in Revelation

Table 8.5: Biblical Roles and Activities of Men

Worshiper
Disciple
Witness
Husband
Father

Leader

Provider

Protector

Mentoring and training men

Exercising spiritual gifts

Hospitality

Participating in public worship

Teaching men, women, and children

Elder (teaching, shepherding, and oversight roles for qualified mature men)

Deacon (servant role for qualified mature men)

Biblical Roles and Activities of Women

It seems that our culture is forever swinging back and forth between two opposite extremes, finding it hard to achieve proper balance. Applied to the issue we've taken up in this book—God's abiding design for men and women—there actually is a balanced biblical position, and it is not one of the extremes of either abusive patriarchy on one hand or autonomous feminism on the other. It is not even the proposed middle ground of egalitarianism where neither the man nor the woman is in charge and where a "consensus model" rules the day. Maybe in theory this consensus model may seem to make some sense, but, as we've seen, Scripture consistently witnesses to the type of loving male-female relationships that assign to the *man* the responsibility to lead, nurture, and care for the woman (with the attendant notion of authority, to be exercised in the context of servant leadership) and to the *woman* the responsibility to honor and respect the man's leadership while coming alongside him as his intelligent partner in fulfilling the calling God has given to humanity at large and to the male-female union, in particular, to "rule" the earth together.

Some Significant Female Roles

Unfortunately, the kind of biblical model we've presented in this book is often cast as diminishing the quality of life and ministry of women. We can see how people could perceive it this way especially in a day

when any sets of boundaries or restrictions are seen as unwelcome obstacles on people's path to unfettered freedom. But Scripture upholds a
different standard than the supremacy of human libertarian freedom:
God's good, wise, and beneficial order that he established and according to which he designed the world. Not only can we see this order
instituted in the opening chapters of Genesis; we see it affirmed and
extolled in books such as Ephesians or 1 Corinthians and through the
rest of the Bible. As biblical Christians, we must be keenly aware that
embracing this kind of message pits us inevitably against the wisdom
of this world, which prevails in our culture. The biblical teaching is
deeply countercultural and will be cast as antiquated, sexist, or worse
by the contemporary media, mainstream political and even many religious institutions, and others.

That said, we must acknowledge that there's unfortunately a certain amount of truth in the charge that conservative churches often
diminish even the legitimate ministry of women. While this may be
done unintentionally, the disparagement of
women's participation in ministry occurs
nonetheless. Whether in the world or in
the church, women therefore continue to be
pressured by a variety of expectations that
are sometimes but not always justified. In
the world, women's role as wife and mother
is often minimized.[9] Yet marriage and moth-

> But Scripture upholds a dif-
> ferent standard than the su-
> premacy of human libertarian
> freedom: God's good, wise,
> and beneficial order that he
> established and according to
> which he designed the world.

erhood are central callings for women in Scripture. We've seen that
bearing and raising children is a foundational and central part of God's
purpose for creating the woman in the first place. For this reason, the
biblical expectation would seem to continue to be that couples have
several children.[10]

Even in the church, women's ministry to other women or children is at times cast as inferior, because their ministry doesn't entail
teaching or authority over men. However, there's nothing inferior
about women ministering to other women or children. To the con-

---

[9] A helpful essay is Mary K. Mohler, "Motherhood Matters," *Journal for Biblical Manhood and Womanhood* 11, no. 2 (2006): 48–55.

[10] For a discussion of related issues such as infertility, adoption, and contraception, see Köstenberger with Jones, *God, Marriage, and Family*, chaps. 7–8.

trary, this kind of involvement is vital, valuable, and biblical. Like men, women are to grow as Christ's disciples, to witness to him, and to engage in mission for Christ, often in conjunction with their husbands. They're also called to practice hospitality and to engage in a variety of good works.[11] What's more, they're to engage in mentoring and training women, as well as to pray, prophesy, and otherwise participate in public worship, exercising their spiritual gifts within biblical parameters.

Women's participation in public worship may take a variety of forms. When we first met, we were part of a church that had a time following the service, moderated by an elder, in which the entire congregation gathered in order to share prayer requests, read Scripture, and voice insights as to what individual members of the congregation (both male and female) thought God wanted the church to do at that particular point in time (cf. 1 Cor. 11:26–33). This is a good model of New Testament church with male oversight and male and female participation in public worship and congregational life.[12] Whatever was said during those meeting was later taken under advisement by the elders of the church for further consideration, and women were consulted in this process as needed and appropriate.

Our study has shown that it's biblically permissible to have women serve as deaconesses and that this was probably a practice in New Testament times. Churches would therefore be well advised to consider whether it'd be wise and appropriate in their context to appoint deaconesses, especially if the church already has male deacons. If so, however, they would need to make sure that the role of deacon (for men as well as women) is properly defined and implemented in keeping with scriptural stipulations for elders and deacons. Any oversight or shepherding responsibility is not biblically to be made part of the

---

[11]On hospitality, see John Piper's sermon, "Strategic Hospitality," http://www.desiringgod.org/resource-library/sermons/strategic-hospitality. Piper explains, "What I mean by strategic hospitality is a hospitality that thinks strategically and asks: How can I draw the most people into a deep experience of God's hospitality by the use of my home or my church home? . . . Who are the people who could be brought together in my home most strategically for the sake of the kingdom?" See also the books and resources listed at the "A Candle in the Window Hospitality Network," http://www.acandleinthewindow.com/Default.aspx?pageId=984465#.UehMytJJMII (accessed July 18, 2013).

[12]Conversely, churches that do not allow women to speak at all in church but limit speaking to men or male heads of household inadequately recognize that the NT texts that speak of women remaining silent address specific circumstances (such as the weighing of prophecies, 1 Cor. 14:33b–36) and are not absolute (see, e.g., 1 Cor. 11:2–16, which makes clear that women prayed and prophesied in that same church in Corinth). See the discussion of 1 Cor. 11:2–16 and 14:33b–36 in chap. 5 above.

role of deacons, whether male or female. Beyond this, women should, of course, share their learning through scholarly or popular writing, teaching in a university or other appropriate settings, and other ways. As a matter of fact, we've referred in this book to several academic and nonacademic books and scholarly articles written by women that have been very helpful to us in our thinking about this topic.

Today, we have a unique opportunity in our churches to nurture a culture in which women feel genuinely appreciated for their unique ministries. Our churches desperately need the ministries of women. Men can't be mothers or wives. Men can't minister to women and children the way only women can. Even in their exercise of hospitality, their practice of good works, their growth as disciples, and their witness in the surrounding culture, women have a unique contribution to make that must not in any way be diminished or go un- or underappreciated. This is itself very important. Beyond implementing the role of deaconess, we'd love to see churches incorporate mature and humble women into the decision making of the local church in appropriate ways.[13] Speaking for myself (Andreas), I've often found the input of my wife or of other humble women to be invaluable. It would be a tragedy for men in the church to ignore this God-given resource of wisdom and insight.

Nevertheless, there will likely be some who will criticize us for affirming the biblical pattern of male leadership. As husband and wife, and as fellow disciples and heirs of God's grace, we're united in our conviction that Scripture teaches a pattern of male leadership but that this pattern, if implemented in keeping with God's design, is not ultimately confining but actually liberating for both men and women. The apostle Paul was right: as women and men, we need each other. By God's design, we truly complement each other in our respective strengths and weaknesses and in our unique contributions to the male-female relationship and to the work of advancing God's kingdom in this world.

---

[13] This may take the form of women sitting in on elders' meetings or in a variety of informal ways of consulting them, especially when decisions made directly affect them. Of course, congregational churches do have a mechanism by which women participate in congregational discussion and voting, though congregational meetings, while helpful and important, are not always the best forum for the type of consultation that we have in mind.

Table 8.6: Women Making Significant
Contributions in Scripture (Selected List)

Eve	First woman, "mother of all living"
Miriam	Prophetess, leads women in worship at the exodus
Deborah	Prophetess, responds in time of national crisis
Ruth	God-fearing Gentile, great-grandmother of King David
Hannah	Godly mother of Samuel, dedicated son to the Lord
Huldah	Prophetess during reign of King Josiah
Esther	Queen, used by God to save the people of Israel from extinction
Elizabeth	Mother of John the Baptist, the forerunner of Jesus
Mary	Mother of Jesus, the Messiah
Mary of Bethany	Sat at Jesus's feet, taking posture of disciple
Mary Magdalene	(Among the) first to see the risen Jesus
Priscilla	With husband Aquila, hosted church in home, instructed Apollos
Phoebe	Deaconess, benefactress, letter carrier of book of Romans
Eunice and Lois	Timothy's godly mother and grandmother

Table 8.7: Biblical Roles and Activities of Women

Worshiper
Disciple
Witness
Wife (companion, helper, partner, advisor)
Mother
Worker (good works in general, work in the home)
Hospitality

Mentoring and training women

Participating in public worship (including praying and prophesying)

Exercising spiritual gifts within biblical parameters (including administration)

Teaching and other ministry to children

Advisor to church leadership (qualified mature women)

Deaconess (servant role for qualified mature women)

Women in the Workplace or in Public Office

One question we're commonly asked when teaching on the subject of women's roles and ministry is, Should women work outside the home? As mentioned above, when it comes to application a variety of cultural, personal, circumstantial, and ethical factors enter in. Beyond this, there is also a larger socioeconomic global dimension.[14] At the same time, there are some universal spiritual parameters that God has assigned to the man and the woman. Ultimately, since the man has responsibility for his family, and the woman's domain is to be primarily a ministry based in her home, the first priority is that a couple embrace this God-given design, to be committed to it in principle, and to strive to make decisions that are in keeping with this principle whenever possible.

There are obviously a limitless number of individual circumstances and exceptions that may be made, and it's completely impossible for us to even begin to address all or even most of those. One caution, however: just because a couple agrees, say, that the husband stays home after the wife has a baby, while she continues to go to work, or because she can make more money than he, doesn't necessarily make it the best decision. In some cases, a couple may need to evaluate their priorities, their lifestyle choices, and even their commitment to honor God's Word and make sacrifices, stepping out in faith and trusting God. Another principle a woman might consider is, Am I giving the best of myself, my best hours and my energies, to those outside of my home? This might not necessarily just include work outside the home, but

---

[14] See, e.g., Kevin Carmichael, "Global Growth May Depend on More Women Working," *Globe and Mail* (Wednesday, July 24, 2013), B2, who says that the key to continued global economic growth is to get more women working.

overly committed ministry responsibilities or excessive time spent online, to give but a few examples.

Some of you reading this may ask, "But what about women in public office? Is there no difference between civic and church polity?" Good question. We would formulate a succinct answer as follows. Old Testament Israel was a theocracy, a political nation ruled by God (whether directly or through a series of rulers or monarchs), and the church is not a political but a spiritual entity. Our argument in this book is that God's design for his people is consistent: men are to lead, women are to intelligently affirm and support male leadership as partners created in God's image. Scripture doesn't directly address the question of whether women ought to pursue positions entailing executive authority such as president or governor. In any case, Christians cannot expect the world that doesn't accept scriptural authority to conduct its affairs in keeping with biblical principles and precepts.

Well, you say, should a Christian woman, from the vantage point of the church and the prescribed roles within it, pursue the presidency or governorship? In making such a decision, she would need to balance the Scripture's teaching on women's roles in the home and church with what she believes God is calling her to do in the public sphere. Would she be able to adequately fulfill her primary God-given roles in both the home and the church? Could she continue to love, support, and enable her husband's leadership and nurture her family and ministry out of her home if she were to take on public office? Though we wouldn't want to answer for everybody, women would likely be wise to exercise restraint in this regard and encourage men to lead if they want to fulfill their essential calling. (Remember Deborah, who recruited and encouraged Barak to take charge as a leader in the nation of Israel during a crisis situation? In this way, rather than taking charge herself, she encouraged and affirmed male leadership.)[15]

Though there are no formal restrictions given in this regard, our concern is primarily for those who are mothers to not neglect their children and family in pursuit of political office (neither should fathers, but there's still a difference in terms of primary calling). This is not to say that women can't be great leaders. It's not primarily a ques-

---

[15] See chap. 2.

tion about characteristics, capability, or competence but about God's design for men and women. There may be a range of perspectives among conservative, Bible-believing Christians at this point, but one thing is clear: if we're prepared to follow God's design in our relationships in every area of life, he'll be honored, and we'll be blessed.

True Femininity

What does it mean to be a woman? In our comments on biblical manhood, we noted stereotypes about what it means to be masculine and how often these ideas owe more to cultural perceptions than to biblical guidance. This is as true for our understanding of femininity as it is regarding masculinity. In our culture, though it is constantly changing, some would conceive of femininity to include some of the following: cute clothes, pink and purple, cosmetics, perfume, beautiful hair, and sex appeal. Many girls are drawn to and encouraged to play with dolls, take ballet lessons, play the flute, try out for cheerleading, pursue certain professions and are generally known to be softer, sweeter, and more sensitive than their male counterparts. Some of these stereotypes are deliberately challenged in our day as we see lines of cosmetics for men emerging and more men entering what might be previously known as feminine professions, such as nursing, but there is still a majority perspective observed in the culture. Is this what it means to be a girl or a woman?

Scripture does indicate that women are "weaker vessels" (in relation to men, 1 Pet. 3:7) and teaches that the woman was created from the man, which may indicate that she is in some sense more dependent on him than he is on her. As far as beauty and sex appeal, Proverbs 31:30 says that beauty and charm are fleeting, but a woman who fears the Lord is greatly to be praised. Proverbs also says that a beautiful woman who lacks discretion is like a gold ring in a pig's snout (11:22). The New Testament, likewise, speaks about the importance of a woman's focus on inner beauty rather than on external jewelry or hair (1 Pet. 3:3–4; 1 Tim. 2:9–10). It's what's on the inside that's lasting and most important. Beauty is only a temporary asset, while godliness has value in this life—maybe more obvious in old age—and in the life to come.

286 God's Design for Man and Woman

For this reason, we'll all do well to impress on our daughters and younger women the surpassing value of cultivating character and godliness. This should be central and balance the concern with the way they look. How much time do they spend standing in front of the mirror, getting dressed, and doing their hair, and how much time do they spend praying, serving, and reading the Bible? That's a tough question for many teenagers and women of any age. As we place cultural stereotypes on what it means to be feminine in the context of what the Bible teaches about femininity, our shallowness and worldliness are often exposed. We realize and must confess that, too often, our working assumption of what it means to be a woman is informed by the world around us rather than by what the Bible teaches.

We rightly deplore the exploitation of women in pornography and women's treatment as sexual objects. Although these abuses mark a clear departure from God's design for women, in their distorted way they still point to God's purpose for women: that in their beauty they bring glory to the one who made them in his image. A woman's dignity doesn't come from her external beauty, male affirmation, or even female empowerment.[16] It comes from being created by God and being loved and valued in Christ. Being loved by God and accepted in Christ is a priceless possession, no matter what a woman's age or level of physical attractiveness. True beauty is defined in the eyes of God, not in the eyes of humans.

What, then, does it mean to be a woman, to be truly feminine according to Scripture? At the heart, it means that women are grounded in God's original design for them as persons created in the image of God and that they're in the process of being restored to that image in Christ. As followers of Jesus, women are called to committed Christian discipleship, to gracious and beautiful submission to authority (including, if they're married, to their husbands), and to faithful Christian witness, service, and mission in the context of their local church and family. Femininity is more than the outfits women wear or the way they do their hair. As Jesus told his followers,

---

[16] On a practical note, see Amy Spiegel, *Letting Go of Perfect: Women, Expectations, and Authenticity* (Nashville: Broadman, 2012); and Carolyn Mahaney and Nicole Whitacre, *True Beauty* (Wheaton, IL: Crossway, 2014).

Do not be anxious about your life, what you will eat or what you will drink, nor about your body, what you will put on. Is not life more than food, and the body more than clothing? . . . Therefore do not be anxious, saying, "What shall we eat?" or "What shall we drink?" or "What shall we wear?" For the Gentiles seek after all these things, and your heavenly Father knows that you need them all. But seek first the kingdom of God and his righteousness, and all these things will be added to you. (Matt. 6:25–33)

John Piper calls "true womanhood . . . a distinctive calling of God to display the glory of His Son in ways that would not be displayed if there were no womanhood." He writes, "Married womanhood has its unique potential for magnifying Christ that single womanhood does not have. Single womanhood has its unique potential for magnifying Christ which married womanhood does not have." Consequently, his advice to women is this: "So whether you marry or remain single, do not settle for a wimpy theology. It is beneath you. God is too great. Christ is too glorious. True womanhood is too strategic. Don't waste it. Your womanhood—your true womanhood—was made for the glory of Jesus Christ."[17]

Conclusion

Hopefully, you've found this closing chapter motivating as we've tried to sketch some possible ways to apply the biblical teaching on manhood and womanhood. We expect that as you begin to apply these truths in your lives and churches, slowly, over time, you may see what we've described take on shape. Men—not all, but some, perhaps even many—will hopefully rise to the occasion with women affirming their leadership. Young people who are beginning to relate as singles according to their biblical design will find opportunity to lay the foundation for marriage, should God provide. Leaders of the church will model and flesh out the vision and roles for manhood and womanhood throughout the ministries of the church. With a tone of encouragement, vision, and grace, many of the men in the church

---

[17] John Piper, "The Ultimate Meaning of True Womanhood," in *Journal of Biblical Manhood and Womanhood* 15 (Fall 2010): 15–18 (the quotes are from p. 18). Repr. from *Voices of the True Woman Movement: A Call to the Counter Revolution* (Chicago: Moody, 2010), based on a message delivered at the True Woman '08 conference.

will begin to gain a sense of hope and vision for what the Holy Spirit can do in and through them, rather than sensing legalistic pressure to "perform" and live up to a standard that seems impossible for them to attain.

Pastors can reinforce this vision whenever appropriate as they teach through biblical books but more intentionally through designing the men's ministry. In this vital role, boys grade six and up could perhaps be included as pastors teach the various facets of biblical manhood and roles and as testimonies and support are given. They might encourage men to work on a family discipleship plan that expresses their vision of how they want to lead their families based on the Spirit's leading and individual family members' gifting, bents, and interests. They could encourage the men in the church to catch a vision for how God might use their family, with its unique makeup, to further his kingdom—Great Commandment *and* Great Commission—by passing the baton of truth to the next generation and, together, making a difference now as a family team.

Likewise, women may meet during the same time period. The primary thrust of these meetings might be defining and encouraging biblical womanhood rather than studying through a book of the Bible. If we are in churches that are preaching consistently through the Bible (often with an added Sunday school hour) and involved in family worship, including study of Scripture, we're already getting a balanced intake of biblical truth, so our limited time as men's and women's ministries may be best devoted to addressing the distinctive roles of manhood and womanhood and their practical application (including young people from about twelve and thirteen and up).

Life-on-life relational mentoring should be at the heart, not the periphery, of a church's vision for ministry and discipleship. Everyone who would like to mentor another person of the same sex or who would like to be mentored should be provided with the opportunity to do so. At times, this will happen spontaneously, but if mentoring is left solely to personal initiative, some people will likely fall through the cracks. For this reason it will be helpful to organize men's and women's mentoring as the core of the men's and women's ministry in the local church. The overall goal should be that everyone in the church catches the vision of living out individual roles as men and women and helping one another to do so, as "iron sharpens iron" (Prov. 27:17).

Does each of us have a Paul and a Timothy, or their female equivalents, in our lives, people we mentor and are mentored by? Are we committed to spending time with like-minded brothers and sisters so we can encourage and exhort one another to live out our God-given roles in our day-to-day lives? Additional Bible studies can be important and helpful, but since our time with men and women separately will always be limited, let's make sure that we spend this time with an intentional focus on helping men and women live out their God-given roles in marriage and the church. Does this sound too idealistic to you? We believe it can happen. We've seen it happen. We pray it'll happen in all our churches.[18]

It would take another book to work out some of these thoughts in greater detail. For now, our job is done. We hope that this volume has sufficiently shown that God's design for men and women is consistent and clear. God made man and woman not merely as undifferentiated individuals; he appointed the man as the leader in the institutions of marriage, family, and the church and created the woman to support the man in his leadership as his intelligent partner. This design undergirded the original creation, and while partially distorted by sin at the fall, it has been redeemed and can be restored in Christ as we walk in his Spirit as his disciples. In these last days, it is God's desire to bring all things back together under the lordship of Christ (Eph. 1:10), including male-female relationships in the home (Eph. 5:21–33) and in the church (1 Tim. 2:8–3:15). While this vision is not the gospel, it is an important part and entailment of the gospel. May we be given the grace to hold in proper tension the truth that in Christ there's no male and female, and yet there are distinct identities and roles given to men and women in the home and the church, for God's greater glory and the good of his people.

---

[18] Thank you so much, Theresa Bowen, for sharing your experiences and insights with us.

Key Resources

Understanding the Family

Köstenberger, Andreas J., with David W. Jones. *God, Marriage, and Family: Rebuilding the Biblical Foundation.* 2nd ed. Wheaton, IL: Crossway, 2010.

———. *Marriage and the Family: Biblical Essentials.* Wheaton, IL: Crossway, 2012.

Sande, Ken, with Tom Raabe. *Peacemaking for Families: A Biblical Guide to Managing Conflict in Your Home.* Wheaton, IL: Tyndale, 2002.

Mentoring Daughters and Young Women

DeMoss, Nancy Leigh, and Dannah Gresh. *Lies Young Women Believe and the Truth That Sets Them Free.* Chicago: Moody, 2008.

Furman, Gloria. *Glimpses of Grace: Treasuring the Gospel in Your Home.* Wheaton, IL: Crossway, 2013.

———. *Treasuring Christ When Your Hands Are Full: Gospel Meditations for Busy Moms.* Wheaton, IL: Crossway, 2014.

George, Elizabeth. *A Girl after God's Own Heart.* Eugene, OR: Harvest, 2010.

———. *A Young Woman after God's Own Heart.* Eugene, OR: Harvest, 2003.

Kassian, Mary. *Girls Gone Wise in a World Gone Wild.* Chicago: Moody, 2010.

Mahaney, Carolyn, and Nicole Mahaney Whitacre. *Girl Talk: Mother-Daughter Conversations on Biblical Womanhood.* Wheaton, IL: Crossway, 2005.

———. *True Beauty.* Wheaton, IL: Crossway, 2014.

Rainey, Dennis, and Barbara Rainey. *Passport to Purity.* Little Rock, AR: FamilyLife, 2004.

Mentoring Sons and Young Men

Hughes, Kent. *Disciplines of a Godly Young Man.* Wheaton, IL: Crossway, 2012.

Mahaney, C. J., ed. *Worldliness: Resisting the Seduction of a Fallen World.* Wheaton, IL: Crossway, 2008.

Rainey, Dennis, and Barbara Rainey. *Passport to Purity.* Little Rock, AR: FamilyLife, 2004.

Mentoring Women

DeMoss, Nancy Leigh, ed. *Becoming God's True Woman.* 2nd ed. Wheaton, IL: Crossway 2008.

Duncan, J. Ligon, and Susan Hunt. *Women's Ministry in the Local Church.* Wheaton, IL: Crossway, 2006.

Furman, Gloria. *Glimpses of Grace: Treasuring the Gospel in Your Home.* Wheaton, IL: Crossway, 2013.

Hughes, Barbara. *Disciplines of a Godly Woman.* Wheaton, IL: Crossway, 2001.

Hunt, Susan. *By Design: God's Distinctive Calling for Women.* Wheaton, IL: Crossway, 1994.

———. *Spiritual Mothering.* Wheaton, IL: Crossway, 1992.

Kassian, Mary A., and Nancy Leigh DeMoss. *True Woman 101: Divine Design.* Chicago: Moody, 2012.

Mahaney, Carolyn. *Feminine Appeal: Seven Virtues of a Godly Wife and Mother.* 2nd ed. Wheaton, IL: Crossway 2004.

McCulley, Carolyn. *Radical Womanhood: Feminine Faith in a Feminist World.* Chicago: Moody, 2008.

Peace, Martha. *The Excellent Wife: A Biblical Perspective.* Rev. ed. Bemidji, MN: Focus, 1997.

VanAtta, Lucibel. *Women Encouraging Women: Who Will Disciple Me?* Portland, OR: Multnomah, 1987.

Mentoring Men

Hughes, Kent. *Disciplines of a Godly Man.* Rev. ed. Wheaton, IL: Crossway, 2001.

Köstenberger, Andreas J. *Excellence: The Character of God and the Pursuit of Scholarly Virtue.* Wheaton, IL: Crossway, 2011.

Mahaney, C. J., ed. *Worldliness: Resisting the Seduction of a Fallen World.* Wheaton, IL: Crossway, 2008.

McKay, Brett, and Kate McKay. *The Art of Manliness: Classic Skills and Manners for the Modern Man.* Cincinnati, OH: How Books, 2009.

Phillips, Richard D. *The Masculine Mandate: God's Calling to Men.* Orlando, FL: Reformation Trust, 2010.

Scott, Stuart. *The Exemplary Husband: A Biblical Perspective.* Bemidji, MN: Focus, 2002.

Appendix 1

The Three Waves

Women's History Survey

> We ask justice, we ask equality, we ask that all civil and po-
> litical rights that belong to the citizens of the United States
> be guaranteed to us and our daughters forever.
>
> —Declaration of Rights for Women (July 4, 1876)

Key Points

1. Our identity as male and female must inevitably be lived out in the context of the culture in which we live. This culture typically rejects what Scripture teaches on biblical manhood and womanhood.
2. It's helpful to understand the impact of feminism on our culture in order to identify its past and present influence on male-female roles in the family and in the church. Feminism's rise came in three major waves: the first from the 1830s to 1920, the second from the 1960s to the 1990s, and the third from the 1990s to the present.
3. Except for secular feminists who exist primarily outside the church and don't address Scripture at all, modern feminists who use Scripture to define male-female roles differ in their approach. They fall into three basic categories: radical (rejection of Scripture), reformist (revision of Scripture), and evangelical (high view of Scripture).
4. Evangelical feminists, while professing a high view of Scripture, nonetheless share certain affinities in method as well as basic belief with other feminists.

There's no question that feminism—a movement concerned with the advancement of women's rights and with the achievement of women's complete parity with men in society, the home, and the church—has had many positive results since its inception almost two centuries ago. Women's status and experience in the Western world, in particular, have been altered for the better in many ways, ending discrimination in various spheres of life through newly instituted legislation and reform. In this way, justice has been served, and women have been lifted from second-class status to genuine equality with men in many ways. At the same time, Bible-believing Christians have come to ask themselves how this massive movement of feminism in its various phases relates to what Scripture teaches on the identity and roles of men and women. The following survey of the successive waves of the feminist movement will serve to canvass the context for our interpretation of gender-related passages in Scripture.

The First Wave of Feminism (1840–1920): Suffragettes and de Jure Feminism

In seeking to understand the context for our study of gender passages in Scripture, there's no better way than to consider the astonishing, even revolutionary, impact feminism has had on Western culture over the past two centuries. Across this period, the feminist movement has irreversibly altered the way people think about themselves and others with regard to what it means to live in our culture as men and women. First, feminism has brought about significant advances in the civic arena (women's legal status, right to vote, etc.). Second, feminism has also exerted a significant religious impact on the church, particularly in its interpretation of gender-related passages in the Bible and the practices resulting from these interpretations.[1] In this book, our primary interest lies in the latter dimension, but because the two aspects are ultimately inseparable, the following survey will touch on both elements.

The first real, significant wave of feminism in the US began in the 1830s and lasted until around 1920 with the attainment of women's right to vote. This wave was part of a worldwide crusade for women's rights. In the early 1800s, typically women were denied many basic

---

[1] For more detailed discussion see Margaret Köstenberger, *Jesus and the Feminists: Who Do They Say That He Is?* (Wheaton, IL: Crossway, 2008), esp. chap. 1.

rights that we commonly take for granted today: voting, education, property rights, and equal pay for equal work. In the 1830s several women rose up and decided to fight for the overturning of laws discriminating against women. The most basic of these was the right to vote, or "suffrage." The right to vote, in turn, was seen as the means and foundation to an even greater end: shaping the laws that governed the lives of women in other areas, such as those regulating the entering of professions traditionally closed to women.

Elizabeth Cady Stanton (1815–1902) and Other Major Leaders

The primary leaders of the first wave of feminism were women themselves, and this movement was supported and formed in churches. Elizabeth Cady Stanton, Susan B. Anthony, Lucretia Mott, Lucy Stone, Angelina and Sarah Grimké, and Frances Willard were significant players.[2] Perhaps most widely known is the contribution of Elizabeth Cady Stanton.[3] Elizabeth was brought up in a strict Presbyterian household in the Old Scotch Presbyterian Church. Her father was a US congressman and New York Supreme Court justice, and as a young woman she attended a school for girls in Troy, New York. In 1840, she married a lawyer and abolitionist and later became the mother of seven children.

Although Stanton didn't appreciate the Bible as inspired by God, she was seriously influenced by Charles Finney's biblical preaching and even described herself as one of his first "victims" during a revival meeting in Troy. Finney and the revivalist movement encouraged social reform, including involvement in the abolitionist movement and the crusade for women's rights. Several of the early women's conventions were actually held in Finney's Tabernacle. Stanton was initially motivated to be involved in the abolitionist movement, but eventually her passion became women's rights.

From her early years, Stanton had experienced discrimination. She lacked opportunity to study Greek and was accepted to the Johnstown

---

[2] See ibid., 18–20.

[3] In her autobiography (Elizabeth Cady Stanton, *Eighty Years and More* [New York: Schocken, 1898]), Stanton recounts the birth of her younger sister when she was four years old, recalling that it was considered a great pity that the child was a girl rather than a boy. When Stanton was eleven, her only brother, Eleazor, died. In the aftermath of his death, Stanton's father said to Elizabeth, "Oh, my daughter, I wish you were a boy!" See also Lisa Frederiksen Bohannon, *Women's Rights and Nothing Less: The Story of Elizabeth Cady Stanton* (Greensboro, NC: Morgan Reynolds, 2001).

Academy only by special arrangement. Colleges were likewise closed to women at the time, so Elizabeth went to Troy Female Seminary where she graduated in 1832. Studying law by reading her father's law books, she took note of how US laws discriminated against women, yet she was unable to become a lawyer herself because women weren't admitted to the bar. Because of her self-training and knowledge, however, she was able to make changes for women through the early feminist movement. Because of her prominence, her views on the Bible became all the more important.

In 1848 the first wave of feminism was formally launched when Stanton, along with Lucretia Mott and others, issued a call for a women's convention to be held in a Wesleyan Methodist chapel in Seneca Falls, New York. Three hundred people attended the convention, and the resulting "Seneca Falls Declaration" was signed by sixty-eight women and thirty-two men. The document, patterned after the Declaration of Independence, started with the words, "We hold these truths to be self-evident: that all men *and women* are created equal." Two weeks later, a second convention took place in Rochester, New York; a third meeting was held in 1850 and then each year (except one) until 1860. It was in 1852 that Stanton joined forces with Susan B. Anthony. The two remained a team for nearly fifty years, with Anthony taking care of finances and Stanton doing most of the writing.

First-Wave Organizations

In the early years, there were no formal women's rights organizations, but because their interests in issues related to social justice converged, the early feminists cast their lot with antislavery, equal-rights groups involved in the abolitionist movement. After the Civil War, the movement to liberate slaves withheld their support from the women's groups, so the budding feminists started their own formal organizations.

The first group, led by Stanton and Anthony, was the National Woman Suffrage Association. It fought for women's rights and an amendment to the US Constitution that would provide women with the right to vote. The other group, the American Woman Suffrage Association, was led by Lucy Stone. In 1890, the two groups merged to become the National American Woman Suffrage Association.

The Bible and Women's Rights

First-wave feminists displayed a range of attitudes toward Scripture. At the height of Stanton's influence, many feminists tended to view the Bible as the chief political obstacle to women's equality and a major hindrance to women's rights. Stanton herself claimed that "the Bible, with its fables, allegories, and endless contradictions, has been the great block in the way of civilization."[4] Such feminists felt that some kind of response had to be made to the Bible because of its "degrading" view of women. For them, Scripture was a purely human book that lacked divine authority but couldn't simply be ignored, because of its influence in the general culture.

Others adopted a less critical stance toward Scripture and focused primarily on using it in order to promote the feminist cause. This often took the form of using biblical passages that showed women as leaders or otherwise portrayed them in a positive light. Yet others, such as Lucy Stone (1818–1893), held that the Bible, as originally intended by its divine author and as rightly interpreted by humans, wasn't truly hostile to women. The problem was not Scripture's teaching itself but the way in which people had misinterpreted the Bible throughout the history of the church.

The Woman's Bible

The Woman's Bible provides a helpful window on first-wave feminism and some of its key proponents. It also served as an inspiration for the second wave.[5] We've already mentioned that first-wave feminists displayed a range of attitudes toward Scripture; this diversity is also characteristic of the contributors to *The Woman's Bible*. Many contributors were moderate in their approach; that is, they sought to accentuate the positive value and contributions of women. A few others, including Stanton, tended to be more critical. It should also be noted that while *The Woman's Bible* was a collaborative effort, Stanton's influ-

---

[4] Elizabeth Cady Stanton, *The Woman's Bible, Part 2: Comments on the Old and New Testaments from Joshua to Revelation* (New York: European, 1898), 9.

[5] See the discussion below. Elisabeth Griffith (*In Her Own Right: The Life of Elizabeth Cady Stanton* [New York: Oxford University Press, 1984], 210), notes that *The Woman's Bible* was a bestseller: "It went through seven printings in six months and was translated into several languages."

ence looms large. She wrote two-thirds of the entire work while the others combined to contribute the remaining third.

Stanton's own view of the Bible appears to have been shaped by several interpreters, particularly the atheist Robert Ingersoll, whose wife was one of the contributors to *The Woman's Bible*. Stanton denied the Bible's inspiration and divine nature, urging people to accept what is good in Scripture and to reject what is evil, foremost the Bible's negative view of women.[6] In Stanton's opinion, the Bible treated women as being of a different class, inferior and subject to men. She proposed to neutralize the Bible's influence by producing her woman-authored Bible, which would expose the Bible's patriarchal bias toward women.

The Woman's Bible was put together by the "Revising Committee" and appeared in two volumes in 1895 and 1898. It's not actually a translation as one might perhaps expect but a series of remarks on portions of the Bible that Stanton and others thought related to women's roles and identity. Stanton herself was not a biblical scholar, so *The Woman's Bible* wasn't the kind of commentary that engaged the original languages and provided an in-depth interpretation of the biblical texts. A few examples will give you a better picture of how *The Woman's Bible* treated Scripture, along with simple explanations of the more likely meaning of the respective biblical texts.

Genesis 1–3. According to *The Woman's Bible*, Genesis 1:26–28 teaches the simultaneous creation of sexes in the image of God, countering the assumption of male supremacy. This assertion, of course, is plainly contradicted by the Genesis 2 account (repeatedly invoked by the apostle Paul), according to which God first created the man and then the woman from the man, with implications for the man's authority in the home and the church.

The plural in Genesis 1:26, "Let *us* make," and the creation of humanity as male and female in God's image in Genesis 1:27, are seen as implying a "feminine element in the Godhead" rather than suggesting "three male personages." Whether or not the plural in Genesis 1:26 is a collective "we" or an anticipation of the New Testament teaching on the Trinity, interpreting the plural as conveying a feminine element

---

[6] Elizabeth Cady Stanton, *The Woman's Bible, Part 1: Genesis* (New York: European, 1895), 33.

in God is entirely unsubstantiated. In fact, God transcends gender, whether male or female.

Genesis 1 and 2 are seen as two contradictory versions of creation, with the first account dignifying the woman and the second having been written by a "wily writer" who added his account to put women in their place.[7] In Genesis 3, Eve is portrayed as strong and courageous, especially when compared with Adam.[8] More likely, however, Genesis 1 and 2 constitute a unified literary narrative, where Genesis 1 narrates God's creation of the universe as a whole and Genesis 2 focuses specifically on God's creation of the man and the woman. There is little in the biblical text to support the notion that Genesis 3 portrays Eve as superior to Adam. Rather, the woman is shown to transgress God's command and to fall into sin, as is made clear by the ensuing judgment. The apparent reason why many early feminists dispute Eve's role in the fall is that they perceive it to threaten their cause. According to Stanton,

> The whole foundation of the Christian religion rests on her [woman's] temptation and man's fall, hence the necessity of a Redeemer and a plan of salvation. . . . Woman's degradation and subordination were made a necessity. If, however, we accept the Darwinian theory, that the race has been a gradual growth from the lower to a higher form of life, and that the story of the fall is a myth, we can exonerate the snake, emancipate the woman, and reconstruct a more rational religion for the nineteenth century, and thus escape all the perplexities of the Jewish mythology as of no more importance than the Greek, Persian, and Egyptian.[9]

In essence, Stanton claims that Genesis 2–3 was a myth fabricated by men in order to discredit women.

Women in the Old Testament. The treatment of Old Testament women in *The Woman's Bible* is frequently at odds with the actual information provided in the biblical text. In 2 Kings 22:13–20 (cf. 2 Chron. 34:22–28), for instance, Huldah the prophetess residing in the college in Jerusalem, is presented as a statesperson and expert in Jewish

---

[7] Ibid., 33.
[8] Ibid.
[9] Stanton, *Woman's Bible*, Part 2, 214.

jurisprudence who advised common people and taught kings while her husband was the humble keeper of the robes. Huldah was indeed a prophetess, but the Bible provides little other information about her. In fact, we know more about her husband than about her, and the little information we have about Huldah is largely in relation to her husband.[10]

With regard to Jezebel, Stanton claims that she, like Eve, was misunderstood, especially by the writer of 1 Kings 21:1–15, who harbored a bias against her because she was from a rival religion. Stanton views Jezebel as brave, fearless, generous, and so wholly devoted to her husband that even wrong is justified to her if she can make him happy.[11] Again, recasting Jezebel as a positive figure is at odds with the biblical message. John, the author of Revelation, chastises the church in Thyatira for tolerating "that woman Jezebel, who calls herself a prophetess and is teaching and seducing my servants to practice sexual immorality and to eat food sacrificed to idols" (Rev. 2:20).

Women in the New Testament. Turning to the New Testament, the same pattern of embellishment continues. Regarding Priscilla, commenting on Romans 16:3–5, *The Woman's Bible* maintains that Paul "virtually pronounces Priscilla a fellow-Apostle and fellow bishop," who together with her husband, "the Apostle Aquila," founded the church of Rome.[12] This, too, is hardly accurate because even though we don't know who founded the church of Rome, there isn't any evidence that it was Priscilla. The author wrote, "Addressing that first Church of Rome . . . Paul indicates the equality of male and female Apostles by mentioning in one and the same category Priscilla and Aquila, Andronicus and Junia," and several others.[13] It is doubtful, however, whether Junia was an "Apostle" with a capital "A" (i.e., to be put on the same level as the Twelve and Paul), and Priscilla and Aquila aren't called "apostles" anywhere in the New Testament.

Phoebe is called "a minister," interpreted as "presbyter, bishop, or Apostle."[14] *The Woman's Bible* contends that Phoebe was "the bishop of

---

[10] Ibid., 81–82; see further the discussion of Huldah in chap. 2 above.
[11] Ibid., 74–76.
[12] Ibid., 153–54.
[13] Ibid., 154.
[14] Ibid.

the Church in Cenchrea, and that she was both a powerful and useful overseer in the episcopate."[15] However, it's without textual warrant to move from the Greek word *diakonos* ("servant") to "minister" (with its modern connotations) and then to "bishop" and "overseer" (*episkopos*). The word *diakonos* describes a nonauthoritative role, whereas *episkopos* conveys the exercise of authority.

As to Paul's instructions regarding women in 1 Timothy 2:9–15, Lucinda Chandler calls them a "tyrannical . . . edict."[16] She claims that Paul wasn't inspired but biased by prejudice and that the teaching of woman as the origin of sin (v. 14) pervaded church history as a poisonous stream (see Stanton's view on Genesis 3 above).[17] However, Chandler's disapproval of Paul's words in 1 Timothy 2:9–15 may reveal a bias of her own.[18]

Feminist Responses to The Woman's Bible. Subsequent to its publication, *The Woman's Bible* elicited a range of responses from various stripes of feminists, not all positive. Among those who expressed concern, some thought the whole venture was mistaken and too radical, while others considered the project a source of division causing controversy at a time when the need was for unity. The North American Woman Suffrage Association initially placed a paragraph in their annual report renouncing Stanton's work, though after much discussion the paragraph was removed.[19] The feminist movement as a whole never officially endorsed *The Woman's Bible*, though many today consider the work to be groundbreaking. On the whole, Stanton's writing and political activism over the years served as a model for other feminists who followed her in her critical stance toward Scripture, and some of the types of interpretations found in *The Woman's Bible* recur (albeit with greater sophistication) in some of today's feminist literature.

Margaret Sanger and Planned Parenthood

Another icon to emerge during the first wave of feminism was Margaret Sanger (1879–1966), an American sex educator, nurse, and founder

---

[15] Ibid.
[16] Ibid., 162.
[17] Ibid., 163–64.
[18] See the discussion of hermeneutical fallacies in appendix 3 below.
[19] Griffith, *In Her Own Right*, 212–13.

of the modern birth-control movement, who coined the phrase "birth control."[20] In 1914, in response to witnessing the negative effects of several self-induced abortions, Sanger started a monthly newsletter, *The Woman Rebel*. In 1916 she opened the first birth-control clinic in the United States and was promptly arrested for distributing information on contraception. The ensuing trial rallied considerable support for her cause.

In 1921, Sanger established the American Birth Control League, which later became Planned Parenthood (Sanger served as its president from 1952 to 1959). Sanger's efforts also contributed to the landmark Supreme Court case legalizing contraception in the United States. Sanger, who died in 1966, has been an extremely influential figure in the reproductive rights movement.

Women's Right to Vote

The first wave of feminism ended in 1920 with the ratification of the Nineteenth Amendment to the US Constitution allowing women to vote. Once women's right to vote was won, the feminist movement fragmented and lost momentum. Not much took place with regard to the feminist cause between 1920 through World War II and the launch of the second wave of feminism in the 1960s. The Great Depression and World War II essentially eclipsed any further activism in pursuit of women's rights.

The Second Wave of Feminism (1960–1990): The Women's Liberation Movement

Social Feminism

Social (sometimes also called "secular") feminism was the direct successor of the first wave of feminism and a child of *The Woman's Bible*. Though many involved with *The Woman's Bible* had strong religious convictions, their main goals were social in nature, centering on the

---

[20] For background information, see Patricia Walsh Coates, *Margaret Sanger and the Origin of the Birth Control Movement, 1910–1930: The Concept of Women's Sexual Autonomy* (Lewiston, NY: Mellen, 2008); Joy Johannessen, "Preface," in Margaret H. Sanger, *What Every Girl Should Know* (New York: Belvedere, 1980); and Jill Ker Conway, ed., *Written by Herself: Autobiographies of American Women: An Anthology* (New York: Vintage, 1992); Emily Taft Douglas, *Margaret Sanger: Pioneer of the Future* (New York: Holt, Rinehart & Winston, 1970); and David M. Kennedy, *Birth Control in America: The Career of Margaret Sanger* (New Haven, CT: Yale University Press, 1970).

procurement of economic and property rights, the elimination of job discrimination, and the attainment of women's right to vote. Second-wave feminists were fighting for many of the same issues, resembling Stanton and other first-wave protagonists in their critical stance toward the Bible. They viewed society as patriarchal, with men exerting power over women and women being subservient and treated as of second-rate importance. Their goal was to set women free from the social bondage of male domination. At times, proponents of the second wave took their cue from Marxist economic theory, which divided humanity into two classes, the rich (capitalists) and the poor (the proletariat), with the former oppressing the latter. Unlike Marxism, however, feminists viewed oppression not only as a function of the possession of economic resources but also as a result of a person's gender as male or female. Thus "women's liberation" describes the feminist goal of setting women free from oppressive male domination in society.

Architects of the Movement

We can gain a clearer picture of the second wave of feminism by looking at some of its leaders: the French writer Simone de Beauvoir, Americans Betty Friedan and Kate Millett, Australian Germaine Greer, and the American feminist Gloria Steinem.

Simone de Beauvoir (1908–1986) was the lifelong companion of philosopher Jean-Paul Sartre. In *The Second Sex* in 1949 (English translation 1953), Beauvoir contended that women had been the victim of male stereotyping in society. By surrounding women with a false aura of mystery, men had cast women as the "Other" in order to justify organizing society as a patriarchy. As an existentialist, Beauvoir believed that gender was not innate but socially determined. She called for a feminist revolution in which women took responsibility for themselves and chose freedom from male dominance. Her volume contained many of the seeds of later feminist thought and laid the groundwork for the movement in the United States.

Betty Friedan (1921–2006) launched the women's liberation movement by publishing *The Feminine Mystique* in 1964. She could have pursued a career as a psychologist but gave it up at the request of a prospective husband whom she never actually married. Having had the opportunity to progress in her profession, she ended up disillusioned as a housewife. "Feminine mystique" described the concept of ideal femininity embodied in the loving, doting housewife whose interests are limited to house, spouse, and children (also known as "the disease with no name" or "the malaise of the suburban housewife").

By "mystique," Friedan meant "myth," contending that the "happy housewife" portrayed at that time in such popular television shows as *Leave It to Beaver* was in fact an illusion. Many women identified with Friedan; her book caught on widely, and the women's liberation movement was born. Friedan proceeded to found The National Organization for Women (NOW). The group quickly became the most effective organization promoting the feminist cause in the public arena and a powerful tool for political activism. Despite the fact that it was plagued by internal dissension, the group endured and fought for women's rights (including abortion), as well as for an equal rights amendment.

Kate Millett (born 1934), another secular feminist, published *Sexual Politics*, a revised version of her PhD dissertation at Columbia University, in 1970, which *Time* called the "Bible of Women's Liberation." Kate's father abandoned the family when she was fourteen years old. Though college educated, her mother had to support the family by selling potato peelers; she later worked as an insurance agent. In her work, Millett explored the dynamics of power in relation to gender and sexuality. Similar to Simone de Beauvoir's argument in *The Second Sex*, Millett advocated the belief that all male-female differences except anatomy are cultural in origin. Eventually, in her autobiographical work *Flying* (1974) Millett admitted she was a lesbian, and from that point on, women's liberation and the gay rights movement progressed in tandem. Lesbianism became part of the feminist agenda.

Australian Germaine Greer (born 1939) studied at Cambridge University and wrote *The Female Eunuch* (1970). Similar to Betty Friedan in *The Feminine Mystique*, Greer attacked the model of meek and drab femininity propagated by male-dominated society as "ideal womanhood." Such a model, according to Greer, castrated women and made them female eunuchs. In a 1971 interview with the *New York Times*, Greer stated, "Women have somehow been separated from their . . . sexuality. . . . Like beasts, . . . who are castrated in farming in order to serve their master's ulterior motives—to be fattened or made docile— women have been cut off from their capacity for action." In *Sex and Destiny: The Politics of Human Fertility* (1984), Greer contended that the nuclear family was a negative environment for women and that the treatment of women's sexuality in Western society was confining and demeaning. The femininity girls were taught to embrace during their growing-up years led them to develop a sense of shame about their bodies, issuing in powerlessness, a diminished sexuality, and a lack of joy. In contrast, Greer advocated total sexual freedom.

Gloria Steinem (born 1934) was another major architect of the women's movement. A one-time *Playboy* bunny, she spoke out against the exploitation of women. At age twenty-two, Steinem had an abortion in London, England, and became a lifelong supporter of abortion rights. She also campaigned for an equal rights amendment. Steinem cofounded the National Women's Political Caucus in 1971. In her "Address to the Women of America," Steinem said of the women's liberation movement, "This is no simple reform. It really is a revolution. Sex and race, because they are easy and visible differences, have been the primary ways of organizing human beings into superior and inferior groups and into the cheap labor on which this system still depends. *We are talking about a society in which there will be no roles other than those chosen or those earned.* We are really talking about humanism."[21] In 1972, she was named "McCall's Woman of the Year." She launched *Ms.* magazine in 1971, which she edited until 1987. Through this venue, the feminist message was made available on a monthly basis at newsstands everywhere. Women in considerable numbers were identifying with these publications. Along with the activity of these leaders, "consciousness-raising groups" regularly met in order to enlighten participants as to their oppressed condition and their need for liberation. These groups focused on introspection and testimonies from their "sisters."

---

[21] *Great Speeches of the Twentieth Century*, vol. 4, *Best of Times, Worst of Times* (Gordon Skene Sound Collection, 1991), speech 10 (emphasis added).

Table A1.1: Major Leaders of Second-Wave Feminism

Major Figure	Key Contribution
Simone de Beauvoir	*The Second Sex* (1949; English trans. 1953); precursor of feminism in the United States
Betty Friedan	*The Feminine Mystique* (1964); first president of NOW (1966)
Kate Millett	*Sexual Politics* (1970), the "Bible of Women's Liberation" (*Time*)
Germaine Greer	*The Female Eunuch* (1970); advocated total sexual freedom
Gloria Steinem	*Ms.* magazine (1971), founder and editor until 1987

The Goals of Second-Wave Social Feminism

Many of the goals of second-wave feminism found expression in NOW's 1967 "Bill of Rights," which included the following eight demands to Congress:[22]

1. Passage of an equal rights constitutional amendment (ERA)
2. Enforcement of the law banning sex discrimination in employment
3. Maternity-leave rights in employment and in social security benefits
4. Tax deduction for home and child-care expenses for working parents
5. Child day-care centers
6. Equal and unsegregated education
7. Equal job training opportunities and allowances for women in poverty
8. Guarantee of women's right to control their reproductive lives

In 1975, the Women's Action Alliance released a document entitled "U.S. National Women's Agenda," which demanded various policies and programs from the government and firms in the private sector. Some people's agenda underlying these documents included the abolition of sex roles, the decentering of traditional marriage and family,

---

[22] http://www.h-net.org/~hst203/documents/nowrights.html.

the legitimization of homosexuality, free universal day care, universal access to abortion, and promotion of the feminist agenda in the schools.[23]

The "Success" of the Women's Liberation Movement

Second-wave social feminism is one of the most successful movements in history in terms of achieving its stated goals. The culture of the United States of the pre-feminist 1950s is worlds apart from the West of the 1990s and beyond. For better or for worse, the women's movement has changed society and all of our lives and language.

The Equal Pay Act was passed in 1963, the same year *The Feminine Mystique* was published. In 1964 Congress passed a civil rights act expressly prohibiting sex discrimination in employment. Abortion laws were liberalized, and in 1973 the Supreme Court legalized abortion in its landmark ruling *Roe v. Wade.* In 1960, 34.8 percent of women were in the workforce; in 2012 it was 57.7 percent. In the 1950s, women made up only 20 percent of college undergraduates; the numbers jumped to 54 percent after women's liberation got underway. Since the 1990s, women have earned more BA, MA, and PhD degrees than men. American society and culture were permanently changed.

While, as mentioned, there were many elements of injustice toward women that were redressed owing to the influence of social feminism, the movement's overall impact hasn't been entirely positive. On the whole, feminism has had a rather negative effect on families, among other reasons because it tends to set women against men and often stereotypes men as oppressors.[24] From a Christian standpoint, however, while removing injustice, whenever possible, is exceedingly important, in the ultimate analysis humanity's main problem is sin affecting both genders, not merely men (though it is granted that men, as leaders, will often use their power in sinful, abusive ways).

Nevertheless, men are not the number-one enemy; sin is. And our sin problem is effectively addressed only by trusting in Christ, who died on the cross in our place for the forgiveness of our sins. This

---

[23]Jim and Andrea Fordham, *The Assault on the Sexes* (New Rochelle, NY: Arlington House, 1977), 53.
[24]See Andreas J. Köstenberger, "Feminism, Family, and the Bible: A Biblical Assessment of Feminism's Impact on American Families," *The Religion and Society Report* 23, no. 1, http://www.profam.org/pub/rs/rs.2301.htm.

truth, in turn, has important social implications for the male-female relationship. In Christ, both men and women are enabled once again to relate to each other in loving ways that respect God's original design (which goes both ways). What women, like men, need the most, therefore, is salvation in Christ, not liberation from all male leadership. True freedom comes only from living in accordance with God's will, and, paradoxically, submission to God and his design for men and women marks the sole path to true freedom.

> "What women, like men, need the most, therefore, is salvation in Christ, not liberation from all male leadership. True freedom comes only from living in accordance with God's will, and, paradoxically, submission to God and his design for men and women marks the sole path to true freedom."

In one sense, at least, the women's movement might be considered passé, not because it is no longer relevant but because social feminism's essential goals have been achieved. Women entered the workforce in large numbers, achieved many of their objectives, and, just like men, could choose to earn their bread by the sweat of their brow. Some feminists, however, as well as others, began to wonder if the cost of attaining equality in every respect was too high.[25] Once women had many of the same opportunities as men, they weren't sure they liked the negative side effects of what they had accomplished.

Religious Feminism

Unlike many social feminists, there were other women during the heyday of the second wave (sometimes called "radical" or "goddess" feminists) who started out in the church—whether in Roman Catholicism or mainline Protestant denominations—but for whatever reason ended up rejecting Christianity.[26] At some point in their lives, these feminists grew more radical and disillusioned with their church. Mary Daly, for example, rejected not only Catholicism but all of Christianity because Vatican II, an important gathering of Roman Catholic ecclesiastical authorities, didn't open up the church to female priests.

---

[25]See, e.g., Susan Faludi, *Backlash: The Undeclared War against American Women* (1991; repr. New York: Three Rivers, 2006).

[26]See Köstenberger, *Jesus and the Feminists*, chaps. 3–5, on Mary Daly, Virginia Ramey Mollenkott, and Daphne Hampson.

In large part, therefore, these feminists became post-Christian and often overtly anti-Christian.

One such feminist, Daphne Hampson, in *After Christianity* chronicled her pilgrimage from working for reform within the Anglican church to concluding that Christianity is completely unacceptable. Many of these feminists found it hard to come to terms with Christianity's teaching concerning the fatherhood of God and the maleness of Jesus. They considered Christianity to be irredeemably patriarchal and were looking for a religion that was more congenial to women. In some cases, their quest for meaning led to goddess worship, involvement in the occult, or a variety of other religious or irreligious practices.

Unlike more moderate voices in the feminist movement (on which see further the discussion below), many of these more radical religious feminists didn't attempt to salvage at least portions of Scripture by seeking to identify positive female role models. Instead, they rejected Scripture in its entirety. In other cases, they radically recast Scripture in keeping with their feminist predisposition. One such example of a feminist who subjected Scripture to thoroughgoing revision was Virginia Ramey Mollenkott. In one of her books, *Sensuous Spirituality: Out from Fundamentalism*, she offered the following "new version" of the Lord's Prayer:

O Birther! Father-Mother of the Cosmos,
Focus your light within us—make it useful:
Create your reign of unity now—
Your one desire then acts with ours,
As in all light, so in all forms.
Grant what we need each day in bread and insight.
Loose the cords of mistakes binding us,
As we release the strands we hold of others' guilt.
Don't let surface things delude us,
But free us from what holds us back.[27]

In this way, some feminists rewrote Scripture, continuing to use religious language while rejecting traditional religion. These feminists

---

[27] Virginia R. Mollenkott, *Sensuous Spirituality: Out from Fundamentalism* (New York: Crossroad, 1992), 26.

chose not to leave Christianity behind completely, because it was part
of their background. Yet for all practical purposes, organized religion
served as a foil for their critique of the oppressive and patriarchal nature of traditional Christianity. In fact, many of these more radical religious feminists moved away from biblical doctrine at virtually every
juncture. While, as mentioned, the feminist movement was sparked by
genuine injustices toward women in the legal realm, the workplace,
and other areas, some of these religious feminists took their agenda
much farther in pursuing liberation from *all* forms of authority, including God and Scripture. These forms of religious feminism therefore constitute a thoroughgoing rejection of every form of authority.

Another type of religious feminism didn't focus so much on total
rejection of Christianity, the Bible, and all forms of authority but strove
for reform (hence the sometime label "reformist feminists"). These
reform-minded feminists are at times known by the label "liberation-
ists" because of their strong roots in liberation theology (a grassroots
movement popular particularly in Latin America, where its proponents aimed to reform exploitative economic relationships).[28] These
reform-minded "liberationist" feminists did not follow the above-
discussed more radical religious feminists in their complete rejection
of the Bible and Christianity. Instead, they believed that there were
aspects of the Bible that could be used to promote feminism and thus
should be utilized.

How, then, should we characterize their approach to Scripture?
The label most often used in this regard is the phrase "hermeneutic of
suspicion," a term applied by Elisabeth Schüssler Fiorenza, the movement's matriarch.[29] This approach advocates looking at Scripture with
suspicion primarily because it was written by men. Nevertheless, these
feminists, as mentioned, drew parts from Scripture they found us-
able in order to propagate their feminist views: the biblical stories of
the likes of Deborah, Ruth, Esther, and others. In addition, feminists
such as Rosemary Radford Ruether supplemented the Bible with other

---

[28] See, e.g., Letty Russell, *Human Liberation in a Feminist Perspective: A Theology* (Philadelphia: Westminster, 1974); Russell, *Becoming Human* (Philadelphia: Westminster, 1982). On reformist feminism, see
Köstenberger, *Jesus and the Feminists*, chaps. 6–10, on Letty Russell, Rosemary Radford Ruether, Elisabeth
Schüssler Fiorenza, Kathleen Corley, and others.
[29] See further appendix 3.

writings that they elevated to the same level as Scripture. Rather than attributing to Scripture divine inspiration, these feminists viewed the Bible as a sacred text similar to the Quran, the Hindu Scriptures, or other sacred writings.[30] In essence, reform-minded feminists such as these were looking for any text that could be used to elevate women.

Within conservative American evangelicalism, another movement arose during the latter part of the second wave, variously called "biblical feminism," "evangelical feminism," or "egalitarianism" (though it should be noted that the concern for egalitarian gender roles is common to all forms of feminism).[31] As feminists, these evangelicals espouse both egalitarianism and biblical inerrancy, holding that Scripture teaches complete male-female equality in essence and role.[32] These feminists claim that the man's leadership role was not part of God's original creation but merely a consequence of the fall.[33] Unlike their more radical religious feminist counterparts who reject Scripture as irremediably male-centered, and unlike their reform-minded fellow feminists who view Scripture with suspicion while selectively using portions in Scripture that present women in a positive light, evangelical feminists believe that Scripture, rightly interpreted, espouses egalitarianism.

While acknowledging that Western Christianity held, throughout its history until recent years, that Scripture affirms male leadership, this group contends that the church has misinterpreted the relevant texts. Rightly understood, evangelical feminists claim, Scripture in fact affirms undifferentiated gender equality. In our biblical-theological survey throughout this volume, we frequently engage the new ways in which evangelical feminists interpret relevant passages in Scripture in order to assess whether their claim to have discovered egalitarian teaching in the pages of Scripture itself (or at least a trajectory moving in an egalitarian direction) can be sustained. In this regard, it is not so much disagreements on interpretive method that surface as differences in specific interpretations of scriptural passages. Also, there

---

[30] See, e.g., Rosemary Radford Ruether, *Womanguides: Readings toward a Feminist Theology* (Boston: Beacon, 1985).

[31] On evangelical feminism, see Köstenberger, *Jesus and the Feminists*, chaps. 11–13.

[32] See, e.g., Letha Scanzoni and Nancy Hardesty, *All We're Meant to Be: A Biblical Approach to Women's Liberation* (Waco, TX: Word, 1974).

[33] See on this chap. 1.

are differences in the way in which we connect the dots, as it were, inductively reconstructing the Bible's own theology with regard to God's design for men and women.

The Third Wave of Feminism (1990–Present): Cultural Goals, Plurality of Voices (Feminisms)

In addition to the first and second feminist waves, we need to consider the so-called third wave of feminism. The beginnings of the third wave can be traced to the early 1990s. According to Rebecca Walker, one of the founding leaders of the movement, "To be a feminist is to integrate an ideology of equality and female empowerment into the very fiber of my life. It is to search for personal clarity in the midst of systemic destruction, to join in sisterhood with women when often we are divided, to understand power structures with the intention of challenging them."[34] Third-wave feminism represents an even more aggressive pursuit of feminine self-realization than previous forms of feminism. It stands completely apart from any guiding Christian values, principles, or beliefs. In this, third-wave feminism builds upon the more extreme dimensions of second-wave secular and/or radical feminism.[35]

While first-wave feminism's focus was on women's suffrage, and the defining causes of second-wave feminism broadened to include reproductive freedom, an equal rights amendment, and educational equality for women, the third wave diversified even further, embracing a variety of causes without "a monolithically identifiable, single-issue agenda that distinguishes it from other movements of social justice."[36]

> "To be a feminist is to integrate an ideology of equality and female empowerment into the very fiber of my life. It is to search for personal clarity in the midst of systemic destruction, to join in sisterhood with women when often we are divided, to understand power structures with the intention of challenging them."
> —Rebecca Walker

---

[34] Rebecca Walker, "Becoming the Third Wave," in *Identity Politics in the Women's Movement*, ed. Barbara Ryan (New York: New York University Press, 2001), 80. Walker authored a defining article for the movement, "Becoming the Third Wave" (*Ms.* 39 [January/February 1992]). She is also the cofounder of the Third Wave Foundation. Other significant spokeswomen include bell hooks [noncapitalization intentional], Katie Roiphe, Naomi Wolf, Jennifer Baumgardner, Amy Richards, and Alison Piepmeier.
[35] The major features and proponents of third wave feminism are chronicled in the two-volume *The Women's Movement Today: An Encyclopedia of Third-Wave Feminism*, ed. L. L. Haywood (Westport, CT: Greenwood, 2005).
[36] "Introduction," in *Women's Movement Today*, xx.

Third-wave feminism continues to crusade for complete legal, political, social, and sexual equality for women, with abortion rights
remaining an important issue. The third wave differs from previous
stages of the feminist movement, however, in its multiculturalism and
concern for justice issues beyond those specifically related to women.

In particular, third-wave feminism reacts against the perceived lim-
itation of previous feminist agendas to white, middle-class women,
contending that "a major part of third-wave identity involves not just
the inclusion of multiple racial and ethnic perspectives but a concern
with multi- and bi-raciality and all of its complications."[37] At the same
time, third-wave feminism aims to address justice issues on a broader
scale: "Feminism in the third wave is a global justice movement acting
on behalf of women's full equality at the intersection of race, class,
gender, and other aspects of identity."[38] As a result, third-wave feminism is concerned not only with gender justice but also with "other,
interrelated forms of justice such as environmental justice, economic
justice, racial justice, and justice around sexuality, religion, and physical ability."[39] This also includes sex trafficking, women's roles and oppression globally, and women's legal rights.

In addition, third-wave feminists are concerned with a plethora of
social issues such as lobbying for marriage equality (i.e., same-sex marriage), same-sex couples' adoption rights, and access to "couples-only"
sperm banks, eliminating race- and gender-based violence, lessening
the negative effects of global capitalism on the poorest of women, and
ensuring that the gains made regarding women's equality in previous
generations are not lost.[40] Other concerns include equal access to the
Internet and technology, HIV/AIDS awareness, sexual abuse of children, self-mutilation, body image, and eating disorders. Third-wave
feminists are also engaged in the area of women's sexual health because women today are more sexually active at a younger age and have
more sexual partners.[41]

---

[37] Ibid., *xviii.*
[38] Caryn D. Riswold, *Feminism and Christianity: Questions and Answers in the Third Wave* (Eugene, OR: Cascade, 2009), 121.
[39] "Introduction," in *Women's Movement Today*, *xxi.*
[40] Riswold, *Feminism and Christianity*, 7–8.
[41] Jennifer Baumgardner and Amy Richards, *Manifesta: Young Women, Feminism, and the Future*, 1st rev. ed. (New York: Farrar, Straus, & Giroux, 2010), 21.

Feminism in its third wave continues to find acceptance in the church. The voices of older feminists such as Elisabeth Schüssler Fiorenza are still heard calling for reform.[42] In a recent collection of essays promoting feminist Christianity, a second-wave evangelical feminist speaks of "a new awakening to the damage done to young women's self-esteem as they are told that God made them to be secondary and subordinate to men, that they may not use their gifts fully in the church, and that it is selfish to aspire to anything more."[43] Evangelical feminists object that women in evangelicalism are still not being "fully treated as co-heirs of the kingdom and image bearers of God" and "preachers are [not] exposing how scripture is misused so that women's voices are being silenced in our churches."[44]

Newer Waves of Feminism (the Present): Diversity, Humor, Literary Sophistication

The arrangement of the feminist movement in three successive waves, while broadly defensible for our present purposes, betrays the fact that surveying the various strands of feminism is hardly an easy task. Gone are the days (if things ever were as simple) where the movement was primarily focused on issues such as the attainment of women's right to vote. As we've seen, some second-wave feminists were primarily concerned with social advances while others focused on religious issues, both positive and critical. Third-wave feminism further extended its reach to a vast variety of issues of concern for women. Doubtless, grouping all current forms of feminism under these "three waves" is hopelessly reductionistic. In our present survey, we can do little more than acknowledge that feminists are exceedingly diverse and defy simplistic categorization.

Satirical Approaches

In particular, it appears that in recent years, with all the advances of first- and second-wave feminism, the tide of feminism is rising once

---

[42] Note her essay, "Critical Feminist Biblical Studies: Remembering the Struggles, Envisioning the Future," in *New Feminist Christianity: Many Voices, Many Views*, ed. Mary E. Hunt and Diann L. Neu (Woodstock, VT: SkyLight, 2010), 86–99.
[43] Letha Dawson Scanzoni, "Why We Need Evangelical Feminists," in ibid., 75.
[44] Kimberly B. George, "The Work Is Not Done: Thoughts from a Third-Wave Feminist," http://www.eewc.com/Articles/work-not-done (accessed September 24, 2012). Thanks are due Chuck Bumgardner for his research assistance on third-wave feminism.

again. Yet rather than being characterized by a strident tone, many who would identify themselves as feminists use a softer, more winsome approach (call it a "new wave" of feminism). This new wave is epitomized by publications such as Rachel Held Evans's *A Year of Biblical Womanhood: How a Liberated Woman Found Herself Sitting on Her Roof, Covering Her Head, and Calling Her Husband "Master."* Rather than stereotyping men as oppressors and taking an adversarial posture, women such as Held Evans employ *satire* in order to expose the foibles of the traditional approach to gender roles that (they believe) is given to excessive literalism.

In her book, which chronicles Held Evans's experiment of trying "a year of biblical womanhood," the author employs what might be termed *reductio ad absurdum*, taking every Scripture passage literally and pointing out what she perceives to be a variety of incongruities between the Testaments. She also identifies biblical commands she considers to be self-evidently absurd when viewed from an "enlightened" feminist perspective (e.g., Prov. 21:9: "It is better to live in a corner of the roof than in a house shared with a contentious woman," NASB). The appeal of this feminism with a lighter touch is that it seems to take the Bible seriously while keeping one's tongue firmly in cheek throughout the process. In the end, Held Evans doesn't reject biblical womanhood altogether, though she returns to her feminist ways.[45]

Literary Approaches

Another "new wave" of feminism epitomizes an increased emphasis on a literary reading of the relevant biblical texts. While these readings exhibit considerable variety, they share in common a close reading of

---

[45]Space doesn't permit detailed interaction here. In short, Held Evans's volume would benefit from a firmer grasp of hermeneutics and biblical theology (the subjects of appendices 2 and 3). In her book, Held Evans treats a passage in Exodus or Deuteronomy in the same way as if it were in one of the Gospels or in one of Paul's letters. However, this approach trivializes and unwittingly misrepresents Scripture's actual teaching on manhood and womanhood because it never sufficiently tries to connect the dots in order to seek to understand a given passage in the context of the larger biblical story line. When Held Evans cites the stipulation in Deut. 22:28–29, for example, according to which a woman and her rapist were required to marry each other without the possibility of divorce, she seems to imply that this is "biblical" in the sense that Bible-believing Christians today still believe this injunction is binding, which is hardly the case. By flattening the biblical teaching as if it were immaterial whether a passage is in the OT or the NT, Held Evans seriously distorts, no doubt unintentionally, the actual biblical teaching on biblical manhood and womanhood. As we attempt to show in this volume, when proper interpretive principles are employed and the biblical-theological development of the scriptural teaching on gender issues is accurately discerned, a pattern of male-female roles emerges that is both consistent and appealing.

texts of relevance to women. In chapter 10 of her book *Jesus and the Feminists*, Margaret discusses this "new face" of feminism as follows:[46]

> The new face of feminism is not that of any one person in the feminist movement. Unlike previous eras in the movement, which were marked by strong personalities, feminism in our day does not have any one recognizable spokeswoman. Instead, feminism is significantly diversified into a variety of strands, many literary in nature. Searches for grand paradigms such as Fiorenza's have largely ceased, and scholars are widely engaged in studies of smaller pericopes [literary units] with no attempt to assemble their findings into a larger synthesis. In many ways, interpretive realism—closer attention to the biblical text—has replaced ideological fervor, though, of course, feminist presuppositions remain a functional nonnegotiable.[47]

We're not able to reproduce Margaret's discussion in full here (though you may want to look it up in her book if you're interested). The essential method of this literary-oriented type of feminism is well described by Dorothy Lee, who studies the presence or absence of female characters and their mode of presentation within specific biblical texts. She writes,

> [Such a] feminist re-reading examines various biblical documents in order to draw women from the shadows, exploring the roles they play (or don't play) and assessing their literary and theological function. . . . Thus the task of feminist exegesis, in this view, is to bring to front stage the female characters of the text, to draw attention to their absence, and to examine the textual presuppositions that shape their characterization.[48]

In her survey of *The Feminist Companion* and other similar literary feminist approaches, Margaret discerns the following unifying themes: (1) a commitment to feminism over Scripture as guiding authority, guided by a quest for women's liberation from the constraints of male hierarchy and a search for positive female role models in Scripture;

---

[46] Köstenberger, *Jesus and the Feminists*, 113–30.
[47] Ibid., 113.
[48] Dorothy A. Lee, "Abiding in the Fourth Gospel: A Case Study in Feminist Biblical Theology," in *A Feminist Companion to John*, vol. 2, ed. Amy-Jill Levine (Cleveland, OH: Pilgrim, 2003), 65 (cited in Köstenberger, *Jesus and the Feminists*, 115, with further bibliographic references to Lee's work).

(2) a critical stance toward Scripture; (3) the use of a variety of literary methods, including deconstructionism and reader-response readings; and (4) a considerable degree of sophistication in literary analysis. As Margaret observes, these new feminist literary approaches must be credited with a proper emphasis on Scripture itself.

At the same time, she notes that many of these studies deal with the text in isolation from the original intent of the biblical authors, or in some other cases in critical opposition to this intent, which has the effect of elevating female experience above the scriptural message. As Margaret puts it, "While the focus on the text in literary feminist approaches is therefore affirmed, the strategy of exposing androcentric bias and of uncovering the hidden liberation potential of texts may have the effect of transposing the textual message in keeping with the reader's own vision, ideals, and ideological commitments."[49] Despite these potential weaknesses, feminist literary approaches have made a positive contribution to our reading of Scripture in that they have sensitized us to women's concerns that some male interpreters may insufficiently recognize in their reading of the text.

Feminist Theory, Theology, and Philosophy: A Very Brief Survey

Before we wrap up our discussion, we'll need to say something about the larger philosophical and theological framework informing feminist theory as it impacts their approach to Christianity at large and to Scripture in particular.[50] The underlying controlling premise of all feminist theology, as mentioned, is the full equality of women to men. Some (if not many) social and religious feminists set aside anything that stands in conflict with this central premise in their quest for women's liberation from all forms of male oppression. Feminist theology, in developing its own theological tenets on topics such as God, humanity, Christ, salvation, and the church, draws on a variety of sources including, but not limited to, the Bible.

You should also know that feminism is by no means limited to

---

[49] Köstenberger, *Jesus and the Feminists*, 126.
[50] This section is based on Margaret E. Köstenberger, "Feminist Theology," in *The Encyclopedia of Christian Civilization*, vol. 2: *E–L*, ed. George Thomas Kurian (Oxford: Wiley-Blackwell, 2011), 926–28; see also Köstenberger, "Feminist Biblical Interpretation," in ibid., 923–26.

North America. Developing feminist theologies within existing cultural and social contexts include the African-American "womanist" and the Hispanic *mujerista* theology as well as emerging feminist theologies from Europe, Latin America, Asia, and Africa. Feminist theology in its various manifestations confronts the issue of authority by calling into question traditional conceptions of gender roles and seeking to address the patriarchal and sexist domination and marginalization of women in all sectors of society. Part of this larger effort is the rethinking of symbols and concepts that were traditionally cast in male terms.

The field of "thealogy," for example, a term coined by Canadian Naomi Goldenberg, critiques male theologizing and urges reflection on the divine in feminine and feminist terms. In keeping with its overall purpose and agenda, thealogy seeks to eliminate patriarchy from mainstream monotheistic religions and strives to promote the equal status and power of female divine, sacred attributes. Thus Daphne Hampson, a British feminist whom we already mentioned, posits a "paradigm of mutual empowerment," while Mary Daly, the former Roman Catholic, calls for decentering maleness from Scripture, Christianity, and even Jesus (despite the fact that he was undeniably male), seeking to recast religion as the human experience of the "power of Being" manifested in all persons.[51]

As briefly discussed above, the reach of feminist theory and revisionist theology extends to virtually every branch of Christian doctrine. Rather than conceiving of God as a trinity consisting of Father, Son, and Holy Spirit, some religious feminists speak of the "divine feminine" and propose goddess worship or other forms of religious beliefs and practices in which women are at the center. This venture, in turn, requires a new set of sacred writings, liturgical practices, and ways of speaking of God. It also entails a recasting of morality and spirituality. Rosemary Radford Ruether, one of the movement's most prolific authors, in her work *Womanguides* provides a feminist "systematic theology" in which she calls for new texts, a new canon, and a new church.[52]

Beyond this, some feminists provide a larger philosophical rationale

[51] Daphne Hampson, *After Christianity* (Valley Forge, PA: Trinity Press International, 1996); Mary Daly, *Beyond God the Father: Toward a Philosophy of Women's Liberation* (Boston: Beacon, 1973).
[52] Radford Ruether, *Womanguides*.

in which they ground their pursuit of gender equality. Their purpose is to overcome traditional philosophy as shaping cultural values, perceptions, and stereotypes of gender. To give but one example, some such feminists focus their critique on the spirit-flesh dualism in Western philosophical (rationalist) thought. Theologically, this Docetic-Gnostic, Platonic hierarchy was addressed and rejected by the first church-wide council in Nicaea (modern-day Turkey) in AD 325, but modern feminists are engaging this philosophical construct once again with an implicit logic of incarnation.[53]

According to these feminists, the problem with traditional Christianity is that it dichotomizes between male and female in ways akin to ancient Gnosticism or Platonism. Only if Christianity is freed from such philosophical strictures will it be able to appreciate the full equality of women to men. In this and many other ways, feminists ground their critique of Christianity and the Bible's teaching on gender in their critique of deeper philosophical structures in Western thought encoded in culture and language. While space doesn't permit us to elaborate, we should remember that much of feminist theory evinces considerable sophistication and must be understood in light of its larger philosophical and theological framework. In the end, however, biblical theology alone holds the reforming promise of feminist thought in its various manifestations.

Conclusion

This appendix has sought to canvass the cultural context for our study of God's design for man and woman in Scripture. We've seen that feminism has had a profound impact on American culture. Without a doubt, much of feminism's results were positive. At the same time, we've also observed that the philosophical and theological soil in which some social and religious feminists sprouted up was insufficiently fertilized with scriptural teaching regarding the divine design for man and woman. We've seen that many social and religious

---

[53] See, e.g., Caroline Walker Bynum, *Fragmentation and Redemption: Essays on Gender and the Body in Medieval Religion* (New York: Zone, 1992), 151, who writes, "*Male and female* were contrasted and asymmetrically valued as intellect/body, active/passive, rational/irrational, reason/emotion, self-control/lust, judgment/mercy, and order/disorder." We owe this quote and some of the material in this paragraph to John Burkett.

feminists have either rejected Scripture altogether or adopted a critical stance toward it, using the portions that support their feminist beliefs while discarding the rest. In so doing, they've chosen to disregard the beautiful design God has for men and women if they're willing to submit to the will of their Creator and to live their lives in keeping with his plan.[54]

Key Resources

Cochran, Pamela D. H. *Evangelical Feminism: A History*. New York: New York University Press, 2005.

Cottrell, Jack. *Feminism and the Bible: An Introduction to Feminism for Christians*. Joplin, MO: College Press, 1992.

Kassian, Mary. *The Feminist Mistake: The Radical Impact of Feminism on Church and Culture*. Wheaton, IL: Crossway, 2005.

Köstenberger, Andreas J., with David W. Jones. *God, Marriage, and Family: Rebuilding the Biblical Foundation*. 2nd ed. Wheaton, IL: Crossway, 2010.

Köstenberger, Margaret Elizabeth. *Jesus and the Feminists: Who Do They Say That He Is?* Wheaton, IL: Crossway, 2008. Chap. 1.

---

[54] A beautiful recent example is Gloria Furman, *Glimpses of Grace: Treasuring the Gospel in Your Home* (Wheaton, IL: Crossway, 2013).

Appendix 2

The Rules of the Game

Hermeneutics and Biblical Theology

> To treat an author's words merely as grist for one's own mill is ethically analogous to using another man merely for one's own purposes.
>
> —E. D. Hirsch Jr.[1]

Key Points

1. *Hermeneutics* is the science and art of interpretation of a text with the goal of determining the biblical author's original meaning.
2. Interpreting the Bible involves the study of a given passage in its individual *historical, literary, and theological contexts* in dependence on the illumination of the *Holy Spirit*.
3. *Biblical theology* seeks to ascertain the unified biblical teaching on a particular topic such as manhood and womanhood by tracing the development of the topic in various biblical books across the entire Bible.

Few things are more important for biblical Christians than knowing how to interpret Scripture correctly. Andreas has devoted a significant part of his scholarly work and ministry to promote sound interpretive methodology, training pastors and aspiring scholars in this field. He's also recently coauthored a book on biblical interpretation, *Invitation to Biblical Interpretation: Exploring the Hermeneutical Triad of History, Literature, and Theology*. In this book, he and his coauthor Dick Patterson spend

---

[1] *The Aims of Interpretation* (Chicago: University of Chicago Press, 1976), 91.

over eight hundred pages spelling out in great detail how to ascertain a biblical author's intended message.

Margaret, similarly, has devoted much of her life and ministry to seeking out and promoting a sound interpretation of Scripture in order to help women find their way in our confusing society and even church life. Her dissertation *Jesus and the Feminists: Who Do They Say That He Is?* evaluates the variety of interpretive approaches employed by different schools of feminism in their portrayals of Jesus's stance toward women. Margaret has a continuing burden to search and apply the Scriptures with courage, conviction, and responsibility.

In *Invitation to Biblical Interpretation*, a great deal of time is spent on studying the historical setting, literary context, and theological message of the various genres in Scripture. Dick and Andreas also discuss outlining a passage, a responsible method for word study, figurative language, interpretive fallacies, and several other important subjects. In this appendix we can hardly hope to duplicate all of this material, nor is this necessary. For our purposes, it'll suffice to introduce you to the importance of hermeneutics and to discuss issues with particular relevance to our subject at hand.

Hermeneutics: What Is It?

Hermeneutics [her-me-noo-ticks] provides the initial key for understanding the biblical teaching on manhood and womanhood, but since *hermeneutics* is not a word we use in our everyday conversations, we'll first need to define the term.[2] What is hermeneutics? Grant Osborne, in *The Hermeneutical Spiral*, defines hermeneutics as "the science and art of biblical interpretation."[3] That's a good basic definition. "Science," or perhaps better, "method," means there are certain ground rules or guiding principles for interpretation, as with any other field of study. We'll discuss these ground rules in more detail in a moment, but some initial examples of these rules are having regard for the historical, literary, and theological context, interpreting words in keeping with their conventional meaning at the time of writing, and observing proper rules of grammar and syntax.

---

[2] Some of this material is adapted from Margaret Köstenberger, *Jesus and the Feminists: Who Do They Say That He Is?* (Wheaton, IL: Crossway, 2008), "Appendix 2: The Nature of Biblical Interpretation," 223–29.
[3] Grant R. Osborne, *The Hermeneutical Spiral*, 2nd ed. (Downers Grove, IL: InterVarsity, 2006), 21–22.

Hermeneutics, however, is more than a science or method; it's also an art. If hermeneutics were just a science, we'd be able to break the interpretive process down into a certain number of steps, which, if followed, would result in the proper interpretation of a given passage. Hermeneutics would then resemble a conveyor belt or assembly line that produces the right interpretation when all the individual steps are followed. Unfortunately, however, that's not how biblical interpretation works. Interpretation also requires empathy (the Golden Rule), creativity, and imagination. This doesn't mean we're free to creatively make things up and imagine the text to mean whatever we want it to mean. I'm sure you've been exposed to some really imaginative—in a negative sense—interpretations of Scripture and cringed at the liberties taken by some in reinterpreting the traditional meaning of a given biblical passage.

What we mean by empathy, creativity, and imagination, taken in a positive sense, has to do, at least in part, with the way in which we often need to fill in the gaps—reading between the lines, as it were—or supplying needed information that is otherwise implied, but not made explicit, in Scripture. As literary theorists will tell you, authors and readers of the same time period and culture typically share what is called a common "presupposition pool," that is, a set of assumptions that "go without saying."[4] We still do the same today. When we have a conversation, we don't tell each other things we know the other person already knows! We understand what people mean in what they say or write because we share the same language, culture, and time period. Successful communication often (though not always!) takes place. The biblical texts, on the other hand, are from different languages, cultures, and times, which makes interpretation considerably more difficult and complex.

The original author and readers didn't need to tell each other things they already knew and agreed upon, but here we are, two thousand years later, in an entirely different culture. We don't share the same culture or presupposition pool with the original author and readers. So how do we bridge this gap? This is one place where personal study

---

[4] See Peter Cotterell and Max Turner, *Linguistics and Biblical Interpretation* (Downers Grove, IL: InterVarsity, 1989), 90–97, for further discussion of presupposition pools.

and the use of study helps (such as commentaries or study Bibles) will prove indispensable. In order to understand the meaning of the text, we'll need to try to re-create the original context. This makes hermeneutics an art as well as a science. (That said, the Christian belief in the inspiration of Scripture, and in the illumination of the Holy Spirit when we read the Scriptures, renders interpreting *biblical texts* unique in certain respects.)

Things have changed quite a bit over the past two thousand years, so we need to do all we can, as it were, to step back in time. This is a tricky endeavor, and some may not even realize that the Bible wasn't originally written in English (it was written in Greek and Hebrew). On one level, that's not a big problem, because virtually all of the English translations we commonly use are very reliable,[5] but lack of awareness of the temporal, cultural, and linguistic gap separating us from the biblical period may wrongly suggest that you and I can read the meaning of a given passage right off the page (which we often can, but not always). At the same time, of course, we shouldn't unnecessarily complicate biblical interpretation, as if people needed to be seminary trained or highly educated in order to understand the Bible. Most of the Bible, certainly the gospel and the plan of salvation, can be easily discerned. However, there's a dimension to understanding Scripture that requires acquiring basic skills in the science and art of biblical interpretation—hermeneutics (direct/naïve vs. mediated/critical interpretation).

The point we're trying to make is that within the larger context of people's overall worldview, hermeneutics is important. Understanding the context is vital to correct interpretation. As our former hermeneutics professor, Robertson McQuilkin, loved repeating, "Context is king!" Even people with a high view of Scripture (those who believe God's Word to be inerrant and authoritative) can misinterpret the text. Your hermeneutic, or approach to the Bible, in conjunction with your overall worldview, will largely determine your conclusions regarding the interpretation of a particular passage, which is why it is so important to know what a correct hermeneutic is. *How* we read shapes and affects *what* we read.

---

[5] For a helpful resource in this regard, see Andreas J. Köstenberger and David A. Croteau, eds., *Which Bible Translation Should I Use? A Comparison of 4 Major Recent Versions* (Nashville: B&H Academic, 2012).

In addition, it's helpful to note that hermeneutics is largely subconscious and not always careful or correct. We all have sets of principles we employ when reading the Bible even if we're not fully aware of what these sets of principles are. (The literary theorist Stanley Fish calls this "subconscious" element in interpreting texts one's "interpretive community," which shapes readers in the way they read a given piece of writing.) For this reason, it's important to reflect *consciously* on the process we use in arriving at a given interpretation, especially on a subject as vital and as controversial as the biblical teaching on gender roles.

Hermeneutics: What Do We Aim For?

In addition to defining hermeneutics, we should also ask a related question, namely, What is the proper goal of hermeneutics? Is it to validate a reader's experience, ideology, tradition, or agenda, or is it to determine the original, authorially intended message of a particular passage, or is it something else? Too often, the approach to understanding Scripture is circular and proceeds along the following lines: "This is what I've *always* believed, so that is what I *want* the Bible to say, and lo and behold, that is what the Bible is actually *saying!*" We start out with our experience, and pre-understanding, and interpret the Bible in light of these. While it is, of course, inevitable that we bring certain presuppositions to the table when interpreting Scripture, we ought to uphold, at least in principle, that interpreting a text means trying to distance ourselves from what we believe in order to understand what another person (in the present case, the biblical author) is saying. Otherwise, we'd be guilty of *eisegesis* (*eis* means "into"), that is, reading our own ideas into the text.

Instead, what should in fact be happening in interpreting any text (including Scripture) or piece of communication is *exegesis* (*ex* means "out of"), where our understanding of a given matter is derived from (out of) the text. Our goal in hermeneutics is ultimately to see the message that is being communicated throughout the Bible. We want to understand what the Bible is actually saying, not what we want it to say. To that end, we need to do our best to truly "listen" to the Bible and be open to the possibility (in some cases, even probability) that the Bible at times may be saying something other than what we already believe. This may challenge our preconceived ideas and cherished convictions, but so be it—that's what it means for Scripture to be our authority.

If we don't adopt this kind of submissive, listening approach to the Bible, we're in grave danger of domesticating it, which is a form of abusing God's Word and robbing it of its authority. Let's not coerce the Word of God into saying something the biblical author never intended to say. To the contrary, the goal of biblical theology is to discern the original meaning intended by the author of a given text of Scripture. This is the proper goal of hermeneutics. To illustrate, some feminists tend to interpret Scripture on the assumption that it teaches male-female egalitarianism, at least in part because this type of reading comports most favorably with their pre-understanding. However, even some feminists today question whether the original authors of Scripture espoused egalitarianism.[6] This kind of reading obviously differs from the hermeneutical approach we're espousing here.

> "Our goal in hermeneutics is ultimately to see the message that is being communicated throughout the Bible. We want to understand what the Bible is actually saying, not what we want it to say."

Table A2.1: Fallacies in the Interpretation of Gender Passages

Fallacy	Description
Invalid distinctions	Obscure vs. plain; culturally relative vs. timeless truth
Testaments in conflict?	Interpreting the Old apart from the New Testament?
Questionable presuppositions	Scripture contains errors, feminism is nonnegotiable
Improper use of background data	Reconstruction of background to override natural reading

---

[6] This is acknowledged even by some egalitarians themselves: see, e.g., John H. Elliott, "Jesus Was Not an Egalitarian: A Critique of the Anachronistic and Idealist Theory," *Biblical Theology Bulletin* 32 (2002): 75–91; John H. Elliott, "The Jesus Movement Was Not Egalitarian but Family-Oriented," *Biblical Interpretation* 11, no. 2 (2003): 173–210; Kathleen Corley, *Women and the Historical Jesus: Feminist Myths of Christian Origins* (Santa Rosa, CA: Polebridge, 2002).

Fallacy	Description
Unlikely word meanings	Dubious word study to support preferred interpretation
Improper trajectories	Inaccurate ways of connecting the dots in Scripture

Years ago, E. D. Hirsch wrote a seminal work, *Validity in Interpretation*, in which he argued that authorial intent is the only proper standard for assessing what constitutes a valid interpretation.[7] Hirsch was an English professor who applied his approach to all literature, secular as well as sacred. He sought to establish a means of determining the

"The Bible displays striking theological unity. It speaks with one voice through the many different voices of the respective biblical authors. In this way, as the Reformers taught us, Scripture interprets Scripture, and we're able to interpret the parts . . . in light of the whole."

most fitting criterion for assessing which interpretation is the most valid. Hirsch's contention was that you can determine the validity of a given interpretation only if you have an independent standard by which to measure the accuracy of varying interpretations: the standard of authorial intent. He wrote:

> Validity requires a norm—a meaning that is stable and determinate no matter how broad its range of implication and application. A stable and determinate meaning requires an author's determining will. . . . All valid interpretation of every sort is founded on the recognition of what an author meant.[8]

Hirsch's point is that even if you might end up disagreeing with another person's interpretation, there should be agreement on a common goal: the pursuit of what the author meant, not what you want the text to mean. Without acknowledging authorial intention and making discerning it the goal of interpretation and the criterion for adjudicating between conflicting interpretations, determining the most valid interpretation of a given passage remains elusive. Kevin

---

[7] E. D. Hirsch, *Validity in Interpretation* (New Haven, CT: Yale University Press, 1967).
[8] Ibid., 126.

Vanhoozer's *Is There a Meaning in This Text?* claims that if the notion of the author "dies," so does the possibility of attainable meaning, and no criterion remains for determining what constitutes valid interpretation.[9]

Not that it'll always be easy to determine authorial intent, but discerning authorial intent remains a valid goal. You may argue that it's difficult to determine authorial intent when a text, such as the Bible, has many authors. In biblical studies, we overcome this hurdle in several ways. First, we affirm the inspiration and activity of one divine Author who was at work through the Holy Spirit in inspiring and guiding the various human authors of Scripture. Second, we work from the final biblical text, understanding it to be inerrant and authoritative, not from hypothetical sources lying behind the text. Third, in the midst of the variety of literary genres and authors, we recognize that the Bible displays striking theological unity. It speaks with one voice through the many different voices of the respective biblical authors. In this way, as the Reformers taught us, Scripture interprets Scripture, and we're able to interpret the parts (any one passage) in light of the whole (i.e., what Scripture as a whole teaches on a given subject). The relevance of this principle for our study of the Bible's teaching on manhood and womanhood should be obvious.

Hermeneutics: How Do We Go About Interpreting Scripture?

To his considerable regret, Andreas didn't grow up playing baseball (no baseball in Austria!). Perhaps this is why now, watching our eleven-year-old son Timothy play on a travel team, Andreas is so intrigued by the plethora of rules (some of them fairly obscure) that continue to surface in a variety of situations. As even the apostle Paul writes, "An athlete is not crowned unless he competes according to the rules" (2 Tim. 2:5). In a similar way, hermeneutics—a set of basic ground rules for proper interpretation—is needed just as rules are needed to play a game. Why do we need rules to play baseball? We could save a good deal of money if we didn't have to pay for umpires to enforce the rules. Why spend the time or energy bothering to learn and adhere to rules? The answer is:

---

[9] Kevin J. Vanhoozer, *Is There a Meaning in This Text? The Bible, the Reader, and the Morality of Literary Knowledge* (Grand Rapids, MI: Zondervan, 1998).

Because that is how you play the game![10] Also, the rules are reasonable and make sense. What would happen in any organized sports competition if the players decided to play without abiding by any set of rules? Chaos would result. It's similar with the interpretation of Scripture.

The overarching ground rule for hermeneutics, within the overall framework of pursuing authorial intent, can easily be stated as follows: interpret every passage in its proper context. Context can be divided into three types: historical, literary, and theological.[11] Regard for context may seem like common sense, but you'll be surprised how often it is disregarded, or insufficiently considered, in biblical interpretation.

The historical context has to do with the background of a particular book and answers questions such as, "Who wrote the book and when, where, and why?" You'll often find helpful discussions of the historical context in Old and New Testament surveys and study Bibles.[12] Proper interpretation requires that in interpreting a given passage, we accurately understand the historical background.

The literary context indicates the placement and function of particular words and sentences within the larger framework of the entire text. This includes the immediate context (what comes immediately before and after our passage in a given book), the broader context of the entire book (what the author's goals for the entire book were and how the various parts fit together), and the literary genre of the book.[13] Different genres themselves require different approaches. You can't accurately interpret an apocalypse as if it were historical narrative, a parable, or a poem!

Finally, the theological aspect of interpretation requires that we seek to understand a particular passage in terms of the theology of a particular author or book (Johannine, Pauline theology, etc.) within the overall teaching of the larger biblical canon (biblical theology).

---

[10] For an interesting account of baseball's origins, see Ron McCulloch, *Baseball Roots: The Fascinating Birth of America's Game and the Amazing Players That Were Its Champions* (Lynchburg, VA: Warwick, 2000).

[11] History, literature, and theology—the hermeneutical triad—are the backbone of the hermeneutics text by Andreas Köstenberger and Richard D. Patterson, *Invitation to Biblical Interpretation: Exploring the Hermeneutical Triad of History, Literature, and Theology* (Grand Rapids, MI: Kregel, 2011. See also Andreas J. Köstenberger, "Reading the Bible in Context," in George Guthrie, *Read the Bible for Life: Your Guide to Understanding and Living God's Word* (Nashville: B&H Academic, 2010), 33–48, where I (Andreas) add "cultural" as a fourth type of context.

[12] If you need help in finding a suitable resource, a useful starting point may be the "Appendix: Building a Biblical Studies Library," in Köstenberger and Patterson, *Invitation to Biblical Interpretation*, 809–32.

[13] E.g., when interpreting Eph. 5:21–33, the immediate context is the command to be filled with the Spirit in 5:18 and to put on the full armor of God in 6:10–18. The genre of Ephesians is that of epistle.

As mentioned, Scripture interprets Scripture. The broader theological context will often help you rule out particular interpretations that are contrary to truth clearly revealed in other parts of the Bible. Being mindful of the theological context of Scripture is vital in discerning the Bible's message on any given subject, including God's design for men and women in the home and in the church.

All three levels of context combine to help us determine what a given word or phrase means. Unlike Humpty Dumpty, who said, "When I use a word, . . . it means just what I choose it to mean—neither more nor less,"[14] we shouldn't make words mean what we *want* them to mean. Rather, we should try to discern what an author meant (authorial intention) when he used a particular word. This will involve examining the most likely conventional meaning at the time (historical context), how the author used the word in other places (literary context), and how the various possibilities fit with what Scripture teaches elsewhere (theological context).

For example, we may ask, How do we know what Paul meant when he said that "women will be saved by childbearing" (1 Tim. 2:15)? We might begin our investigation of what Paul meant in this passage by studying his use of the expressions "saved" and "childbearing" in the Pastoral Epistles (e.g., "saved" in 1 Tim. 4:16 and "childbearing" in 1 Tim. 5:14), as well as in the broader Pauline corpus (Pauline literature and theology) and elsewhere in the New Testament. Also, we learn more by observing proper rules of Greek grammar and syntax (literary context).[15]

Similarly, what did Paul mean when he wrote, "I do not permit a woman to teach or to exercise authority over a man" (1 Tim. 2:12)? Paul's statement can be interpreted as, "I don't permit a woman to teach in a domineering manner," in which case he would be prohibiting a woman's abuse of authority along the lines of, "Don't be overbearing in your teaching." Is this what Paul meant? Or does it mean that a woman shouldn't teach men in the local church? A careful study of the historical, literary, and theological contexts will be vital in discerning Paul's message.[16]

---

[14] The reference is to Lewis Carroll's *Through the Looking Glass*, chap. 6. The story continues: "The question is," said Alice, "whether you can make words mean so many different things." "The question is," said Humpty Dumpty, "which is to be master—that's all."

[15] See chap. 6 above.

[16] See chap. 6 above.

Proper interpretation must carefully investigate and correctly determine the historical, literary, and theological contexts of any given passage. Much of this may seem elementary and obvious, but this is the place where many fail.

The Fruit of Sound Hermeneutics: Biblical Theology

What should be the outcome of our discussion of hermeneutics? Sound biblical interpretation involving a study of the history, literature, and theology of a given passage or sets of passages will issue in biblical theology.[17] Biblical theology, simply put, is the theology of the Bible. At one level, of course, this definition begs the question, "The theology of the Bible according to whom?" However, we're not implying that biblical theology renders interpretation unnecessary but rather contend that sound hermeneutics must inexorably lead to an appraisal of biblical theology on a broader scale. In biblical theology, the interpreter is seeking to determine, across the entire canon (theology), what the various authors of the Bible believed in their own historical context (history) and on their own terms (literature).

The Swiss-German theologian Adolf Schlatter penned the following helpful comments regarding biblical theology:

> In speaking of "New Testament" theology, we are saying that it is not the interpreter's own theology or that of his church and times that is examined but rather the theology expressed by the New Testament itself. We turn away decisively from ourselves and our time to what was found in the men through whom the church came into being. Our main interest should be the thought as it was conceived *by them* and the truth that was valid *for them*. We want to see and obtain a thorough grasp of what happened historically and existed in another time.[18]

Schlatter called this project "the historical task," which is properly complemented by the "doctrinal task" of systematizing the Bible's

---

[17] For a survey of the different ways in which contemporary interpreters conceive of and practice biblical theology see Andreas J. Köstenberger, "The Present and Future of Biblical Theology," *Themelios* 37 (November 2012), http://thegospelcoalition.org/themelios/article/the_present_and_future_of_biblical_theology (accessed June 28, 2013). See also Edward W. Klink III and Darian R. Lockett, *Understanding Biblical Theology: A Comparison of Theory and Practice* (Grand Rapids, MI: Zondervan, 2012).
[18] Adolf Schlatter, *The History of the Christ*, trans. Andreas J. Köstenberger (Grand Rapids, MI: Baker, 1997), 18 (emphasis original).

teachings on the various subjects it addresses. Interpreting Scripture is a historical enterprise because God's revelation was revealed in the context of history.[19]

The context of the entire canon is important for biblical theology because, for example, even if (for argument's sake) Deborah served as a judge and exercised real authority in ancient Israel, it's important to understand what happened in this case, when it happened, what the situation was in ancient Israel, and how Deborah's actions fit with what precedes and what follows canonically. We should resist the tendency to extrapolate illegitimate conclusions from isolated incidents and to lodge unwarranted claims concerning the leadership of women in the church today (more on this in the following appendix). We need to be sensitive to the time and the place at which a given event took place and is recorded in the Bible and be nuanced in drawing appropriate implications for today.

This biblical-theological approach that pays careful attention to the development of biblical themes is sometimes referred to in terms of "progressive revelation" or as "redemptive history." Because of the progressive nature of God's self-revelation, not everything in the Bible has equal weight. There's a sense in which the New Testament and Paul's teaching explain more fully an issue such as the role of men and women in the church than a passage found earlier in Scripture (though we also maintain that God's plan for men and women in the Bible is entirely unified). God is consistent, and so the message of the Bible will ultimately be found to cohere and not contradict itself. Biblical theology helps us understand the message of the Bible as it gradually unfolds across the canon. There's still a place for *systematic* theology— gathering passages together topically regardless of where they appear in the Bible—but the interpreter will most likely be subject to error if the biblical-theological work isn't done first.

In engaging in biblical theology at large, the interpreter must also be sensitive to the respective biblical genre(s) represented by a given text or set of texts. Didactic passages are often more determinative or conclusive than references in historical narratives. Take Priscilla's

---

[19] For a fuller treatment of biblical theology, see Köstenberger and Patterson, *Invitation to Biblical Interpretation*, chap. 15.

teaching of Apollos, recorded in the book of Acts (a narrative depicting the history of the early church), for example. What are we to make of the mention of Priscilla as teaching Apollos at one occasion in the book? Some would infer from this that women should be able to teach men in the church today without any restrictions, but this is a giant leap. We need to be very careful not to jump to conclusions concerning women's involvement in teaching and leadership roles in the church based on the limited evidence supplied by the reference to Priscilla in the Acts narrative. Likewise, it would be illegitimate to cite examples from a given Old Testament legal text (e.g., the stipulation that a woman marry the man who raped her) without acknowledgment that most of those texts are no longer directly applicable in the church today.

We also should be slow to assume that if something is a burning issue today, it was necessarily a pressing matter in the first century. Interpreters who wrongly assume that their questions and concerns are identical to those of the biblical writers often end up misinterpreting a passage by using proof texts out of context.

Why is biblical theology essential? It's needed because it helps us understand the broad biblical message, developments over time, and how each particular text and its theology fit in with the broader biblical story line and larger theology. If the question arises, therefore, whether 1 Timothy 2:12 is an isolated passage dealing with the question of women in local church leadership, it is immediately apparent that in 1 Timothy 2:13–14 Paul is invoking Genesis 2 and 3 and is thus building on a broad stream of biblical revelation throughout the entire canon. It is the Bible in its totality, from Genesis to Revelation, that contains and presents God's plan for gender roles. This understanding is at the heart of the burden of biblical theology, and is the central premise underlying the approach in this book. Unfortunately, many misunderstand, misrepresent, or fail to appreciate the significance of keeping the story line of Scripture in mind when interpreting individual passages in the Bible. Discussions of 1 Timothy 2:12 should therefore acknowledge that Paul there articulates and applies what's been explicitly taught and implicitly assumed throughout Scripture.

In understanding and explaining God's design for men and women, we need to learn to appreciate the broad plan and big picture of Scripture with regard to gender roles. In a controversial district court ruling, a California judge, Vaughn Walker, overturned a vote defining marriage as between one man and one woman, opining that the exclusion of same-sex couples from marriage is "an artifact of the time when the genders were seen as having distinct roles."[20] Contrary to the judge, however, the notion of gender roles is not antiquated. Hopefully, this appendix has provided you with a sufficient understanding of the necessity of hermeneutics and biblical theology.

Key Resources

Fuhr, R. Alan, and Andreas J. Köstenberger. *Inductive Bible Study: A Method for Biblical Interpretation.* Nashville: B&H Academic, forthcoming.

Guthrie, George. *Read the Bible for Life: Your Guide to Understanding and Living God's Word.* Nashville: B&H Academic, 2010.

Köstenberger, Andreas J., and Richard D. Patterson. *Invitation to Biblical Interpretation: Exploring the Hermeneutical Triad of History, Literature, and Theology.* Grand Rapids, MI: Kregel, 2011. (Note: an abridgment is currently in preparation.)

Köstenberger, Margaret Elizabeth. *Jesus and the Feminists: Who Do They Say That He Is?* Wheaton, IL: Crossway, 2008. Chap. 2.

Osborne, Grant R. *The Hermeneutical Spiral: A Comprehensive Introduction to Biblical Interpretation.* 2nd ed. Downers Grove, IL: InterVarsity, 2006.

---

[20] Cited in editorial, "Marriage Is a Constitutional Right," *New York Times*, August 4, 2010.

Appendix 3

Proceed with Caution

Special Issues in Interpreting Gender Passages

To obliterate our God-given gender distinctions (or to follow Marxism or other social theories in declaring all such distinctions to be no more than social conditioning) on the flimsy grounds offered by postmodern humanism is an affront and basic alteration to the message of the cross.

—Robert Yarbrough[1]

A hermeneutics of suspicion seeks to explore the liberating or oppressive values and visions inscribed in the text by identifying the androcentric patriarchal character and dynamics of the text.

—Elisabeth Schüssler Fiorenza[2]

Key Points

1. Special hermeneutical issues related to feminism and the interpretation of gender passages include the reconstruction of history, epistemology, the role of the reader, the biblical canon, the alleged patriarchal nature of Scripture, and the difference between evangelicalism and fundamentalism.
2. Hermeneutical pitfalls in feminist interpretation include drawing invalid distinctions, interpreting the Old Testament apart from the

---

[1] Robert W. Yarbrough, "Progressive *and* Historic: The Hermeneutics of 1 Timothy 2:9–15," in *Women in the Church*, 2nd ed., ed. Andreas J. Köstenberger and Thomas R. Schreiner (Grand Rapids, MI: Baker, 2005), 144.
[2] *But She Said: Feminist Practices of Biblical Interpretation* (Boston: Beacon, 1992), 57.

New, questionable presuppositions, improper use of historical background material, and drawing on unlikely word meanings.

In appendix 2, we laid out the rules of the game—how to interpret
Scripture correctly and responsibly. In this third appendix, we'll take a
closer look at several additional, more advanced hermeneutical issues:
(1) three general overarching hermeneutical principles (a listening hermeneutic, the two horizons of Scripture, and the need for interpretive
restraint); (2) six particular interpretive issues related to the interpretation of gender-related passages in Scripture; and (3) six common
hermeneutical fallacies in dealing with biblical gender passages.

General Hermeneutical Principles

Several basic principles will help any interpreter understand the author's originally intended meaning through an analysis of the historical, literary, and theological contexts: a listening hermeneutic, a
distinction between the two horizons (ancient and modern) in Scripture, and interpretive restraint.

A Listening Hermeneutic

Adolf Schlatter, a conservative Swiss theologian, argued for a hermeneutic of perception in which the goal is to see what is actually there.[3]
We're sure you've heard some sermons in your life where the preacher
was waxing eloquent on points that were not even in the text. The matter was certainly in the preacher's head but absent from the passage
that was being preached. Schlatter encouraged interpreters to immerse
themselves in the text through lengthy and repeated readings in order
to find out what is there. A submissive, "listening" approach is an inner
disposition that we ought to bring to the task of interpreting Scripture.
Because we're so busy in our North American culture, not to mention
other obstacles, we often don't take the time to ponder and wrestle with
what's actually there in the text before us. Not that it's always wrong to
try to read between the lines, but first you and I need to start out with
a clear understanding of what's actually there in the text.

---

[3] Adolf Schlatter, *The History of the Christ*, trans. Andreas J. Köstenberger (Grand Rapids, MI: Baker,
1997), 18.

Take John 3:16, for example. Andreas has written several commentaries and a number of articles on John's Gospel but just last year noticed something in this well-known passage that he'd never before realized was there. Specifically, it occurred to him that John, when recounting Jesus's conversation with Nicodemus, the Jewish rabbi, put a major emphasis on God's love for the world, which would have been deeply countercultural because Jews in Jesus's day believed that God loved them and hated non-Jews.[4] Seems obvious enough. So why didn't Andreas see this all along? Because it wasn't there? No, because he'd assumed he already knew what the passage says. Apparently, there was more truth to be found through repeated reading and sustained study of Scripture. We don't want to be so full of ourselves or so certain that we already know what a text means that we fail to see what's actually there. Our primary goal is to find out what Scripture is actually saying and to humble ourselves sufficiently to consider that the Bible will often challenge us to change our preconceived ideas and align them with Scripture.

> "Our primary goal is to find out what Scripture is actually saying and to humble ourselves sufficiently to consider that the Bible will often challenge us to change our preconceived ideas and align them with Scripture."

The Two Horizons

A second hermeneutical principle is that of distinguishing between the two horizons of biblical interpretation, ancient and modern. Interpreters often get ahead of themselves on precisely this point. First, we want to interpret what Paul (or another biblical writer) said, regardless of whether we like it, whether it fits with our theology, or whether it's in keeping with modern culture. When people collapse the two horizons, they ask only, "What does this passage mean to me?" Fortunately, by the grace of God, we often still arrive at a valid application to our present circumstances, but ideally proper interpretive procedure requires that we first understand the original setting and authorial intention. In order to safeguard the authority of Scripture and the accuracy of

---

[4] See Andreas J. Köstenberger, "Lifting Up the Son of Man and God's Love for the World: John 3:16 in Its Historical, Literary, and Theological Contexts," in *Understanding the Times: New Testament Studies in the Twenty-First Century*, ed. Andreas J. Köstenberger and Robert W. Yarbrough (Wheaton, IL: Crossway, 2011), 141–59.

modern application, it's important to maintain the distinction between the original message in the past and our present-day application.

To give but one example, let's not be so naïve as to think that Paul's letter to the Ephesians was written directly to you and to me. It wasn't. To be sure, self-centered interpretation and application are common in our self-absorbed, narcissistic society, but such a hermeneutic will often lead to misinterpretation. We're fond of singing of how Jesus died for "me, even me." In many of our contemporary praise songs, everything is about "me." It's sometimes hard for us to realize that there were other people in view in the Bible. The various books of Scripture weren't written directly to you and us. This doesn't deny the fact that you and we are very special in God's eyes and that he loves each of us very much, but when we approach the text, we must realize that even though Scripture was written for us, it was not written directly to us as its first, original readers.[5] This calls for a distinction between the ancient and contemporary horizons of Scripture.

Interpretive Restraint

A third hermeneutical principle concerns the importance of interpretive restraint. As mentioned, we need to acknowledge our own biases and presuppositions and refuse to exceed the evidence. Even if we're convinced regarding the validity of a particular interpretation, we mustn't confidently claim interpretive conclusions that are unsupported by reasonable arguments or present the case as if it were stronger than the text warrants. The best interpretation will be the one that makes the most sense of all the available evidence. We need humility because we could be wrong, and at some point or another, we probably will be.

Particular Issues Related to Feminism[6]

Next, let's look at several issues that relate particularly to the interpretation of biblical passages on gender roles.

---

[5] John Walton, *The Lost World of Genesis One* (Downers Grove, IL: InterVarsity, 2009), 9, cogently makes this point in reference to the text of Genesis 1: "The Old Testament *does* communicate to us and it was written for us, and for all humankind. But it was not written *to* us. It was written to Israel. It is God's revelation of himself to Israel and secondarily through Israel to everyone else" (emphasis original).

[6] For more detailed discussion of these points see Margaret Köstenberger, *Jesus and the Feminists: Who Do They Say That He Is?* (Wheaton, IL: Crossway, 2008), chap. 1.

Table A3.1: Hermeneutical Issues Related
to Gender Passages in Scripture

Issue	Key Question
Reconstructed history	How do we know what really happened?
Epistemology	How do we know anything at all?
The role of the reader	What is the reader's role in interpreting Scripture?
The biblical canon	Which books are included in the biblical canon?
Patriarchy	Does Scripture have a bias against women?
Evangelicalism vs. fundamentalism	Is a nonfeminist view narrow-minded and bigoted?

Reconstructed History

Can we ever know what really happened in history? Even if interpreters agree on the hermeneutical importance of historical background material, how can we know what actually took place? Some people are greatly troubled by the fact that we weren't there when the Declaration of Independence was signed and thus cannot be certain that this event really took place. How do we know, short of being eyewitnesses, that this kind of event actually happened or that there really was a George Washington? We assume the historicity of these matters based on reliable information, but, at least in theory, we cannot absolutely prove historical facts. Some scholars stress the elusiveness and subjectivity of history. They allege that because all history is interpreted history, it'll never be objective. Take Josephus, for example. He is one of the major historical sources for the second-century BC Maccabean revolt and first-century AD Judaism, but his background and agenda at times tend to diminish his objectivity. Or take history textbooks as another example. More often than not, they reflect political ideology and aren't written from an entirely objective vantage point.

The helpful point made by all such arguments is that we can't and shouldn't blindly trust any historian or given historical account without proper verification. To the extent that this is possible, we should always refer back to primary sources that include firsthand eyewitness accounts of the events that are described. Fortunately in the case of the biblical documents, such as the Gospels, this is exactly what we have in Scripture. Two of the four Gospels claim authorship by a member of Jesus's closest circle of followers, the Twelve (Matthew and John), and the other two are based on the testimony of one of its members (Mark, on Peter's testimony, according to church tradition) or other eyewitness testimony (Luke; cf. Luke 1:1–4). Thus we can be confident that the Gospels present us with reliable information about Jesus and the events they portray. The same can be said for the book of Acts, the letters included in the New Testament, and the book of Revelation, which records visions received by the apostle John on the island of Patmos (Rev. 1:9). In the case of historians such as Josephus, of course, we must be careful and discerning and wherever possible seek to corroborate information he provides by other sources.

The issue of reconstructed history often surfaces in debates about the interpretation of gender-related biblical passages. Feminists typically claim that history, including biblical history, was for the most part written by males and is therefore pervasively androcentric, or male-centered. What many feminists therefore believe they must do is excavate the buried memory of all the female figures that was lost and forgotten because the men who wrote the history weren't interested in the lives and activities of these women or wanted to suppress them. Because of this, those feminists feel the need to build up a counter-history ("her-story") in support of women in their class struggle against men. When dealing with those kinds of feminists, this will often be one of the driving issues. They'll claim that we can't trust the history of the Bible because it was written by men and because it's tainted by an irredeemable patriarchal bias, especially in historical narratives. It's true that Scripture was written by men. It's hardly true, however, that the male writers of Scripture wrote with the purpose of oppressing women. This view is largely an imposition of feminist ideology onto the way in which Scripture has come down to us. Alleging male bias by itself is certainly not legitimate grounds for feminists rewriting history in such a way that it's more to their liking. When pressed against other ancient sources, the biblical documents stand up very well. While they do reflect a male perspective, this doesn't mean that they falsify history. People can arrive at such a negative conclusion only when they illegitimately impose their anti-male feminist bias onto the biblical documents.

Epistemology

How do we know anything at all? Is truth relative, occasional, and subjective, or is it objective and absolute? How do we know something is true? As mentioned, many radical and reformist feminists emphasize the subjective nature of knowledge, and they do have a point. Even though Christians firmly believe that truth is absolute and objective, our *apprehension* of it *is* subjective. Admit it or not, the fact is that all of us are subjective. We know things only as people who've been shaped by our particular background and experiences. Feminists are wrong, however, when they use their experience heavy-handedly to determine what Scripture can or can't say or to make it say what they want it to say based on their feminist presuppositions. They're right in asserting that we all read Scripture with our own lenses shaped by our individual backgrounds but wrong in elevating experience as the final arbiter of truth. Scripture is divine revelation; the Holy Spirit guides our interpretation; our community, the church, helps us interpret Scripture correctly; and ministry in the world opens our eyes to different perspectives and approaches. There are a lot of ways in which we can transcend our limitations as individuals (all of which require humility and a willingness to submit ourselves to truth claims outside ourselves).

In order to salvage the idea of absolute truth, we don't need to go to the opposite extreme of utter subjectivism by claiming that we possess complete objectivity. Such claims are born out of ignorance or naïveté and lead to dogmatism. Many people today—certainly, most scholars—will laugh at you if you claim that you're objective and always know for certain what the text means. Just because truth is absolute doesn't mean we can know everything absolutely or perfectly. Fortunately, scholars in the field of hermeneutics have wrestled to come to terms with these epistemological questions and the natural limitations we have in the process of acquiring knowledge. These issues are not just relevant for biblical interpretation but pertain to philosophy, science, and many other disciplines as well. While we can't know a matter fully or absolutely, we can know our subject matter—the Bible—sufficiently in order to understand and apply it.[7] This is also true with regard to God's design for biblical manhood and womanhood. We've done our study of Scripture in the confidence that through diligent study we can come to know and subsequently apply what is God's plan for men and women. If we're open to Scripture, we can be confident that God's revelation will guide us with lucidity and authority.

The Role of the Reader

What is the role of the reader in biblical interpretation? When we emphasize that our primary pursuit ought to be for the intent of the author, this may sound as though the reader is completely irrelevant in the interpretive process. On the other side of the spectrum, feminists often contend that the reader's experience is primary. Correspondingly, there is often little concern in feminist exegesis for what the author originally meant because he was male, untrustworthy, abusive, deceptive, oppressive, and so forth. Female readers and "enlightened" male readers need not be unduly preoccupied with seeking to discern the biblical author's intent but instead focus on the reader and what strikes her as relevant in a given text.

In response, Kevin Vanhoozer helpfully discusses the morality of reading.[8] He argues that respect for the author and what he intended to communicate is ultimately a moral issue. It's immoral and unethical for a reader to be unconcerned about an author's intended meaning. Try telling your spouse, friend, or coworker that you don't care about what he meant to convey and see how that works for you! We imagine that such a glib dismissal of authorial intent would not go over very well. If you're going to discard what the Bible says in any case, why

---

[7] Kevin J. Vanhoozer (*Is There a Meaning in This Text? The Bible, the Reader, and the Morality of Literary Knowledge* [Grand Rapids, MI: Zondervan, 1998]) discusses epistemology in much greater detail. He grounds his hermeneutic in the Trinity. See also the discussion of "critical realism" in N. T. Wright, *The New Testament and the People of God*, Christian Origins and the Question of God 1 (Minneapolis: Fortress, 1992), chap. 2.
[8] Ibid.

even study it? Some feminists treat studying the Bible merely as a res-cue operation in an attempt to salvage what they can from references to women such as Deborah or Priscilla. It's inconsistent and indefen-sible, however, to pick and choose the passages we like and ignore the rest. Radical or reformist feminists generally don't sufficiently reflect on why we, or they, should study Scripture at all.

That said, the undue emphasis on the role of the reader by many feminists can help us appreciate the role of the reader in conservative, evangelical interpretation. The reader's response to the text was part of the author's intention in the first place. The author wanted his text to be read. Epistles were person-to-person communication and not abstract manifestos. The author intended to convey information, pres-ent issues, and influence, persuade, and motivate his audience. In a few cases, Paul tried to communicate something, failed, and tried again (2 Thess. 2:1–12; cf. 1 Thess. 4:12–5:11). Why did the Gospel writers in-clude some pieces of information and omit others? Part of the reason was theological, but another criterion was what the authors perceived to be the need of their given audience. While readers didn't determine what the author wrote, the author took his readers into account. We'll elaborate on this further below.

The Biblical Canon

The biblical canon is a big issue for radical and reformist feminists who, for the most part, don't like the books we have in the Bible. Some reject the whole Bible because they don't like any of it. Others don't like certain books and want to remove some books and include others. Rosemary Radford Ruether, a Roman Catholic feminist, has written a systematic theology in which she proposes the formation of a new canon.[9] Because the current Bible contains books that are irredeemably oppressive, she argues, we need a new canon and a new Bible. Lest you think the differences between evangelicals and radical or reformist feminists are the result of mere minor disagreements over the inter-pretation of particular passages, some radical feminists don't stop there but reject entire books of the Bible. An interpreter's view of Scripture

---

[9] Rosemary Radford Ruether, *Womanguides: Readings toward a Feminist Theology* (Boston: Beacon, 1985).

is foundational to interpretation, and this is a clear point of division between evangelical and radical and reformist feminist hermeneutics.[10]

Another issue related to canon is the relationship between the Old and the New Testaments. Feminists frequently cite instances in the Old Testament where women weren't treated as on par with men and interpret these passages in light of their own feminist outlook. They find this portrayal of women unacceptable and extrapolate from these Old Testament references that the Bible as a whole is patriarchally biased and oppressive to women. However, these feminists don't sufficiently appreciate the fact that there's a progression in Scripture that moves from creation to the fall to a period between the fall and the coming of the Messiah and finally to the church age. The Old Testament passages that those feminists single out as portraying a negative view of women seek to regulate life in a sinful, post-fall state prior to the coming of Christ. But, as mentioned, if anyone wants to know what the Bible teaches regarding God's original purpose for men and women or regarding the restoration of his purposes in Christ, they should go first of all to Genesis 1 and 2 or Ephesians 5, not to Exodus or Leviticus (though rightly understood in its larger framework, all of Scripture's teaching is consistent).

> "The father was the hub, and like the spokes of a wheel, life in the extended household revolved around him. He wasn't just an authority figure; he was at the heart of the family and provided support, protection, nurture, and other benefits."

Patriarchy

Does the Bible—especially the Old Testament—embrace an outmoded cultural system of gender roles? We need to come to terms with this frequent assertion and be able to address it because it's a fundamental premise of feminists as they approach the Bible. Remember the California judge who overturned a vote defining marriage as between one man and one woman on the grounds that marriage is "an artifact of the time when the genders were seen as having distinct roles"? Does the Bible, then, have only antiquarian interest for us? On what basis are we still looking to the Old Testament as an authority on gender roles

---

[10] Köstenberger, *Jesus and the Feminists*, 224–25.

when patriarchy was a cultural system that has long been superseded? These questions call for a satisfactory response.

As mentioned, characterizing the Old Testament teaching on gender roles as patriarchy that invariably entails abuse, oppression, and domination is potentially misleading.[11] The ruling aspect of the father has often been exaggerated, while in fact his overall centrality in the life of the family is much more prominent. The father was the hub, and like the spokes of a wheel, life in the extended household revolved around him. He wasn't just an authority figure; he was at the heart of the family and provided support, protection, nurture, and other benefits. Historically, the Old Testament portrays male headship in ancient Israel in more benevolent terms as a way for God to provide for a family by supplying protection, provision, and care.

Evangelicalism vs. Fundamentalism

When Margaret defended her doctoral dissertation on feminist hermeneutics, two of the four members of her dissertation committee were feminists. At one point, it looked like she might not get her degree, having devoted the better part of eight years to study without any formal recognition of her work. The committee was deadlocked, when a majority was needed for her to pass. The two feminists on the committee were insistent that Margaret shouldn't be awarded a degree from their university because of her beliefs on gender roles. In their view, Margaret was a fundamentalist, a militant, radical gender jihadist who was probably pro-slavery, pro-apartheid, and so forth. Once Margaret realized the nature of these objections, she was able to point out that she's not a fundamentalist but an evangelical. She certainly isn't pro-slavery! Nor is she advocating male supremacy.

In fact, there's an important difference between evangelicalism and fundamentalism. There's a widespread stereotype concerning fundamentalism as a cultural and sociological phenomenon. We don't have space here to discuss the history of the evangelical movement and its relationship to fundamentalism, but the interested reader would

---

[11]See chap. 1. Cf. Daniel I. Block, "Marriage and Family in Ancient Israel," in *Marriage and Family in the Biblical World*, ed. Ken M. Campbell (Downers Grove, IL: InterVarsity, 2003), 33–102. See also Rebekah Josberger, *Between Rule and Responsibility: The Role of the 'ab as Agent of Righteousness in Deuteronomy's Domestic Ideology*, PhD dissertation, The Southern Baptist Theological Seminary (2007).

do well to start with the works of George Marsden and Mark Noll.[12] Some people think that if you're opposing feminism, you are a fundamentalist, and you may need to distance yourself from some of their preconceived notions regarding religious fundamentalism in order to gain a hearing. We must continually insist that we're advocating a nonegalitarian view of gender roles not on the basis of some sociological phenomenon (fundamentalism) but on theological and biblical grounds that can't easily be dismissed or stereotyped on sheer humanistic terms.

Fallacies in the Interpretation of Gender Passages

There are several hermeneutical pitfalls to which interpreters often succumb, especially when interpreting passages related to gender roles.[13] A brief discussion of these fallacies will help us avoid such missteps when interpreting gender-related passages. Some of these may appear a bit technical, so if you like, you can skip this discussion and return to it at a later time and move on to the section on biblical theology.

Invalid Distinctions

At times interpreters are tempted to make distinctions that aren't warranted by the texts themselves. One such invalid distinction is that *between obscure and plain passages*. This distinction often is made with regard to 1 Timothy 2:12 and Galatians 3:28, but this procedure is highly precarious. Who says that one of these passages is more obscure than the other? Obscure to whom, and why? Is one text labeled "obscure" simply because a given interpreter doesn't like it? Would the text have been obscure to Timothy or the original recipients? This distinction is often highly arbitrary and results in the undue marginalization of passages of Scripture, devolving into a canon-within-the-canon approach that dismisses certain passages from consideration for dubious reasons.[14]

---

[12] George M. Marsden, *The Outrageous Idea of Christian Scholarship* (New York: Oxford University Press, 1997); Mark A. Noll, *Between Faith and Criticism: Evangelicals, Scholarship, and the Bible in America*, 2nd ed. (Grand Rapids, MI: Baker, 1991).

[13] For more detailed discussion of these hermeneutical pitfalls, see Andreas J. Köstenberger, "Gender Passages in the NT: Hermeneutical Fallacies Critiqued," *Westminster Theological Journal* 56 (1994): 259–83, http://www.biblicalfoundations.org.

[14] "Canon-within-the-canon approach" means essentially that interpreters illegitimately pick and choose which passages they like better and then dismiss others they don't like on the grounds that the passages they happen to agree with are more central or more important.

Another common invalid distinction is that between culturally relative and universally normative passages. This is related to the former point. All of what Paul and the other biblical writers say is directed to particular people at a particular historical point in time but by God's providence is useful and applicable for us today. Paul doesn't seem to indicate that his instructions concerning women in the church were culturally relative. What more could he have done in 1 Timothy 2:12 than root his point in the order of creation (v. 13)? Both passages—Galatians 3:28 and 1 Timothy 2:12—are reasonably clear *and* are occasional; *both* are addressed to a specific context yet have abiding relevance. In addition, Paul's letters to Timothy and Titus were specifically written to establish permanent principles for church life. In the same literary unit as 1 Timothy 2:12, Paul stipulated qualifications for church leaders (1 Tim. 3:1–12) that are widely used in the church today and called the church "a pillar and buttress of the truth" (v. 15). The claim that 1 Timothy 2:12 is culturally conditioned while the qualifications for church leaders in 1 Timothy 3:1–12 are abiding and normative is inconsistent. Galatians 3 is not exclusively timeless, abstract, and normative any more than 1 Timothy 2 is exclusively occasional and culturally relative. As we'll see further below, in Galatians 3 Paul was dealing with the particular historical issue of the Judaizers requiring circumcision and in that context established abiding principles.

The same invalid distinction can also be expressed as a distinction between paradigm passages and passages of limited application. This distinction, likewise, results in a canon within a canon where the interpreter is free to pick which passages are palatable to modern culture and neglect those that aren't. Amazingly, "paradigm passages" end up being ones that support the interpreter's position while "passages of limited application" are those that don't fit her views. But what basis or warrant is there for putting passages in those respective categories? It seems that they're often categorized on the basis of what fits an interpreter's presuppositions. Galatians, contextually interpreted, has very little to do with the role of women in the church or home. It's unfortunate that some feminists misinterpret important passages of Scripture because their particular concerns with regard to gender equality and women's liberation from male domination override proper regard to historical, literary, and theological context.[15]

Testaments in Conflict?

A second hermeneutical pitfall involves interpreting the Old Testament apart from the New or pitting the two Testaments against each other. This happens all the time. We recently heard a "conservative" scholar argue that Genesis 1–3 has nothing to do with gender but instead is about community. Paul didn't seem to think so, because he readily refers back to Genesis 1–3 when addressing the role of men and women in the church. Apart from the fact that the above-mentioned dichotomy is false (the passage is about both gender and community), the kind of community we're talking about here is between male and female. This scholar was trying to interpret the Old Testament apart from the New. We must avoid the tunnel vision that says, "We're only interpreting the Old Testament." It's also important to keep in mind that in cases where we have a New Testament passage interpreting an Old Testament one, the New Testament's interpretation is authoritative.

One example of this hermeneutical pitfall in action is the proposed reinterpretation of the phrase "helper fit for him" in Genesis 2:18, 20 in terms of equality or congenial equals, resulting in translations such as "equal opposite him." We've heard all sorts of glosses that attempt to get the attention off the idea of "helper," but Paul obviously didn't read "helper fit for him" in Genesis 2 as merely conveying the notion of congenial equals. In 1 Corinthians 11:8–9 he wrote, "Man was not made from woman, but woman from man. Neither was man created for woman, but woman for man." Paul goes on to stress that both are important, so he was certainly not a misogynist (one who holds women in contempt). Now if Paul—a New Testament writer—saw a distinction in roles in Genesis 2, it's illegitimate for us today to ignore the New Testament and to interpret "helper" in Genesis 2:18, 20 as conveying undifferentiated equality without a role distinction between men and women.[16]

---

[15] Some egalitarians even distort the teaching on the roles of the members of the Trinity in order to support their views. This is even more serious than misrepresenting the biblical teaching on the role of men and women. See Bruce Ware, "Tampering with the Trinity: Does the Son Submit to His Father?," *Journal of Biblical Manhood and Womanhood* 6 (Spring 2001): 4–12.

[16] Lest some think we are singling out evangelical feminists, there is some confusion even among conservatives. See Mark A. Weathers, *How to Pray for Your Wife* (Wheaton, IL: Crossway, 2006), 35–36.

Paul Jewett, a one-time professor at Fuller Seminary, published one of the earliest evangelical feminist works, entitled *Man as Male and Female*.[17] He caused quite a stir among evangelicals who held to a high view of Scripture when he came out and claimed that Paul was a chauvinist and at places was wrong. Most evangelical feminists, however, will not normally lodge such claims but instead seek to interpret (or reinterpret) biblical texts in a way that is consistent with their egalitarian views, often claiming to have discovered that the original authorial intent underlying a given passage was egalitarian. Radical or reformist feminists, by contrast, may simply contend that Paul was wrong or that the two Testaments contradict each other.

Questionable Presuppositions

A third hermeneutical pitfall involves questionable presuppositions, particularly the presupposition of feminism. Many feminists approach the interpretation of Scripture with the conviction that feminism overrides anything else and that Scripture must either be interpreted in such a way that it is consistent with feminist ideology or be rejected. Even evangelical feminists (who profess belief in the inerrancy of Scripture) start out with a presupposition of undifferentiated male-female equality that sets the framework for their interpretive decisions and as a result can't legitimately claim to be truly inductive in their approach (though, of course, we all have our framework for interpretation, and no one can legitimately claim to be purely inductive). Those who regard Scripture as authoritative ought to desist from making feminism a bedrock presupposition in their hermeneutic. It's hard to see how an interpreter can credibly claim to be open to the teaching of Scripture on a given issue while subscribing to a set of beliefs that rule out certain interpretations at the very outset.

Improper Use of Background Data

A fourth hermeneutical pitfall involves the improper use of background data. One example we discussed in greater detail above involves the interpretation of 1 Timothy 2:9–15. As mentioned, some interpreters

---

[17] Paul K. Jewett, *Man as Male and Female* (Grand Rapids, MI: Eerdmans, 1975).

claim that Paul is only dealing with the issue of women in the church in the way in which he does in this passage because Ephesus was a feminist society. In other cities such as Corinth or Thessalonica, they contend, things were different, and Paul wouldn't have written the same instructions to these churches. The problem with this argument, however, is that responsible historical research shows that Ephesus was not a feminist society but resembled other major cities in the first-century Greco-Roman world.[18]

What's more, even if we assume for argument's sake that Ephesus was a feminist society, this still wouldn't change our interpretation of 1 Timothy 2. The interpreter still must determine whether a given piece of background information is relevant to interpreting the passage. There are plenty of contextual indications in 1 Timothy 2 and the surrounding chapters that Paul is *not* limiting his instructions simply to Ephesian society. He isn't giving instructions only for women in Ephesus but is instructing Timothy, based on principles drawn from the foundational Old Testament passages in Genesis 1 and 2, concerning roles in the home and in God's household, the church (see 1 Tim. 3:15; cf. 1 Tim. 2:8–9: "In every place . . . likewise also that women . . .").

Unlikely Word Meanings

The fifth hermeneutical pitfall concerns unlikely word meanings. One obvious example is the meaning of the Greek word for having or exercising authority, *authentein*. In a book entitled *I Suffer Not a Women*, Richard and Catherine Kroeger claimed that the Greek word actually meant "to proclaim oneself the author of."[19] They contended that there were some women in Ephesus who argued they were first in creation and the men were created from them, and Paul was addressing only that specific heresy among some women in Ephesus. The problem is that there's no reliable historical or linguistic evidence for such an interpretation of *authentein* in first-century Ephesus at all! In fact, many other evangelical feminists seem embarrassed by the Kroegers' argumentation, and you'll find very few current evangelical feminist

---

[18] S. M. Baugh, "A Foreign World: Ephesus in the First Century," in *Women in the Church*, 2nd ed., ed. Andreas J. Köstenberger and Thomas R. Schreiner (Grand Rapids, MI: Baker, 2005), 13–38.

[19] Catherine C. and Richard C. Kroeger, *I Suffer Not a Woman* (Grand Rapids, MI: Baker, 1992).

scholars supporting their interpretation. It's not good scholarship to propose word meanings that lack supporting linguistic evidence.

Improper Trajectories

A final fallacious approach to Scripture when interpreting gender-related passages is that of positing trajectories of doubtful value. An example of this is William Webb's "redemptive movement" hermeneutic. In his book *Slaves, Women, and Homosexuals*, Webb compares the scriptural teaching on these three topics with a view toward whether the Bible's teaching on these subjects is static or dynamic.[20] With regard to slavery, he finds clear evidence that the Bible progressively moves from slavery as acceptable (Old Testament) to hints that slavery should be surmounted (New Testament). He argues that it was only in the period subsequent to the completion of the canon of Scripture—in fact, much more recently in the Western world—that humanity has come to realize that slavery must be abolished. Hence, we mustn't stop where the Bible stops—at mere hints that slavery should be done away with—and project the end point of the biblical trajectory in determining what is normative biblical teaching for today.

With regard to homosexuality, Webb finds that both the Old and the New Testaments condemn it, so that Scripture is static (no development or progression) in this regard. The question therefore arises: Is the biblical teaching on women more like its stance toward slavery (which is dynamic) or its approach to homosexuality (which is static)? According to Webb, the answer is somewhere in between, but on the whole, Scripture's trajectory on women is more like that regarding slavery; it is dynamic. What this means is that rather than looking to the canon of Scripture for a definitive word on the subject, we must extrapolate the trajectory and then follow it beyond Scripture to its logical end point—egalitarianism. Webb himself finds in the New Testament what he calls a "soft patriarchy," though, as mentioned, his

[20] William Webb, *Slaves, Women, and Homosexuals: Exploring the Hermeneutics of Cultural Analysis* (Downers Grove, IL: InterVarsity, 2001). For cogent critiques of Webb see Benjamin Reaoch, *Women, Slaves, and the Gender Debate: A Complementarian Response to the Redemptive-Movement Hermeneutic* (Phillipsburg, NJ: P&R, 2012); Wayne Grudem, "Should We Move beyond the New Testament to a Better Ethic? An Analysis of William J. Webb, *Slaves, Women, and Homosexuals: Exploring the Hermeneutics of Cultural Analysis*," *Journal of the Evangelical Theological Society* 47 (2004): 299–346; and Thomas R. Schreiner, "Review of *Slaves, Women, and Homosexuals*," *Journal of Biblical Manhood and Womanhood* 7 (2002): 41–51.

ultimate authority rests not in the New Testament but in the end point of his posited trajectory.

However, while certainly creative and hermeneutically sophisticated, Webb's "redemptive movement" hermeneutic is deeply problematic.[21] While he deserves credit for focusing attention on some of the difficult issues arising from Old Testament passages that can't be applied literally by people in the church today, Webb's proposal illegitimately dethrones the canon of Scripture as final authority. However, only Scripture is inspired, not the perceived trajectories by a given interpreter such as Webb. Rather than connect the dots in a way that places authority outside of

> "Specifically, a biblical-theological approach understands that we find in Scripture a movement from God's original design for man and woman to the fall and its consequences to the period prior to the coming of the Messiah to the Messiah's arrival, death, and resurrection to the church age and to the eternal state."

Scripture, it's preferable by far to understand the redemptive-historical dimension of the Bible without resorting to Webb's "redemptive movement" hermeneutic. Specifically, a biblical-theological approach understands that we find in Scripture a movement from God's original design for man and woman to the fall and its consequences to the period prior to the coming of the Messiah to the Messiah's arrival, death, and resurrection to the church age and to the eternal state.

Within this framework, it's certainly possible, even necessary, to understand the limitations of a given law regarding women, or a practice involving women, during Old Testament times that is not authoritative today. Jesus's coming and the Spirit's arrival have ushered in a new age that moves beyond Old Testament practice toward the restoration of God's original design for man and woman as narrated in the opening two chapters of Genesis. Importantly, while this way

---

[21] See, e.g., Daniel I. Block, who writes, "It has been claimed that the move from Old Testament to New Testament times witnessed increasing acceptance of women in leadership, even among the community of faith (Webb). Without prior commitment to this view, it is difficult to recognize such developments in the New Testament. The New Testament knows of no female elders." He continues, "The exceptions to this androcentric pattern involve female deacons . . . and prophets. . . . But this is precisely the pattern witnessed in the Old Testament." Block's conclusion: "Although women are engaged in *ad hoc* ministry situations and in practical spiritual service, claims of their involvement in positions of governance depend on arguments from silence. And if one reads the biblical texts with a 'redemptive-movement hermeneutic' the New Testament provides little if any evidence of the erosion of the androcentric patterns of leadership found in the Old Testament." "Leadership, Leaders in the New Testament" (unpublished paper provided courtesy of the author) 10–11.

of reading Scripture in its progressive unfolding also involves a certain type of dynamic, the movement is not open-ended as in Webb's proposal but has as its endpoint, at least as far as the church today is concerned, a restoration of the male pattern of leadership rather than unfettered egalitarianism. At the same time, the type of male leadership in the church (and in the home) that is propagated in the New Testament is that of loving, self-sacrificial service, without displacing the man from his position as the one who's in charge of the familial household as well as of God's household, the church.

Key Resources

Köstenberger, Andreas J. "'Biblical Hermeneutics: Basic Principles and Questions of Gender' by Roger Nicole and 'Hermeneutics and the Gender Debate' by Gordon D. Fee." *Journal of Biblical Manhood and Womanhood* 10 (Spring 2005): 88–95.

———. "Gender Passages in the NT: Hermeneutical Fallacies Critiqued." *Westminster Theological Journal* 56 (1994): 259–83.

Köstenberger, Margaret Elizabeth. *Jesus and the Feminists: Who Do They Say That He Is?* Wheaton, IL: Crossway, 2008. Chap. 2.

Reaoch, Benjamin. *Women, Slaves, and the Gender Debate: A Complementarian Response to the Redemptive-Movement Hermeneutic.* Phillipsburg, NJ: P&R, 2012.

Helpful Resources

Block, Daniel I. "Leader, Leadership, OT." Pages 620–26 in *New Interpreter's Dictionary of the Bible*, Volume 3: *I–Ma*, edited by Katharine Doob Sakenfeld. Nashville: Abingdon, 2008. A very thorough survey of leadership terminology in the Old Testament, including a section on women and leadership.

Campbell, Ken M., editor. *Marriage and Family in the Biblical World*. Downers Grove, IL: InterVarsity, 2003. See especially the excellent essay by Daniel I. Block, "Marriage and Family in Ancient Israel," on pages 33–102. See also Andreas J. Köstenberger, "Marriage and Family in the New Testament," on pages 240–84.

Cottrell, Jack. *Feminism and the Bible: An Introduction to Feminism for Christians*. Joplin, MO: College Press, 1992. An older but still helpful critique of feminism from a biblical perspective. See also Cottrell, *Gender Roles and the Bible: Creation, the Fall, and Redemption: A Critique of Feminist Biblical Interpretation*. Joplin, MO: College Press, 1994.

Doriani, Dan. *Women and Ministry: What the Bible Teaches*. Wheaton, IL: Crossway, 2003. Simple and straightforward but wise presentation by a scholar with extensive pastoral experience in churches of various sizes. After doctoral research in church history with focus on the Puritan family, the author developed expertise in New Testament and ethics.

Furman, Gloria. *Glimpses of Grace: Treasuring the Gospel in Your Home*. Wheaton, IL: Crossway, 2013; *Treasuring Christ When Your Hands Are Full: Gospel Meditations for Busy Moms*. Wheaton, IL: Crossway, 2014. The author is the wife of a cross-cultural church planter and mother of four young children. *Glimpses of Grace* is an inspirational volume designed to encourage women to live their lives for the glory of God.

Grudem, Wayne. *Evangelical Feminism and Biblical Truth: An Analysis of More Than 100 Disputed Questions*. Wheaton, IL: Crossway, 2013. First published

2004 by Multnomah. Set of responses to evangelical feminist arguments from a complementarian perspective. See also Grudem, *Evangelical Feminism: A New Path to Liberalism?* Wheaton, IL: Crossway, 2006.[1]

Hove, Richard. *Equality in Christ? Galatians 3:28 and the Gender Dispute.* Wheaton, IL: Crossway, 1999. A thorough, undisputed, and compelling study of Galatians 3:28, "There is neither . . . male nor female, for you are all one in Christ Jesus." Argues that the passage's emphasis is on *unity in Christ,* not *equality in role.*

Köstenberger, Andreas J., with David W. Jones. *God, Marriage, and Family: Rebuilding the Biblical Foundation.* 2nd ed. Wheaton, IL: Crossway, 2010. Survey of the biblical teaching on marriage, parenting, and a host of related subjects. Abridged as *Marriage and the Family.* Wheaton, IL: Crossway, 2012.

Köstenberger, Andreas J., L. Scott Kellum, and Charles L. Quarles. *The Cradle, the Cross, and the Crown: An Introduction to the New Testament.* Nashville: B&H Academic, 2009. A useful survey of the historical background, literary context, and theological message of each of the twenty-seven books of the New Testament.

Köstenberger, Andreas J., and Richard D. Patterson. *Invitation to Biblical Interpretation: Exploring the Hermeneutical Triad of History, Literature, and Theology.* Grand Rapids, MI: Kregel, 2011. A thorough yet practical study of the various rules of interpreting different Old and New Testament genres.

Köstenberger, Andreas J., and Thomas R. Schreiner, editors. *Women in the Church: An Analysis and Application of 1 Timothy 2:9–15.* 2nd ed. Grand Rapids, MI: Baker, 2005. Third edition. Wheaton, IL: Crossway, forthcoming in 2015. Looks at the important passage 1 Timothy 2:9–15 from every conceivable angle and concludes that in this passage Paul does not permit women to teach or exercise authority over men in the church.

Köstenberger, Margaret Elizabeth. *Jesus and the Feminists: Who Do They Say That He Is?* Wheaton, IL: Crossway, 2008. A thorough critique of feminist interpretations of Jesus's view of women surveying radical, re-

---

[1]See also Andrew Wilson, "Is Egalitarianism a Slippery Slope? It Depends." http://thinktheology.co.uk/blog/article/is_egalitarianism_a_slippery_slope_it_depends (accessed June 12, 2013), who argues that of four types of egalitarianism (exegetical, experiential, trajectory, and kingdom-now), some (exegetical, kingdom-now) aren't on a slippery slope while others are.

formist, and evangelical feminism. Conclusion: feminists are conflicted in their view of Jesus, and efforts to portray Jesus as feminist have been unsuccessful.

Laniak, Timothy S. *Shepherds after My Own Heart: Pastoral Traditions and Leadership in the Bible.* New Studies in Biblical Theology 20. Downers Grove, IL: InterVarsity, 2006. Together with Tidball (see below), a helpful study of the biblical theology of leadership (though Paul is largely neglected owing to his sparse use of shepherding language).

Piper, John, and Wayne Grudem, editors. *Recovering Biblical Manhood and Womanhood: A Response to Evangelical Feminism.* Wheaton, IL: Crossway, 1991. This is the classic tome on complementarianism, featuring a collection of essays on the relevant biblical passages as well as broader related contributions.

Reaoch, Benjamin. *Women, Slaves, and the Gender Debate: A Complementarian Response to the Redemptive-Movement Hermeneutic.* Phillipsburg, NJ: P&R, 2012. Along with similar critiques by Wayne Grudem, Thomas Schreiner, and others, Reaoch provides a thorough refutation of William Webb's "redemptive movement hermeneutic."

Sandom, Carrie. *Different by Design: God's Blueprint for Men and Women.* Fearn, Ross-shire, UK: Christian Focus, 2012. Sandom, associate minister for women and pastoral care at St. John's Church, Turnbridge Wells, UK, is a critic of the impact of feminism, feminist hermeneutics, and the results of these movements in the church.

Saucy, Robert L., and Judith K. TenElshof, editors. *Women and Men in Ministry: A Complementary Perspective.* Chicago: Moody, 2001. Along similar lines as *Recovering Biblical Manhood and Womanhood*, a helpful presentation of the biblical teaching on manhood and womanhood by a team of authors.

Severance, Dianna Lynn. *Feminine Threads: Women in the Tapestry of Christian History.* Fearn, Ross-shire, UK: Christian Focus, 2011. Treats women's presence and contribution to the church in every age, including the New Testament period. Seeks to rehabilitate the biblical prominence of women in ministry.

Smith, Claire. *God's Good Design: What the Bible Really Says about Men and Women.* Kingsford, NSW, Australia: Matthias Media, 2012. One of a growing number of books by women who understand, and may have been part of, one or more of feminism's three waves. Takes a look at biblical passages on men and women, particularly on marriage.

Tidball, Derek. *Skilful Shepherds: Explorations in Pastoral Theology.* 2nd ed. Leicester, UK: Apollos, 1997. Along with Laniak, a very useful study of the biblical theology of leadership focused on shepherding terminology. Excels in his biblical-theological approach and in his treatment of individual books of Scripture.

Note: In addition to the above-mentioned resources, see also "For Further Study: Helpful Resources," in Köstenberger with Jones, God, Marriage, and Family, pages 289–311.

General Index

plain passages, 326, 346; invalid
distinction between paradigm
passages and passages of limited
application, 347–48; questionable
presuppositions, 326, 349; unlikely
word meanings, 327, 350–51
Genesis, book of, 253; debates concern-
ing the creation narrative in, 26n3
Gentiles, 119, 128
Gideon, 51, 241
Gnosticism, 199, 200
God: as creator, 24–2537; as *Elohim*,
26n3; as Father, 82; as helper,
36–37, 38–39; as the paradigm for
leadership, 75; as *Yahweh*, 26n3
*God, Marriage, and Family: Rebuilding the
Biblical Foundation* (A. Köstenberger
and Jones), 17n4
Goldenberg, Naomi, 318
Gomer, 52
Gospel of Thomas, 200n12
Gospels, the, 81–82. *See also the specific
Gospels*
great commandments, the, 276
Great Commission, 84, 276
Greer, Germaine, 304–5, 306
Grenz, Stanley J., 41n31
Griffith, Elisabeth, 297n5
Grimké, Angelina, 295
Grimké, Sarah, 295
Grudem, Wayne, 170n15, 182, 247n14
gynaikeios (Gk. "the feminine" or "fe-
male," "femininity"), 246
gynaikos (Gk. "women" or "deacons'
wives"), 225–26
gynē (Gk. "woman" or "wife"), 206n21,
207, 220

Hamilton, Victor P., 40n30, 45
Hampson, Daphne, 309, 318
Hannah, 65, 65n15, 70, 282
Harvey, Paul, 238–39
Hebrews, book of, 240–43, 261; Abraham and Moses in, 241; comparison of Jesus with both Moses and
Joshua in, 240; David in, 241–42;
"Hall of Faith" in, 240–41, 242,
243; Jesus as the great high priest
of his people in, 240; main focus
of (Jesus), 240; Sarah and Rahab
in, 242

Held Evans, Rachel, 246n10, 315,
315n45
hen (Gk. "one"), 164–65
Hensley, Adam D., 179n26
hermeneutical principles: acknowledge
personal biases and presuppositions and refuse to exceed the
evidence, 338; distinguish between
the ancient and contemporary
horizons of Scripture, 337–38; see
what is actually there, 336–37
hermeneutics: and authorial intent,
327–28; definition of, 322–25;
and eisegesis, 325; and empathy,
creativity, and imagination, 323;
and exegesis, 325; goal of, 325–28;
overall ground rule for (interpret
every passage in its proper context
[historical, literary, and theologi-
cal]), 328–31; and presupposition
pools, 323; and the Scripture
interprets Scripture principle, 328.
See also hermeneutical principles
"hermeneutics of suspicion," 91n10,
310, 335
Herodion, 144
heterodidaskaleō (Gk. "to teach different
doctrine"), 201n14
Hirsch, E. D., Jr., 321, 327
Holy Spirit, 72; the command to be
filled with the Spirit, 185–86;
guidance of, 263, 265; and the
inspiration of Scripture, 328; and
prophesying, 141, 142
homosexuality, 53–54, 55, 72, 259; as
a breach of God's creation design,
53; death as a punishment for in
the Levitical holiness code, 54; in
Sodom and Gomorrah, 54
hooks, bell, 312n34
Hosea, 52
hospitality, 136–37, 280, 280n11
house table, 180; in the book of 1 Peter,
244; in the book of Ephesians,
180, 189
Hove, Richard, 164n5, 167, 168n10
Hubbard, Moyer, 216–17n40
Hugenberger, Gordon P., 207n27
Huldah, 66, 68–69, 69, 259, 282, 300;
portrayal of in *The Woman's Bible*,
299–300

in Christ), 181–82; in the context
of Ephesians 1:9–10, 5:18, and
6:10–18, 185–86; and the erroneous interpretation of mutual
submission, 182–84
Paul, on male-female unity in Christ
(Gal. 3:28), 162–63, 168–69; background of, 163–64; in the context
of Galatians 3, 165–67; the meaning of the Greek word *hen* ("one"),
164–65; relationship between the
couplets Jew/Gentile, slave/free,
male/female, 167–68
Pauline circle, 123, 124, 125, 132, 143,
144, 157
Payne, Philip B., 39n28, 179n26, 209n29
Pennington, Jonathan, 81n4
Pentateuch, 59n5
Persis, 146, 152–53
Peter, 85, 86, 87, 89, 123, 124, 136, 249;
confession of, 86, 105n23
Philemon, 137, 146
Philip, 85, 87, 89
Philip's daughters, 65n15, 69n24, 141,
142
Phoebe, 138, 146, 150–52, 151n25,
152n27, 226–27, 282; portrayal of
in *The Women's Bible*, 300–301
Piepmeier, Alison, 312n34
Piper, John, 280n11, 287
Planned Parenthood, 302
Plato, 247n15
Pliny the Younger, 229n53
poimēn (Gk. "shepherd"), 249, 249n24
polygamy, 50–51, 55, 71, 72, 259; allowance for in the Old Testament, 72;
among first-century Jews, 222; in
the Greco-Roman world, 222
polygyny, 71, 72
Pontius Pilate, 95
presbyteros (Gk. "elder"), 249
priests (Old Testament), 57–58, 64,
66, 76–77, 259; and the role of
women, 64–65
Prisca. *See* Priscilla
Priscilla, 123n3, 125, 137, 140–41,
140n15, 143, 146, 147, 148–50, 155,
282, 332–33; portrayal of in *The
Woman's Bible*, 300
proistēmi (Gk. "to rule"), 225
prophecy, 134, 141; New Testament
prophecy, 69n24, 142, 142n16,

179–80; Old Testament prophecy,
142, 142n16; prophetic utterance
as the word of God itself, 142n16;
and women, 65n15
prophets and prophetesses (Old Testament), 57–58, 65–66, 65n15, 69,
69n24, 77, 250, 259; appointment
of by God, 66; the nature of a
prophet's authority, 66; and the
revelation of God's will, 66
prostatis (Gk. "helper" or "patroness"),
150, 151
Proverbs, book of, 73; on wisdom, 265;
women in (as personifications of
virtues and vices), 73, 255
Pudens, 146

Quarles, Charles L., 163n4, 169n13,
180n31, 197n4, 243n4
Quartus, 144
queen mothers (Old Testament), 63–64

Rabbi Yose ben Yohanan, 104n19
Rachel, 70
Rahab, 70, 241
Rebekah, 70
Rehoboam, 51
repentance, 72, 80
Rest of the Story, The (Harvey), 238–39
Reuben, 52
Revelation, book of, 252–55, 261;
authorship of, 340; the church as a
bride in ("the wife of the Lamb"),
254, 255; Israel as a woman
clothed with sun, moon, and
stars in, 254, 255; the unbelieving
world as "the great prostitute" in,
254–55, 255
Richards, Amy, 312n34
Riesner, Rainer, 105n21
Roe v. Wade (1973), 307
Roiphe, Katie, 312n34
Romans, book of, references to indi-
viduals at the end of, 150, 150n20
Ruether, Rosemary Radford, 82n7, 310,
318, 343
Rufus, 144
Ruth, 70, 110, 282

Sailhamer, John H., 28nn7–8, 29n9,
34n20, 36n22, 47nn42–43, 48n45
salvation, 72, 80, 214

Samaritan woman, 102, 103–4, 116, 119
Samaritans, 104, 116
Samson, 241
Samuel, 59, 65, 66, 241
sanctification, 214
Sanger, Margaret, 301–2
Sapphira, 134
Sarah, 70, 241, 246
Sartre, Jean-Paul, 303
Satan, 27, 70; God's judgment on after the fall, 46–47, 47n40; role of in the fall, 42–43, 43n34
Saul, 59
Scanzoni, Letha Dawson, 314
Schlatter, Adolf, 331–32, 336
Schreiner, Thomas R., 33n18, 39n28, 151n25, 167n8, 174, 177, 205–6, 206nn21–22, 209n32, 210–11n33, 214
Schultz, Ray B., 151
Schüssler Fiorenza, Elisabeth, 91, 91n10, 314, 335
Scripture: inerrancy of, 328; inspiration of, 328; theological unity of, 328
Scripture, application of, 262, 337; and circumstantial factors, 264; and cultural factors, 263; and ethical factors, 264–65; four essential steps of, 262–63; guidelines for application, 262–63, 262n2; and personal factors, 263–64
Scripture, interpretation of. *See* hermeneutics
Second Sex, The (Beauvoir), 303
"Seneca Falls Declaration" (1848), 296
Sensuous Spirituality: Out from Fundamentalism (Mollenkott), 309
Serpent. *See* Satan
servant leadership, 188–89, 278
Sex and Destiny: The Politics of Human Fertility (Greer), 305
sex/sexual union, 36, 40; beauty of, 55
Sexual Politics (Millett), 304
shame and honor, 175n21
Sheldon, Charles M., 79–80
shepherding, 76, 90
Silas, 123, 124, 131, 131–32, 138, 249
Silvanus. *See* Silas
Simon (of Cyrene), 155–56
Simon Peter, *See* Peter
Simon the Zealot, 86, 88

sin, 50, 50n49, 69; as the fundamental problem of humanity, 72. *See also* fall, the
skeuos (Gk. "vessel"), 246
slave-free distinction, 166n7
slavery, 92n13
Slaves, Women, and Homosexuals (Webb), 351–52
Smith, Carol, 64n14
Snodgrass, Klyne, 162
Social Gospel movement, 80
Sodom and Gomorrah, sin of, 54
Solomon, 51, 59, 62
sōphronizō (Gk. "to train"), 232
Sosipater, 144
sōzō (Gk. "to save"), 214–15, 217n40; in the "diabolical passive" voice, 216; range of meaning associated with in the New Testament, 215; in secular Greek, 215
Spencer, Aída, 188n41
Spencer, William, 188n41
spiritual warfare, 47, 186, 275
Stanton, Elizabeth Cady, 26n3, 295–96, 295n3, 296; view of the Bible, 297, 298
Steinem, Gloria, 305, 306
Stone, Lucy, 295, 296, 297
submission. *See* Paul, on head coverings and submission to authority (1 Cor. 11:2–16); Paul, on headship and submission in marriage (Eph. 5:21–33)
Sumner, Jim, 36n24, 171n16
Sumner, Sarah, 36n24, 171n16
Susanna, 93, 106, 139
synathleō (Gk. "to contend"), 156, 156n35
synergoi (Gk. "fellow workers"), 156
Syntyche, 147, 156–57
Syrophoenician woman, 110, 111
systematic theology, 332

Tabitha. *See* Dorcas
Tamar, 110
Taylor, Justin, 107n24
teknogonia (Gk. "childbearing"), 213–14, 217n40; as a synecdoche, 214, 219
Tertius, 144
Thaddaeus, 85, 88
"thealogy," 318
Theophilus, 127, 139
Thomas, 85, 87–88, 89

in the Old Testament, 69–70; in Paul's churches, 145–57; significant female roles, 278–83; silence of in church, 280n12; status of Old Testament times, 71–74; true femininity, 285–87; as "weaker vessels," 246–47, 247n19, 285; the women near the cross and at the empty tomb in the Gospels, 107–8; women's ministry programs, 288–89; in the workplace or in public office, 283–85. *See also* men and women; wives; women teaching or having authority over men in the church (1 Tim. 2:12); women, as deacons (1 Tim. 3:11); women, older, and the training of young women (Titus 2:3–5); women's domestic and familial role (1 Tim. 2:15)

women teaching or having authority over men in the church (1 Tim. 2:12), 195–96, 199–200; cultural background of (first-century Ephesus), 197–99, 211–12; the framework for interpreting 1 Timothy 2:12, 195–96, 205; interpreting 1 Timothy 2:12 in context, 205–12

women, as deacons (1 Tim. 3:11), 225–27, 280–81; exegetical arguments for, 227–29; relevance of, 227, 229–30

women, older, the characteristics that they are to impart: being busy at home and being kind, 233–34; love for husband and children, 232–33; self-control and purity, 233; submission to husbands, 234

women, older, and the training of young women (Titus 2:3–5), 230, 231–32; characteristics of older women, 231; and the church as the family of God, 230–31. *See also* women, older, the characteristics that they are to impart

Women's Action Alliance, "U.S. National Women's Agenda" (1975), 306

women's domestic and familial role (1 Tim. 2:15), 212–13, 217–19; messianic interpretation of, 212; what "childbearing" means, 213–14, 219; what "saved" means, 214–16, 219

worship, appropriate conduct for men and women in the public assembly gathered for, 206–10, 218–19

Wright, N. T., 29n10, 90n9, 105n22, 113n27, 136n9, 157n36, 163n3, 168, 170n14, 178n25, 198n9

WWJD (2010), 80

WWJD bracelets, 80

Yarbrough, Robert W., 92n13, 166n7, 251n29, 335

Year of Biblical Womanhood, A: How a Liberated Woman Found Herself Sitting on Her Roof, Covering Her Head, and Calling Her Husband "Master" (Held Evans), 315, 315n45

Zacchaeus, 96, 97, 98

zealots, 88

Zebedee, 86

Zenas, 146

zera (Heb. "seed"), 36n22

Scripture Index

Confronting the Latest Cultural Challenges to God's Plan for Marriage and Family

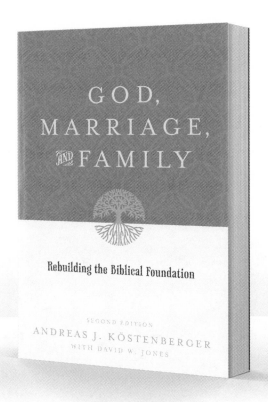

"The special value of this book lies in its pervasive exposition of Scripture. We are adrift in a sea of speculation without this. I am thankful for the book. I plan to give it to my grown children."

JOHN PIPER, Founder, desiringGod.org; Chancellor, Bethlehem College and Seminary

"Sensible, balanced, and biblical, this is a sound and timely summary of the Bible's teaching on some of the most basic and yet controversial topics in today's world. I highly recommend it."

MARK DEVER, Senior Pastor, Capitol Hill Baptist Church, Washington DC; President, 9Marks

"In an era when too many Christians listen more intently to television therapists than to the Bible on the question of the family, this could be one of the most significant books you ever read."

RUSSELL D. MOORE, President, The Ethics & Religious Liberty Commission; author, *Tempted and Tried*

For more information, visit crossway.org.

Download a **FREE** study guide for
God's Design for Man and Woman
at **crossway.org/GDMW**